INVESTMENT ANALYSIS
AND MANAGEMENT

INVESTMENT
ANALYSIS
AND
MANAGEMENT

John W. Bowyer, Jr., D.B.A.
Professor of Finance
Washington University

Third Edition

1966

RICHARD D. IRWIN, INC.
Homewood, Illinois

Third Edition

First Printing, September, 1966
Second Printing, August, 1967
Third Printing, August, 1968
Fourth Printing, February, 1969

Library of Congress Catalog Card No. 66–24589

Printed in the United States of America

To Inge, Karen and Linda

Preface

The major changes made in this revision of *Investment Analysis and Management* were to add more materials on personal financial and investment planning. Chapters on investment planning and programming also were added.

The chapters on security analysis were again revised and updated to reflect many changes and improvements in analytical technique. The chapter on investment mechanics underwent a major revision. The author is particularly indebted to R. Charles Goodwin of Goldman, Sachs and Co. for his assistance in revising this chapter as he prepared the first draft of the revised chapter. The chapters on analysis of insurance companies and finance companies has been revised substantially. The author is indebted to Dean Arthur W. Mason, University of Denver, for many helpful suggestions in revising the chapters on insurance companies and to William Gerard, Liberty Loan Company, and to J. Marvin Elliott, Elliott Finance Company, for their comments and assistance in revising the chapter on banks and finance companies. I also wish to acknowledge the assistance given by my colleague, Merle T. Welshans, and Keith B. Johnson, University of Connecticut, who read sections of the manuscript and contributed materials for the revision.

Appreciation must also be expressed to the following people: W. Gene Gerard and Edward A. White, White and Company; James D. Vernon, Smith, Moore and Company; Charles F. Bealke, Tower Grove Bank and Trust Company and F. R. Reiter and James Corbett, General Contract Finance Corporation. In addition, I would like to express my appreciation to Miss Shirley Kraft and Mrs. Gloria Becker for secretarial assistance in preparing the manuscript.

St. Louis, Missouri
June, 1966

JOHN W. BOWYER, JR.

vii

Table of Contents

1. SCOPE AND NATURE OF INVESTMENTS 1
   THE VIEWPOINT OF THE INVESTOR. WHY STUDY INVESTMENTS. WHY SAVE AND INVEST: The Allocation of Savings. Investment Choices. CLIMATE FOR SAVINGS AND INVESTMENT: Nature of Investment. Economic Uncertainty and Investment.

2. PERSONAL FINANCIAL AND INVESTMENT PLANNING 10
   THE INCOME PATTERN: Illustration of an Income Pattern. PERSONAL INVESTMENT REQUIREMENTS: Premature Death as a Requirement. How Much Life Insurance? Disability as a Requirement. Nature of Medical Expense Insurance. Nature of Disability Income Insurance. Retirement as a Requirement. Unemployment and Other Contingencies as a Requirement. Other Planning Considerations.

3. INVESTMENT POLICY FACTORS 26
   THE NATURE OF RISK: Financial Risk. Purchasing Power Risk. Interest Rate Risk. Market Risk. TAX CONSIDERATIONS: Special Treatment of Capital Gains. LIQUIDITY CONSIDERATIONS: Other Aspects of Marketability. PERSONAL CONSIDERATIONS.

4. CHARACTERISTICS OF INVESTMENT MEDIA—INSTITUTIONAL FIXED-
   DOLLAR CONTRACTS 39
   INVESTMENT CHARACTERISTICS OF INSTITUTIONAL DOLLAR CONTRACTS. SAVINGS AND LOAN ASSOCIATIONS. COMMERCIAL BANKS AND MUTUAL SAVINGS BANKS. LIFE INSURANCE AND ANNUITIES AS INVESTMENTS: The Nature of Pure Life Insurance. The Origin of Cash Surrender Values. The Level Premium Plan as the Cause of Reserve Accumulations. Annuities as Investments. Purchasing Power Risk Exposure of Annuities and Life Insurance. U.S. SAVINGS BONDS.

5. CHARACTERISTICS AND VALUE OF INVESTMENT MEDIA—
   CORPORATE BONDS 55
   CORPORATE BONDS: Type of Security and Asset Protection. Methods of Recovering Principal. Interest Payment Provisions. Conversion Provisions. THE VALUE OF BONDS: The Valuation Process. Bond Value Variables. Value, Yields, and Length to Maturity. Quality Reflected in Yield.

6. CHARACTERISTICS AND VALUE OF INVESTMENT MEDIA—COMMON
   AND PREFERRED STOCK 76
   CHARACTERISTICS OF COMMON STOCK: Voting Rights. Par Value. Preemptive Rights. Warrants. VALUE OF COMMON STOCK: Intrinsic Value—Present Value of Dividends. Intrinsic Value—Multiple-of-Earnings Approach. Growth Stock Valuation. Book Value. Market Value. CHARACTERISTICS AND VALUE OF PREFERRED STOCK: Claim on Income. Participation Provision.

Voting Rights. Claim on Assets. Call and Sinking Fund Provisions. Preferred Stock Yields. Variations in Preferred Stock Quality.

7. INVESTMENT PROGRAMMING 100

LIFE INSURANCE AND INVESTMENT PROGRAMMING: The Purpose of Life Insurance. What Kind of Life Insurance? The Choice of Policies. Choosing a Life Insurance Company. RETIREMENT AND THE INVESTMENT PROGRAM: The Fixed-Dollar Contract Program. The Equity Program. The Balanced Program. The Program after Retirement. STABILITY AND LEVEL OF INCOME AND INVESTMENT POLICIES. FEDERAL INCOME TAXES AND INVESTMENT POLICIES. QUALITY AND THE INVESTMENT PROGRAM.

8. SOURCES OF INFORMATION 118

FACT VERSUS OPINION: Free Advice. Mail-Order Investment Counsel. COMPANY DATA SOURCES: Use of Standard Financial Services. Sources Supplementary to the Manuals. Supplements to the Accounting Record. INDUSTRY DATA SOURCES: Basic Characteristics Industry Statistics. GENERAL ECONOMIC AND MARKET DATA SOURCES: Basic Economic Data. Summary of Basic Data Sources. SOURCES OF INFORMATION ON SOURCES. READING THE FINANCIAL PAGE: The News and Stock Prices. Security Prices. Money Rates and the Banking Situation. Public Finance.

9. INVESTMENT MECHANICS AND THE SECURITY MARKETS 150

PRIMARY MARKETING OF SECURITIES: Public Sale of Securities. Private Placements. SECONDARY MARKETS FOR SECURITIES: The Stock Exchanges. The Over-the-Counter Market. Inactive Issues. Secondary Offerings. TRANSACTIONS ON THE STOCK EXCHANGE: Types of Orders. Stop Orders. Delivery. Brokerage Commissions. The Monthly Investment Plan. Buying on Margin. Selling Short. Puts, Calls, Straddles, and Spreads.

10. INTRODUCTION TO SECURITY ANALYSIS 174

DEFINITION OF INVESTMENT ANALYSIS: APPROACHES TO SECURITY ANAYLSIS: Market Analysis. Intrinsic Value Approach. Qualitative Analysis. Quantitative Analysis. Importance of Market Price Fluctuations. Summary. SECURITY ANALYSIS PROCEDURE: Preliminary Screening. Industry Analysis. COMPANY QUANTITATIVE ANALYSIS: Ratio Analysis. Analytical Reference Standards. Comparability of Financial Statement Data. Importance of Interpretation. COMPANY QUALITATIVE ANALYSIS: Qualitative Information Sources. Management Interview.

11. ANALYSIS OF INDUSTRIAL SECURITIES—THE INDUSTRY 195

ECONOMICS OF INDUSTRY GROWTH. STAGES OF INDUSTRY DEVELOPMENT. INDUSTRY GROWTH AND ITS INVESTMENT IMPLICATIONS: Large Capital Investment as Limiting Factor. Patents, Trademarks, and Customer Goodwill. CAUSES OF CHANGE IN INDUSTRY PROSPECTS: Technology and Industry Prospects. Changes in Buying Habits of Consumer. Population Characteristics and Industry Growth. Foreign Competition and Industrial Growth. SPECIAL FACTORS IN INDUSTRY ANALYSIS: Governmental Actions. Commodity Prices as a Factor. Industry Cyclical Characteristics.

12. ANALYSIS OF INDUSTRIAL SECURITIES—FINANCIAL STATEMENTS . . 218

INTRODUCTION TO FINANCIAL STATEMENT ANALYSIS: Familiarization with Accounting Practices. Preparation of Statements for Analysis. Choice of Tools of Analysis. Importance of Interpretation. THE BALANCE SHEET: Current Assets. Cash and Its Equivalent. Receivables. Inventory. Fixed Assets. Liabilities. Short-Term Debt. Deferred Income. Long-Term Debt. Capital

Funds. Contractual Equity Value Factors. Consolidated Balance Sheets. THE INCOME STATEMENT: Sales. Cost of Operations. Cost of Goods Sold and Inventories. Depreciation Charges. The Cash Earnings Concept. Debt Service Analysis. Extraordinary Items.

13. ANALYSIS OF INDUSTRIAL SECURITIES—FINANCIAL STATEMENT ANALYSIS AND INTERPRETATION 246
MEASURES OF GROWTH. MEASURES OF PROFITABILITY. MEASURES OF EARNINGS QUALITY. MEASURES OF WORKING CAPITAL ADEQUACY. MEASURES OF CREDIT CAPACITY. DIVIDEND PAYOUT RATIO. FINAL SELECTION MEASURES.

14. ANALYSIS OF TRANSPORTATION SECURITIES—RAILROADS AND AIRLINES 262
CHARACTERISTICS OF THE TRANSPORTATION INDUSTRY. FREIGHT TRANSPORTATION MARKET. PASSENGER TRANSPORTATION MARKET: Railroads and Passenger Traffic. RAILROAD INDUSTRY: Railroads and Their Competitors. Regulation of Rail Rates and Service. Work Rules and Cost of Operation. Merger Movement. Summary. Analysis of Railroad Financial Statements and Operations. The Balance Sheet. Measures of Plant and Equipment Utilization. Traffic Analysis. The Income Statement. Analysis of Operating Expenses. Analysis of Other Income. Analysis of Fixed Charges and Debt. Analysis of Claims of Bonds. Analysis of Fixed Charges. Analysis of Maturities. Criteria for Selection. AIRLINES: Financial and Operating Characteristics. Assets. Capitalization. Analysis of Operations and Profitability. Regulatory Environment. Airline Growth Prospects.

15. ANALYSIS OF PUBLIC UTILITY SECURITIES 296
PUBLIC UTILITY REGULATION: Rate-Making. Rate Base. Rate Base and the Investor. THE ELECTRIC LIGHT AND POWER INDUSTRY: Industry Growth. Regional Growth. Cyclical Stability and Competition. Analysis of Electric Utility Financial Statesments and Operations. SELECTION OF SECURITIES: Times-Fixed-Charges-Earned Ratio. Common Stock Selection.

16. SPECIALIZED ANALYTICAL TECHNIQUES—INSURANCE COMPANIES . . 321
LIFE INSURANCE COMPANIES: Nature of Life Insurance Company Operation. The Source of Policy Reserves Life Insurance Company Costs. Acquisition and Operating Costs. Net Gain from Operations. Book Value of Stocks of Life Insurance Companies. Adjusted Book Value. Importance of Growth. Summary. PROPERTY AND CASUALTY INSURANCE COMPANIES: Profits of Property and Casualty Companies. Measures of Underwriting Experience. Emphasis on Investment Income. Earnings Adjustments. The Balance Sheet. Liabilities. Adjusted Book Value. Selection and Adjusted Book Value.

17. SPECIALIZED ANALYTICAL TECHNIQUES—INVESTMENT COMPANIES . 347
NATURE OF INVESTMENT COMPANIES: Differences in Form of Organization. Differences in Capital Structure. Differences in Investment Objectives and Policy. Differences in Systematic Purchase Plans. Purchasing and Closing Costs. SELECTION CONSIDERATIONS: Management Appraisal—Open-End Investment Companies. Evaluation of Management Performance in Closed-End Companies. Investor's Experience Indexes. Effect of Purchasing and Closing Costs. Effect of Federal Individual Income Taxes.

18. SPECIALIZED ANALYTICAL TECHNIQUES—BANKS AND FINANCE COMPANIES 366
COMMERCIAL BANKS: The Balance Sheet. Capital Structure. Capital-Risk

Asset Ratio. Loan-Deposit Ratio. Profitability Analysis. Gains and Losses on Securities. Summary. FINANCE COMPANIES: Investment Characteristics. The Financial Statements. Analysis of Operations. Selection Measures.

19. GOVERNMENT AND FOREIGN SECURITIES 386

MUNICIPAL BONDS: General Characteristics. Investment Characteristics. Marketability of Municipal Bonds. Analysis of Municipal Bonds. Legality. Measures of Ability to Pay. Importance of Efficient Fiscal Management. Economic Characteristics of the Area. Revenue Bonds. Other Types of Municipals. U.S. GOVERNMENT SECURITIES: Marketable Direct Obligations, Nonmarketable Securities. Bonds of Government Corporations and Agencies. Risks of Government Securities. FOREIGN SECURITIES: Political Stability and Government Regulation. Transfer Problems.

20. THE PROBLEM OF TIMING INVESTMENTS 409

APPROACHES TO PROBLEM OF TIMING. FORECASTING MAJOR ECONOMIC TRENDS: Use of Business Indicators in Forecasting. Limitations of Data. TECHNICAL MARKET ANALYSIS: The Dow Theory. The Odd-Lot Theory. The Confidence Index. The Advance-Decline Line. Summary. THE FORMULA PLANS: The Equalizing Formula Plans. The Dollar-Averaging Formula Plan.

21. ALTERNATIVES FOR THE INVESTOR—PORTFOLIO ADMINISTRATION . . 440

PORTFOLIO ACQUISITION: Media Selection. Media Quality. Capital Appreciation versus Current Income. Capital Gains and the Portfolio. Growth Stocks and Capital Gains. Income Taxes and the Portfolio. Income Taxes and Growth Stocks. Need for Liquidity. Other Selection Considerations. INVESTMENT PORTFOLIO SUPERVISION: Portfolio Supervision and Timing. Security Analysis and Timing. Tax Switching. Aids in Portfolio Supervision.

APPENDIX 1. ELEMENTARY MATHEMATICS OF STATISTICS AND FINANCE . 463

APPENDIX 2. INCOME SAVINGS AND EXPENDITURES OF PEOPLE WITH FOUR OR MORE YEARS OF COLLEGE 487

INDEX 489

CHAPTER **1**

Scope and Nature of Investments

THE VIEWPOINT OF THE INVESTOR

The conventional course in investments generally has as a prerequisite certain basic courses in finance and accounting. These courses usually involve an examination of financial institutions, the problems and techniques of business or corporate financing, and business financial management. The student's vantage point in these studies is usually as a manager of a business. The subject matter is concerned with, among other things, the best method of solving the firm's financial problems and selecting the most favorable type of financing. In this role of business financial manager, he nearly always is a borrower of funds and seldom a lender; he is generally the seller of an equity interest in a business and is not often a purchaser.

Since each financial asset is a bargain between the business financial manager and the investor, the study of investment management and analysis makes it necessary for the student to reverse his position. As business financial manager, the student had available to him all the information concerning the firm's operations. In contrast, the investor in his relationship with businesses is usually viewing financial transactions as an outsider. His dealings with the business are nearly always as a creditor or an absentee owner. Unless the investor has a substantial interest in the business, the management does not feel compelled to share all the information available. A certain amount of information is customarily shared with investors in annual and other periodic reports, but on the whole, the management regards the investor as an outsider who is trying to maximize his income. To achieve his objectives, the investor must usually bargain for his rights with a business which has a vastly superior economic power. The investor reinforces his bargaining position by analyzing the in-

1

vestment opportunities offered to him by business financial managers. He scales down the superior bargaining position of the business financial manager by exercising his privilege or right to reject any or all of these opportunities offered to him. This power of rejection or selection forces the financial manager to offer only those opportunities that will meet the requirements of the mass of investors who make the market.

The investors further exercise their influence over the business financial manager after the initial sale of securities by trading those creditorship or ownership securities they hold. Successful management is rewarded by relatively high security prices, which is an invitation for continued sale of corporate securities to provide funds for expansion. On the other hand, poor management is usually denied access to the market or is offered access on very unfavorable terms.

If the investor fails to analyze investment opportunities before purchase, he is not using the bargaining tools available to him. The key to successful investing is careful selection and valuation of available investment opportunities. This examination and analysis involves three chronological segments—past performance, present condition, and future prospects. Although an investor is only interested in the future performance of the firm, later discussion will show that the starting point in estimating the future is the past performance of the business.

WHY STUDY INVESTMENTS

A student of investment management and analysis may be motivated to study the subject either because of desire to enter some phase of the investment business or to acquire the knowledge necessary to manage his own investments. The material in this book should serve as an introduction to the subject and should satisfy the needs of either group.

A person who studies investments with the idea of possibly entering some phase of the investment business has two general avenues available to him. He may enter the securities distribution end of the business as a customer's man or salesman with a brokerage house, investment banking firm, or mutual fund; he may select as his career security analysis, in which case he would become a security analyst. These two career choices are not mutually exclusive, because any good brokerage house customer's man has some knowledge of security analytical techniques and frequently makes recommendations to customers. Conversely, the security analyst who works for a brokerage house may be allowed to have his own customers which he may service. However, the distribution and analysis functions, even in those financial institutions that are basically distributors of securities, are usually separated, with the customer's man performing one group of services and the analyst another.

The customer's man is an employee of a brokerage or investment banking house. His basic function is to provide the link between customers and security markets. However, a secondary function, often a vital part of his job, is to give recommendations to clients. The second function is usually an important part of the first. That is, the customer's man's success in building his clientele is often based on the soundness of the advice he gives to clients. The customer's man may do his own research and analysis as the basis for his recommendation. Usually, he relies on the work of the firm's research department, supplemented by his own study of current news and estimates of customer needs.

The person interested in security analysis as a career has a far wider choice of employers. His function as an analyst is to select after analysis suitable securities for any one of a wide variety of investors. He may be employed by a brokerage house, an investment banker, an investment counselor, an investment company, an investment advisory service, an insurance company, or a commercial bank.

Irrespective of who his employer is, the security analyst must determine whether or not securities about to be purchased or those presently held are overvalued or undervalued in terms of current market price. He advises the management to either buy or sell the security, depending on the situation. When employed by a financial institution, the analyst performs a function slightly different than when he is investing for himself. The individual investor not only makes the appraisal of the security but also determines whether the security is suitable for his portfolio and conforms to his investment policies. The professional analyst generally only makes a recommendation as to the relative valuation of the security, and the final investment decision is made by an investment committee of the institution.

Most people study investments so that they may acquire sufficient knowledge to intelligently invest their own savings. Possibly, the individual investor may wish to rely on his own broker or an investment counselor to select his investments. Even in such cases, he should have sufficient knowledge and understanding of investment management and analysis to judge an adviser's knowledge and competence.

WHY SAVE AND INVEST

If an individual studies investments, it must be assumed that he has funds to invest. One might ask the more basic question: Why save? The purpose of saving is to provide for future economic contingencies. The general financial goal of the individual is to provide an income for the members of his family as long as they are dependent on him. In normal circumstances, a man will provide sufficient income to support his family.

The motivation for saving is to provide for the family if one's income is interrupted by death, disability, retirement, or some other contingency, such as unemployment. The provision for these things and current expenditures both must be provided for out of one's income. The need to save to provide for these contingencies is usually a most pressing problem, since when the need for savings and insurance to cover these contingencies is greatest, the income is smallest. The nature of this problem and its solution is discussed in Chapter 2.

The Allocation of Savings

The personal financial management problem is the allocation of income between current needs and savings. The personal investment management problem is the use of savings in the most efficient manner to cover the contingencies that may interrupt income. In later chapters, there will be a discussion of the problems associated with allocating savings for life insurance premiums, disability insurance premiums, and a retirement fund. Most of the discussion in this book is concerned with problems surrounding the choice of investment media for the retirement fund.

Investment Choices

In the investment of the retirement fund, the individual has two broad choices. These choices are fixed-dollar contracts and equity investments. Fixed-dollar contracts are those investments in which the investor is legally entitled to receive for his commitment the return of his original investment plus a limited return in the form of interest. Equities, on the other hand, refer to ownership investments, such as real estate holdings or ownership of a business. A U.S. government savings bond is an example of a fixed-dollar contract; the original investment plus interest is returned to the investor after a predetermined number of years. In contrast, a share of common stock is an equity investment; a fractional ownership interest in a corporation is acquired with the idea of participating in the profits, if any, of the company. There are several different types of equity investments. The investor may purchase real estate, go into a business himself, or purchase common stock in a corporation without intending to actively participate in management. The problems of investing in real estate or real estate mortgages, or owning and operating a business involve special considerations better covered in books and courses devoted exclusively to that subject. Therefore, the discussion of equity investments will be confined to corporate securities held by the nonmanagement-type investor.

Fixed-dollar contracts may be classified into two groups: (1) direct fixed-dollar contract investments, such as U.S. government savings bonds, and (2) indirect or institutional fixed-dollar contracts, such as commercial bank savings deposits.

These institutional fixed-dollar contracts have increasingly become an important investment media in the last 10 years. The data in Table 1–1 show that individuals, each year, have increased their holdings of institutional fixed-dollar contracts, particularly savings accounts. The increase in direct investments in securities amounted to only $7.7 billion in 1964, or the same increase as in 1955, while savings accounts in financial institutions increased by $23.7 billion in 1964. Savings accounts are more popular with individual investors because of the simplicity of administering this type of investment.

Investment in corporate securities, particularly common stock, is probably inadvisable for the average untrained investor because of the problems of selecting securities and timing purchases. For this reason, the discussion in the following chapters is concerned primarily with these problems of security analysis and investment portfolio administration. However, some attention is given to the more pedestrian investments of the savings deposit type with financial institutions.

TABLE 1–1

Annual Net Change in Financial Assets of Households

Year	Savings Associations	Mutual Savings Banks	Commercial Banks	Credit Unions	Life Insurance Reserves	Pension Fund Reserves	Credit and Equity Instruments	Total
			Billions of Dollars					
1955	$ 4.9	$ 1.8	$ 1.7	$ 0.4	$ 3.0	$ 5.5	$ 7.7	$25.0
1956	4.9	1.9	2.2	0.5	3.4	6.0	7.5	26.4
1957	4.8	1.7	5.2	0.5	2.8	6.6	6.9	28.4
1958	6.1	2.3	5.3	0.5	3.1	7.3	3.9	28.5
1959	6.6	1.2	3.0	0.5	3.4	8.3	12.6	35.6
1960	7.5	1.4	3.3	0.6	3.3	8.1	1.0	25.2
1961	8.8	1.9	6.8	0.7	3.4	8.6	4.1	34.3
1962	9.4	3.1	11.5	0.7	3.8	8.9	4.2	41.5
1963	11.0	3.3	7.6	0.9	4.3	10.1	7.2	44.4
1964	10.5	4.2	8.1	1.1	4.8	10.1	7.7	46.5
			Percentage Distribution					
1955	19.6%	7.2%	6.8%	1.6%	12.0%	22.0%	30.8%	100.0%
1956	18.6	7.2	8.3	1.9	12.9	22.7	28.4	100.0
1957	16.8	6.0	18.2	1.8	9.8	23.2	24.2	100.0
1958	21.4	8.1	18.6	1.8	10.9	25.5	13.7	100.0
1959	18.5	3.4	8.4	1.4	9.6	23.3	35.4	100.0
1960	29.8	5.5	13.1	2.4	13.1	32.1	4.0	100.0
1961	25.7	5.5	19.8	2.0	9.9	25.1	12.0	100.0
1962	22.6	7.5	27.6	1.7	9.1	21.4	10.1	100.0
1963	24.8	7.4	17.1	2.0	9.7	22.8	16.2	100.0
1964	22.7	9.1	17.5	1.9	10.4	21.8	16.6	100.0

Source: United States Savings and Loan League, *Savings and Loan Fact Book, 1965*

CLIMATE FOR SAVINGS AND INVESTMENT

The attitudes toward saving vary considerably over a period of time. These changes in attitude depend on the individual's estimate of future economic and political conditions.

Generally, individual investors have not been influenced too much by changes in the political climate, because in U.S. history there has been no major political upheaval, such as has been experienced in other countries, to dramatically affect the value of investments and the incentive to save. Political instability can reduce the incentive to save and invest in claims stated in terms of the national currency or in contracts whose validity is dependent on the retention of the national government. For example, the lack of stability in some Latin-American governments causes many investors to decline investments in those countries.

Nature of Investment

Investment is the commitment of funds with the hope of gain. The gain may take different forms, such as current money income or capital gain. The need for an income is to compensate the investor for giving up control and use these funds for a period of time. Since any gains as well as the original investment will be received in the future, investment involves risk or the possibility of loss, because any future commitment involves the possibility of loss or risk. Therefore, the definition of investment is the commitment of funds with the hope of gain which includes compensation for risk.

That an investment carries risk does not accurately express the idea, as risk suggests only the possibility of loss. Actually, an investment involves uncertainty or the possibility of both gain and loss.[1] With a good investment, the possible gain presumably is more than sufficient to compensate for the assumption of the risk of loss. The sources of uncertainty are discussed more fully in Chapter 3.

Economic Uncertainty and Investment

The U.S. investment climate is primarily affected by economic uncertainties. The individual's appraisal of the future economic climate profoundly affects his willingness and ability to save and the type of claims he is willing to hold. Periods of economic recession tend to cause individuals to shift their savings from equities or shares of ownership to creditorship obligations, such as savings deposits or bonds. For example, it may be noted from the percentage distribution of annual net change in financial assets of households that the relative interest in securities diminished in 1960 after a decline in stock prices in that year. In addition, the results of the *1959 Survey of Consumer Finances* noted that "there were marked shifts in the types of financial assets that consumers acquired in 1958 as compared with 1957."

The fear of financial insecurity which stems from an economic recession and its symptoms—unemployment, loss of overtime pay, and shorter hours—causes individuals to save more proportionately and to spend less.[2] The amount of financial assets increased, and the

---

[1] George Heberton Evans, Jr., and George E. Barnett, *Principles of Investment* (New York: Houghton Mifflin Co., 1940), chap. iv. This chapter is an excellent treatment of risk, uncertainty, and the compensation for uncertainty.

[2] "Saving and Financial Flows," *Federal Reserve Bulletin*, August, 1959, pp. 822–23.

preferences for the types of assets changed. During the recession year of 1958, the individual tended to shift his investments to bank deposits and other fixed-value claims, while purchases of bonds and common stock which could be sold in the market declined sharply.

The tendency of the investor to shift from equity claims to evidences of debt during periods of economic adversity indicates one of the major investment management problems—that is, the problem of timing purchases and sales of securities. The perverse timing indicated by reducing or selling holdings of marketable securities, particularly equities, during periods of falling market prices is indicative of the effects of the economic climate on the individual investor's actions. In fact, the belief that the average investor consistently sells common stock at the wrong time and purchases them at the wrong time is the basis for one theory of timing common stock investments discussed in Chapter 20.

SUMMARY

The study of investment management and analysis frequently requires that the student reorient his thinking. The customary position of a business manager is reversed, and the investor is in on the other side of the bargaining table.

In one sense, the study of investments is premature in many cases. The necessary first step is saving funds before investment, and this becomes a problem for the individual. The motivation for saving for most individuals is strong, but it is evident from later discussion that the problem of investing does not normally arise until the individual is past the age of thirty. Even after funds are saved, most investors do not invest in securities, but shift the investment management problem to financial institutions. This tendency to use financial institutions as the basic investment media is probably the result of the inability or unwillingness to analyze, select, and manage a securities portfolio. Therefore, the individual who has an education in investment management and analysis has acquired knowledge that is possessed by relatively few people.

REVIEW QUESTIONS AND PROBLEMS

1. What are the major differences in emphasis in the study of investment management and business financial management?

2. What are the general career choices of a student of investments?

3. Distinguish between direct and indirect investments by individuals.

4. The word "investments" has more than one meaning, depending on the context. Distinguish between the usage of the term by the economist and by the investor.

5. If successful investment decision-making is an art or skill based on previous experience and an element of chance, what reason is there for studying investments?

6. The National Federation of Financial Analysts Societies has an educational program and campaign to require security analysts to meet certain minimum standards. What would be the advantages and disadvantages, if any, of such standards? What should be the minimum educational requirements?

7. One thinks of saving and investing as "laying away for the future." Could one purchase a piano or automobile and come within this definition?

8. What are the two basic contractual forms of investment media?

9. What is meant by the climate for saving and investment?

CHAPTER **2**

Personal Financial and Investment Planning

Personal investment and financial planning are closely related. The investment plan is a part of the overall personal financial plan.

To fully understand the interrelationship of financial and investment planning, it helps to think of a man's family as a self-contained economic unit. The family is usually dependent on a single income producer, the man of the family, for its income. The economic responsibility of this income producer is to provide an income for himself and his dependents during their lives. This means that normally he must support his children until they are eighteen to twenty-one years of age, and his wife and himself for the rest of their natural lives.

The income producer has no problem in discharging his responsibility as long as he is in good health and is employed. If he were positive that he would be the last surviving member of his family and would be gainfully employed until his death, the family could spend all the income provided by him. The problem is that the income flow to the family may be interrupted by various personal hazards. These hazards are: (1) premature death, (2) disability, (3) retirement, and (4) involuntary unemployment. The existence of these hazards makes it necessary for the income producer to provide alternative sources of income for his family if his normal income is interrupted. It is not necessary to replace *all* the income when the head of the household is nonproductive. It is necessary to provide only sufficient income to meet living expenses. The family usually divides its income between (1) current expenditure needs and (2) savings and insurance premiums. Obviously, the amount needed for future living expenses would be less than the income of the family, because it would not be necessary to continue to save and pay insurance premiums to provide for these hazards. For example, in the event of the death of the income producer, there would be no need to

10

continue paying life insurance premiums. (It is assumed that no life insurance is carried for those members of the family who are not producing an income.)

To provide for these future expenditure requirements, the income producer has three types of protection: (1) accumulated family assets and voluntary insurance programs, (2) employer and union benefits, and (3) compulsory government programs. In this book, we are primarily concerned with the problems associated with investment of family assets and selection of proper types of private life insurance. It is necessary, however, to recognize that other benefits do reduce the need for the income producer to provide for these future expenditure requirements. For example, in the case of the social security program, he has been compelled to make partial provision for the contingencies of death and retirement through a series of involuntary contributions such as social security taxes and unemployment compensation taxes.

THE INCOME PATTERN

To realize the full economic impact of income loss from one of the hazards mentioned previously, it is necessary to calculate the income loss. That is, each investor has a considerable value as an economic man because of the income he will generate during his lifetime. The economic value of a man is dependent on (1) the level of income, (2) the pattern of income, and (3) the length of working life. The effects of the level-of-income and the length-of-working-life factors on the economic value of a man are obvious.

A man who works 40 years for an average annual income of $10,000 a year obviously has a greater economic value than a man who only receives $5,000 a year with the same working life.

Differences in the pattern of income receipts also have a profound effect on the economic value of a man. The effects of these differences in the patterns of income stem from the fact that present incomes are more valuable than future incomes. That is, a dollar received today is more valuable than a dollar to be received five years from today. Therefore, the total life income of a highly skilled worker may be the same as the total life income of a college graduate. The economic value of the skilled worker, however, may be greater than the economic value of the college graduate, because the skilled worker receives his income at relatively constant amounts over his lifetime, while the college graduate has a relatively low income in his early working years and a greater one in later years.

Illustration of an Income Pattern

To illustrate the value of the income loss to the family, it is useful to compute the economic value of a man as an income-producing unit for his family. In the following example, we have computed the value of the average college graduate using as income data the median incomes of persons with four or more years of college. In the illustration in Figure 2–1, we assume that this hypothetical college graduate begins work at twenty-two years of age and retires at age sixty-five.[1] The figure shows the pattern of money incomes and the present value of these incomes. Our composite college graduate will receive $473,924 in income, based on 1963 data.[2] The present value of those incomes discounted at 4 percent is $199,054.

This life value estimate is useful in investment planning. For example, if our college graduate died, his family would be losing an income-producing unit with an income potential of about $475,000. Obviously, this income loss must be replaced for the family to continue as a social and economic unit. It may be replaced by the wife's remarrying, but a man cannot plan on covering this contingency in this way. A more conventional approach would be life insurance for the man of the family. The question of how much life insurance will be more fully discussed later. However, if the total economic life value were replaced, the family would have to carry life insurance equal to the present value of $475,000, which is about $200,000, less the present value of social security benefits and other family investments.

There is not, however, any need to replace the entire life value of the income producer of the family unless (1) the family was spending all its income, and (2) the income producer was spending none of his own income before his death. It is unlikely that this would be true. Generally, the family will have been spending some income for insurance premiums to provide protection against the life hazards of death and disability. Obviously, after the death of the income producer, these expenditures would not have to be continued. In addition, some of the income would be used by or consumed by the

---

[1] See also Appendix 2 for tables showing detail.

[2] These income data were taken from *Consumer Income, Income of Families and Persons, 1963*, U.S. Bureau of Census, Department of Commerce.

FIGURE 2–1

**Cumulative Income and Cumulative Total Present Value of
Income of College Graduate, Age Twenty-two**

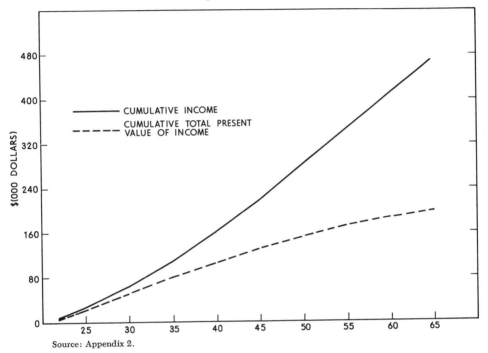

Source: Appendix 2.

income producer. In the event of his death, there would be no necessity to replace this portion of his income. The amount of the income that must be replaced is:

GROSS INCOME — INCOME TAXES — FUTURE EXPENDITURE REQUIREMENTS
(SAVINGS AND LIFE INSURANCE PREMIUMS) = CURRENT EXPENDITURES

Therefore, the maximum amount of income that must be replaced in the event that income is interrupted is not the total income but the amount the family is currently spending for consumption or current expenditures.

In order to determine the value of the economic loss to the family, what must be computed is present value of the current expenditures. For illustrative purposes, we have computed the present value of the current expenditures of a college graduate. It is assumed in the following illustration that our hypothetical college graduate saves 5 percent of the first $5,000 of income, and 30 percent of any excess.[3]

Whether the assumed rate of savings is sufficient to cover the future expenditure requirements is dependent on (1) the rate of growth in the value of these savings and (2) the family's scale of living. As the family becomes accustomed to a particular scale of living, the objective of the investment plan is to allow the family to continue that scale of living in the future. Naturally, the lower the present scale of living, the smaller will be the amount of income required to maintain it in the future and the greater will be the residue from income which will be available to provide for these future contingencies. As mentioned earlier, the process of proper financial planning is to achieve a proper allocation of income between current and future expenditures. One of the most difficult problems is to control the family's scale of living and its level of expenditures. The importance of attaining some sort of a balanced allocation of income is evident from the material in Table 2–1.[4] In this illustration, the college graduate has available $87,128 in savings over his lifetime. A recapitulation of our college graduate's financial position at various age levels is shown in Table 2–1.

The current expenditures of our college graduate over his lifetime

TABLE 2–1

Cumulative Incomes, Expenditures, and Savings, at Various Age Levels, for a Person with Four or More Years of College, Beginning Work at Age Twenty-two

	Income	*Expenditures*	*Savings*
25	$ 25,776	$ 23,043	$ 2,733
30	64,202	56,191	8,011
35	109,523	94,166	15,357
40	161,652	136,956	24,696
45	219,026	183,367	35,659
50	280,964	232,974	47,990
55	344,644	283,799	60,844
60	409,124	335,185	73,938
65	473,924	386,796	87,128

Source: Appendix 2.

[3] Joseph M. Belth, "Dynamic Life Insurance Programming," *Journal of Risk and Insurance*, Vol. XXXI, No. 4, pp. 542–43. This is an excellent article on using the life economic value approach in life insurance programming.

[4] An immutable law of family economics seems to be that family expenditures will rise to the level of a man's income no matter how high it goes. A higher level just seems to arouse their competitive spirit to spend, not their incentive to save.

are $386,796, and the present value of these expenditures discounted at 4 percent is $165,045. (See Appendix 2.) In other words, if the college graduate were to become disabled or die, his family would need $165,000 to replace his lost income if they are to continue living in the manner to which they have become accustomed.

PERSONAL INVESTMENT REQUIREMENTS

The head of the household must have either savings or insurance to provide a capital fund of $165,000. If this capital fund is invested to yield an average annual return of 4 percent and the capital fund is used up or consumed in the process, the family would have an income flow that would approximate their current expenditures. Therefore, the crux of the financial planning problem is to allocate income between current expenditures and savings in order to satisfy present wants and needs and adequately cover future contingencies. The investment planning problem is to allocate these savings in a way that will most effectively cover the hazards that may adversely affect the family's income. These hazards, mentioned earlier, are (1) premature death, (2) disability, (3) retirement, and (4) involuntary unemployment and other contingencies.

Premature Death as a Requirement

A major contingency that must be covered by the investment plan is that a man will not live long enough to completely fulfill his economic responsibility of providing his wife and dependent children with an income during their lives. The death of the income producer causes an immediate termination of his income. The personal consequences of the termination of the family income are obviously nil, but the effect on the family can be catastrophic.

The economic impact on a family of income termination is more a matter of when it happens. If the income producer dies after retirement and has an adequate retirement fund, the economic impact is not too great. The more serious situation is the premature death of the family income producer during the earlier years of his working life, particularly if there are children or other dependents.

For example, let us assume that our hypothetical college graduate gets married when he is twenty-two years old, and he marries a woman who is also twenty-two years old. They have their first child at the age of twenty-four and the second child at the age of twenty-six, and the husband dies at the age of thirty. The family would sustain a substantial financial loss from the death of the husband. The present value of the future income at age thirty is $209,320. At the age of thirty, the family has total savings of only $8,011, which would not provide sufficient income for the family to meet future expenditures. (See Table 2-1.) Since no estate exists from savings, it must be provided by life insurance. In the event of the investor's death and an inadequate life insurance program, the investor's wife has the alternative of working or remarrying.[5] If there are small children in the family, the situation without adequate life insurance is even more complicated, as the wife has difficulty in working and at the same time caring for the children.

It may be noticed in Table 2-1 that the present value of family expenditures declines as time passes. In the event that a man and wife live past the productive period of the man's life, there is less reason to emphasize income termination at death. His children are presumably no longer dependent on him. If the man cannot work or has retired, the financial loss to his wife in the event of his death is limited essentially to burial expenses. In this case, life insurance probably would not be essential. For example, the total current expenditures remaining at age sixty are only about $40,000, and their present value is substantially less, so if the income producer died at age sixty, the income loss would be relatively small.

How Much Life Insurance?

In the event of premature death, it seems that the investor should have sufficient life insurance, or its equivalent, to replace at least the lost income or, more precisely, the present value of current expenditure requirements. Actually, the investor does not have to purchase that amount of life insurance because of the survivors' benefits provided by the social security program. Through involuntary contributions or taxes, the investor has "purchased life insurance" or life value protection. The survivors' benefits under social security are shown in Table 2-2.

The life insurance required can be reduced by the amount of these

---

[5] One could formulate a law of life insurance programming which postulates that the amount of life insurance a man carries should be an inverse relationship to the relative attractiveness and marriageability of his wife.

TABLE 2–2

Social Security
Monthly Survivors' Insurance Payments

Average Yearly Earnings after 1950	Widow, Widower, Sixty-two or over or One Aged Parent Alone	Widow under Sixty-two and One Child	Widow under Sixty-two and Two Children
$ 800	$ 40.00	$ 60.00	$ 60.00
1,200	48.70	88.50	88.50
1,800	60.30	109.60	120.00
2,400	69.30	126.00	161.60
3,000	78.40	142.60	202.40
3,600	86.70	157.60	236.40
4,200	95.70	174.00	254.00
4,800	104.80	190.60	254.00

social security death benefits. For example, if we assumed that our graduate died at age thirty his wife would receive $254 a month ($3,048 a year) until the oldest child reached eighteen years of age. Then, the family would receive $190.60 a month ($2,287.20 a year) until the youngest child reached the age of eighteen. After that time, social security benefits would terminate until the widow reached the age of sixty-two.

To illustrate the effect of social security benefits on life insurance needs, the present value of family expenditures of our college graduate at age thirty is $169,374. (See Appendix 2.) The present value of the social security benefits is $39,957.[6] The life insurance equation is: present value of current family expenditures, less present value of social security survivors' benefits, less other assets equals life insurance needed.

In this example, the life insurance needed would be about $130,000. ($169,374 less $39,957 = $129,417.) We assumed here that there were no "other assets" or that the members of the family were not able to generate any income themselves.

Disability as a Requirement

The economic effects of the income producer's disability parallel the effects of death, because in both cases there is an income loss to the family. The economic impact of disability of the head of the

---

[6] Appendix 2.

household on the family income is usually greater than death. The reason for this is that not only has the income of the income producer stopped but also medical expenses that may be large and continuing are usually associated with the disability. That is, there is usually a two-fold economic effect of total disability—income loss and medical expenses.

Generally, the economic effects of these hazards may be covered by insurance. The investor may purchase health and accident insurance to relieve his family of the medical and hospital expense burden. To cover the income loss, disability income insurance may be purchased. Most families now have accident and health insurance, with the widespread coverage offered by various Blue Cross and Blue Shield plans. However, disability income insurance, which provides an income during periods of total disability, is much less common. This insurance protects the investor against loss of income resulting from accidents or illness. Protection is afforded because the insurance pays benefits or an income to the insured while he is disabled. These disability income policies usually do not provide benefits that will cover the entire income loss, because there would be no incentive for the insured to work if the benefits were as much or more than his earnings. As indicated from the previous discussion, disability income insurance in this amount would not be necessary. The amount of benefits should be roughly the same as the current expenditure requirements of the family. The investor in the example discussed previously would need an amount equal to only 65 percent of his income to cover his current expenditures. This percentage of income would fall within the normal limits of coverage, which are about 60 to 75 percent of the insured's income.

Of course, the investor may decide that he wants to assume the risk of total disability himself and save the cost of insurance. Many people do take this attitude, since 60 million wage earners had hospital insurance, while only 47 million had some type of loss-of-income coverage.[7] An investor may decide that he "can't afford" this insurance. It is questionable whether he "can afford" to be without it if one considers the severity of the consequences of being without this coverage. In addition, the investor should recognize that the frequency of long-term disability is high. For example, at age thirty-two

---

[7] *Sourcebook of Health Insurance Data* (New York Health Insurance Institute, 1965), pp. 12 and 23.

the probability of having a long-term disability are 3.45 times the chances of dying; "at age forty-two, 3.01 times; and at age fifty-two, 2.28 times."[8]

TABLE 2–3

Comparison of Chances of Long-Term Disability with Chances of Death at Quinquennial Central Ages

Age at Time of Disablement	Number per 1,000 Still Disabled at End of 3 Months	Number per 1,000 Dying at the Given Age	Changes of Disability Compared with Death
22	6.64	1.86	3.56 to 1
27	6.57	1.99	3.30 to 1
32	7.78	2.25	3.45 to 1
37	9.81	2.80	3.50 to 1
42	12.57	4.17	3.01 to 1
47	16.76	6.36	2.63 to 1
52	22.72	9.96	2.28 to 1
57	32.38	15.54	2.08 to 1
62	46.66	24.31	1.91 to 1
67	67.16	38.04	1.76 to 1
72	103.01	58.65	1.75 to 1

Source: Robert Osler, "Programming Health Insurance," *Life and Health Insurance Handbook*, ed. Davis W. Gregg (Homewood, Ill.: Richard D. Irwin, Inc., 1964).

Equal to, if not more important than, the frequency of total disability is its severity or average duration. Generally speaking, the number of disabilities that last longer than 24 months is so small that it is hardly worth insuring against. For example, the current morbidity—rates of disability—tables indicate that at the age of thirty-five, of those disabled at the end of a 30-day waiting period, only 2.6 percent were still disabled at the end of 24 months.[9] Of course, it is of little consolation to the investor totally disabled for 10 years to say that he is a statistical freak. However, as a practical matter, the investor may not feel that the cost of insuring for periods longer than two years is worth the added premium.

Nature of Medical Expense Insurance

Medical expense insurance policies may be placed in two broad groups. First, there is the basic or "first dollar" coverage, which pays for hospital and medical expenses from the first day of confinement and for rendering of professional services for surgical procedures.

---

[8] Robert W. Osler, "Programming Health Insurance," *Life and Health Insurance Handbook*, ed. Davis W. Gregg (Homewood, Ill.: Richard D. Irwin, Inc., 1964), p. 845.

[9] *Ibid.*, p. 849.

These policies have no deductible provision in that they pay the first dollar of hospital and surgical expense much like the Blue Cross–Blue Shield policies.

The other category of medical expense policies is major medical coverage. These policies do not cover the first dollar of medical expense, but they usually have deductible and coinsurance provisions. The deductible feature usually provides that the insured pay the first $50 or $100 of any claim. (The deductible amount may be any amount, depending on the contract.) The coinsurance will then pay a specified percentage of the claim, usually about 80 percent over the deductible amount, up to $10–15,000. Major medical expense insurance is designed to provide protection against catastrophic medical expenses.

The two types of coverages may be combined to provide complete hospital–surgical care insurance. The basic plan would pay all costs up to the deductible amount, and the major medical insurance would pay for the catastrophic losses. Normally, if the investor had to choose between the coverages, he would find the major medical insurance most suitable. The average investor has, by definition, accumulated a capital fund; therefore, he is usually in a position to pay out the first $100 to $200 of a medical expense loss. He needs to insure against the large catastrophic loss. For this reason, major medical expense insurance is the most suitable type of insurance for the average investor, since he has the funds to handle the small loss.

Nature of Disability Income Insurance

Disability income insurance is designed to cover the income loss from disability. There are many different provisions in the standard disability income policy. The major features that would be of concern to the average investor are: (1) the waiting period before benefits start, (2) the renewal provisions, and (3) definitions of disability.

The conventional disability income policy pays benefits after an elimination or waiting period of a specified time. This waiting period is usually 7, 30, 60, or 90 days. The longer the waiting period, the shorter the period the insurance company is obligated to pay benefits and, consequently, the lower the cost of the coverage.

Another key feature in these policies is with respect to the renewal of the policy. The renewal provisions may state that the policy is (1) cancelable or (2) noncancelable. A cancelable policy is renewable at the option of the insurance company and may be canceled by the company at any time with written notice. The noncancelable policy allows the insured to continuously renew his policy until reaching a specified age, usually age sixty-five. However, the noncancelable policy usually limits the total amount of benefits that may be received for each disability. For example, the policy may provide that the company is obligated to pay benefits for a maximum period of two years, and at the conclusion of this time the benefits would terminate.

The third major provision deals with the definitions of disability. A person is disabled under the terms of most policies when he is unable to perform his occupation. If the policy provides benefits for a period of time longer than two years, it may provide that the disability after one or two years would be defined as inability "to perform the duties of any gainful occupation."[10]

Disability income policies may have any combination of these provisions, plus other salient features. The only way to determine what is being purchased is to inspect and carefully read the policies. Each investor usually can find a policy to fit his individual needs. Three questions that the investor should have answered about any disability income policy are:

1. How much does it pay?
2. How soon does it pay?
3. How long does it pay?

As a general rule, the investor should lengthen the period before benefits start, and should use the saving in premium to increase the monthly benefit payments after they start and to lengthen the period for which they are paid. This plan is practical, because while the first one to six months' income loss from disability is usually not catastrophic, long and continuous disability is catastrophic and the investor should have insurance coverage.

Retirement as a Requirement

Retirement as an investment requirement stems from the need to provide an income that will allow the investor and his wife to live in the manner to which they are accustomed. For example, Appendix

---

[10] John H. Miller, "Individual Disability Income Insurance," *Life and Health Insurance Handbook, op. cit.,* p. 251.

2 shows that the college graduate at the retirement age of 65 will have an income of $12,960, and current expenditures of about $10,000. The life expectancy of a woman at age sixty-five is another 16 years, of a man another 13 years.[11] Social security benefits would allow our investor $2,287.20 a year. Consequently, the investor would be required to have a retirement fund that would provide an income of about $7,700 a year for at least 13 to 16 years.

It is not realistic for a person to assume that he can live only from the income from investing the retirement fund. Assuming an average return of 4 percent, the investor would need a retirement fund of $192,500, which he might accumulate with good investment management. However, the retirement plan should be designed to include consumption of capital as well as current investment income. A conservative approach to solving this problem after retirement is to purchase an annuity which will pay an income to the investor and his wife for the rest of their lives. If purchased at age sixty-five, the cost of a single premium annuity, which would pay $7,700 a year, would be about $132,600. There are also other approaches to the solution of this problem of investing the retirement fund in order to fulfill the investment objective. These approaches will be discussed fully in later chapters.

Unemployment and Other Contingencies as a Requirement

Unemployment is not a major financial hazard for the college graduate, since for this group the probability of unemployment is relatively low. It is, however, a contingency which is, for the most part, unforeseeable, and it is a loss that is not voluntarily insurable. There are some government unemployment insurance programs, but the benefits are not usually large enough to replace the income loss of the average investor. As a consequence, the investor must provide funds to meet this requirement out of his savings.

In addition, the investor may wish to save for some short-term requirements that are not usually so important as the long-term requirements discussed earlier. These foreseeable requirements include such things as the education of children, purchase of a car, and down payments on a house or other consumer goods.

---

[11] *Life Insurance Fact Book, 1965* (New York: Institute of Life Insurance, 1965), p. 97.

The investor also should maintain some liquid funds to cover these requirements and unforeseeable contingencies. It is often suggested that the investor maintain an emergency fund in amount equal to about two to six months' income after taxes. In many cases, an emergency fund of this size is a needless luxury, because there is little or no return on funds held as cash or cash equivalent. The funds for emergencies usually can be provided by borrowing, at a relatively modest rate, on life insurance or other liquid assets. The costs of such infrequent loans are usually more than offset by the gains from having otherwise idle emergency funds invested.

Other Planning Considerations

The investment requirements outline the investor's general needs for life insurance, disability income insurance, retirement funds, and emergency funds. To complete his investment plan, he must estimate the approximate amounts of savings he will allot to satisfy each of these requirements and the policies he will adopt toward the various investment considerations. The accuracy of the estimate of how much he should save for retirement, how much life insurance he should have, and so on, is dependent on consideration of a number of personal economic and social characteristics. These characteristics include age and health of the investor and number and ages of his dependents. These characteristics affect his current requirements as well as his investment requirements.

SUMMARY

Age and level of income and expenditures are the key considerations in investment planning. That is, each investor has considerable personal value as an economic man because of his earnings potential. If the investor begins work at the age of twenty-two and plans to retire at the age of sixty-five, he has roughly 2,236 weeks of productive effort for sale. The sale of this productive effort by the man in the example shown on page 14 would provide total incomes in excess of $473,000. The income from the sale of this productive effort is used by him to fulfill his responsibility of providing for himself and his dependents.

During the early years of his adult life, the investor typically saves little, since his income is usually lowest and his current expenditure requirements usually proportionately highest during that period.

This is also the period during which the risks of disability or death are low, because of the investor's age. Retirement as an investment requirement often is not seriously considered.

Even though the risk of death or total disability is low, the economic effects of death or total disability may be catastrophic, particularly if there are children or other dependents. It is obvious that at this age savings are practically nonexistent, but the family, in the event of the income producer's death, must have an income from the estate. Total disability is even more catastrophic when there is not adequate insurance coverage, because the wife has no acceptable income alternatives, yet the family income has ceased.

At an early age, the investor should begin saving for retirement and building an investment fund. The rate of savings should increase at about the age of thirty and continue to increase to about the age of fifty-five, at which time the rate and amount of savings should begin to level off. Then, after retirement, the investor usually spends all his income and, in most cases, consumes most of his capital fund.

REVIEW QUESTIONS AND PROBLEMS

1. What is the primary objective of a personal financial and investment program?

2. What are the personal hazards which may interrupt the family income flow?

3. What types of protection are available to cover the economic effects of these personal hazards?

4. The economic value of a man is dependent on what factors?

5. Under what set of circumstances might it be possible for a plumber to have a higher economic life value than a brain surgeon? Discuss fully.

6. Why is it not necessary for the family to replace the entire life value of a man at his death?

7. If the average annual income of a college graduate was $8,000, what would be his life value if his future income pattern was similar to that shown in Table 2–1 on page 14?

8. How much life insurance should a man carry if he has no dependents?

9. Why is the economic effect of permanent total disability greater than the economic impact of premature death?

10. Why should a major medical insurance policy with a deductible provision be most suitable for a college graduate?

11. What are the major features of disability income insurance which are of most concern to the investor?

12. If government unemployment, medical insurance, and retirement programs are developed, would there be any need to continue to save and invest?

13. What effect does the age of the investor have on his attitude toward life insurance coverage? Disability income insurance coverage?

CHAPTER **3**

Investment Policy Factors

The development of the investment program is the attempt to satisfy the requirements of the investor after determining the relative importance of various investment policy considerations. These investment policy considerations include the investor's attitude toward risk, taxes, liquidity, and other miscellaneous factors. The relative importance of each of these factors in an investment program may be determined after a review of the investor's requirements and characteristics.

In this chapter, we will discuss these investment policy considerations. Most attention will be given to the risk considerations, because they are basic in investment policy formulation and programming. Tax, liquidity, and other considerations would be considered as secondary to the primary factors of uncertainty and risk of loss in the formulation of most investment programs.

It must be pointed out that these policy considerations are related to one another to such an extent that a change in policy toward risk would very likely also affect a change toward income. For purposes of this discussion, these considerations will be treated as separate entities.

THE NATURE OF RISK

The term "risk" is used here in the popular sense. Risk arises from situations where the outcome is subject to chance, but the cause of the chance and the probability of a particular outcome can be estimated within reasonable limits. It is assumed that the investments the investor is concerned with are of this type. There are some investments with which information is so imperfect or is lacking that the probable outcome can not be estimated. These commitments involve

26

a total speculation as to their outcome and the uncertainty involved would not be included in this definition of risk.

Risk in investment literature usually means the risk associated with probability of loss due to the impaired profitability or solvency of the company. This "risk" is called financial risk. Securities which carry a minimum of financial risk are considered to be relatively safe or high-grade investments. When an investment is considered to be a high-quality commitment, the probability of loss of the dollar amount of the investment from variations in the financial fortunes of the business is small.

One of the problems in investment management is that attempts to minimize financial risk usually result in the assumption of other types of risk. The investment may be a safe investment in the popular sense. However, it may not be safe with respect to (1) losses of purchasing power of dollar payments, (2) declines in value because of changes in the level of interest rates, and (3) losses from the forced sale of the investment at temporarily depressed market prices.

The inevitability of risk assumption causes us to become obsessed with it. This concern with risk is a natural one, because no rational person wants to lose money. However, this probability or chance of loss of dollar amounts and purchasing power of investments is ever present when funds are committed to any venture. The investor may knowingly but not willingly assume risk. He goes to great lengths to reduce possible risks. He does this by intelligent investment management and analysis. In one sense, one could logically refer to investment management and analysis as risk management and analysis. To properly manage these risks, each investor must know the nature of (1) financial risk, (2) purchasing power risk, (3) interest rate risk, and (4) market risk.

Financial Risk

Financial risk is the decline in the value of an investment because of impairment of solvency or unprofitability of the business. As mentioned earlier, the popular notion of risk is financial risk. When there is a discussion of risk in brokerage house literature, financial risk is usually meant.

The probable reason for the emphasis of financial risk in financial literature is that its unwise assumption can result in serious consequences for the investor. Losses from the assumption of financial risk are often permanent and total losses. These total investment losses arise when a corporation becomes insolvent or unable to pay debts. Insolvency usually requires that some definite action be taken to satisfy the claims of creditors of the business. This action may be (1) a voluntary readjustment in the capital structure or (2) a judicial reorganization of the business. When court action is required, the investor, particularly the common stock investor, often suffers a complete loss. In other cases, there may be a voluntary readjustment of financial difficulties which does not require court intervention and is not usually so drastic. Such voluntary readjustments usually do not result in total losses to investors.

Losses due to the impaired profitability of a business are far more frequent and generally less permanent in nature. Insolvency is usually accompanied by impaired profitability. However, a corporation may have a temporary decline in earning power without impairing solvency. Usually, the reduced earnings are caused by conditions that are temporary or that may be corrected by the management. Reduction in earning power is usually the result of such things as changes in level of business activity, reduced product demand, or increased costs of operation. Corporations that manage to maintain solvency usually recover from these setbacks in earnings, and the value of their securities frequently returns to their former level. Actually, the basic purpose of security analysis is to appraise the degree of financial risk involved. Later chapters will deal intensively with these problems.

Purchasing Power Risk

The conservative investor may attempt to avoid financial risk by investing in high-grade bonds, savings deposits, or similar investments. In his attempt to minimize financial risk and preserve the dollar value of his investments, he exposes himself to the purchasing power risk or the probability of loss in the power of these dollars to buy goods and services.

Since World War II, the purchasing power of the dollar has declined nearly 50 percent. The investment effect of this is obvious from this illustration. An investor who wished to save for his son's education could have bought a $1,000 U.S. Savings Bond, Series E, in 1948 for $750. The government would promise to repay him $1,000 in 1958. At maturity in 1958, he would surrender the bond for payment and receive $1,000, or a dollar gain of $250. The investor would have paid a minimum income tax of 20 percent of the gain, or $50, and the net dollar gain would have been only $200. Therefore, in 1958 he would receive his original investment of $750 plus the net increase of $200, or a total of $950. However, during the 10-year period from 1948 to 1958, the consumer price index increased from 102.8 to 123.5, or an increase of 20 percent. The value of his investment in 1958 in terms of 1948 dollars was $759.05, or a net gain of $9.05. This increase in the price level had the effect of decreasing his yield, in real terms, from in excess of 3 percent per annum as advertised by the U.S. government to slightly over $1/10$ of 1 percent per annum. The net result of this effort to avoid financial risk was exposure to purchasing power risk and loss of most of the real value of the income over the 10-year period.

TABLE 3–1

**Consumer Price Index, Unadjusted
Selected Years, 1929–65**
(1957–59 = 100)

1929	59.7	1959	101.5
1933	45.1	1960	103.1
1941	51.3	1961	104.2
1945	62.7	1962	105.4
1956	94.7	1963	106.7
1957	98.0	1964	108.1
1958	100.7	1965	109.9

Source: *Federal Reserve Bulletin.*

One can conclude from Table 3–1 that the purchasing power values of fixed-dollar contracts have been impaired by increases in the price level. From 1945 to 1958, a relatively short span of 13 years, investors experienced a decline of about 38 percent in the value of fixed-dollar contracts. Since that time, the purchasing power of the dollar has been relatively stable, or, at least, the rate of increase in the price level has diminished.

One should exercise caution in appraising the effects of the purchasing power risk, because it is easy to lose perspective. If the price level rises for a few years, the investor may get swept up in a tide of emotionalism which causes him to believe that prices can go in only one direction.

However, in the history of the United States the price level has decreased in as many years as it has increased. In addition, the cumulative magnitude of the increases in purchasing power of the dollar have almost equaled the cumulative decreases up to 1945. (See Table 7–3, page 108.) Since 1945, obviously, we have had a significant deterioration in the purchasing power of the dollar. (See Table 3–1.)

Management of purchasing power risk does not normally receive the attention it should, because it is the most difficult to recognize at the time of occurrence. The investor often is not aware of the slowly increasing level of prices until after the real value of his investment has deteriorated. This is in contrast to financial risk where failure of a corporation to maintain earnings or solvency is almost immediately recognizable.

The purchasing power risk affects only those investors who have plans to spend their savings for goods and services. The investment plans of financial institutions, such as commercial banks whose obligations to depositors are in the form of fixed-dollar contracts, are not directly affected by changes in the price level. Their only requirement is to repay a given number of dollars to their depositors at the time they have agreed; they are not required to restore a given fund of purchasing power.

Interest Rate Risk

Variations in the level of interest rates cause fluctuations in the price of marketable bonds. The probability of loss in the value of an investment from a change in interest rates is called the interest rate risk. The average individual investor would not be concerned with the interest rate risk as a major investment hazard, because he would not usually be a holder of marketable bonds. The fixed-dollar contract portion of the individual investor's program usually would be institutional fixed-dollar contracts, such as cash value of life insurance and savings deposits. However, there are instances where the purchase of marketable bonds by the individual investor would be highly desirable. For example, the purchase of tax-exempt municipal bonds by the investor in the high income tax brackets might be most advantageous.

An investor in high-grade bonds not only is exposed to the purchasing power risk, but also, in addition, he may experience a loss if the general level of interest rates rises. For example, a person who invested $5,000 in U.S. Treasury $3\frac{7}{8}$ percent bonds at the high in 1960 would have paid $5,055 for them. If the investor had been forced to sell these bonds at the low price in 1960, he would have sold them for $4,604 and would have experienced a loss of $451, or about 9 percent.

The interest rate risk can be managed more easily than either financial or purchasing power risk, because (1) interest rates rise and fall over a relatively short period of time, (2) the investor would not experience a money loss unless he purchased marketable bonds, and (3) a loss on bonds is realized only if the bonds are sold. In the example above, the worst that could happen to the investor, if he holds the bond to maturity, is that he will receive a $3\frac{7}{8}$ percent return on his investment. If there were a rise in interest rates, his loss would be an opportunity loss if he held the bond to maturity.

Market Risk

The financial, interest rate, and purchasing power risks are basic considerations in the determination of investment value. The previous discussion of these risks and their relationship to the value of investments assumes that investors collectively, the market, recognize and properly appraise changes in these risk considerations. Such an assumption is unrealistic. Investors tend to overcompensate for changes in these risks. The changes in market prices are usually started by evidence that the future will bring a change in relative investment opportunities. However, investor psychology may cause him to miscalculate the magnitude of the change in relative investment opportunities or, at least, to overestimate or underestimate the significance of the change. The irrationality in the securities markets may cause losses unrelated to the basic risks discussed before. This risk is called the market risk.

The market risk in common stock is much greater than it is in bonds. Common stock value and prices are related in some fashion to earnings. Current and prospective dividends, which are made possible by earnings, theoretically should be capitalized at a rate that will provide yields to compensate for the basic risks. On the other hand, bond prices are closely related to changes in interest rates on new debt. Stock prices are affected primarily by financial risk considerations which, in turn, affect earnings and dividends. However, stock prices may be strongly influenced by mass psychology, by abrupt changes in financial sentiment, and by waves of optimism or pessimism. The size of the spread between bond yields and stock yields may possibly provide a rough index of the degree of optimism or pessimism prevailing in the stock market. The extremely unstable relationship between yields on common stocks and yields on high-grade bonds shown in Figure 3–1 indicates the changes in investor

FIGURE 3–1

Comparative Yields on Moody's AAA Corporate Bonds and Moody's 125 Industrial Common Stocks, 1928–64

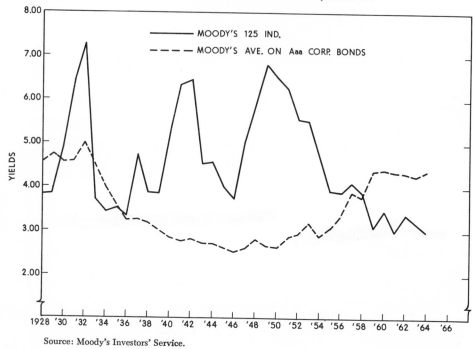

Source: Moody's Investors' Service.

sentiment toward the basic risks. Conventionally, the yield on common stock should be roughly equivalent to the interest rates on high-grade bonds plus a premium for financial risk. Financial risk for a large group of common stocks should be a relatively constant factor. As a consequence, the yield spreads between common stock and bonds should fluctuate within a very narrow range. However, an inspection of the material in Figure 3–1 shows that the yield spread has fluctuated over a wide range.

Market Risk and Inflation. Market risks to this point have been related to financial and interest rate risk considerations. One of the major influences on security prices in recent years has been the purchasing power risk. The widely heralded price inflation has made investors conscious of purchasing power risk. This mass investor consciousness has made individual investors relatively unwilling to hold cash or fixed dollar contracts. The specter of inflation has resulted in investors' bidding up the prices of common stocks so that traditional price-earnings and yield relationships appear to be no longer valid. This is a significant market risk factor. Removal of the threat of inflation may cause investors to overcompensate in the other direction and force a drastic reduction in common stock prices. It appears that investors have assumed that price inflation will tend to increase earnings, and these increased earnings will provide a basis for higher stock prices and permit a larger dividend income. It appears in some cases that investors may have overestimated the impact of price inflation.

TAX CONSIDERATIONS

Federal individual income tax rates are so high that income taxes nearly always receive some consideration in making investment decisions. In 1965, the effective tax rates rose, on a graduated scale, from 14 percent of the first $500 of taxable income ($1,000 in the case of a husband and wife filing a joint return) to a maximum of 70 percent on that portion of taxable income in excess of $100,000. ($200,000 in the case of a married couple filing a joint return). These rates apply to "ordinary income," such as salaries, dividends, and interest, including the excess of the net short-term capital gains over the net long-term capital losses. The distinction between short term and long term is based on the length of time that elapses between the purchase of a security and its subsequent sale. Capital gains or losses resulting from the sale of securities or other assets that have been held for more than six months are long term. Those assets held less than six months are short term.

Dividends are treated separately. The first $100 of each taxpayer's dividends are excluded from income. A husband and wife filing a joint return may exclude $200 in dividends if each of them has received $100 or more in dividends from qualifying corporations within the taxable year. The remainder of the dividends included in gross income entitles the taxpayer to a credit against his tax equal to the lesser of: (1) 2 percent of the dividends included in gross income; (2) 2 percent of taxable income; (3) the tax for the year, before all credits.

Total income tax liability is computed by taking successive portions of ordinary taxable income and applying against each portion the percentage tax rate that is defined by law as appropriate. These percentages increase with each successive segment of income. The highest effective tax rate applicable to the tax portions of any taxpayer's income may be called the "marginal" rate. It represents the additional number of cents the person would pay to the government if he were to add one more dollar to his income. We have already noted that it can amount to as much as 70 cents for a single person with an income of $100,000 or more per year. The effect of the individual income tax on taxable income is shown in Figure 3–2.

FIGURE 3–2

Effect of Taxation on Total Taxable Income
Federal Income Tax Rates, 1965

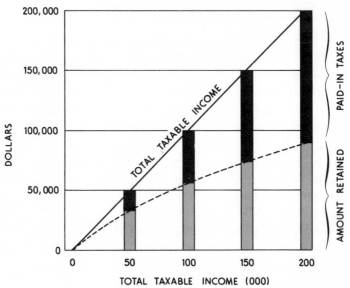

Special Treatment of Capital Gains

Capital gains and losses, including those that may arise from the sale of securities, are given special treatment. Where there is an excess of net long-term capital gains over net short-term capital losses subject to tax, a special maximum tax rate of 25 percent applies against this reported amount. When the taxpayer would pay less taxes by including 50 percent of capital gains in ordinary income, he is permitted to do so, and the special rate of 25 percent applicable to long-term capital gains may be ignored.

Capital losses may be used to offset capital gains. Initially, long-term transactions are separated from short-term transactions. If there is a net short-term gain, that is, short-term gains exceed short-term losses and a net long-term gain, the long-term gain is taken into account to the extent of only 50 percent; the short-term gain is fully taxable. If the short-term transactions within the year result in a loss smaller than the net long-term gain, that loss must be offset against the net long-term gain before applying the 50 percent factor. Similarly, if there are a net short-term gain and a net long-term loss, one must offset the loss against the gain. If the aggregate of all capital transactions within the year results in a loss, that loss may be deducted from ordinary income to the extent of $1,000; the excess may be carried forward into succeeding years, and may offset the individual taxpayer's short-term or long-term capital gain, plus his other taxable income to the extent of $1,000, until it is used up.

For a person in any tax bracket, but particularly for those in the higher brackets, there is obviously a distinct advantage in being entitled to report his securities gains as long-term capital gains. But investors whose incomes are not in the higher tax brackets should avoid letting tax considerations overrule more fundamental considerations concerning proper selection and timing in the purchase and sale of securities. The investor should remember that, when good judgment dictates, it is better to take a capital gain now and report it as short-term gain than to wait for six months only to discover that the capital gain has disappeared.

LIQUIDITY CONSIDERATIONS

Liquidity is the ability to meet cash needs on short notice. Complete liquidity can be assured only by holding all investment funds as cash balances. Obviously, to be practical such a course of action would be too expensive in terms of sacrificed income. Therefore, every investor must consider the amount of cash or cash equivalent he must hold.

The investor usually segregates his funds into cash balances and investment funds. The cash balances are assumed to be sufficient to meet all foreseeable needs. The liquidity consideration arises from the ability of the investor to accurately forecast his cash needs. If he can forecast them fairly accurately, there is no real liquidity problem. Liquidity is an investment consideration when there is a possibility of cash needs in excess of normal balances. When such a situation is likely to arise, needed additional liquidity must be built into the investment portfolio.

Investment portfolio liquidity is attained by (1) marketability and (2) maturity. Marketability is the degree to which securities can be sold without appreciable loss as a result of the forced sale. The point is that almost anything is marketable or salable at some prices, but a security is considered marketable when it is readily salable at close to its current market value.

Bond investments may be liquidated by holding them to maturity as well as by selling them in the market. Therefore, relative liquidity of investment funds may be accomplished by holding a certain portion of the portfolio in short-term obligations. Holding short-term obligations does not always insure needed liquidity, because cash needs are frequently immediate. These unplanned needs for funds often cannot wait for some future maturity date, irrespective of how close it may be. Therefore, the investor must rely primarily on marketability for needed liquidity.

The terms "marketability" and "liquidity" are not, however, synonymous. Complete liquidity can be achieved only when the investment can be sold without appreciable money loss. An investment may be marketable, yet fluctuate in price. Therefore, a security is relatively liquid when it is marketable and has price stability.

Other Aspects of Marketability

The marketability of securities also tends to minimize the risks of investment and to increase collateral value when the securities are used as collateral for a loan. Risk is reduced through marketability. Risk is reduced through marketability because of the investor's ability to correct errors in judgment and analysis by promptly disposing of the security. A most hopeless investment situation is one in which an investment has not worked out and for which there is no market. The investor is absolutely defenseless against loss, because the security's lack of marketability does not enable him to reverse his decision. This situation usually arises with promotional ventures or when a company's stock is held by a few people.

Sometimes, the investor may have a need for cash, and yet does not wish to liquidate his holdings. He may borrow the funds, using his securities as collateral. The collateral value or percentage of value that the lender will lend will be determined by the relative marketability and price stability of the securities.

PERSONAL CONSIDERATIONS

Various personal factors must be considered in formulating an investment policy. The more significant are (1) ability to supervise investments and (2) temperament of the investor.

A major consideration in the formulation of investment policy is the investor's ability to analyze, select, and supervise his investments. This ability is dependent on the education, experience, and temperament of the investor. In addition, the investor must have adequate time for supervision of his portfolio.

The importance of this consideration varies with the primary policy objectives of the investor. The more financial risk that is assumed, the more careful attention the investor must give his investment portfolio. It is not meant to suggest that the investor should commit funds to any investment without supervision. However, the amount of supervision required tends to vary with the type and quality of securities held. Obviously, it takes more time to properly manage a portfolio of speculative common stocks than it does to handle a fund invested in short-term U.S. government bonds. Therefore, the investor should decide how much time he will have to devote to the management of his investments. The individual investor's time may be limited due to the pressure of business or his employment. In these situations, the investment program should be built around investments that require minimum supervision.

Assuming that the time for supervising investments is available, the investor should have an adequate background in economics, finance, and accounting if he is to properly supervise a portfolio of securities. An understanding of the monetary and banking system and the effect of its actions on interest rates, business conditions, and the market prices of securities is indispensable to the investor. The need for a knowledge of modern accounting practices in the analysis of securities will be evident from the discussion in later chapters.

The temperament of the investor is obviously a major policy consideration in some cases. A person's attitude toward risk assumption is affected by his emotional stability. All people dislike losing money and are fearful of loss. For this reason, they analyze securities to determine the risk they are assuming and the probable gain or loss from the investment. This is a rational approach to the management of risk.

Some people, however, have an irrational fear of loss. These investors panic when the market value of their securities drops below what they originally paid for them. In many such cases, they either sell out at the slightest price decline or worry about the value of their holdings. As a general rule, investors should follow investment policies that enable them to be relatively free of worry. They should follow the maxim, "you should always sell off to the sleeping point," even if this action involves selling all security holdings, because chances are that programs which cause excessive concern to investors are probably the wrong ones for them.

REVIEW QUESTIONS AND PROBLEMS

1. Discuss the statement that risk and income are inseparable factors.
2. United States Savings Bonds are frequently advertised as the best securities investment in the world for the individual. In what sense is this statement true? What are the fallacies?
3. Losses from the interest rate risk are not real losses unless the bonds are sold, because the investor can always recover his investment if a decline in the bond price is only from interest rate changes. Discuss this statement.
4. Why are the financial, interest rate, and purchasing power risks considered to be long-run value considerations and the market risk a short-run value consideration?
5. Discuss the proposition that $100 in current income received in equal annual payments over ten years is more valuable than $100 in capital gains realized in a lump sum at the end of ten years.
6. The terms marketability and liquidity are not synonymous. Why not?
7. An investor states that he must earn $2.00 to equal $1.00 in capital gains after taxes. What is his marginal income tax rate?
8. Is the provision for special treatment of capital gains of any significance to the investor who is not in the higher marginal income tax brackets?
9. What are the more important personal considerations in formulating investment policy?
10. If all investors had perfect information and knowledge of the value of securities, would there be any fluctuations in market prices of these securities? If not, why?
11. Which of the risks, purchasing power or financial risk, would be probably most significant to the investor who is 75 years of age?
12. What is the fallacy in the idea that persons in the highest income tax brackets are best able to assume financial risk irrespective of their age?

CHAPTER **4**

Characteristics of Investment Media—
Institutional Fixed-Dollar Contracts

As noted in Chapter 1, an investor may choose either fixed-dollar contracts or equity investments. These fixed-dollar contracts are alike in that they are promises to repay the investor his original investment, plus periodic interest payments.

The investor has two broad choices in selecting dollar contract investment media. He may purchase bonds or mortgages directly or he may entrust his funds to a financial intermediary or institution that will, in turn, make the direct investments. If the investor chooses to invest directly, he has the problem of selecting the quality and type of medium best suited for his needs. The investor may choose to avoid this problem of analysis and quality determination; or in that case he would invest his funds through a financial intermediary, such as a commercial bank.

Institutional investment media and bonds have different investment characteristics. Most institutional investment media today have a negligible degree of financial risk, while bonds vary considerably in quality. The investments of most financial institutions of the savings-deposit type are regulated as to quality and type, and the investor's savings are often insured by an agency of the federal government. The investor in bonds does not have this complete assurance that his funds will be returned to him at maturity. In addition, these institutional-type investments have a common characteristic which distinguishes them from other types of investments. These investments characteristically do not fluctuate in value, because there is no market for them. There is no market because institutional fixed-dollar contracts usually can be liquidated by the investor on relatively short notice.

39

Seven major savings media are normally included in this fixed-value asset classification: (1) savings and loan associations, (2) mutual savings banks, (3) commercial banks, (4) credit unions, (5) U.S. savings bonds, (6) postal savings, and (7) life insurance and annuities. Credit unions and postal savings are relatively unimportant, as savings media, and their characteristics will not be covered in this chapter. U.S. savings bonds are not "bonds," because they have fixed value and are readily convertible into cash; therefore, they will be discussed along with the savings deposit institutional fixed-dollar contracts and life insurance.

The fixed-dollar contract investor who wishes to invest directly will generally be interested in bonds. It is also possible for such investor to invest in real estate mortgages. However, it is normally not practical because of the problem of determining the quality of these mortgages. Quality determination of bonds is relatively standardized, requiring no special knowledge, while determination of mortgage quality requires a knowledge of real estate appraisal. As a consequence, we will confine our discussion of dollar contracts to the characteristics, risks, and value of institutional media and bonds.

INVESTMENT CHARACTERISTICS OF INSTITUTIONAL DOLLAR CONTRACTS

It is possible for the individual investor to build his entire investment program around institutional fixed-dollar contracts by depositing his funds in savings institutions and/or purchasing certain types of life insurance. A program that relies exclusively on fixed-dollar contracts as investment media is not usually a good one because of the extreme exposure to purchasing power risk. The possible extent of these potential losses is evident from the discussion in Chapter 3.

The holder of any type of dollar contracts is subject to purchasing power losses. Any dollar contract almost guarantees that the holder will suffer a loss from price level increases if the contract is held for any length of time. Of course, the investor is able to reverse his investment position when he uses one of the institutional investment media; consequently, he can minimize his risk of financial loss. In this same instance, the investor also pays for this minimal risk by receiving less income.

The introductory discussion would indicate that the investment characteristics of these various fixed-value media are the same. Although the investment characteristics are similar, there are significant differences in yield or rate of return and, in some cases, differences in quality. It may be noted from the data shown in Table 4–1 that the rate of return on these fixed-value investments fluctuates with the general level of interest rates.

In addition, the fixed-value dollar contracts offered by the various financial institutions do sometimes vary in quality. Usually, either these institutions have their deposits insured by an agency of the federal government and/or their operations are strictly supervised by an agency of the federal government or the state governments. There is, however, a wide variation in the stringency of this supervision. As a consequence, the investor should always investigate the reputation of the institution before investing, and should appraise the quality of supervision if the institution is subject to only state supervision. The following discussion of these fixed-dollar-value investment media will outline the potential areas of financial risk.

SAVINGS AND LOAN ASSOCIATIONS

The typical savings account in a savings and loan association appears, as a matter of practice, to be quite similar to a savings account in any other institution. The account is evidenced by a passbook or a certificate. Customarily, the savings account holder can withdraw or liquidate his account on demand.

Technically, a holder of a deposit in a savings and loan association is not a depositor; he is a part owner in the association. In other words, he has an equity interest in the association, particularly if it is a mutual savings and loan association. As an equity interest holder, he has the right to vote in the election of directors. However, the average savings account holder does not concern himself with the operations of the association and considers himself a depositor. This attitude results because, customarily, the savings account holder can withdraw or liquidate his account on demand. However, the charter of the association may, and usually does, allow the officers to require a 30- to 60-day written notice for the withdrawal of funds. Generally, the notice would be required only if the association were experiencing a period of cash stringency. During such periods of cash stringency, the notices of withdrawal are filed and paid out in the order of filing. The investor should keep in mind that it is not mandatory for the association to pay the requested funds after expiration of the 30- to 60-day period; these funds are paid only as the cash becomes available.

The risk of loss to an investor whose savings are in a savings and

TABLE 4–1

Average Annual Yield on Selected Types of Investments, 1930–64

Year	Savings Accounts in Savings Associations	Savings Deposits in Mutual Savings Banks	Time and Savings Deposits in Commercial Banks	U.S. Government Bonds	State and Local Bonds	Corporate (Aaa) Bonds
1930	5.3%	4.5%	3.9%	3.3%	4.1%	4.5%
1931	5.1	4.4	3.8	3.3	4.0	4.6
1932	4.1	4.0	3.4	3.7	4.6	5.0
1933	3.4	3.4	3.4	3.3	4.7	5.5
1934	3.5	3.1	3.0	3.1	4.0	4.0
1935	3.1	2.7	2.6	2.7	3.4	3.6
1936	3.2	2.5	2.0	2.5	3.1	3.2
1937	3.5	2.4	1.8	2.6	3.1	3.3
1938	3.5	2.3	1.7	2.6	2.9	3.2
1939	3.4	2.2	1.6	2.4	2.8	3.0
1940	3.3	2.0	1.3	2.2	2.5	2.8
1941	3.1	1.9	1.3	2.0	2.1	2.8
1942	3.0	1.9	1.1	2.5	2.4	2.8
1943	2.9	1.9	0.9	2.5	2.1	2.7
1944	2.8	1.8	0.9	2.5	1.8	2.6
1945	2.5	1.7	0.8	2.4	1.7	2.5
1946	2.4	1.7	0.8	2.2	1.6	2.4
1947	2.3	1.7	0.9	2.3	2.3	2.9
1948	2.3	1.8	0.9	2.4	2.3	2.8
1949	2.3	1.9	0.9	2.3	2.1	2.6
1950	2.5	1.9	0.9	2.3	2.0	2.6
1951	2.6	2.0	1.1	2.6	2.0	2.9
1952	2.7	2.3	1.1	2.7	2.2	2.9
1953	2.8	2.4	1.1	2.9	2.8	3.2
1954	2.9	2.5	1.3	2.5	2.4	2.9
1955	2.9	2.6	1.4	2.8	2.6	3.1
1956	3.0	2.8	1.6	3.1	2.9	3.4
1957	3.3	2.9	2.1	3.5	3.6	3.9
1958	3.38	3.07	2.21	3.43	3.36	3.79
1959	3.53	3.19	2.36	4.07	3.74	4.38
1960	3.86	3.47	2.56	4.01	3.69	4.41
1961	3.90	3.55	2.76	3.90	3.60	4.35
1962	4.08	3.85	3.14	3.95	3.30	4.33
1963	4.17	3.99	3.33	4.00	3.28	4.26
1964	4.19*	4.10	3.47	4.15	3.28	4.40

* Estimated.

Sources: Savings and loan associations: effective rate of dividends, i.e., dividends distributed relative to average savings balance, based on data of members of FHLB System; mutual savings banks: "per deposit" rates reported by National Association of Mutual Savings Banks; commercial banks: effective interest rate, based on data of Federal Reserve Board and Federal Deposit Insurance Corporation; bond yields: Moody's Investors Service.

Reprinted from *Savings and Loan Fact Book, 1965* (Chicago: United States Savings and Loan League, 1965), p. 16.

loan association is relatively small. These institutions are required to confine their investments to mortgages; the size of each mortgage and its quality are restricted by law and by the examination standards of state or federal regulatory authorities. In most cases, the savings account holder is protected against financial loss up to $10,000 because of insurance of accounts by the Federal Savings and Loan Insurance Corporation. Insurance is required for all federally chartered savings and loan associations. However, state chartered associations may obtain insurance only on application and approval by the Federal Savings and Loan Insurance Corporation. In a substantial number of cases, the state savings and loan associations are not insured. At the end of 1963, insured savings and loan associations were 69 percent of all associations and accounted for 96 percent of the total savings and loan assets.[1] In other words, 31 percent of all savings and loan associations are not insured. It would be inadvisable to place funds in savings and loan associations not federally insured without a thorough analysis of their lending policies and practices.

Since the share account holder is a part owner rather than a creditor of the association, liquidity of the account and rate of return are not guaranteed. The share account holder may ask for return of his money. Failure of the association to meet his request does not result in the account holder's having a claim against the saving and loan insurance corporation if the reason is the illiquidity of the association. The Federal Savings and Loan Insurance Corporation insures against loss from insolvency and capital impairment but does not guarantee liquidity of insured share accounts.

As part owners, the return paid is a dividend rather than interest, and is not guaranteed. The dividend is payable only when deemed advisable by the board of directors. However, the rate of return on savings and loan association share accounts generally has been higher than the return on other institutional-type fixed-dollar contracts. These returns, shown in Figure 4–1, have varied from 2 to 4½ percent in recent years.

COMMERCIAL BANKS AND MUTUAL SAVINGS BANKS

The investment characteristics of savings accounts of mutual savings banks and commercial banks are essentially the same. These institutions receive deposits which maintain a fixed value and may be liquidated on short notice, usually 30 to 60 days. As a matter of practice, these banks usually pay these accounts on demand.

The commercial bank and the mutual savings bank have signifi-

---

[1] *Savings and Loan Fact Book, 1964* (Chicago: United States Savings and Loan League, 1964), p. 85.

44   *Investment Analysis and Management*

FIGURE 4–1

**Average Annual Yield on Savings at
Major Financial Institutions**

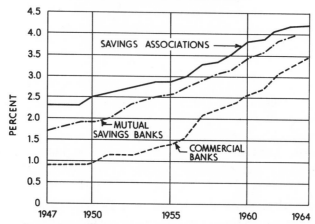

Source: *Savings and Loan Fact Book, 1965* (Chicago: United States
Saving and Loan League, 1965), p. 17.

cantly different forms of organization. In the mutual savings bank,
the account holders are technically owners, but they have no voting
rights. The mutual savings bank is operated by a self-perpetuating
board of trustees. However, the account holder does hold a quasi-
creditor relationship to the mutual savings bank, because his account
must be paid in cash after expiration of a notice period. The commercial bank savings depositor is a creditor; and the payment to him
is interest, while the mutual savings bank account holder receives
"dividends" at a rate fixed by the trustees.

Presently, the rate of interest that can be paid on commercial bank
savings deposits is restricted to 4 percent.[2] There is no similar restriction on the rate paid by their major competitors—mutual savings
banks or savings and loan associations. The yield on commercial bank
deposits is, as a consequence, slightly lower than these competing
institutions.

Deposits in commercial banks and mutual savings banks have been
accepted as having unquestioned safety. These institutions are carefully supervised, and the types and quality of investments they may
make are carefully regulated. This supervision and regulation of

---

[2] In December, 1965, commercial banks were permitted by regulatory authorities to
pay up to 5½ percent interest on certificates of deposit with a maturity of 30 days or
longer.

investments and operations minimizes the risk of loss from depositing funds with these institutions.

Generally, the risk of loss from bank failure is further minimized by the insurance of deposits up to $10,000 for each depositor. A few commercial and mutual savings banks are not insured. On December 31, 1963, there were 14,092 operating commercial and savings banks in the United States, and 13,621 banks, or about 97 percent, were insured by the Federal Deposit Insurance Corporation.[3] These insured banks accounted for approximately 98 percent of deposits in all banks.[4] It is not likely that an investor would experience a loss because of deposit in a noninsured bank, but it is possible and should be checked routinely by the investor. In the 29 years from 1934 to 1962 inclusive, 125 noninsured banks with $58 million in deposits closed because of financial difficulties.[5]

LIFE INSURANCE AND ANNUITIES AS INVESTMENTS

The basic purpose of life insurance, in most investment programs, is to protect those dependent on the insured from hardship in the event of his death. Most life insurance policies or contracts provide, in addition, a saving element. We may make major errors in investment planning and programming if we fail to distinguish between the pure functions of life insurance and life insurance as an investment. The best way to prevent this error is to be able to recognize life insurance in its pure form and when it is also an investment.

The Nature of Pure Life Insurance

The life insurance company enters into a contract providing that the company will pay a person—the beneficiary—a specified sum of money in the event of death of the insured. The consideration for life insurance companies issuing this policy is a fixed annual payment or premium.

This premium is really a form of a wager or bet between the insured and the insurance company. This wager is clearly evident with pure insurance or term insurance. To illustrate, let us assume we purchase

---

[3] *Annual Report of the Federal Deposit Insurance Corporation for the Year Ended December 31, 1963* (Washington, D.C.: Federal Deposit Insurance Corporation), p. 3.

[4] *Ibid.,* p. 19.

[5] *Ibid.,* p. 27.

a term or pure insurance contract at age thirty-five. How does the life insurance company handle this policy?

Pure insurance, in the form of a wager that any particular individual thirty-five years of age will not die during the year, can be offered by an insurance company, because it places the same wager on the lives of, let us say, 100,000 individuals, all thirty-five years of age. Available mortality tables show how many individuals of that age will die during the year. According to the Commissioners' 1958 Standard Ordinary Table, based on experience from 1950 to 1954, 251 individuals out of 100,000 will die during the first year. Obviously, the premiums per $1,000 paid by those fortunate enough to live must be great enough to pay death claims on account of the 251 who die. At age thirty-six, a larger number—264 out of 100,000 individuals—will die.[6] Clearly, the premium that must be collected from the survivors in any age group must increase with age. There is no way to avoid this increasing cost of pure insurance as one grows older. One-year renewable term insurance, for example, requires an increased premium each year.

If only one-year term life insurance policies were written, life insurance would not be an investment medium, because all premiums would be utilized to pay death benefits and operating expenses of the life insurance company. Most life insurance contracts are written for the whole life of the insured rather than for a specified term of, for example, one year.

The purchaser of any whole or ordinary life insurance policy must begin to consider life insurance as an investment medium, because the company accumulates the premiums into policy reserves to pay future death benefits. The ordinary life policy, the most common form of whole life insurance, is actually a combination of pure insurance and a saving and investment medium. The insurance company can keep the premium level only by collecting more than enough to provide pure insurance in the earlier years. The excess is used to build a savings fund, called the "cash surrender value of the policy," and this value is actually a part of the payment made in event of death. The amount of pure life insurance thus declines every year. A $1,000 policy when first taken out constitutes $1,000 of pure insur-

---

[6] Another way of viewing the problem is that out of the original 100,000 persons age thirty-five only 99,749 will survive until age thirty-six, and 0.265 percent of the survivors, or 264, will die at that age, leaving 99,485 survivors at age thirty-seven.

ance. In later years when the policy has a cash surrender value of, let us say, $400, the insurance company is providing only $600 of pure insurance.

The Origin of Cash Surrender Values

For all whole life insurance policies, the company must accumulate premiums in policy reserves to pay future death benefits. The example in Figure 4–2 shows the accumulation of reserves for $1,000 of whole ordinary life insurance on 10,000 people aged twenty, and follows the reserve accumulation premium payments and ultimate disposition of the policy reserves of this group. It may be noted that with successive declines in premiums paid the policy reserves continue to climb until the group reaches the ages of fifty–fifty-nine. Reserves continue to increase because of the interest income from investment of the reserve accumulations. The amounts shown in the bottom line of Figure 4–2 are the funds available for investment. In this example, the reserve accumulations are invested at 2½ percent, which accounts for the interest income.

The cash surrender values of these life insurance policies are the total amount of the policy reserves after payment of death benefits. For example, during the first 10-year period (ages twenty–twenty-nine), the group of insureds in Figure 4–2 paid in premiums of $1,234,200 and earned $152,111 in interest on the investment of reserves accumulated during that period for a total of $1,386,311. During this 10-year period, 282 persons died, and death benefits amounting to $282,000 were paid, leaving a fund of $1,104,311 at the end of the period. This fund or reserve accumulation of $1,104,311 represents the total of the cash surrender values available to the 9,718 surviving insureds. In other words, each of the surviving members of this group has an investment in life insurance cash surrender values amounting to $113.63 ($1,104,311 divided by 9,718 insureds).

The Level Premium Plan as the Cause of Reserve Accumulations

The basis for these reserve accumulations which create cash surrender values is the level premium plan. To describe the level premium plan, it may be helpful to review the way life insurance premiums are calculated.

For a young person, the cost of insurance would be small because

FIGURE 4-2

History of 10,000 Life Insurance Policyholders All the Same Age; Each Purchased $1,000 of Ordinary Life at Age 20

Mortality Table Used: Commissioners Standard Ordinary; 2½ Percent Interest; Net Annual Premium $12.49

10 YEAR PERIODS	AGE 20–29	AGE 30–39	AGE 40–49	AGE 50–59	AGE 60–69	AGE 70–79	AGE 80–89	AGE 90–100
NUMBER LIVING AT BEGINNING OF PERIOD	10,000	9,718	9,284	8,523	7,124	4,778	1,911	227
TOTAL PREMIUMS PAID DURING PERIOD (DOLLARS)	1,234,200	1,191,657	1,121,543	994,411	767,985	433,626	123,871	8,723
TOTAL INTEREST EARNED ON INVESTMENTS DURING PERIOD (DOLLARS)	152,111	439,924	731,977	952,505	964,673	655,900	210,923	15,971
NUMBER OF PERSONS DYING DURING PERIOD	282	434	761	1,399	2,346	2,867	1,684	227
TOTAL OF DEATH BENEFITS PAID DURING PERIOD (DOLLARS)	282,000	434,000	761,000	1,399,000	2,346,000	2,867,000	1,684,000	227,000
FUND AT END OF PERIOD AFTER BENEFIT PAYMENTS (DOLLARS)	1,104,311	2,301,892	3,394,412	3,942,328	3,328,986	1,551,512	202,306	–0–

Source: R. Wilfred Kelsey and Arthur C. Daniels, *Handbook of Life Insurance* (New York: Institute of Life Insurance, 1949), pp. 43–44. Reprinted by permission.

the probability of death or mortality risk at early ages is relatively small. Each year, the mortality risk would increase, and life insurance would become increasingly expensive until the premium would be almost prohibitive for persons in the older age groups. Because of these changes in life insurance premiums from early life to late life, the level premium plan was instituted. With this plan, the premiums on life insurance remain the same throughout the lifetime of the policyholder. During the early years, premiums are relatively greater than the mortality cost, or the cost of paying death benefits, and the premiums in the later years much less than the death benefits (see Figure 4–2). Without the level premium plan, there would be a relatively small reserve, because premium payments would approximate annual death benefit payments, as mentioned earlier. It is obvious from the material in Figure 4–2 that the level premium plan results in the accumulation of substantial policy reserves or cash surrender values. The amount and rate of the policy reserve accumulation varies with different types of insurance policies. For example, the reserve accumulations for term insurance are relatively small, while some other types of insurance are primarily insured savings plans.

Annuities as Investments

An annuity is a regular monthly or annual receipt of money. The word here, however, is used to designate the contract of an insurance company to make such payments of money. If the payments are guaranteed as long as the recipient lives, the contract is known as a "life annuity." Such contracts are desirable as a means of providing retirement income for a man of limited means, because they permit him to consume his capital as well as the interest income without any fear of exhausting his capital. The insurance company is able to make such a contract because it knows how many years a man of any designated age is likely to live. Since it knows the average life expectancy of a large group of individuals age sixty-five, for example, for every $1,000 of capital turned over to the insurance company by people of that age the company can guarantee payments which, allowing for interest income, would exactly exhaust the capital fund in that number of years. The losses incurred by payments to those who live longer than average expectancy are made up by gains from those contracts with individuals who live less than average-length lives. If one must die in order to win from a life insurance policy, one must live longer than average in order to win from the insurance company in an annuity. Even if he loses, the only actual financial loss, of course, is to the heirs, and this may be more than offset by the peace of mind of the annuitant as long as he lives. If both parties to the marriage contract are living at retirement age, it is possible to buy a joint annuity with a provision that two-thirds of the amount payable to both will be payable to the survivor if either partner dies.

Investment Characteristics. These annuities may be purchased by paying (1) a single premium or (2) a series of periodic payments over a number of years, usually annually, until the annuity matures. Such annuities may be purchased out of funds that have been saved and invested in savings banks, government securities, or in any other investment media. Sometimes, a home that was originally purchased to care for a growing family can be sold, the husband and wife can move to an apartment, and the proceeds of the sale can be used to meet the more pressing need for an annuity to provide retirement income.

It is obviously prejudicial to the interests of residual heirs for a retired couple to invest a greater amount in life annuities than is necessary to provide an assured and adequate dollar income, taking into account their total financial resources. But for the person who has a small fund of savings to invest, buying an annuity may be the only way he can be assured of an adequate and steady income for the balance of his life. At age sixty-five, for example, a man can get an annual income amounting to about $7\frac{1}{2}$ percent on his investment in an annuity, with payments made monthly. This is about $1\frac{1}{2}$ times what he could get by investing in high-grade fixed-income securities.

One must not forget that the reason for this higher yield is the investor's willingness to assume, not the risk of a capital loss, but the *assurance* of a complete capital loss at death. Once enough annuity contracts have been purchased to assure a steady dollar income sufficient to cover the costs of an adequate standard of living, from the viewpoint of the heirs, any other kind of investment of the additional investment funds available, no matter how risky, is better than an annuity.

Purchasing Power Risk Exposure of Annuities and Life Insurance

The risks of a total capital loss with annuities and life insurance are negligible, but as with any fixed-dollar contract there is a major exposure to purchasing power loss. The suitability of the conventional annuity as an investment medium for retirement is dependent on the stability of the price level and the value of the dollar.

A recognition of the purchasing power risk caused the Teachers' Insurance and Annuity Association to develop a novel solution to the problem of purchasing power risk exposure. They developed a variable annuity, College Retirement Equities Fund (CREF). "A variable annuity is an annuity providing periodic payments, the dollar amount of each payment being determined from period to period primarily in accordance with the then current earnings and market value of a portfolio of equity assets, especially common stocks."[7] The variable annuity shifts the emphasis from a stable dollar income to the annuitant to a relatively stable amount of purchasing power. The CREF plan requires its participants (college professors) to invest at least one half of their retirement savings in a fixed-dollar annuity issued by Teachers Insurance and Annuity Association. The professor has at retirement two annuities—one a fixed-dollar annuity which provides a fixed-dollar income, the other a variable annuity which provides an income that varies in dollar amounts from year to year.[8]

U.S. SAVINGS BONDS

Generally, bonds are marketable and, as a consequence, fluctuate in value or are variable value fixed-income investments. A notable exception is U.S. savings bonds. These bonds are a fixed-value investment and are nonmarketable. Thus, U.S. savings bonds will be discussed along with other fixed-value investments.

These savings bonds are designated as a savings media for individuals. Two different types of bonds, known as Series E and Series H, are available for purchase (Table 4–2). These bonds are not transferable and are registered in the name of the purchaser. They may be purchased by any investor other than commercial banks.

Series E bonds are discount bonds, since they are sold at 75 percent of maturity value and appreciate in value to the face amount at the end of seven years. These bonds yield 4.15 percent from the date of purchase to the maturity of seven years. The investor is limited in

---

[7] William C. Greenough, "Variable Annuities," *Life and Health Insurance Handbook*, ed. Davis W. Gregg (2d. ed.; Homewood, Ill.: Richard D. Irwin, Inc., 1964), p. 554.

[8] *Ibid.*, p. 555.

TABLE 4–2

United States Savings Bonds
(Sold on and after June 1, 1959)

	Series E	Series H
Type:	Appreciation.	Current income.
Dated:	First day of month in which payment is received by an authorized issuing agent.	First day of month in which payment is received by a Federal Reserve Bank or the U.S. Treasury.
Maturity:	7 years from issue date.	10 years from issue date.
Cost per $1,000:	$750.00.	$1,000.00.
Maturity value per $1,000:	$1,000.00.	$1,000.00.
Yield to maturity:	4.15% a year compounded semi-annually.	4.15% a year payable by varying semi-annual Treasury checks.
Redemption:	By owner at any time not less than 2 months from issue date.	At par by owner on 1 month's written notice after 6 months from issue date.
Denomination (maturity value):	$25, $50, $75, $100, $200, $500, $1,000, $10,000, $100,000.*	$500, $1,000, $5,000, $10,000.
Registration:	In the name of adults or minors, also coowners or beneficiaries; persons or organizations, public or private, as fiduciaries; public or private organizations, including corporations, partnerships, associations, public bodies, but not commercial banks.	Same as Series E.
Limitation on purchase per calendar year:	$10,000 maturity value.	$20,000.
Exchange:	May be exchanged for Series H.	
Purchase place:	U.S. post offices, Federal Reserve Banks, Treasury Dept., commercial banks, and other qualified agencies.	Federal Reserve Banks, Treasurer of the U.S.

* $100,000 for certain employee savings plans.
Source: *Securities of the United States Government, Twenty First Edition, 1964,* The First Boston Corporation, p. 65.

the amount of bonds he can purchase to $10,000 maturity value or $7,500 purchase price in any one calendar year.

Series E bonds can be redeemed on demand after they have been held for two months, but the redemption values are set up so that the holder "loses" if he redeems the bonds before maturity. The redemption value increases slowly at first and then at faster rates as the bonds get nearer maturity. If the investor redeems a Series E bond after holding it for only a few years, he receives a yield of much less than 4.15 percent and thus loses a possible future yield of more than 4.5 percent. There is no question about the liquidity of these bonds, but the yield is very low in the event of early redemption. Consequently, the bonds are not a good source for investing emergency funds. In addition, they cannot be pledged as collateral for a loan, since the bonds are not marketable or transferable.

The Series E bond is not suitable for the investor who needs a current cash income from his investment. In fact, one of the more attractive investment features of Series E bonds is the ability of the investor to defer taxable income by electing to pay federal income tax in the year in which the bonds mature. As a consequence, the investor may postpone payment of taxes on the interest income from Series E bonds for at least seven years. In addition, the investor may elect to not present the bonds for payment at maturity and accept an automatic extension up to 10 years after maturity. On these extended bonds, federal income taxes may be postponed for 17 years.

The Series H bonds are designed for the current income investor. These bonds are issued and are redeemable at par or face value. The bonds must be held at least six months from date of purchase before they can be redeemed. They are then redeemable on one month's written notice. The Series H bond provides a yield of 4.15 percent over the 10-year period to maturity, with lesser yields in the earlier periods. These bonds pay interest to holders semiannually on a scale similar to the rate of value appreciation of Series E bonds. Series H bonds may be purchased by all investors, except commercial banks, up to $20,000 a year.

SUMMARY

Most individual investors invest the bulk of their savings with financial institutions such as commercial banks, life insurance companies, and savings and loan associations. Contractually, there are usually limitations on the rights of the investors to withdraw funds from these institutions. These limitations are usually in the form of written notice 30 to 60 days in advance of withdrawal of the funds. Practically, however, most of these institutions will release savings deposits on demand, because they feel that their failure to do so would hinder their ability to attract new funds for investment.

With such institutional investments, the investor has almost complete reversibility. In times of general economic adversity, which may be the very time he would need his funds, he might have a short wait for his funds. However, maintenance of a reversible position is a matter of alternatives. If the investor is unwilling to invest in these financial institutions because of possible restrictions on withdrawals, what is the alternative? The only asset that is generally more liquid is cash itself. If the investor insists on being free at all times to choose between consumption or investment of his savings without waiting or possible loss, his only choice is to hold his savings in cash. Holding cash does not provide any guarantee that the investor will not suffer some loss. He may be free of financial losses, but he still may incur a purchasing power loss as well as the loss of any return that might have accrued to him if he had invested the funds.

REVIEW QUESTIONS AND PROBLEMS

1. Why is the loss from interest rate changes minimized with institutional fixed dollar contracts?
2. Why should the yield on savings and loan share accounts be generally higher than the yields on savings deposits of commercial banks?
3. Discuss the relative liquidity of a commercial bank saving's deposit and a savings and loan share account.
4. How would it be possible that there is little if any cash value accumulation for a five-year term life insurance policy, but there may be a substantial cash value accumulated for a term to age 65 life insurance policy?
5. Why is there no physical examination of the applicant required for an annuity yet one is usually required for life insurance?
6. How could U.S. Savings Bonds be used to advantage by an investor in a high marginal income tax bracket?
7. What are the major differences between Series E and Series H U.S. Savings Bonds?
8. What are the major advantages of an annuity to an investor?
9. What is the level premium plan and what is the relationship of this plan to cash value accumulations?

CHAPTER **5**

Characteristics and Value of Investment Media—Corporate Bonds

Those investors who wish to invest in fixed-dollar contracts directly rather than through financial institutions will usually select bonds as the medium for investment. Bonds may be classified by (1) length to maturity, (2) type security, (3) method of recording ownership, and (4) type of issuer. All these classifications are used and may have meaning to the bond investor.

Bonds are classified as to length of time to maturity as (1) short term (1 year or less), (2) intermediate term (1 to 10 years), and (3) long term (10 years and over). These classifications are not well-defined ones and vary considerably. They are helpful, however, in discussing differences in rates of return, as will be seen later.

Ownership of bonds may be recorded by specific name (registered bonds) or by bearer (bearer bonds). Most bonds are bearer bonds with attached coupons which are detached and presented semi-annually for interest payments. The interest on registered bonds is usually paid by check semiannually to the registered owner.

Bonds may be issued by (1) corporations (corporate bonds), (2) state and local governments (municipal or public bonds), (3) the federal government (Treasury or government bonds), (4) agencies and instrumentalities of the federal government (agency bonds), and (5) foreign governments and foreign corporations (foreign bonds). Many of the basic contractual and value characteristics are common to all types of bonds, irrespective of who issues them.

The bond, like all forms of indebtedness, is a promise to pay. Its legal claim against the assets and earnings of the issuer is the same as any other form of indebtedness unless there are specific contractual provisions to the contrary. The corporate bond has certain contractual characteristics that make it distinctive from government bonds and from other forms of indebtedness. Therefore, for purposes of this discussion, a basic distinction will be made between corporate bonds and the other types mentioned above. The characteristics of corporate bonds will be discussed here, along with the valuation process used for all types of bonds. Certain special characteristics of bonds issued by governmental units are described in Chapter 19.

CORPORATE BONDS

Most forms of indebtedness, private and public, are contracts involving two parties, the borrower and the lender. Corporate bonds usually involve three parties, the borrower, the lender, and a trustee. The promise to pay, the bond, is the basic contract between the borrower and lender. In addition, a supplementary contract, called the indenture, outlines and usually restricts the rights of the individual bondholder. The indenture is restrictive, because it prevents the bondholder from directly proceeding against the corporation if he feels that the provisions of the contract are not fulfilled. The reason for this restriction is that there are usually many bondholders and it is not practical to enter into this detailed agreement with each one. Consequently, the indenture is executed with the trustee, who acts on behalf of the individual bondholders and has the responsibility of seeing that the terms of the contract are enforced.

The contractual terms and characteristics of corporate bonds are as varied as the ingenuity of the issuers and their investment bankers. Therefore, a detailed cross classification of all types of bonds available to investors would be voluminous. However, certain basic bond indenture provisions are significant to every bond investor. This indenture, or contract, includes essential contractual provisions which have a direct bearing on the value of the bond as an investment. Some of the more important provisions cover: (1) type of security and asset protection; (2) methods of recovering principal, maturity, and sinking fund provisions; (3) interest payment provisions; and (4) special provisions, such as conversion privileges. Since these contractual provisions have an effect on the value and quality of the bond as an investment, study of these provisions is an essential part of the investment analysis of bonds.

Type of Security and Asset Protection

The asset protection provisions of the bond indenture are significant only when the issuer gets into financial difficulty. The asset protection is the bondholder's second line of defense, because the principal and interest of the bond can be paid only with the cash generated from the operations of the corporation. The relative security or asset protection only assures the bondholder a better bargaining position in the event the issuing corporation gets into financial difficulty.

The basic classifications of bond security are (1) secured, (2) unsecured, and (3) subordinated. A secured bond is one in which the corporation has specifically pledged some of its assets as security for the bond issue. In contrast, unsecured bonds do not have a specific pledge of assets as security. These unsecured bonds are not without security, because they do have a general claim on all unpledged assets. Subordinated bonds are also unsecured, but, in addition, their claim on assets generally is subordinate to all other credit claims of the corporation, both secured and unsecured.

Secured Bonds. The corporation may pledge any of its assets as security for a bond issue. The long-term nature of corporate bonds makes it impractical to pledge certain assets, such as inventory and receivables. For this reason, corporations most commonly pledge (1) plant and equipment or (2) securities, i.e., stock or bonds in another corporation. When plant and equipment is pledged as security, the bond is called a mortgage bond. If securities are pledged, it is referred to as a collateral trust bond.

Real estate or plant and equipment are most frequently used as security for the bond issue. The legal instrument used to pledge these assets is the mortgage or deed of trust. The mortgage provides that in the event of default the title to the property is transferred to a trustee for the benefit of the bondholders. Theoretically, the mortgaged property, after it is seized by the trustee, can be sold to satisfy the bondholder's claims. However, as a practical matter, the corporate assets are seldom broken up and sold piecemeal, because the corporate assets are more valuable in their present use. Generally, the corporation is reorganized by the courts, and the bondholders receive new securities in the reorganized corporation. A specific pledge of assets as security for the indebtedness gives the bondholders a superior position in reorganization proceedings. However, the mortgage bondholder is by no means assured that the value of the new securities he receives in the reorganized corporation will be equal to the value of his original investment.

Although mortgage bonds are the most common types of secured bonds, the corporation may pledge assets other than real property. For example, bonds secured by the pledge of other securities are also available for investment. A corporation may own the stock of a subsidiary and may pledge this stock as well as other securities it owns as security for the bond issue. These securities are deposited with the trustee as collateral security. The bonds are called collateral trust bonds. Of course, the collateral might be any intangible asset of value, such as bonds or mortgages, as well as common and preferred stock of subsidiary corporations. For example, Realty Collateral Corporation sold 5 percent collateral trust notes, due in 1981, which were secured by FHA insured first mortgages on residential properties. The more common type of collateral trust bond is the Pennsylvania Company 5¼ percent collateral trust bonds, due in 1985, which are secured by common stock of railroads operated by the parent, Pennsylvania Railroad.

Unsecured Bonds. Unsecured bonds are called debenture bonds. These debenture bonds have a general claim against all the corporate assets with the exception of those assets specifically pledged to secure other debt. In many situations, these bonds may have as much asset protection as they would if there were a specific pledge of assets. This protection is provided by a clause in the bond indenture or contract which prevents the issuance of other debt with a prior claim on the assets. If none of the assets of the corporation are pledged, the debenture holder has, in effect, a first claim on all assets. This protective clause usually provides that the issuer will not create any mortgage on any of its assets unless provision is made that the outstanding debentures "shall be equally and ratably secured." This clause usually has an escape hatch for the issuer which exempts all existing mortgages and allows other pledges in certain circumstances, such as new property additions.

Subordinated Bonds. In some cases, corporations have marketed bonds with a claim on assets and income that is junior to debenture bonds as well as other debt. In fact, finance companies have issued more than one class of subordinated bonds. For example, Midland-

Guardian Company, a finance company, had outstanding three classes of subordinated debt, shown in the debt structure as of December 31, 1965.

	(in thousands)
Short-term senior debt	$ 91,517
Long-term senior debt	72,900
Subordinated debt	16,534
Junior subordinated debt	8,450
Capital debt	5,000
	$194,401

The junior subordinated debt has a claim that ranks below the subordinated debt, and the capital notes are junior to both classes of subordinated debt.

Subordinated long-term debt is a relatively recent development in corporate financing. It seems that issuance of these subordinated debentures results because the interest on debt is fully deductible as a business expense, while the dividends on preferred stock are paid from after-tax income. Consequently, instead of preferred stock, these subordinated debentures have been offered to investors rather frequently in recent years because of their lower after-tax cost.

From an investor's standpoint, these subordinated debentures are roughly equivalent to a prior preferred stock, because their relative claim on the assets and earnings of the corporation is junior to other debt and senior to all equity issues. However, these bonds are still debt, and the corporation must pay the interest and principal when due, while payment of preferred dividends is discretionary.

Subordinated bonds usually carry with them an inducement for their purchase, such as warrants to purchase common stock, a conversion privilege, or a high interest rate. This practice of including sweetners is most prevalent with industrial corporations. Financial institutions, commercial banks, and finance companies borrow on a subordinated basis without any inducement other than slightly higher interest rate. For example, none of the subordinated debt of the Midland-Guardian Company is convertible.

Methods of Recovering Principal

A bondholder may recover the principal amount of his investment in bonds by three methods: (1) sale in the market, (2) call by the corporation, and (3) maturity. Of these three methods, the investor may initiate the recovery only by sale of the bond in the open market.

The decision to sell the bonds is entirely that of the investor. Of course, the investor has no assurance that he will recover his entire investment by selling in the open market, because the market price will depend on the general level of interest rates and the quality of the bond.

The mechanics of the sale of bonds will be discussed in Chapter 9. The concern here is with the contractual provisions, call and maturity, which directly affect recovery of the principal of bonds. These provisions are conditions which the investor accepted when he purchased the bond. After purchase of the bond, the investor cannot normally accelerate the maturity or force the corporation to call the bonds.

Call Provisions.   The bond indenture usually includes a provision that enables the issuer to retire the debt before maturity by calling the bonds for payment. Most corporate bonds are callable, usually at a price stated in the bond indenture—commonly a price or premium of 3 to 12 percent above the principal amount of the bond. This premium is to give the investor recompense in the event of an early call. The point is that if the issuer exercises his call provision, it is normally not to the advantage of the investor. The issuer usually will call only when he can get a lower coupon rate on a replacement bond issue. On the other hand, the call price places a ceiling on the price of the bond, because a purchaser of a bond at a price above the call price runs the risk of an immediate loss from a call. For example, the Public Service Electric and Gas $5\frac{1}{8}$ percent first mortgage bonds, due 1989, were selling for 105 at a time when the equally secured 5 percent first mortgage bonds, due 2037, were selling for 110. The lower coupon rate, longer-term bond was selling at a higher price because it was noncallable while $5\frac{1}{8}$ percent bonds had a call price of 105.

The amount of the call premium depends on market conditions. When the general level of interest rates is relatively high, the issuer may have to offer a large premium or make the bond noncallable for a long period of time after issuance. For example, the Sears Roebuck Acceptance Corporation 5 percent debentures issued in 1957 were not callable before January 15, 1970. The inclusion of a provision for delaying the call of bonds for a number of years is necessary to make them salable, because investors want assurance that the bonds will not be called at a later date and refunded at lower interest rates.

Maturity and Sinking Fund Provisions.   Nearly all bonds have maturity dates when the outstanding bonds must be paid. The bonds may mature either (1) in a lump sum or (2) in installments over the life of the bonds. The bond issue that matures in installments or in a series is referred to as a serial bond. Usually, a portion of the serial bond matures each year. This method of extinguishing bonded indebtedness is normally used in financing railroad equipment (equipment trust certificates) and in state and local government bond issues.

A more common method of reducing the size of the debt before maturity is through use of a sinking fund. The usual type of sinking fund requires an annual deposit with the trustee of a certain sum of money, or its equivalent in principal amount of bonds, sufficient to retire a specified percentage of the issue. Failure to meet such payment can constitute an act of default. The indenture may provide that in lieu of cash sinking fund payments the company may get credit for additions to the property securing the bond issue. This practice is accepted on the theory that such additions increase the asset protection of the bonds. The cash sinking fund payments unquestionably increase the value of the bond issue, because the payments are nearly always used to reduce the amount of bonds outstanding. The trustee may use the proceeds to purchase the bonds in the open market or may call the bonds for the sinking fund. The method of acquisition would depend on what price would be the lowest.

The maturity or length to maturity is the time that must elapse before the corporation pays the principal of the bond to the investor. Bonds are loosely classified as short, medium, or long term. These terms have different meanings to different investors. To a bank, a short-term bond has a maturity of under 5 years, a medium-term bond has a life of 5 to 10 years, and a long-term bond has a maturity of over 10 years. To the individual investor, a short-term bond may be considered one with a life of 10 years or less, and a long-term bond one with a maturity of 20 to 25 years. During periods of low interest rates, it is obviously to the advantage of the borrowing corporation to issue bonds with long maturities and vice versa. Conversely, investors will try to bargain for longer maturities during periods of tight money and high interest rates, and will require elimination of the call provision or a higher call premium, as was mentioned earlier.

Interest Payment Provisions

Most bond issues provide that the interest be paid semiannually at a fixed rate. For example, the interest on the Public Service Electric and Gas 5⅛ percent bonds mentioned earlier must be paid semi-annually or the bond is in default.

The interest on some bonds is variable, and payment is dependent on earnings. These bonds are called income bonds. The interest payment provisions for these bonds usually provide that payment will be made up to a stipulated percentage if earned. If earnings are available for only a partial interest payment, a partial payment usually must be made with the deficiency accumulating. For example, the interest on the Trans World Airline 6½ percent subordinated income debentures is paid only if earned. Any unpaid interest accumulates and must be paid out of subsequent accruing available net income.

These bonds usually arise from a corporate financial reorganization or recapitalization. In a number of instances, income bonds have been issued and sold as new financing. The TWA issue mentioned above was sold as new financing in 1961.

Conversion Provisions

A convertible bond is one which contains a provision for an exchange of the bond for shares of stock at the option of the bondholder. These provisions usually require an exchange for common stock, but in some instances, the exchange has been for preferred stock.

In recent years, there has been increased use of convertible bonds by corporations in new financing. During periods of rising interest rates and tight money, corporations offer this inducement to persuade investors to accept a lower interest rate. In addition, marginal companies must offer the conversion privilege to investors, irrespective of the level of interest rates, to get market acceptance of the issue.

These convertible securities offer an opportunity to the investor to have the prior position and income of bonds and the possibilities of capital appreciation of the common stockholder. The investor, of course, does not get this conversion privilege without sacrificing income. The conversion privilege usually results in a lower yield for the security than the investor would receive from an investment of comparable quality that does not have this feature. For example, Carrier Corporation 4⅛ percent bonds, due in 1982, are convertible into common stock. These bonds were selling to yield 4.5 percent on November 30, 1964. These bonds were rated as medium quality. Medium-quality bonds were selling to yield, on this date, 4.93 percent.

Investors in these bonds were willing to sacrifice 0.43 percent in yield for the privilege of converting the bonds into 16.15 shares of common stock per $1,000 bond until February 1, 1967.

The value of a convertible bond is dependent on (1) its value as a debt instrument, and (2) the value of the common stock into which it is convertible. If the conversion price of the common stock is considerably above the present market price of the stock, the conversion privilege is of little value, and the convertible bond sells at a price that reflects its value as a debt instrument. To illustrate these dual value characteristics, Figure 5-1 shows the price of the FMC Corporation common stock and $3\frac{1}{8}$ percent convertible bonds, due in 1981. The figure shows that the price of the bonds rises more rapidly than the price of the common stock on the upswing. With the downturn, the price of the bond declines more rapidly than the price of the common stock during the early stages of the decline. During the later stages of the decline, the price of the bond begins to level off, while the price of the common stock continues on down for a time. At this later stage, the price of the bond indicates that the conversion privilege is of little value, and the market is valuing the bond as a debt instrument.

The investor should always appraise the value of the bond independent of the conversion privilege. If he decides that basically the security is a good value, then he can decide whether he is willing to sacrifice the income necessary to have an option on the common stock of the company. The value of this option or conversion privilege is dependent on the length of time the conversion privilege is exercisable and the relationship of the market price of the common stock to the conversion price.

A convertible bond selling at a substantial premium over its basic value as a bond should not be purchased unless the investor wants to become a holder of common stock. The reason is that most convertible bonds are callable, and the corporation may force conversion by calling the bond. Conversion would be forced, because the call price of the bond would be less than the converted value of the bond.

Investors in convertible bonds sometimes do not realize the premium they are paying for the conversion privilege. They believe that they are buying a senior security that will have value as a bond and, in addition, capital appreciation if things go well. However, if the common stock of the company has little prospect for appreciation, the investor may pay a premium for an option that has little value.

FIGURE 5-1

FMC Corporation Convertible Subordinated Debentures and Common Stock, End-of-Month Bid Prices, September, 1961–September, 1965

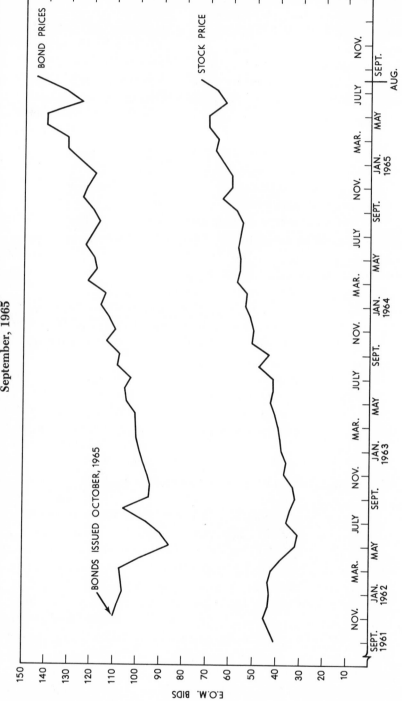

THE VALUE OF BONDS

The Valuation Process

The value of a bond is dependent on three factors: (1) the total money payments that will be received in future, (2) the rate at which these money payments should be discounted to arrive at their present value, and (3) the relative certainty that they will be received in accordance with the contract. For example, the investor wants to purchase a $1,000 bond with a seven-year maturity and a coupon or contractual rate of interest of 4 percent annually. The expected proceeds from this bond would be (1) a stream of payments of $40 per year (4% × $1,000) and (2) the lump-sum receipt of the bond's face value of $1,000 at maturity. The total money payments received by the investor will be $1,280. Obviously, the investor would not pay $1,280 today for $1,280 to be received in the future, because he would not receive any payment for use of his money over time. Therefore, the investor would pay only $1,000 for this bundle of future payments totaling $1,280. The reason is that the investor could invest $760 at 4 percent compounded annually and would have a lump-sum payment of $1,000 at the end of seven years. As a consequence, he obviously would not pay $1,000 for a $1,000 lump-sum payment if it is worth only $760.

Similarly, the investor would not pay $280 for the $280 in interest payments. The present value of these future interest payments is obviously not $280, but an examination of a present value table will show them to be worth $240 ($40 × 6.003). In summation, the investor finds that this $1,000 bond is worth $760 for the lump sum payment at the end of the period and $240 for the stream of interest incomes to be received over the seven-year period.

Bond Value Variables

The value of a bond will vary in the marketplace. The variables that will cause changes in the market price of a bond are: (1) changes in the pure interest rate, which is the rate of return that investors demand for putting their funds in an investment that has an absolute minimum of risk; (2) the premium for risk, which is the payment for assuming the risk of possible interruption of the stream of future money payments. The bond will tend to increase or decrease in price to reflect changes in the pure or basic interest rates. The causes of change in the basic interest rate are the supply and demand for funds. These factors will be discussed in Chapter 19.

The bond will also vary in value because of changes in the degree of risk involved. In the preceding discussion of the 4 percent, seven-year bond, the assumption was made that the 4 percent rate did not include any payment for possible default by the corporation of its contractual obligation. As a practical matter, there is an element of financial risk in all bonds. To the extent that there are now added risks of default, the interest rate of the bond should be higher than the basic rate of 4 percent. The investor will demand an added return to compensate him for this risk. How much higher the rate should be is a question the analyst can determine by comparing yields of bonds of similar quality in the market.

For a bond of particular quality, the market may demand a differential of only $\frac{1}{2}$ percent to compensate for the financial risk. Why does the market demand a premium of only $\frac{1}{2}$ percent? Presumably, the premium for added risk is related in part to experience in the past, which indicates that on the average only a moderate percentage of bonds of such quality actually default. As the degree of financial risk increases, the premium for risk that investors will demand will increase.

In summary, the bond will tend to increase or decrease in price to reflect changes in the pure or basic interest rates, or the changes in evaluation of the financial risk, or both. The current market price of the bond will tend to be at a level that will provide a yield or rate of return to the investor roughly equivalent to the yield on bonds of similar quality.

Value, Yields, and Length to Maturity

The three types of returns or yields used in bond valuation are (1) coupon rate or contractual yield, (2) current return or yield, and (3) yield to maturity. The first of these is the coupon rate or contractual yield stated in the bond contract. For example, with a $100 face value, 3 percent bond, the coupon rate or contractual yield is 3 percent. If this bond is selling at 90 in the market, the yield on a current return basis is 3.33 percent ($3 \div 0.90$). But if the bondholder holds to maturity, say for 20 years, he will at that time receive an additional $10, which must be taken into account in computing the yield of his bond to maturity. Since this money will not be received until the end of the 20-year period, its present value is, of course, less than $10. The true yield to maturity would be 3.71 percent. A similar calculation is necessary when a bond is bought at a premium. Assume that a 3 percent bond maturing in 20 years is purchased at 105. The current return is about 2.86 percent, but the yield to maturity is less, because at maturity the payment of $100 principal involves a capital loss of $5.00. The computation of yields to maturity is described in the mathematical appendix. However, bond yield tables are available to aid in computing yields to maturity.

The relationship between yields and maturities may be clarified by reference to Figure 5–2. This figure shows how varying the length of maturity affects the yield to maturity of three bonds with different coupon interest rates when each bond sells at a price that gives the same current return of 3.33 percent. Thus, as shown in the figure, a 3 percent bond selling at 90 and maturing in 20 years gives a yield to

FIGURE 5–2

Yields to Maturity of Bonds of Varying Maturities and Coupon Rates Selling on the Same Current Return Basis of 3.33 Percent

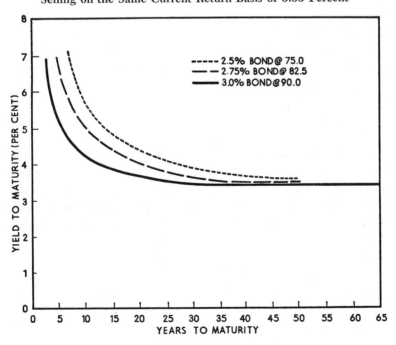

maturity of 3.7 percent; a 2½ percent bond with the same maturity date selling at 75 yields 4.4 percent to maturity, although both give the same current return.

The nearer the date of maturity, the less the price of a bond fluctuates with changes in market rates of interest, always assuming, of course, that there is no doubt in the minds of buyers concerning the ability of the issuer to pay the principal when due. Let us use again the example of a $100 3 percent bond that matures in 20 years. If interest rates in the capital markets should rise to 3.71 percent, this bond would drop in price to 90. If, however, the same bond had a maturity of 5 years instead of 20, it would decline in price to only 96.79 in order to show a yield of 3.71 percent. Conversely, if interest rates in the capital markets should drop to 2.68 percent, the 20-year bond would rise in price to 105 to reflect this yield, while a 5-year bond need rise only to 101.29 to provide this yield. In periods of rising interest rates (which means lower bond prices), it is to the advantage of the investor to hold short maturities, and in periods of falling interest rates, to hold long maturities. Because of the long-term cycle in interest rates, the choice of the correct policy to pursue is of utmost importance, particularly for those portfolios that are exclusively in bond investments.

The yields on bonds of the same quality will tend to vary with length of time to maturity. It appears logical to expect lower yields on shorter maturities, because there is less risk of variation in market price and there is a shorter wait to get liquid funds for reinvestment if interest rates rise. For example, in January, 1965, the yield to maturity on U.S. Treasury bonds due within one year was 3.77 percent compared to a yield of 4.70 percent for government bonds maturing in 1970.

A bond issue which matures serially illustrates the manner in which yield increases as maturity lengthens, because the element of quality is eliminated. This issue consists of serial bonds maturing annually over a 48-year period. The earliest maturity (one year) shows a yield of 1 percent. The yield increases 0.25 percentage points each year as maturity increases by one year, but the gains in yield decline as the longer maturities are approached. These yield relationships are shown in the approximate smooth curve shown in Figure 5–3. As indicated, the yield is sharply increased during the early maturities, but the rate of increase tapers off after the sixth year. After the twenty-fifth year, the rate of increase is so small that it offers little inducement to purchase maturities extending beyond this point.

FIGURE 5–3

Bond Yields as a Function of Maturity

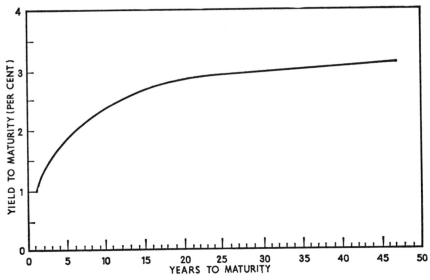

The yields on short-term debt tend to vary more widely than the yields on long-term debt. As credit becomes more stringent, both the long-term and short-term yields will tend to rise; the shorter term rises by a greater amount, perhaps even moving above the long-term rate during periods of severe credit stringency. For example, in 1965 the demand for funds for business expansion and Federal Reserve Board monetary actions, along with an ample supply of long-term funds, caused the spread between short-term and long-term rates to narrow to less than 1 percent.

Unfortunately, an investment in high-grade bonds per se does not assure the investor that he will succeed in attaining market stability, because the prices of such bonds move inversely with the market rate of interest, and these price changes can be very substantial. The actions of the U.S. Treasury and the Board of Governors of the Federal Reserve affect the general level of interest rates. There is a more detailed discussion of these actions and the changes in the supply of money and interest rates in Chapter 19. As illustrated in Figure 5–4, which traces the changes in yields on high-grade bonds, the cycle of changes in interest rates is of long duration and can show substantial amplitude. A change of 1 percent seems relatively small, but a 3 percent 30-year bond would decline from 100.0 to 82.6 a drop of 17.4 percent, if the market rate of interest were to rise from 3 percent to

FIGURE 5-4

Long- and Short-Term Interest Rates

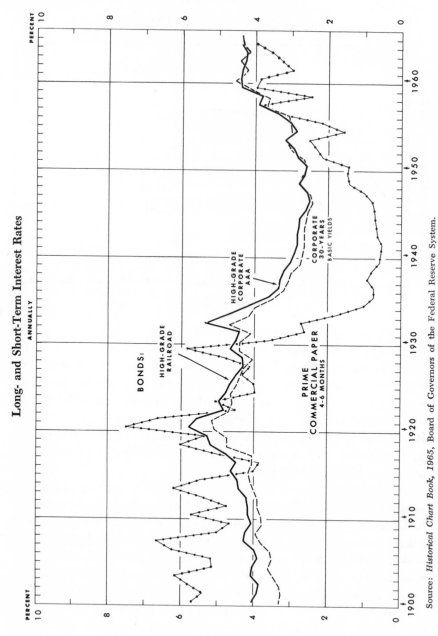

Source: *Historical Chart Book, 1965*, Board of Governors of the Federal Reserve System.

4 percent. Therefore, the investor must decide what phase of the cycle of interest rates prevails currently. If he believes there is a good chance of a rise in the trend of interest rates, he should confine his investments in high-grade bonds to those of short maturities, since the pull of maturity will prevent the price of the bond from being greatly affected.

The investor cannot count on adequate warning to make his changes in maturities leisurely. Changes in the level of interest rates may come abruptly, as can be observed in Figure 5–4.

When the course of interest rates is not clear, the investor may minimize his risk by staggering the maturities of high-grade bond-holdings. Where such a course is not feasible because of the small size of the investment, the investor should hedge his risks by investing in medium-term bonds of about five to ten years' maturity. Unless he is speculating on declining interest rates, the investor would be better advised in general to avoid bonds with excessively long maturities, for the prices of these bonds can decline substantially when interest rates rise.

Quality Reflected in Yield

As mentioned before, the contractual characteristics of a bond do not determine its quality. The issuing corporation must be analyzed to make a quality determination. A debenture of a strong company, for example, would be a better investment than a mortgage bond of a weak company. The investor should not be unduly impressed by the descriptive title "first mortgage bond." A first approximation of the quality of a bond is provided by the ratings given by such organizations as Moody's and Standard and Poor's. These two rating systems, most commonly employed, use letters to indicate levels of quality. For example, the Standard and Poor's bond quality rating system divides bond into two broad classes. One class is interest-paying bonds. The other class is bonds on which no interest is paid either because the bonds are in default or because they are income bonds. The interest-paying bonds are assigned quality ratings in eight classifications, ranging from AAA for the highest quality to CC for the lowest. Bonds on which interest is not being paid are rated C, DDD, DD, and D.

Another indication of quality is legality. Many trustees, insurance companies, and banks are restricted in their corporate bond investment to issues that are declared legal for investment by states in which they reside. To qualify as "legals," bonds must pass certain requirements that have been set by the state. Because of the rigidity of law and lack of judgment involved in administration, some very sound securities are denied legality, and some of rather dubious quality may make the legal list. For this reason, legality is not such a good test of quality as the ratings, but it is an important market price factor because banks and insurance companies are the major buyers of the better-quality bonds. If a bond should fail to meet the legal requirements, buying power for the bond is greatly diminished, and its market price may, consequently, be adversely affected.

High-quality bonds are those rated BBB or higher by Standard and Poor's or Baa or higher by Moody's. These bonds are usually eligible as investments for financial institutions. The market value of these bonds tends to vary only with fluctuations in the open market interest rates. The yield differential between the highest rated and lowest rated bonds is relatively narrow. The yields for composite bonds by rating at the year-end 1965 were the following:

Moody's Ratings	Yield (Percent)	Standard and Poor's Rating	Yield (Percent)
Aaa	4.73	AAA	4.69
Aa	4.82	AA	4.79
A	4.89	A	4.87
Baa	5.04	BBB	5.06

The market value of lower-grade bonds—those with a quality rating below BBB—is also affected by changes in the general level of interest rates. The market value of these bonds is additionally affected by changes in the credit rating of the issuer, and usually is more responsive to the prospects for the issuer than to money market changes.

When a bond is purchased for the specific purpose of attaining safety and stability of principal, it is essential that the investor recognize this distinction and confine himself to high-grade bonds. Too often the lure of a larger income leads to investment in lower-grade bonds, which seem perfectly safe during periods when these marginal companies experience good earnings. However, these bonds often drop sharply in price during periods of recession.

As a general rule, the investor should not consider higher yields from lower-grade bonds as adequate compensation for risk if, as a matter of investment requirements and policy, he cannot afford to assume the risk. To the extent that the investor can afford to assume the risks of buying any lower-quality bonds, perhaps in the hope of capital gain in addition to higher yield, the bond buyer will play close attention to the size of the yield spread in trying to attain proper timing in purchase and sale. A historical record of yield spreads between high-quality and medium-quality bonds is shown in Table 5–1.

TABLE 5–1

**Annual Average Excess Yield of BBB Over AAA Utility Bonds
(Expressed as a Percentage)**

Year	Excess Yield (Percent of AAA Yield)	Year	Excess Yield (Percent of AAA Yield)
1930	29	1948	13
1931	40	1949	17
1932	57	1950	17
1933	68	1951	16
1934	56	1952	16
1935	48	1953	14
1936	42	1954	15
1937	49	1955	10
1938	60	1956	12
1939	56	1957	17
1940	43	1958	18
1941	28	1959	10
1942	25	1960	11
1943	20	1961	11
1944	19	1962	9
1945	13	1963	9
1946	13	1964	7
1947	12	1965	8

Following the 1929 stock market crash, business conditions worsened and affected the corporate credit, and the yield on lower-grade bonds rose more than that of high-grade bonds. In other words, the price of lower-grade bonds declined more than the prices of high-grade bonds. This rise in yield reached its peak in 1933, and the yield spread then declined as business recovered. The 1938 recession caused the spread to rise to a point almost as high as it was in the depths of the depression in 1933. The spread thereafter resumed its decline, which carried through the post-World War II and post-Korean war periods. During this second period, which bottomed out in 1955, the excellent business conditions and monetary ease caused lower-grade bonds to show a yield only about 10 percent greater than high-grade bonds. The yield spread has become even narrower during the period of unprecedented prosperity of 1961–65. The yield spread was only 7 percent at end of 1964. The spread between the yields on lower-grade and high-grade bonds might be used as an indication of investor confidence. When business is good and there is confidence in corporate credit, the yield on lower-grade bonds tends to approach that of high-grade bonds. When doubt enters the investor's mind, the spread widens.

The record of yields indicates the substantially higher return that is generally available from lower-grade bonds, but they should be purchased for speculation only when the differential yield is quite wide. That is, they should be bought during periods of business recession and sold during periods of prosperity. A very careful analysis must be made of the issuing company and the differential yields. In the post-World War II years, for example, the yield on lower-grade bonds, averaging only about 13 percent above that of high-grade bonds, suggested that low-grade bonds were probably not attractive even for the speculator.

SUMMARY

An investment analyst should investigate the legal characteristics of the bond issue. This step would involve an examination of the contractual provisions related to (1) security, (2) call, (3) maturity and sinking fund, and (4) conversion provisions of the bond contract. These legal characteristics have a bearing on the financial risk assumed in the purchase of a bond, since they affect such important matters as the relative claim on the income and assets of the corporation.

The primary problem in analysis is to provide the basis for valuation of the bond. The variables affecting the value of a bond include (1) the length of time to maturity, (2) the financial risk involved, (3) the market rate of interest, and (4) the coupon rate of interest on the bond. Length to maturity, financial risk, and coupon rate are matters that may be determined by analysis of the bond contract and the issuing firm. The market rate of interest, the interest rate risk factor, involves external analysis of the supply and demand for funds and the factors affecting them.

REVIEW QUESTIONS AND PROBLEMS

1. Basically what is the legal difference between corporate bonds and the long term debt of a proprietorship or a partnership?
2. In the event of a default on corporate debt, what action may a bondholder take against a corporation?
3. If the assets pledged to secure a bond issue is the investor's second line of defense, what is the first line of defense?
4. What types of assets are generally pledged to secure a bond issue?
5. What is the basic difference between a secured and an unsecured bond?
6. Under what conditions would a corporation probably issue bonds that were noncallable?
7. Why would two bond issues with the same current return have greatly differing yields to maturity?
8. Is it possible to speculate in high-grade bonds? Explain.
9. In February 1966, Northrop Corporation convertible subordinated 5 percent debentures were selling for 153. These bonds were convertible into Northrop common stock at $19.25 per share. The common stock was selling for $27.00 per share. How much would the stock have to increase in price to make it profitable for debenture holders to convert?
10. Isn't there a contradiction between a bondholder's desire for a sinking fund provision and a high call price?
11. Does the yield curve for bonds slope downward or upward? What determines the slope of the yield curve?
12. What characteristics of bonds relating to quality, maturity, and call price should an investor seek who believes that an economic recession is imminent and that interest rates are likely to fall?

CHAPTER **6**

Characteristics and Value of Investment Media—Common and Preferred Stock

An equity or ownership interest in a corporation is evidenced by common stock and preferred stock. The equity interest of the common stockholder is directly comparable to the ownership of a house, a partner's interest in a partnership, or any similar private property right. The holder of the basic equity interest usually has two fundamental rights: (1) control of the management of assets owned and (2) the residual profits after all current prior and limited claims are satisfied.

These two rights have a direct bearing on the investment value of common stock. Control of management enables the common stockholder to select management that will vigorously attempt to maximize the residual profits available to the common stockholder. In turn, the size and certainty of these residual profits have a bearing on the investment value of the common stock. Therefore, it is evident that the characteristics and the valuation of common stock are closely linked.

Preferred stock also represents an equity or ownership interest. The preferred stockholder, however, is not entitled to the same rights and claims as the common stockholder. The preferred stock investor generally exchanges his rights to participate in management and his unlimited share of residual profits for a prior claim to assets in liquidation and to corporate income. In other words, he accepts limitations on his income and other rights of ownership in order to secure certain preferences.

The value of a preferred stock is dependent on the special features accorded it by the articles of incorporation. These features are concerned with (1) claim on assets in liquidation, (2) claim on income, (3) voting rights, and (4) call features. Certain combinations of legal characteristics may make a preferred stock a "debt-like" instrument,

76

and other combinations may make it an "equity-like security." The later discussion of preferred stock will develop these differences and their effect on the value of the preferred stock.

CHARACTERISTICS OF COMMON STOCK

Common stockholders have residual claims on assets and earnings after prior claims of bondholders and preferred stockholders have been met. Common stock earnings and dividends will fluctuate; the degree of fluctuation depends on the character of the industry and the enterprise, the amount of senior capital in the form of debt, and the amount of preferred stock ahead of the common stock. Common stockholders usually, but not always, exercise voting control of the corporation and elect the board of directors who, in turn, select the officers.

Voting Rights

The common stockholders usually control the affairs of the corporation, since they usually have the voting power. In some cases, there is more than one class of common stock, and only one class of stock has the voting right. For example, Plymouth Rubber Company has two classes of common stock which are identical in all respects, except that Class A common stock has voting rights and Class B common stock is nonvoting. In this manner, it is possible to retain control of a company with a relatively small investment while obtaining funds for expansion by the sale of nonvoting stock. Such securities have become relatively rare. The New York Stock Exchange, for example, has refused since 1926 to list nonvoting common stock. In these days of widely diversified ownership of stock, voting power often is not of real importance to the investor anyway. Most of the larger corporations are controlled by managements that own relatively small amounts of the stock. Nevertheless, the power to vote possesses a strong latent threat to curb or prevent management abuses that might otherwise arise.

Par Value

Common stocks may have a par value, a nominal stated value, or no par value. The par value of a common stock indicates the minimum amount of capital originally subscribed by the stockholders, and addi-

This Week magazine, October 4, 1959. Reproduced by permission.

"And please don't refer to me as a common stockholder!"

tional shares cannot be sold for less. If the common stock is sold for more than par, the excess is placed in a capital surplus account. The more realistic view of no-par stock is that the par value is only a legal fiction and that common stock represents, not a stated amount of dollars, but a share in ownership. Additional stock can be issued at the current market rate. From the viewpoint of the investor, the distinction between par and no-par stock is of no practical significance.

One benefit of a corporate organization compared with investments as a sole proprietor or partner is that the stockholder's liability is limited to his capital contribution in the corporation. Occasionally, if corporations have sold stock at less than its par value, the company can, by means of an assessment, require the stockholder to contribute the difference between the original sale price and the par value. This type of financing was formerly rather common in mining ventures. Assessable common stock is a rarity in present-day corporate finance.

Preemptive Rights

State laws or corporate charters frequently provide that stockholders (usually common stockholders alone) have a prior right to purchase additional common stock, or securities convertible into common stock, which may be issued by the corporation. This privilege is called a preemptive right.

The preemptive right is designed to protect the common stockholder against dilution of his proportionate interest in the business. New stock issues may cause a dilution in the existing stockholder's proportionate share in the net worth of the corporation and earnings of the corporation, and will cause a dilution in relative voting power. The issuance of new stock at a price higher than book value per share would, of course, increase the book value of the existing common stock. In addition, if the corporation invests the proceeds from the sale of the new common stock to yield a rate higher than the yield on the old common stock there would be no dilution in earnings. However, the sale of new voting common stock to any outsider will result in dilution of voting control. As described earlier, the voting control factor is not usually a major consideration.

The issuance of new stock by means of privileged suscription rights granted to existing stockholders is a common financial practice, even when stockholders do not possess preemptive rights. In such cases, the new stock is offered at a price substantially below the market price of the old stock. The stockholder may retain his proportionate share in the equity by subscribing to new stock. He may sell his rights in the market to someone else if he does not want to purchase additional stock.

Value of Rights. If new stock is offered at a price below the market price, the rights have a value. Judging how the valuation of rights affects the stockholder's position is helpful in deciding whether to sell the rights. To illustrate the procedure in valuing rights, assume that a company has 600,000 shares of stock outstanding; they sell for $20 a share in the open market and earn $2.00 a share. The company wishes to raise $2 million of new capital through sale of additional common stock to existing stockholders, offering them a privileged subscription.

The company could effect this sale in various ways. For example, it could sell 200,000 shares at $10 a share (plan A) or 400,000 shares at $5.00 a share (plan B). Both plans would have the same effect on the investor who exercised his rights. These plans would likewise have the same effect on the investor who sold his rights, although his total investment in the business would be reduced by varying amounts. The effects of these plans on the investment position of an owner of 60 shares of old stock are shown in Table 6–1. The shares outstanding before the issue of additional stock are designated "old stock." The additional shares issued, as well as all outstanding shares after the new issue has been completed, are called "new stock."

TABLE 6-1

Analysis	Assuming Exercise of Rights		Assuming Sale of Rights	
	Plan A	*Plan B*	*Plan A*	*Plan B*
Original number of old shares held	60	60	60	60
Number of new shares acquired	20	40	nil	nil
Total number of new shares held	80	100	nil	nil
Market value of original holding of old stock ...	$1,200	$1,200	$1,200	$1,200
Cost of new stock acquired	$ 200	$ 200	nil	nil
Total investment in new stock	$1,400	$1,400	$1,050	$ 840
Proceeds from sale of rights	nil	nil	$ 150	$ 360
Earnings per share of new stock	$ 1.75	$ 1.40	$ 1.75	$ 1.40
Total earnings on stock held	$ 140	$ 140	$ 105	$ 84
Total earnings as a percentage of investment	10%	10%	10%	10%

The results shown are based on the assumption that the corporation will be able to earn on the new money invested in the business the same return it was already earning on the total market value of the old stock. This assumption is also implicit in the formula for computing the theoretical value of the rights a stockholder receives under a privileged subscription plan. The investor must analyze the facts to determine whether this assumption is warranted. To the extent that the assumption is not consistent with the facts, or the investor's opinions as to the facts, the market value of rights will deviate from their theoretical value.

To compute the theoretical value of a right, the investor can use the formula: $V = (M - S) \div (N + 1)$. This formula is valid only during the period when rights are sold, and is discussed in Appendix 1. Each old share is always entitled to one right. Thus, in the example in Table 6-1, the investor who owns 60 shares has 60 rights, even though these rights under plan A entitle him to purchase only 20 new shares. In the formula, V is the value of a right; M stands for the market value of a share of old stock; S, for the subscription price of the new stock; and N, for the number of old shares necessary to obtain the privilege of buying one new share. Under plan A, in which the stockholder would be offered one new share at $10 for every three old shares he held, the theoretical value of one right would be $2.50, or $(20 - 10) \div (3 + 1)$.

Whether rights should be exercised or sold is, of course, a question that cannot be answered by means of a formula. The basic issue is whether the company will be able to employ the new money profitably. Determining this may involve not only an appraisal of management but also an estimate of future business conditions and price levels. For example, the new stock may be sold in a market that is valuing the stock so conservatively that a high yield is indicated. Yet, the proceeds from the new stock issue may be invested in plant and equipment, which may return less profits per dollar invested than the company earned prior to the expansion. Investment of the additional money is not necessarily a favorable development, because the smaller return on the new expansion tends to dilute the future earning per share. If careful analysis indicates that the stockholder should not increase his investment in the company by exercising his rights, this is evidence that he probably should have sold his original holdings of stock before new financing took place.

So far, as timing problems are concerned, it is a more conservative procedure for the investor who intends to sell to do so early rather than gamble on market fluctuations through delay. If he intends to exercise his rights, however, he can lose nothing by waiting until a time near the expiration date, and he may possibly gain if adverse developments, such as precipitous market decline, cause the rights to become valueless.

Warrants

Warrants, like rights, are options to buy other securities, usually common stock, at a stated price. They arise in a manner somewhat different than rights. They are usually sold in conjunction with other securities that might not be readily marketable without the speculative appeal of an attached warrant or, in the case of bonds, could not be sold with a reasonable interest rate. Warrants may be either detachable or nondetachable. Only if the warrant is detachable may the investor resell it separately from the security with which it was issued. Some warrants represent perpetual options. Others expire at a definite time stated in the option. The issue of warrants in connection with the sale of preferred stocks or bonds is usually an indication that these securities could not be sold on their own investment merits or reasonable terms.

The number of warrants available to investors is relatively small.

Because warrants fluctuate in wider market swings than the common stocks on which they have an option, they represent a good speculative medium for purchase in anticipation of a rise in the general market. If timing of purchase is faulty, however, a greater proportionate loss can be suffered in the event of a decline in the general market.

Sometimes, the price of the common stock may be so low in relation to the price at which the warrant is exercisable that the price of the warrant appears worthless. Although the warrant may be apparently worthless on this basis, the option privilege has a value that enables the warrant to command a price beyond the value indicated if exercised immediately. For example, Pacific Petroleums, Ltd., sold $5\frac{1}{2}$ percent sinking fund debentures in April, 1958, and attached 20 warrants to each $1,000 bond. These warrants were detachable and exercisable on November 1, 1958. Each warrant entitled the holder to purchase one share of common stock of Pacific Petroleums, Ltd., at $19 a share until March 31, 1968. The common stock is listed on the New York Stock Exchange, and the warrants are listed on the American Stock Exchange. On October 15, 1965, the price of the common stock was $10.37 per share, which was less than the price each warrant holder would have to pay for the stock if he exercised his option. The warrant would seem valueless in these circumstances, but on that same day investors were paying $5.25 for each warrant. These investors were willing to pay $5.25 for a warrant that was apparently worthless, because it enabled them to control a share of stock, that was paying no dividend, with less funds than the price of the stock itself. Undoubtedly, these investors believed that the price of Pacific Petroleums common stock will exceed $24.25 a share before expiration of the warrant on March 31, 1968, because they invested in the warrant and will be required to pay another $19 when they exercise the warrant.

When the common stock sells at only a fraction of the price at which it could be purchased by exercise of the warrant, the warrant still has some value. When the common stock on which the warrant has an option goes beyond the option price, the warrant possesses a real value in addition to the speculative value of the option. But when this point is reached, the price of the warrant tends to move up more slowly relative to further rises in the price of the common stock. The possibilities of large percentage gains are sharply diminished, while the chances of large percentage losses are enhanced.

VALUE OF COMMON STOCK

There are many concepts of value of common stock.[1] The more commonly used concepts of common stock value and common stock valuation are (1) book value or net asset value, (2) market value, and (3) some form of "appraised" or "intrinsic" value based on determination of the present value of the future earnings of the company. The investment analyst and the investor are concerned most with determination of an intrinsic value based on a present-worth analysis.

Intrinsic Value—Present Value of Dividends

In the previous discussion of bond value, it was noted that the two important elements to be considered in the valuation process are (1) total money payments that will be received in the future and (2) rate at which these payments should be discounted to arrive at their present value. Common stock valuation by this method cannot be so precise as bond valuation, because the characteristics of common stock cause these elements used in the valuation process to vary widely. Therefore, the valuation of common stock presents some special problems.

The first problem is to determine the rate at which future dividends of the common stock should be discounted. It is relatively easy to determine the basic or pure interest rate. The problem is to determine the premium for financial risk. This problem arises because the premium for risk in the discount rate cannot logically be related to a past record of defaults, because common stock offers no contractual promise to make payments. Where there is no contract, there cannot be a default.

The income for the common stockholder is dividends. The investor should increase the discount rate sufficiently to compensate for the added financial risk the common stockholder assumes. The investor can never determine this rate precisely. He knows that the discount rate should be higher than the current yield on high-grade bonds, but

---

[1] See Nicholas Molodovsky, "Valuation of Common Stocks," *Readings in Financial Analysis and Investment Management*, ed. Eugene M. Lerner (Homewood, Ill.: Richard D. Irwin, Inc., 1963), pp. 246–88.

the question is how much higher. An indication of the discount rates is provided by the pattern of common stock yields in the past. It may be noted from Figure 6–1 that the yields have varied from about 3.5 percent in 1929 to 7.5 percent in 1931. In other words, these data indicate that the future dividends of common stocks should be discounted at a rate somewhere between 3.5 percent and 7.5 percent.

The difficulty of estimating future income payments outweighs the problem of selecting the discount rate. As mentioned previously, the income payments to the common stockholder are in the form of dividends. Although dividend payments frequently show more stability than earnings, the trend of the company's current earnings is followed closely by investors, because changes in earnings usually forecast changes in dividends. Estimation of future dividends on the basis of the current trend of earnings may be a sound procedure for the near future, but the value of a common stock depends on the sum of discounted dividend payments for a long period of time.

The importance of errors involved in estimating the exact earnings and dividends for any specific year very far in the future is minimized because the present value of any specific payments to be made far in the future is very small. Thus, a dividend of $2.00 to be paid 10 years from now is worth today only $1.22 on a 5 percent yield basis, and one payable 20 years from now is worth only 74 cents. This indicates that one need not be particularly discouraged because he cannot name the exact pattern of dividend changes year by year over the distant future. It is difficult enough to try to estimate the average level of earnings and dividends.

While it is not necessary to estimate the specific pattern of dividend changes year by year, it is extremely important to be assured that an approximate average level of dividends will be paid for a long period of time. This is important, because a common stock provides for no end payment or return of capital, as does a bond. It is possible, of course, to view every corporation as going through a life cycle of growth, maturity, and decay, with some chance of an end payment to stockholders on liquidation. But the length of time over which dividends will be paid is more important than the amount of the end payment.

The problem is to forecast dividends into the future. The analyst has the problem of appraising the future prospects of the company. One may object to this procedure on the basis that such long-run

FIGURE 6-1

Stock Yields

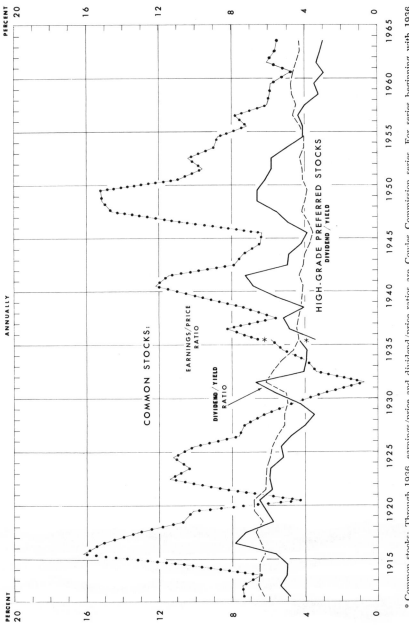

* Common stocks: Through 1936, earnings/price and dividend/price ratios are Cowles Commission series. For series beginning with 1936, dividend/price ratio is an annual average of monthly yields for the Standard and Poor's Corporation's 500 stock index (90 stocks before 1957); and earnings/price ratio is an annual average of quarterly data for the same stocks, based on seasonally adjusted quarterly earnings at annual rates and end-of-quarter prices.

Preferred stocks: Yields are annual averages of Standard and Poor's monthly figures.

Source: *Historical Chart Book, 1965*, Board of Governors of the Federal Reserve System.

forecasts are inaccurate. Admittedly, such a valuation process is not precisely accurate. What are the alternatives? Either the estimate of future incomes is made, or the stock is bought without full consideration of its probable value, or the investor must turn to another valuation method. This is the most scientific basis for arriving at the intrinsic investment value of common stock, but it is difficult to use in practice because of the pitfalls involved.

One of the pitfalls of this approach to common stock valuation is that the investor is often unduly influenced by the current yield or rate of return. For example, the investor purchases a share of common stock for $20; it yields 10 percent because it pays a $2.00 dividend. Currently, the yield may be 10 percent, but a thorough analysis of the industry and the company may indicate that in all probability this dividend cannot be maintained for many years. Current brokerage house literature often perpetuates the tendency of investors to depend on current yields, because in it the current year's dividend is divided by the market price, and it is stressed that the investor will receive that rate of return on the stock if he purchases it. This method implies that the dividend will be paid forever, while, actually, the value of the stock is dependent on the average return that will be received over a long period of years.

In summary, it would be remembered that the valuation of common stock is an art. Choice of the proper discount rate at which to value average future dividends and the estimate of future dividends is a matter of judgment. The premium for financial risk that the investor will demand will be a decision made after a careful analysis of the company and will reflect his confidence in his estimate of the future earnings potential of the company, because dividends cannot be paid without earnings.

Determination of the intrinsic value of common stock based on the present value of future dividends presents a number of difficulties. A major shortcoming is that the payment of dividends is dependent on the earnings the company generates. Therefore, another approach to this intrinsic value determination is to base it on the present value of future earnings rather than dividends. This approach is called the multiple-of-earnings or capitalization-of-earnings approach to common stock valuation. The difficulties of using the present-value approach in valuing common stock suggests that investors base the value of stock on a multiple of earnings or capitalization of earnings.

Intrinsic Value—Multiple-of-Earnings Approach

The more conventional and, in many respects, more practical approach to the valuation of common stock is to value it as a multiple of earnings. That is, the investor estimates future earnings and decides that the value of the stock is so many times earnings. This multiple of earnings is usually expressed as a price–earnings ratio, which is the price of the stock divided by the earnings. For example, if a company's stock is selling for $20 a share and the earnings are $2.00 a share the price–earnings ratio is 10, or the stock is selling for 10 times earnings. The investor is interested in projecting this price–earnings ratio into the future. This projection involves (1) an estimate of future earnings, and (2) selection of the proper multiple. These two elements are the focal points of common stock valuation using this approach.

Estimating future earnings is as difficult and hazardous as estimating future dividends, but in some respects it can be done more accurately because the investor does not have to evaluate and forecast the future dividend policies of the companies. Some companies, as a matter of policy, may decide to restrict dividends and retain earnings, while others may not. However, the investor can be sure that the company will attempt to maximize earnings, and company policies will not restrict the average future earnings.

The estimate of average future earnings is a product of security analysis which will be discussed in later chapters. A practical method of estimating average future earnings is to use an average of the past five or ten years' earnings. The use of past earnings assumes that the past performance of the company is indicative of its future performance. Such an assumption is dangerous without a thorough analysis of the company. After the investor has analyzed the company and appraised its future prospects, he must decide whether:

1. The future average earnings will approximate the past average earnings.
2. The future average earnings will be higher than the past average earnings.
3. The future average earnings will be less than the past average earnings.

The multiple the investor will use in valuing the common stock will be a reflection of his estimate of future earnings. He may decide that common stock of a company in a certain industry should be valued at between five and ten times present earnings. If the investor's appraisal of the company's prospects indicates that the future average earnings will be less than past average earnings, he selects a multiplier nearer five rather than one near ten. Conversely, if he feels that prospects are such that future earnings will be higher than past earnings, he selects a multiplier near ten.

To illustrate, both company A and company B have had a five-year average earnings of $2.00 per share. Analysis of company A shows it is relatively certain to increase average earnings in the future to $4.00 per share or, at least, to show a sizable increase in earnings. On the other hand, the analyst decides that the future average earnings of company B will remain at approximately $2.00 a share. Obviously, in valuing the stock of company A the investor would use a multiple of earnings higher than one he would use for company B.

The question still remains as to what should be the earnings multiplier. The most practical way to approach this problem is to determine the range of earnings multipliers for the industry of which A and B are a part, based on the historical range of price–earnings ratios. For purposes of this discussion, it is assumed that companies A and B are typical industrial enterprises.

Average Annual Price–Earnings Ratios,
Standard and Poor's, 500 Stocks
1945–64

1945—16.33	1955—11.50
1946—17.69	1956—14.05
1947— 9.36	1957—12.89
1948— 6.90	1958—16.64
1949— 6.64	1959—17.05
1950— 6.63	1960—17.09
1951— 9.27	1961—21.06
1952—10.47	1962—16.68
1953— 9.69	1963—17.62
1954—11.25	1964—18.08

An examination of the price–earnings ratios of industrial common stocks published by Standard and Poor's, an investment advisory service, indicates that in the 19-year period, 1945–64, industrial common stock has sold as low as 6.63 times earnings and as high as 21.06 times earnings.

Using the range-of-earnings multiples of 6 to 21 times, the investor must select the specific multiples for the earnings of companies A and

B. The solution to this problem is the key to successful investing in common stock. The proper multiple is purely a matter of investor judgment based on analysis of the company.

Growth Stock Valuation

Generally, the market has valued common stock at prices 10 to 20 times current earnings per share, as we noted in previous discussion. These common stock values are based on the general assumptions that (1) the future earnings of these companies will increase at a relatively constant, modest rate, and (2) a substantial proportion of these earnings will be paid out in dividends. This 10 to 20 times earnings range has been considered the "normal" limits for common stock prices, and situations selling at above 30 times earnings would probably be overpriced.

In recent years, a new type of common stock investment situation has arisen, or, at least, the investment literature has begun to recognize it as a special case or a departure from the "normal" situation. This is the growth stock.

A growth stock situation has two characteristics: (1) retention of a high percentage of earnings or low dividend payout and (2) a prospective high rate of return on these reinvested earnings. The effect of this policy on the common stock is to increase the net asset value of the common stock and to increase the future earnings at a compound rate of growth. For example, a company earns $5.00 per share of common stock that has a net asset value of $50. The company has a 10 percent rate of return on net asset value. If the company decides to pay out 50 percent of earnings, or $2.50 a share, the net asset value and earnings will increase by a compounded annual rate of 5 percent. As a consequence, the net asset value at the end of the first year will be $52.50, and earnings will increase to $5.25 a share, and so on. This example ignores some elements of mathematical accuracy, but it is sufficient to illustrate the point.[2]

Using this technique to select growth companies, one could hardly justify some common stocks that have sold for 70 to 80 times earnings. These growth situations generally have not only the two char-

---

[2] For a more detailed discussion, see Ralph E. Badger, "Investment Growth, Is It Overvalued?" *Financial Analysts Journal*, Vol. IXX, No. 1 (January–February, 1963); and Douglas A. Hayes, "Techniques for Appraising Growth Rates," *Financial Analysts Journal*, Vol. XX, No. 4 (July–August, 1964).

acteristics enumerated above—retention of earnings and constant rate of return—but also the prospects of an increasing rate of return. For example, the rate of return would increase from 10 percent in the first year to 15 percent in the second year and so on. This increased rate of return is justified on the basis of such things as prospective increases in product demand, improvements in technology, or new product development.

To arrive at a reasonable value for a growth stock is difficult, because often so much is dependent on the success of new, untried products and technologies. The typical pattern for a growth stock is a slow, gradual increase in the annual earnings of the company, then an acceleration in the rate of return on equity with substantial increases in earnings, and finally a leveling off.[3] In some cases, there is an actual decline in rate of return and earnings per share in the later stages of growth development, with disastrous results to the investors.

Book Value

Sometimes, in investment sales literature reference is made to the fact that a company has a book value of $60 per share of common stock and is presently selling in the market for $25 a share. The implication is that this particular stock must be undervalued. This particular stock with high book value relative to market value may be undervalued, but is this abnormally high book value in relation to the market value a good indicator of undervaluation?

To reach a conclusion on the reliability of book value in deciding whether or not a share of common stock is a good investment, the investor should first understand the nature of book value. Book value is computed by deducting total prior claims from total assets, which leaves the net worth available to the common stockholders. The book value per share is then computed by dividing this net worth available to common stockholders by the number of shares of common stock outstanding.

Generally accepted is the notion that there is no direct relationship among the book value of a share of common stock, its market price, and its intrinsic value.[4] One can present considerable empirical evi-

---

[3] Charles C. Holt, "The Influence of Growth Duration on Share Prices," in *Elements of Investment, Selected Readings*, ed. Hsiu-Kwang Wu and Alan J. Zakon (New York: Holt, Rinehart & Winston, Inc., 1965), pp. 194–204.

[4] Frank E. Block, "The Place of Book Value in Common Stock Evaluation," *Financial Analysts Journal*, Vol. XX, No. 2 (March–April, 1964).

dence to support this contention. A recent study of the relationship of book to market price of the 30 common stocks that make up the Dow-Jones Industrial Average showed little relationship between these two value measures.[5] During this period, 1949–62, these stocks had a market value which varied from 67 percent to 41.4 percent of book value.

What does the book value of a common stock reflect? Since assets are usually valued at depreciated cost on corporate balance sheets, the book value is not likely to vary closely with earning power or market value. To effectively use book value as a tool, an analyst must make a host of adjustments.[6] In the articles cited, Mr. Block's major point is that book value sets a long-term limit on earnings, and book value should be considered in analysis.[7] Investment analysis of common stock is usually a short-term problem involving projections of from one to five years. Therefore, book value as a measure of investment may be helpful only if a company is a merger or liquidation prospect.

Market Value

The market price of a common stock represents a consensus of opinion on its value. The investor may tend to accept this price as the best available evidence of an equilibrium or normal value, because it is a consensus of possibly hundreds of prospective and actual buyers and sellers of the stock. Of course, an acceptance of this pattern of thinking is self-defeating, because many investors do not rationally appraise the value of a common stock before purchase.

The concepts of common stock value are discussed primarily because the judgment of everyone tends to be distorted by current events. Investor's judgment can be and usually is influenced by emotion. Emotional binges are the primary explanation for rapidly rising stock prices and their counterpart, falling stock prices. The problem the investor has is to refrain from accepting the going market price of a stock as the best available evidence of an equilibrium or normal value. The investor must be wary of acceptance of market appraisals of a common stock, particularly when prospects for the company are good. It may be that the price of the stock already reflects the pros-

---

[5] Frank E. Block, "A Study of the Price to Book Relationship," *Financial Analysts Journal*, Vol. XX, No. 5 (September–October, 1964), p. 110.

[6] Block, *op. cit.*, pp. 30–31.

[7] *Ibid.*, p. 29.

FIGURE 6-2

Stock Prices and Trading

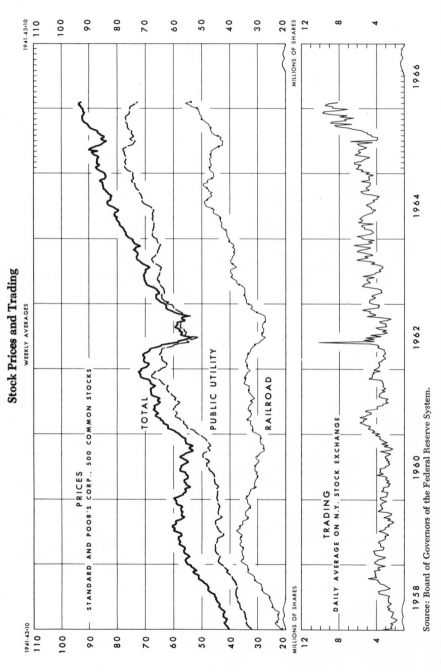

Source: Board of Governors of the Federal Reserve System.

pect of a gain in earnings. In addition, a change in prospective business conditions may bring a decline in the price of the stock in spite of increased earnings. Therefore, it is vitally important that the investor preserve his independence of judgment and not be influenced too greatly by the short-run market forecasts.

The material in Figure 6–2 shows the fluctuations in stock prices for the period 1957–65. It is obvious that in stock prices there are significant fluctuations of considerable amplitude. The trend line shows that investors, on the average, would have experienced substantial appreciation over this period. However, trying to evaluate short-term stock market action is an art that will be discussed in Chapter 20.

CHARACTERISTICS AND VALUE OF PREFERRED STOCK

The rights and privileges of preferred stock are set forth in the charter of the corporation. Preferred stock represents an ownership interest, since the corporation may not be compelled or is not obligated contractually to pay anything to the preferred stockholders. Often, the preferred stock does have certain preferences which make it similar to bonds, since both have a prior claim on the assets and income of the corporation.

There is considerable variation in the nature and form of these preferences. Sometimes, there may be what appear to be striking similarities between bonds and preferred stock; and in other cases, there are combinations of characteristics that cause the preferred stock to be more like common stock. Of course, whether the preferred stock has debt-like characteristics or equity-like characteristics will have an effect on its investment value. The essential features of preferred stock, mentioned earlier in the chapter, which have an effect on its investment value include (1) relative claim on income, (2) voting rights, (3) relative claim on assets, and (4) call features.

Claim on Income

The returns to preferred stock are dividends. The dividends on preferred stock are paid only when declared by the board of directors. The directors need not declare a preferred dividend, even if it is earned. The undeclared dividends of preferred stock may accumulate, depending on whether the preferred stock is (1) cumulative or (2) noncumulative. Dividends on cumulative preferred stock accrue to the credit of the stock for future payment to the extent that they are not paid on the regular payment date. It should be reemphasized that the preferred stockholders cannot legally enforce payment of arrearages of dividends. However, these arrearages must be paid before dividends can be paid on common stock. These dividend arrearages can get quite large. For example, in 1965 Pittsburgh Steel Company had two preferred stock issues outstanding; one issue, 5½ percent prior preferred, had $22 of dividends in arrears, and the other issue, 5 percent class A preferred, had $20. There are usually valid reasons why preferred dividends are passed for such long periods. The basic reason is usually poor earnings performance.

The dividend history on many issues of noncumulative preferred stocks is such that, as a general rule, they should be avoided by the investor. If the dividends on noncumulative preferred stock are passed because of a lack of earnings, they are forever lost. The investor is in a situation that provides him with a limited return when corporate earnings are high and no return when corporate earnings are low or nonexistent. It is a sort of heads-I-win, tails-you-lose proposition.

For that matter, there is some question whether the management is required to pay dividends on noncumulative preferred stock even when the dividends are earned. Although it is generally thought that the dividend is lost if it is not paid, such is not necessarily the case. Various state laws provide, unless nullified by the charter of the company, that dividends on noncumulative preferred stock, if earned, must ultimately be paid before dividends can be paid to the common stock. When there are no state laws governing the matter, noncumulative preferred stockholders have no claim on past dividends that have been earned but not paid.[8] This legal doctrine seems to have been reinforced by dismissal in May, 1950, of a suit by holders of noncumulative preferred stock of the Illinois Central Railroad, in which it was contended that dividends should be cumulative to the extent earned.

Participation Provision

In some cases, a preferred stock is participating, which means it is entitled to dividends in addition to a limited percentage or dollar

---

[8] *Wabash Railroad* v. *Barclay*, 280 U.S. 197 (1930).

amount. For example, Standard Fruit and Steamship Company $3.00 cumulative participating preferred stock is entitled to annual dividends of $3.00, and, in addition, this preferred stock will receive four times any amount paid to the common stock. The common stock of Standard Fruit is on a 40 cent annual dividend basis. As a consequence, the preferred receives $4.60.

From this example, it is evident that the participating provision of preferred can be quite valuable. In some cases, the participation is limited to a specified additional payment over and above the normal dividend. One cannot make any meaningful generalization on these participating provisions; therefore, the investor must evaluate each separately.

Voting Rights

Preferred stock may be (1) voting, (2) nonvoting, or (3) contingent voting. Generally, preferred stock is nonvoting or contingent voting. Contingent voting means that the preferred stock has the right to vote in some adverse circumstances, such as passage of a dividend. The rationale for allowing the right to vote in these circumstances is that if the prior position of the preferred stockholder has not given him his income then he should be allowed to actively participate in management.

The basis for not allowing the preferred stock to vote is that the preferred stock is in a relatively secure position and, therefore, the preferred stock should have no right to vote except in the special circumstances described above. Normally, the voting rights of the preferred stock have no investment significance, because in most cases the management of the company will attempt to comply with the terms of the corporate charter relating to the payment of preferred stock dividends and the other rights of preferred stockholders. However, the investor should buy a preferred stock with adequate voting rights if it is available and has the other desired characteristics.

Claim on Assets

Most preferred stock issues have preferences over common stock in liquidation of corporate assets. Usually, the preferred stock is entitled to a fixed amount plus any accumulated dividends when the liquidation is involuntary. If the corporate liquidation is voluntary, the preferred stockholder is usually given a premium payment plus par value and accumulated dividends, say 105 to 115 percent of par value or a fixed sum. This provision usually has little investment significance.

Call and Sinking Fund Provisions

Nearly all preferred stock issues have some call provision. Call prices on preferred stocks tend to be higher than on bonds. It is not unusual to see call premiums ranging up to 15 percent of par value. The call premium is usually lower than this, probably averaging around 5 percent of par; and, in some instances, provision is made for reduction of the premium at stated intervals until the premium disappears. The amount of the call premium generally reflects market conditions. For example, in 1957, Northern Natural Gas Company issued a 5.80 percent preferred stock, which bore a call premium of 15 percent above par. When the sale of preferred stock in the past has been very difficult, either because of general market conditions or the credit position of the issuing company, some companies have been forced to offer stock that is noncallable.

In some instances, the retirement of preferred stock is systematically provided for through a sinking fund. Sinking funds for preferred stock originated during the last 20 years. In earlier years, a preferred-stock sinking fund was a rarity. However, sinking funds have been used frequently since World War II as a device to sell new preferred issues. The annual sinking-fund payments tend to range from 1 percent to 5 percent of the issue; 2 percent probably is the most common figure. In some cases, sinking-fund payments are made only if earned. In other cases, payments cumulate if earnings are insufficient to meet them currently. Some charters provide that in case of failure to meet required sinking-fund payments preferred stockholders shall be given a vote or the right to elect a certain portion of the board of directors, but in many cases no penalty is specified. Presumably, even if earnings were available for the sinking fund, the payment could be passed and cumulated without penalty if the cash needs of the corporation so required.

Preferred Stock Yields

Preferred stocks are similar to bonds in one respect, because the income payable to the investor is limited. A fundamental difference between a preferred stock and a bond is that the preferred stock has no maturity, even though it may be retired through a sinking fund. Also, because a preferred stock is not a debt it is never secured by a lien or by collateral. It is not easy to go further than this in drawing a distinction between a bond and a preferred stock. Some bonds, such as income bonds, have most of the characteristics of preferred stocks, except for maturity. This difficulty of definition arises because preferred stocks are essentially compromise securities designed to attract investors who want a safer and more stable income than that provided by common stocks. For the issuing company, they do not have the disadvantage of bonds because they have no maturity that might come at an awkard time, and because dividends may be omitted in times of poor business without resulting in default.

Because of this compromise in quality, high-grade preferred stocks should have a substantially higher yield than high-grade bonds, and until recent years this was the case. More recently, the yield differential between them has narrowed significantly from 1.26 in 1950 to .06 in 1963. This narrowing in yields is, in large part, the result of the favorable tax treatment given to preferred and common stock dividends. This favorable tax treatment stems from the fact that only 15 percent of the dividends paid by one corporation to another are taxable. As a consequence, the effective corporate tax rate on preferred dividends of those in the highest corporate tax bracket (48 percent) is 7.2 percent. Therefore, the effective yield of a high-grade preferred stock at the end of 1963 would be 3.99 percent (4.30×92.8 percent), and on high-grade bonds the yield would be 2.20 percent (4.24×52 percent).

Since preferred stocks have no maturities, their yield is computed on the basis of current return. Lack of maturity makes them subject to a greater decline in price than bonds if interest rates go up and, conversely, allows them to enjoy a greater price appreciation if interest rates go down. As an example of the relative effect of firming interest rates, the reader may recall that a 3 percent 20-year bond selling at par would decline in price to 90 if the interest rate were to rise 0.71 percentage points. If the yield on a 4 percent preferred selling at par were to rise this much, the price would drop to 85.

Variations in Preferred Stock Quality

Although attempts have been made to give preferred stocks ratings similar to bond ratings, no satisfactory system of rating has been, or probably can be, devised. In various states, preferred stocks that meet certain requirements are considered legal for investments by trust funds. The necessarily rigid requirements tend to make the legal list a rather poor measure of investment merit. At one time, for example, for purely technical reasons, General Motors Corporation's preferred stock, one of the highest-grade issues available, was removed from the legal list of a certain state for a few years. Legality, moreover, is not so much a market factor in preferred stocks as in bonds because of the relatively small proportion of institutional buying of preferred stocks.

The quality of preferred stock varies between high-grade preferreds, on which dividend payments are almost a certainty, to the lower-grade preferreds, on which the dividend payments depend on general business conditions and the prospects of the individual company. With high-grade preferreds, the investor assumes mostly interest rate risk, because market prices tend to vary inversely with interest rates. Low-grade preferreds are also affected by interest rate changes, but the effects of these changes are sometimes overshadowed by changes in financial risk.

In most circumstances, lower grade preferred stocks are not desirable investment media for the individual investor. The limited income of preferred stock places the investor in a position of assuming considerable financial risk for which he cannot be properly compensated. In these cases, the investor would be better off to invest in the common stock of the company. Common stock investment would not result in appreciably more financial risk, and the investor would be able to share in any future good fortunes of the company without the limits placed on the preferred stockholder.

REVIEW QUESTIONS AND PROBLEMS

1. What is the distinction between rights issued in connection with a privileged subscription and warrants?

2. In March, 1966, Massey-Ferguson, Ltd. issued rights to purchase additional shares of common stock at $24.25 a share. Five rights were required to purchase one share of new stock. The last sale of the old stock on March 16, 1966, before it went ex-rights was $30.125. At what price would you expect the rights to sell? Express the price of the stock to the nearest eighth and the price of the right to the nearest sixteenth.

3. Under what conditions would it be equitable to present stockholders

if a corporation made a public offering of additional common stock at current market price? Below market?

4. You are offered your choice of an investment in a $1,000 bond convertible into common stock at $100 a share and a $1,000 bond with nondetachable warrants which entitle you to purchase 10 shares of stock for $100 a share any time before the maturity of the bond. If the bonds were identical in all other respects, which would you choose?

5. Under what circumstances would book value be a fair measure of the investment value of common stock?

6. If the value of common stock is dependent on earnings, why is it that the common stock of companies without earnings still has a market value?

7. "A" Company has had a record of excellent earnings and outstanding future prospects. The company has announced, however, that it will not pay dividends for at least 60 years. Would this stock have any value to you?

8. If every investor had perfect knowledge of all value factors of a common stock and evaluated these factors rationally, would there be a market price for the stock?

9. What benefits, if any, does a preferred stockholder obtain from earnings that are retained by the corporation?

10. What characteristics of a preferred stock may make it similar to bonds?

11. If a preferred stock has no maturity date, why would it have a sinking fund?

CHAPTER **7**

Investment Programming

The investment program is the next link in the investment management process. The investment program is the allocation of the investor's savings in a manner that will help him most effectively to meet his goal of providing an income for members of the household during their lifetimes or as long as they are dependents. As may be recalled from the discussion in Chapter 2, in normal circumstances the head of the household will provide sufficient income to meet current expenditures. In this chapter, we are concerned with the most effective and efficient investment of the savings, giving full weight and consideration to various investment policy considerations.

In review, the purpose of saving is to enable the investor to cover situations that may cause an interruption in the family income flow. The situations or investment requirements, discussed in Chapter 2, that should be met from these savings are: (1) premature death, (2) disability, (3) retirement, and (4) involuntary unemployment and other contingencies.

The investor has a wide range of investment choices for commitment of his savings. These range all the way from cash to the most speculative common stock. However, for purposes of this discussion, there are three basic media: (1) insurance, (2) fixed-dollar contracts, and (3) equities.

In the choice among these basic investment forms, there are investment policy considerations concerned with policies toward (1) risk, (2) income, (3) income taxes, and (4) liquidity. The primary policy consideration is the posture to be assumed toward the investment risks: (1) financial risk, (2) purchasing power risk, (3) interest rate risk, and (4) market risk.

In summary, a simple statement of the investment program objective is to invest the savings so as to maximize returns, minimize risk, and provide maximum liquidity to the investor. The investment program represents a compromise among these policy considerations.

In certain instances, the choice of media to meet the investment requirement is obvious. For example, the most efficient method of meeting the disability requirement is through purchase of disability income and health and accident insurance. The insurance that will be discussed in this chapter will be life insurance, since the use and effectiveness of disability income insurance was covered in Chapter 2. Therefore, the life hazards that we will be concerned with here are premature death, retirement, and other contingencies.

LIFE INSURANCE AND INVESTMENT PROGRAMMING

In the discussion of investment requirements, it was pointed out that it is necessary for a man's family to have an estate to provide an income at his death. A man may not have lived long enough to build up an estate adequate to care for his wife and dependent children. Therefore, it is necessary to have a means of establishing an immediate estate in the event of the income producer's premature death.

The primary purpose of life insurance is to meet this contingency. The investor should take a portion of his savings and buy life insurance with it. Since any savings used to purchase life insurance cannot be used for other investment purposes, certain questions must be resolved. What is the purpose of life insurance in the investment program? What kind of life insurance should be bought? How much life insurance is needed?

The Purpose of Life Insurance

Life insurance may provide the investor with (1) protection against the economic hazards of premature death, and (2) a means of savings or investment. The nature of the life insurance contract, discussed on pages 45–49, gives rise to the savings or investment element. Since the basic purpose of the life insurance contract is to provide protection, the investor should make a separate decision concerning whether or not he wants to use life insurance as an investment medium.

The investor should recognize that the basic purpose of life insurance is to provide protection. In the allocation of his savings, the investor should first purchase adequate protection; then the use of life insurance as a medium for investment should be examined. Unquestionably, it can be used as a means of investing a portion of the investor's savings. Since the savings element of life insurance is a fixed-dollar contract, examination of the suitability of life insurance as an investment will be postponed until a later discussion of investment of the retirement fund and fixed-dollar contracts.

What Kind of Life Insurance?

Individual life insurance is available in a wide variety of policy contracts. These policies are designed to fit different needs, and companies use a wide variety of descriptive names in order to differentiate their product. However, it is helpful to know that all of them are combinations or permutations of four basic types of life insurance policies: (1) term, (2) ordinary or straight life, (3) limited payment life, and (4) endowment. These life insurance policies differ mainly in the relative portions of the premium dollar that go for protection and savings.

Term Insurance. This policy provides protection for a specified term or period of years. It offers the same protection as all the other types of policies if the insured person dies while the policy is in force. It may be purchased for any number of terms, such as five-year term, ten-year term, or even term to age sixty-five. This means that a five-year term policy provides insurance for five years. When that term ends, the policy expires without any cash values, and the protection ends.

Because of the temporary nature of life insurance, this type has no cash values. As a consequence, there is no savings element, and the premiums at a given age are lower than for other types of insurance. The premium is approximately equal to the mortality cost for the insured's age group. Therefore, if a term policy is renewed for consecutive periods, the annual premiums increase and become very high in later years. For example, the cost of term insurance at age twenty is $8.75 per $1,000, but the premium rises to $20.10 at age fifty. (See Table 7–1.)

The insured is able to purchase the most insurance per premium dollar with term insurance. However, the problem with this type of insurance is that since it is temporary insurance it expires. In addition, the investor might have a continuing need for insurance and might not be insurable after the expiration date. The investor may

TABLE 7–1

**Approximate Annual Premium Rates for $1,000 of Each of
Four Types of Life Insurance Policies***

Bought at Age	Straight Life	Limited Payment, 20-Payment	Endowment, 20-Year	5-Year Term, Renewable
18	$15.80	$25.55	$48.85	$ 8.65
20	16.50	26.45	48.90	8.75
25	18.45	28.45	49.05	8.90
30	21.00	31.25	49.40	9.25
40	28.50	39.45	51.40	12.20
50	45.65	50.40	56.55	20.10

* Rates shown are approximate premium rates for life insurance protection for men. Rates for women are somewhat lower because of women's somewhat lower mortality. Rates of participating policies would be slightly higher, but the cost would be lowered by annual dividends. Nonparticipating policy rates would be somewhat lower than those shown, and no dividends would be paid.
Source: *Policies for Protection*, Institute of Life Insurance, New York.

purchase term insurance that is renewable with a medical examination but, as suggested above, at higher rates.

Ordinary or Straight Life. Ordinary life insurance provides coverage for the life of the insured, and premiums are payable as long as the policy is in force. This policy is the least expensive type of permanent insurance. (See Table 7–1.) It is the most flexible type of insurance policy. The investor can plan his insurance expenditure, since the contract is permanent and the premium is level or does not increase during the life of the insured. In addition to providing protection, a cash value is accumulated, which provides the insured with liquidity.

Limited Payment Life. This type of policy is a permanent kind of insurance. The premiums, however, are paid only for a limited number of years. For example, a 20-payment life insurance policy states that premiums are payable for only 20 years, after which the insured has the life insurance in force for the rest of his life or until he cancels it.

Naturally, a limited payment life policy is more expensive than comparable term or ordinary life coverage, because the insured pays premiums for only a set number of years on a policy that provides insurance for life. The shortness of the premium-paying period naturally results in a higher premium for comparable protection.

Endowment Life. The endowment life insurance policy is an insured savings plan. The investor is purchasing a fixed-dollar contract, with the full amount of the contract guaranteed if the insured dies before the end of the period. Thus, a $10,000, 20-year endowment policy provides that at the end of the period the insured is paid the full amount of the policy. If the insured should die before the end of the 20-year period, the $10,000 would be paid to the beneficiary.

As was the case with the limited payment life policy, this plan is primarily a savings plan. Because of the shortness of the period and the rapid savings buildup, the premiums for this type of policy are the highest. The premium for $1,000 of straight life insurance at age eighteen is $15.80, while for 20-year endowment the premium is $56.55.

The Choice of Policies

As mentioned earlier, the primary purpose of life insurance is to provide funds for the family if the income producer does not live to retirement. The permanent forms of life insurance also provide the investor with a means of savings for retirement through the accumulation of cash values. In addition, these cash values may be used as quick recourse or emergency funds for unforeseen contingencies such as involuntary unemployment.

In choosing the type of life insurance, the investor should always place primary emphasis on providing the protection needed. When funds are limited, it seems logical that the investor buy the insurance that will provide the most protection per dollar of premium. Therefore, the young married man will probably be most interested in buying renewable term insurance, because it will enable him to protect his family with the least cost when savings are the lowest.

There are two major disadvantages to this course of action. First, if the investor has a continuing need for life insurance throughout his lifetime, he will be faced with increasing premium rates. Second, permanent insurance does force the investor to save at a time when saving is difficult, thereby providing emergency funds during the early years. For these reasons, most investors will find straight life insurance the most satisfactory.

Choosing a Life Insurance Company

Life insurance companies use a number of different descriptive titles for their life insurance policies. These policies are usually one of the basic types described above, or some combination of them. The companies use these different descriptive titles for merchandising purposes. In other words, the insurance offered is essentially the same from one company as from another.

There may be a substantial difference in the cost of life insurance. The gross premiums charged for a particular kind of life insurance are fairly uniform. That is, the premium for $1,000 of ordinary life insurance with company A will be about the same as it will be with company B. The net cost of $1,000 of ordinary life insurance may differ substantially among companies.

Computation of the net cost of life insurance takes into account the dividends paid on the policy and the increases in cash values. The size of the dividends are a function of (1) the company's ability to control expenses, (2) a better mortality experience than expected, and (3) a better return on the company's investments than anticipated. Of course, the investor cannot estimate what these amounts are going to be any better than the company can. Therefore, to make an analysis of what company's life insurance is the best buy, the investor must analyze the past performance and assume that the future will be about the same as the past has been.

To calculate the average cost per $1,000 of life insurance in the past, the investor can use the following formula:

GROSS PREMIUM − DIVIDENDS = NET PAYMENTS LESS CASH VALUE
AT END OF PERIOD = NET COST

For example, an insured who bought $1,000 of ordinary life insurance in 1945, at age twenty-five, from Company A would have paid $334.80 in premiums by 1964. During this 20-year period, 1945–64, the company paid $52.15 in dividends. The net payments (premiums less dividends) for the $1,000 of ordinary life insurance has been $282.65. The accumulated cash values are $231. Deducting the cash values of $231 from the net payments of $282.65, the net cost of the $1,000 of ordinary life insurance is $51.65 for 20 years.

A comparison of the relative costs of $1,000 of ordinary life insurance for Company A and Company B is shown in Table 7-2.

It is obvious that among various companies there are differences in the costs of the same kind of life insurance. These calculations for most major life insurance companies are published annually in the *Flitcraft Compend.*

This method of computing life insurance costs may have some shortcomings. The major one is that it does not take into account the time value of the cash paid and received by the insured, even though the net cost of two policies may be the same. A policy with a low gross premium would be more valuable than one that arrived as the same net cost by paying larger dividends.

TABLE 7–2

**Comparison of Net Cost of $1,000 Ordinary Life Insurance,
Two Hypothetical Life Insurance Companies
Experience of 1945–64**

	Company A	Company B
Annual premium	$ 16.74	$ 20.55
20 premiums	334.80	411.00
Dividends, 20 years	52.15	152.16
Net payments, 20 years	282.65	258.84
Cash value, 20th year	231.00	230.50
Net cost of $1,000 insurance	51.65	28.34

Assumed: 25 years of age at issue for a $5,000 policy.

In spite of the shortcomings, this method is the simplest and seems best for the average life insurance purchaser. More sophisticated and more complex methods of computing life insurance costs are available.[1]

RETIREMENT AND THE INVESTMENT PROGRAM

The savings the investor has available for accumulation of a retirement fund may be invested in (1) equities and (2) fixed-dollar contracts. Choice of the types of investment media depends primarily on the policies he assumes toward the various risks. The investor generally will approach the consideration of risk by first deciding which risks and how much of these risks he can reasonably assume. Then, he will decide which combination of media—equities or fixed-dollar contracts—is most suitable.

Financial risk is usually a dominant policy factor in the formulation of any investment program. Probably second in importance is the purchasing power risk, but the effects of purchasing power risk losses

---

[1] Joseph M. Belth, "Cost of Life Insurance to the Policyholder," *Journal of Insurance*, Vol. XXVIII, No. 4 (December, 1961), p. 24.

are more gradual and are not usually so devastating as financial risk losses. The interest rate and market risks are not major considerations for the individual investor because of their short-run nature. This assumes that the investor maintains adequate liquid reserves and is able to wait out temporary drops in security prices.

There are a number of investment programming choices. The choices vary with differences in the investor's age, his income tax position, and whether or not he already has a capital fund for retirement or must accumulate one. An investor who at an early age has a capital fund, received possibly through inheritance or good fortune, has programming problems different than those of one who must accumulate the capital fund for retirement.

The initial choices in investment media are between fixed-dollar contracts and equities. There are numerous other considerations, such as shadings of financial risk and compensation for risk. Initially, in the discussion that follows the choices will be limited to a fixed-dollar contract program and an equity program.

The Fixed-Dollar Contract Program

An investment program that uses fixed-dollar contracts as its media is tempting to the person who is not temperamentally suited to common stock investment. In fact, an investment program made up of institutional fixed-dollar contracts often is referred to as a conservative one. The claim of conservatism stems from the defensive position taken toward the financial and interest rate risks. It is true that such a program would eliminate the likelihood of sudden large capital losses with just a minimum amount of investment judgment.

However, increases in the price level can seriously errode the value of a fixed-dollar contract investment program. Over a lifetime, it is almost a certainty that the investor will experience some purchasing power loss if he invests in only fixed-dollar contracts. Since 1900, there has been only one period, 1920–1933, of a rise in the purchasing power of the dollar. The balance of the time, purchasing power has been declining.

If one considers that the average span of a man's working life and retirement is slightly over fifty years, there has been no period since 1808 in which an investor would not have experienced some purchasing power loss. (See Table 7–3.)

TABLE 7–3

Major Trends in the Purchasing Power of the Dollar
(Changes of 25 cents or more)

Declines	Number of Years	Percent Decline	Range of Decline	Amount of Decline	Average Decline Per Year
1808–1814 6		39	$ .87–.53	$ .34	$.057
1834–1836 2		22	1.24–.97	.27	.135
1860–1865 5		54	1.34–.62	.72	.144
1897–1920 23		70	1.75–.53	1.22	.053
1932–1958 26		64	1.26–.44	.82	.032

Rises	Number of Years	Percent Rise	Range of Rise	Amount of Rise	Average Rise Per Year
1814–1830 16		134	$.53–1.24	$ .71	$.044
1839–1843 4		36	.97–1.32	.35	.088
1865–1896 31		182	.62–1.75	1.13	.036
1920–1932 12		138	.53–1.26	.73	.061

Source: Philip Braverman, "The Purchasing Power of the Dollar," *Banking*, December, 1964.

The Equity Program

An equity investment program would tend to eliminate the short-comings of a fixed-dollar contract program since equities tend to rise and fall with changes in cost of living. Changes in the value of equities, such as common stocks, are not perfectly correlated with price level changes. (See Figure 7–1.) It is obvious that equities do provide some protection against the purchasing power risk.

It does not seem wise, however, to invest everything in equities, since fluctuations in common stock prices are too pronounced to allow the investor to rely on them for stable value and income, particularly when he is nearing retirement. Some of the hazards of market risks and financial risks can be removed by diversification. The investor can smooth out the fluctuations in market price by diversifying over time or spreading purchases over time. The advantages of diversifying over time are available only if he stays with a long-range program of capital accumulation and common stock purchase. The problems of timing common stock purchases and techniques for solving the timing problem are discussed in Chapter 20.

The nature of the timing hazard is best illustrated by discussing what happens when timing of investment is poor. In the discussion up to this point, it has been assumed that the investor has an accumula-

FIGURE 7–1

The Common Stock Index, Standard and Poor's (500 stocks),
and the Bureau of Labor Statistics Consumer Price
Index, 1928–64

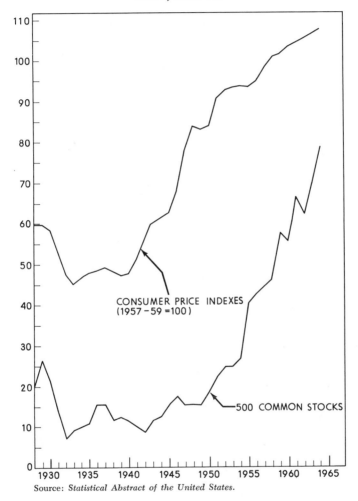

Source: *Statistical Abstract of the United States.*

tion investment program. The investor who has an existing capital
fund to invest has a different set of problems. If he attempts to diversify overtime and to average the price of his purchases, he may lose
income and the chance for capital appreciation. On the other hand,
if he invests the entire fund at one time, he runs the risk of deteriora-

tion in the value of his portfolio. For example, if an investor had invested $10,000 in common stock in 1929, the market value of his portfolio would have dropped to $2,600 by 1932.[2]

The investor who is nearing retirement and has invested his capital fund in common stocks over time has much the same problem as the lump-sum investor. How does he liquidate? Equities are an excellent medium for investment if the investor does not have to "cash out" when the market is seriously depressed. This investment program could be liquidated in the same way in which it was accumulated— that is, over time. The problem is that this technique might cause accelerated liquidation of the portfolio with disastrous results. To illustrate, let us assume that the investment program was designed to provide the investor with a retirement income of $500 per month. The program is designed to provide an income from portfolio income from his investments and capital consumption. At the beginning of retirement, the capital consumption is rather modest, but it would obviously accelerate in the later years of retirement. If common stock prices were low at the beginning of the retirement period, the investor would be compelled to liquidate a larger portion of capital fund than planned, and he might outlive his funds.

Since the investor cannot be sure of the price level of equities or the level of the cost of living, the obvious conclusion is to develop a program that provides for both equities and fixed-dollar contracts.[3]

The Balanced Program

The investment program that includes both fixed-dollar contracts and equities purchased over time seems to be the best approach to the investment of savings for retirement. The approach advocated by the Greenough study was to have a constant ratio of 50 percent invested in fixed-dollar contracts and 50 percent in equities. This constant-ratio approach seems to be overly conservative. It would seem that a variable ratio of common stocks and fixed-dollar contracts would be a better investment program pattern, with a larger portion of the portfolio in common stock in the earlier years and a gradually reduced common stock commitment as time passes.

When the investor begins, it seems that almost all his retirement

---

[2] William C. Greenough, *A New Approach to Retirement Income* (New York: Teachers Insurance and Annuity Association of America, 1955), p. 15.

[3] *Ibid.*, p. 45.

fund should be invested in common stock. He should have an aggressive policy toward financial risk. Such a policy almost automatically results in a defensive policy toward purchasing power risk because of the tendency for common stock prices to rise and fall in sympathy with consumer prices.

As the investor approaches the age of fifty-five to sixty, the portfolio should be made up of almost equal parts of equities and fixed-dollar contracts, such as bonds and savings deposits. The shift in investment policy from aggressive assumption of financial risk to a more moderate policy should be a gradual one.

The Program after Retirement

The investment requirements of the investor nearing or at retirement age are usually apparent. He needs a stable flow of purchasing power from his investments. Program formulation and investment media selection are often difficult. The retired investor's program should provide for preservation of the dollar amount of the investment fund and a maximum stable investment income. This defensive policy toward financial risk almost always results in a maximum exposure to the purchasing power risk. The retired investor has a dilemma, because almost any policy he follows results in an unwanted exposure to some risk. His general policy should be, as mentioned earlier in the discussion, to accept the exposure to the purchasing power risk rather than chance a total loss from the assumption of unwarranted financial risks.

The retired investor may decide to forego the desired stability of income in order to hedge against the purchasing power risk by balancing his holdings of bonds and preferred stock and common stock. Such a policy would be, in a sense, a no-defense investment program. This approach admits that there is no completely satisfactory solution to the retired investor's policy problems, and it attempts to avoid the problem by equalizing the exposure to the purchasing power and financial risks.

This balanced program also reduces exposure to the interest rate risk as contrasted with the possible losses from interest rate changes if the investor has concentrated his investments in high-grade bonds. The risk of loss from interest rate changes is a secondary consideration in the investment program development of the individual investor. The cyclical nature of interest rates discussed in Chapter 5 reduces the possibility of loss from interest rate changes unless the investor is forced to liquidate his holdings.

STABILITY AND LEVEL OF INCOME
AND INVESTMENT POLICIES

The investment program patterns described previously are conventional ones that reflect the probable actions of the average economic man. A number of special circumstances might cause an investor to deviate from these conventional patterns. Two of the more important factors are the stability and level of income and the influences of the federal income tax.

The previous discussion of investment program policies assumes that the investor has a relatively stable income. Those that have unstable personal incomes or tend to have large incomes for a few years and then drop to a lower income level, such as professional athletes or actors, naturally would deviate from the conventional pattern. In a sense, these investors are already subject to greater-than-average economic hazards. As a consequence, these individuals would normally tend to be more defensive toward financial risk, because each year of income constitutes an indeterminate amount of the life income.

Frequently, owners of businesses have through their ownership already assumed considerable financial risk. Because of this, the term "businessman's risk," sometimes used in brokerage house literature, seems to be contradictory. A businessman's risk is usually a security that involves considerable financial risk. The contradiction arises because as a matter of policy many businessmen have fluctuating personal incomes, and their business investment already subjects them to the possibility of large financial loss. Therefore, the purchase of low-quality and speculative securities would add to an already aggressive financial risk position.

In contrast, many investors have relatively fixed incomes and stable employment, such as college professors or government employees. People in these stable fixed income occupations frequently follow a defensive financial risk policy. Such a course of action is the height of folly, because a defensive financial risk policy usually results in additional exposure to the purchasing power risk. In fact, these investors would tend to have a double exposure to purchasing power losses, because their salaries usually lag behind price level increases.

Retired people frequently do not have any income except from their investments and social security benefits. These retired people are usually old, and the effect of age differences on investment policies was discussed previously. However, they often have other special investment policy problems, because there is often a basic conflict in objectives. For example, the retired investor does not have sufficient income to maintain the scale of living to which he is accustomed. This situation may be the result of poor financial and investment planning during the income-producing years. Possibly the purchasing power of his investments has been reduced by an increase in the price level. To remedy this income deficiency, the retired investor is often tempted to buy higher-yielding securities, which would be an aggressive financial risk policy. Yet, he cannot afford to assume more financial risk. The only way to resolve this conflict is to accept modest annual purchasing power losses and, as suggested earlier, to follow a program of planned consumption of investment principal.

FEDERAL INCOME TAXES AND INVESTMENT POLICIES

The ultimate objective of investors is to obtain, both before and after taxes, the maximum amount of investment income commensurate with the risk assumed. In some instances, the dominant consideration in investment program planning is the effect of the federal tax on investment income. The higher the taxable income, the greater the influence federal taxes have on the investment program. For example, the different treatments of capital gains and current income, discussed in Chapter 3, often causes the investor in the higher income tax brackets to avoid current income if he has a free choice between current investment income and capital gains.

To support this contention, a study of the influence on investment program policies of federal taxation on individual incomes indicated that the degree of influence tends to vary directly with the size of the investor's income.[4] This study indicates the percentage of the investors questioned who said that their investment program policies were affected by federal income taxes.

However, this study indicates that the impact of federal taxes, particularly income taxes, is not so great as commonly thought. The

---

[4] J. Keith Butters, Lawrence E. Thompson, Lynn L. Bollinger, *Effects of Taxation: Investments by Individuals*, Harvard University, 1953, pp. 34–36.

controlling factors seem to be such things as age, stability of employment, and family responsibilities. Federal taxes do however, cause investors to take more extreme policy positions after the general course of action has been determined. That is, those investors who were interested in capital gains and followed an aggressive policy toward financial risk tended to become more aggressive as their incomes increased in size. Conversely, those investors who were relatively unwilling to assume financial risk tended to become more conservative as size of income and taxes increased.

The logic of an investor with a large income taking a defensive position toward financial risk is that the high rate of income tax payable on the increments in his income makes it difficult to amass wealth. Consequently, this investor feels that the avoidance of financial risk and the preservation of principal is more important than attempting to increase his general investment fund by assuming more financial risk.

QUALITY AND THE INVESTMENT PROGRAM

In the discussion thus far, it has been assumed that all types of investment media are uniform in quality. However, it is obvious that there are wide variations in the quality of investment media.

The investor's primary problem after selecting the type of media suitable for attainment of his investment objective is to determine the quality of the media. As mentioned earlier, the investor can determine the quality of investment media, particularly securities, only after analysis. The evaluation of quality is a subjective judgment. The investor may rely on various rating systems supplemented by a superficial analysis, or he can make his own careful, detailed analysis. In any event, the most difficult problem facing the investor is to accurately match quality in terms of financial risk with his ability to assume financial risk.

For purposes of exposition, the quality of securities will be classified as high grade, medium grade, and speculative. The emphasis in quality determination is on financial risk. It refers to the possibility of impairment of the portfolio's dollar value because of corporate financial stringency. Although it is possible to lose some of the dollar value of the fund due to the interest rate risk or market risk factors, such losses need not necessarily be permanent ones. The age of the investor affects his ability to assume risk and withstand loss. All losses, whether they are losses of purchasing power of the investment or the money value of the investment fund, tend to have a greater impact on older people's financial positions than they do on those of younger people. The nature of the life-income cycle increases the effect of these losses on the older man. It is obvious that the older man has less total earning power than the younger man, because the older man has fewer years of working life remaining.

Typically, the average annual income of the individual increases until the investor is about fifty years of age and then begins to decline. Therefore, the effect of losses on older people, particularly those past fifty years of age, is compounded not only by the fact that these older people have fewer remaining years of productive life, but also because the remaining years are years of declining annual income. Since the older investor cannot afford a substantial capital loss, he will tend to adopt a defensive policy toward financial risk.

It is questionable whether securities of low quality, both equities and fixed-dollar contracts, ever should be included in the portfolio of the investor. Probably, such investments should be considered only when the investor is relatively young, say less than thirty-five, and has both the time and strength to recoup the losses he may experience. If the young investor is not in good health or has a rather erratic income, the media selected should be of medium or high quality only.

After age thirty-five, the investor should confine his investments to those of high and medium quality. Any losses are more difficult to recoup. It is paradoxical that as the investor's judgment should be improving because of experience his loss in earning capacity due to the passage of time has reduced his ability to utilize this experience profitably. As the investor grows older, his accumulated experience will not offset the hazards of a large loss which would result from the assumption of excessive financial risk. For example, after the investor reaches age fifty-five his remaining life income is small, and even if he chooses to remain active the possibility of permanent disability and the resultant forced retirement are so great that he should confine his investments to those of the highest quality.

The investor's quest for higher quality investments tends to expose him to the purchasing power and interest rate risks. The question is which hazard—a potential loss from financial risk or a purchasing power risk loss—is the more significant to the retired investor. If one analyzes the nature of the two hazards, it is obvious that the dangers of assuming the financial risk of low- and medium-grade securities in order to increase income and possibilities of capital appreciation generally outweigh the possible purchasing power losses. The average annual increase in consumer prices over the last 50 years has been less than 2 percent. The life expectancy of a man retiring at age sixty-five is 12.90 years, therefore the attrition in the value of a portfolio from the purchasing power risk would be, on the average, about 25 percent before death. Thus, the possibility of purchasing power losses for the retired investor is probably less than the financial risk that would have to be assumed to reduce its effect.

REVIEW QUESTIONS AND PROBLEMS

1. If life insurance is designed to replace income loss to the family because of premature death, would there be any justification for life insurance for a man that is retired?

2. Is there any need for life insurance on children or wives? If so, what is the justification for it?

3. If an investor believes that he can invest the difference in the premium on term life insurance and straight life insurance and achieve better results than if he purchased straight life insurance, what arguments are there against such a course of action?

4. The purchase of limited payment life insurance and endowment life insurance almost guarantees loss by the investor. Discuss this statement.

5. If the premiums charged by two life insurance companies are the same, could there be any difference in the cost of the insurance? What are the factors that control the difference?

6. John Jones is a bachelor, age 49, who does seasonal work as a handyman at a major league baseball park. He earns $4,000 a year after taxes. At the present time, he is not saving any of his income nor does he have any insurance except health and accident insurance. He states that he does not need to save for retirement and does not need any other insurance because Social Security will take care of him in his old age and his employment assures him of income to retirement. Criticize his plan and conclusions.

7. Professor John Jones, age 47, has a wife and a 16-year-old daughter. His net worth is approximately $75,000, and he has a $2,000 term life insurance policy which expires at age 65. In addition, he has a retirement annuity which will provide him with a retirement income of roughly one-half of his present income. Most of his other assets are

savings deposits in commercial banks. Criticize his program and make suggestions for change, if any.

8. A letter from Dr. Smith, a dentist, asks, "Should I invest my savings of $50,000 in common stock?" Dr. Smith is retired and is 70 years of age with no dependents. He states that his current income from the $50,000 invested in U.S. Government bonds is not sufficient to live on. Would you recommend investment in common stocks? If not, why not? What would you recommend to Dr. Smith?

9. John and Mary Ellis are a young married couple with two children, ages 3 and 5. John has a congenital heart defect. He has no savings, life insurance, or disability income insurance. There is available $1,000 each year for savings, purchase of life or disability income insurance. The premiums on insurance would be high, because John is a substandard risk. John plans to save the $1,000, because he can only purchase a $20,000 five-year level term insurance policy for a $1,000 annual premium and he feels that he is a better risk than that. Do you agree with his conclusions? If not, why? What would you recommend that he do?

10. What is a "business man's risk"? What is the investment policy contradiction in this term?

11. Why could it be argued that every college professor should follow a moderately speculative investment policy?

12. What is the fallacy of a balanced investment program of 50 percent invested in fixed dollar contracts and 50 percent invested in equities at all ages?

CHAPTER **8**

Sources of Information

Space of necessity, limits any attempt to discuss the sources of information upon which intelligent investment decisions are based. The subject is so vast that one cannot hope to provide within the confines of a single chapter an exhaustive enumeration and description of specific sources. Yet, a discussion that is confined to vague generalities will be of little help to the investor who is seeking to educate himself by actually consulting original sources. In a sense, the subject matter of this chapter must be learned by examination of the material. But an attempt will be made to provide a sample of specific sources which will, in turn, lead to many more.

The many different sources of information may be classified for purposes of discussion into the following groups: (1) general economic and market data, (2) industry data, and (3) company data. Each of these classifications of data will be discussed separately in this chapter. However, it will be evident to the reader that the sources of data are not mutually exclusive. For example, the effect of some of each classification is reflected in common stock prices. It should be realized that this classification is used only to facilitate the discussion that follows.

The individual investor who is attempting to do his own investment research, perhaps on a part-time basis, cannot hope to make use of all the varied types of information available. Adequate investment research is time-consuming, and some branches are highly specialized. Because investment research is concerned not only with a study of the past but also with what is happening currently or is likely to happen in the future, investment data must be kept current. Even large investment organizations doing independent research may well rely in part on specialized research done currently by other organizations. Various types of services such as field reports, current comparative statistics on major companies in particular industries, business forecasts, and technical analysis of stock market prices are offered to subscribers for a fee.

The typical individual investor cannot afford to subscribe to all these various services. The discussion of certain sources of information not readily available to the individual must, therefore, be viewed as merely an attempt to suggest a few of the sources utilized by professional investment research organizations. On the other hand, the enumeration of other sources of information readily available to the individual investor should not be construed as a suggestion that the individual can necessarily make effective use of the information, particularly in the matter of forecasting business conditions.

FACT VERSUS OPINION

In analyzing securities, the analyst is seldom concerned with a scarcity of data, except in certain special situations. The basic problem is to find data that are both significant and accurate. The masses of available data must be sifted to eliminate material that is not of controlling importance. This process involves the exercise of judgment. Relevance of data and validity of data sources are qualitative considerations of the first importance, because the soundness of investment conclusions is, of necessity, tied to the quality of the data used.

Free Advice

Many individual investors prefer to seek information consisting of opinions rather than facts. Many are unable to distinguish between fact and opinion. These approaches are perhaps natural, because security analysis is not only a time-consuming process but also an art in which proficiency can be attained only after considerable study and experience. A major danger arises, however, because the typical investor insists that he get his information free, and it is frequently worth what it costs—nothing. The major source of free opinions is from brokerage firms. The investor should not rely solely on this source, particularly if the investor is not capable of making an independent critical analysis. It is not meant to suggest that all professional investment advice for which a fee is charged is dependable or worth the price that is asked. In fact, it is not advisable for the investor to refuse to investigate any sources of information which are free.

Brokerage firms and investment bankers are often excellent sources for certain types of information. If a firm has acted as the investment banker for certain corporations and has close personal contacts with the management, it may be in a position to furnish information on monthly earnings, trend of new orders, budgets for future sales, management attitudes, and other facts that the investor could obtain only, if at all, by personal interviews with corporate executives. In addition, brokers who try very hard to give advice that will make money for their clients sometimes originate ideas which may prove valuable to investors or speculators who are able to subject these opinions to independent critical scrutiny by further research. But the fact remains the brokerage advice is incidental to the function of acting as an agent in the purchase and sale of securities. The brokerage function is not designed to serve as an adequate substitute for continuous investment management.

Even among the routine opinions contained in brokerage wires, reports, and market letters, there are many evidences of high-quality investment research. The investor must not forget that the free advice handed out by brokerage houses, whether by word of mouth or the printed page, is for the purpose of inducing trading in securities so that brokers may earn larger sales commissions. The advice may be offered in perfectly good faith, but it is often nothing more than sales literature. For the investor who is unable to undertake his own independent investment analysis, no rule of thumb can be offered for distinguishing the reliable brokerage opinions from those that may be unreliable. Financial firms may be constantly in close contact with managements of a large number of important corporations, yet the facts are sometimes garbled. Even when they are not, the recommendations based on these data sometimes prove to be extremely poor because of a failure to properly analyze and interpret the facts.

Even if all brokerage opinions were uniformly based on high-quality research, there would still be the danger of adverse timing. Brokers make money during bull markets, when trading volume is good, optimism prevails, and stock prices are high. It is natural that wishful thinking will color brokerage opinions with the more optimistic hues. Only after stock prices have risen substantially, suggesting a further upward move, do research staffs grow larger and the bulletins of free advice to buy securities show an increase.

Brokers sometimes advise sale of securities. They make commissions on sales as well as purchases. Few brokers, however, succeed in following up their initial advice to buy a particular security with a subsequent recommendation to sell. Even if the original advice to buy proves correct, the investor will seldom be warned when he should take his profit through sale. Indeed, the sophisticated investor who is aware of the optimistic bias of brokerage opinion will condition himself to become ever more skeptical of brokerage advice as it increases in volume. On the other hand, when trading volume is low and brokers lose interest in offering free advice, the investor may be forced to take the initiative in getting access to basic information that brokerage firms are sometimes in a position to provide.

Mail-Order Investment Counsel

Investment counsel is one solution to investment management problems. It is a professional service that furnishes more than specific data and opinions. The investment counselor provides personal guidance in the selection of investment media. However, investment counsel is generally not available to the smaller investor, because of the burdensomeness of the minimum fees charged by investment counseling firms. The nature and use of professional investment counselors will be discussed in more detail in Chapter 21.

The challenge of this problem of providing adequate advice to the small investor has caused certain research organizations, including some of the standard financial services, to offer mail-order investment counsel. A survey made in 1963 estimates that 327 different investment advisory services prepare and issue periodical investment publications, and 278 prepare and issue special investment reports and analyses.[1] Essentially, many of these services are attempts to "rate" common stocks, which the investor often finds difficult to evaluate. Although the basic research may be complete, the investor should be made aware of some of the problems involved. They can be discussed without surveying in detail the relative merits of the different types of services available.

---

[1] H. C. Walter (ed.), *Investment Information and Advice; A Handbook and Directory* (Whittier, Calif.: FIR Publishing Co., 1964).

In the first place, the personal contact between client and investment counselor is lost. This means that an attempt is made by the research organization to rate common stocks without reference to the peculiar needs of each individual investor. Secondly, the recommendation or the rating given to each stock is accompanied by only a very brief explanation of the reasons. Most of the ratings will cluster in the neutral category of "satisfactory," "above average," or some similar designation. Obviously, a great deal of analysis still remains to be done by the subscriber.

Stock ratings may on occasion result in adverse timing and selection if the investor is not prepared to protect himself by an independent analysis. A stock-rating agency may, unconsciously perhaps, center most attention on those stocks that are likely to rise in price because of favorable developments that seem likely to take place in the near future. It may happen that only after a stock has already risen substantially will the danger of missing a winner loom so large as to cause the agency to change its rating to "buy." In some cases, special clients of the research organization receive advice concerning probable favorable developments before the general public gets the same information.

One of the research organizations that make specific recommendations on common stocks is Arnold Bernhard and Company, Inc., which publishes *The Value Line Investment Survey*. This service provides basic data as well as ratings on over 600 leading stocks. One unique feature of this service is the monthly *Special Situation Reports*. These reports make specific recommendations on common stocks of companies that have unusually good prospects or some outstanding feature which will contribute to future earnings.

COMPANY DATA SOURCES

Use of Standard Financial Services

Before consulting the basic sources of information on various topics, an analyst may obtain most of the basic data relating to a particular company and its securities from financial services. A good first source is the *Handbook of Commercial, Financial and Information Services.*[2] Another basic source will probably be one of the so-called

---

[2] Walter Hansdorfer (5th ed.; New York: Special Libraries Association, 1956).

"manuals." These are published by Moody's Investors Service, and by the Standard and Poor's Corporation. The investor will be able to find the manuals in the better libraries. Most commercial banks also subscribe to one or more of these publications.

Even if the investor has no particular company in mind but merely wishes to investigate the investment opportunities available in a particular industry, the manuals are a convenient source of information. Moody's *Manual of Industrial Securities,* for example, provides a list of all companies operating in each of a large number of industries. Moody's publishes annually five separate manuals, each of which is limited to securities of a particular industry group. One manual covers government and municipal obligations; another deals with securities relating to banks, insurance companies, investment companies, and real estate; another with public utilities; another with railroads; and, finally, a separate volume for all the other "industrial" securities.

Standard and Poor's makes no such segregation in its manuals, which are classified alphabetically. They are bound volumes of loose-leaf sheets which permit filing of revised basic information on each company as it becomes available. Both agencies, however, have an additional loose-leaf service to report current news items relating to all the companies covered by the manuals. These supplementary sheets are issued periodically, along with a cumulative index. With a lag of only a day or so behind the daily newspapers, these supplements enable the investor to review all the pertinent news relating to a particular company. A similar loose-leaf service with a cumulative index is provided to report news of dividends paid or declared.

For detailed information on Canadian industries and companies, the Maclean-Hunter Publishing Company publishes manuals by specific industries. For example, each year they issue a *Survey of Oils,* a *Survey of Mines,* and *Survey of Industrials.* These surveys give reviews of industry activities, price ranges on stocks and pertinent detailed company information.

The procedure in obtaining basic information on a company and its securities will thus be, first, to consult the basic description in one of the manuals; second, to supplement this with a study of news and interim financial reports in the "current" volumes; and, finally, to consult the dividend book. To help in deciding whether recent action on dividends implies a change in policy compared to the previous year, the investor can review the pattern of dividend declarations in the year before, which will be summarized in a special publication generally found bound with the current loose-leaf sheets in the dividend book.

The basic information provided in the manuals includes the history of the company and its subsidiaries, a description of the type of business and products, a statement of location and size of plants, and comparative income statements and balance sheets for a period of several years. For those companies that have been required to make annual reports to the Securities and Exchange Commission, Moody's *Industrial Manual* reports income and balance sheet accounts in considerable detail. The record can be reviewed for about seven years on a strictly comparable basis, because all the figures are taken from the reports to the Securities and Exchange Commission.

For smaller companies that may not have filed reports with the commission, comparative accounts are shown in Moody's for only about two years. Strict comparability is not assured, because the data are taken from annual reports to stockholders. In such cases, Standard and Poor's may be a better first source, because in that manual will be found a digest of the record according to Standard and Poor's own uniform method of classifying statistics relating to income and financial condition. The digest lacks some of the detail to be found in Moody's manual, but the record is extended back over a longer period of years. To compile a more detailed record from Moody's for smaller companies, it is often necessary to consult manuals published in earlier years. Sometimes, a comparison of the accounting record as reported by each of the major financial services will suggest matters that should be investigated further, but the investor should realize that any attempt to completely reconcile the apparent divergencies in reporting is frequently frustrating and generally not too rewarding. However, the careful analyst will probably rewrite the historical record to suit his own analytical needs after consulting more than one source and after a careful reading of all detailed footnotes explaining the financial record as published in the manuals.

Other information to be found in the manuals under the basic description of a company consists of a list of officers and directors, a description of the securities in the capitalization of the company, and the annual price range (high and low) of these securities for a period of years in the past. In some cases, statistics on physical output of commodities will be given. It is obvious that this description in the manuals applies to the typical "industrial" company. Similar pertinent information may be found in the manuals when the company is a railroad or a public utility.

In Chapter 5, reference was made to bond ratings provided in the manuals published by the various investment services. Ratings are published for common and preferred stocks as well as bonds. The symbols used by the statistical agencies to rate bonds are not uniform. Beginning with the highest quality, Moody's ratings proceed from Aaa to Aa, Baa, and so on. Standard and Poor's rates the highest-quality bonds AAA, and proceeds to AA, A, BBB, BB, and so forth on through C. While the lower ratings may not be entirely dependable, objective measures of variations in investment quality, the four highest ratings have a special significance. These four highest ratings usually indicate that the bond is of a quality suitable for institutional investment.

The common and preferred stock ratings are not so widely used as the bond ratings. These ratings are used primarily as screening devices to weed out for analytical consideration common and preferred stocks that obviously do not meet the specifications of the investor's policy. Their derivation is usually limited to one or two pertinent quantitative factors, such as dividends and earnings. For example, Standard and Poor's Corporation publishes common and preferred stock ratings in its *Stock Guide*. These ratings are alphabetic indications, A+, A—, B+, B, B—, etc., of an earnings and dividend index trend. The index measures the stability and growth of dividends and earnings.

Sources Supplementary to the Manuals

Prices. It is obvious that for certain purposes the information in the manuals is not sufficient. For example, to get the current price of a bond or stock it is necessary to consult the financial page of the daily newspaper or the market section of one of the financial newspapers such as the *Wall Street Journal* or the *Journal of Commerce.* Sometimes, the past record of market prices will not be complete in the manuals. Perhaps the analyst wants to know something of the recent trends in prices and volume of trading or wants to extend the record further back into the past. For such purposes, the current and back numbers of the monthly *Bank and Quotation Record*[3] are useful.

---

[3] New York: William B. Dana Co.

especially for unlisted stocks and bonds. The Maclean-Hunter Publishing Company publishes *The Financial Post,* a Canadian weekly financial newspaper that carries detailed price information on companies whose stock is listed on the Montreal and Toronto Stock Exchanges.

For listed industrial stocks and bonds, a convenient source of annual high and low quotations for a 10-year period is the center "blue section" of Moody's *Industrial Manual. Moody's Bond Record,* which appears twice monthly, also gives past extreme price ranges for 7,000 issues, some of which are unlisted. Sometimes a convenient source of statistics on past price history for unlisted stocks is *Standard and Poor's Over-the-Counter and Regional Exchange Stock Reports.* Most of these services are available at the offices of brokerage houses.

Management. Having reviewed the basic information in the manuals and established the past price history of the security under investigation, the careful analyst investigates other sources of information on the company and its management. A biographical record of officers and directors can sometimes be obtained in *Who's Who in America,*[4] *Who's Who in Commerce and Industry,*[5] or *Poor's Register of Directors and Executives, United States and Canada.* Published notices of annual meetings of the corporation and solicitations of proxies contain information on salaries of management, bonus plans, and business affiliations of officers or directors. The matters at issue in the solicitation of proxies will often reveal attitudes of management, as will questions asked and debates occurring at annual meetings of stockholders. The analyst cannot attend the annual meetings unless he is already a stockholder, but sometimes the meetings are reviewed in the press. An increasing number of corporations themselves publish summaries of what takes place at annual meetings.

The manuals will reveal which underwriting firms and commercial banks have been associated with the firm in the past. Sometimes, a check with these financial firms will enable the analyst to get an opinion on the quality of management. The analyst will remember, however, that "street" opinions regarding management are sometimes biased. The opinions of professional public relations representatives hired by a corporation are of necessity biased in favor of

---

[4] Chicago: A. N. Marquis Co.
[5] *Ibid.*

management. However, the analyst should consult all sources that may provide information, keeping in mind the possible bias.

The problems of appraising the quality of management are discussed in Chapter 10. However, the investor can gain some notion of management's appraisal of the company's prospects by examining the purchases and sales of a corporation's stock by its officers and directors. These transactions are reported monthly by the Securities and Exchange Commission in an *Official Summary of Security Transactions and Holdings*. The more signicant transactions may be reproduced in the financial page of a newspaper as well. The analyst will follow such transactions with considerable interest, but they are not necessarily an indication of a change in the course of a corporation's fortunes.

Supplements to the Accounting Record

Listing Statements. The analyst may wish to supplement the accounting records published by the financial services. If he has access to the New York Stock Exchange library and the stock is listed, he may find additional details in the official listing statement required by the New York Stock Exchange. This may be of some help in interpreting financial statements, because the listing statement contains a summary of the policies of the corporation relating to accounting matters. The reports required by the Securities and Exchange Commission may also be a source of detail. In particular, the so-called annual "10-K" reports, on file at the stock exchange library but appearing somewhat later than stockholders' reports, may provide details not available elsewhere. These reports are particularly valuable in revealing details on expenditures for new plants and equipment and the extent to which old plant is being retired.

The Prospectus. A particularly valuable source of information is the prospectus. When a corporation makes a public offering of stocks or bonds, it is required to issue a statement regarding the purpose of the issue, the nature of the business, the past record of earnings, recent changes in asset position, the company's position in the industry, the importance of patents, and many other matters that are of vital concern to the analyst. Before it appears in final form with the offering price of the security printed on it, a preliminary edition may be issued. Such a preliminary prospectus has some red lines of printing across the pages and is called a "red herring." The analyst may obtain a copy of a prospectus or a red herring from one of the financial firms underwriting the new issue or participating in its sale, or he may consult it at one of the brokerage offices. Financial libraries file back copies of all prospectuses relating to a particular corporation, and the analyst may use them as material for historical study. A prospectus is a particularly valuable source of information, because it is likely to be dependable in view of stiff penalties for misrepresentation. In a prospectus, a corporation may be forced to reveal for the first time certain types of information that have been well-guarded secrets for years.

Reports to Stockholders. In some cases, annual reports to stockholders may be the only type of information available to supplement the statistical record found in the manuals. Even when other sources of information can be obtained, the analyst may wish to consult annual reports, because they may provide additional pertinent information. The statistical material presented in annual reports is often accompanied by a commentary on the results of operations for the year and on management's appraisal of the company's prospects.

The content of annual reports is steadily improving. However, there is a conflict between the needs of the analyst and the desires of the typical investor. The companies are now providing a popular type of presentation, which is oversimplified to such an extent that it does not provide some of the basic information needed by the analyst. Each analyst, depending on his approach, may find that even the most complete annual reports do not give him the exact information he needs. Some corporations provide separate statistical supplements for the analyst.

The better annual reports may be inadequate because financial statements fail to provide sufficient detail. For example, inventories may be reported as a lump sum instead of classified as raw materials, semifinished goods, and finished goods. In the income statement, depletion may be lumped with depreciation; sizable amounts of nonoperating income or expense may be unexplained. There is, of course, a limit to the amount of detail that can be reproduced in a report. Some types of information, such as detailed breakdown of sales to various types of markets, may be withheld for competitive reasons.

Another shortcoming of annual reports is that a great many words may be wasted on business forecasts, expressions of appreciation, and reaffirmations of belief in the future of America, while vital information concerning major problems confronting the company and the policy that management has adopted to meet them is not included.

Annual reports are often late in appearing. In some cases, they may be published three or four months after the close of the fiscal year. The time consumed in getting an audit of accounts perhaps makes such delays unavoidable. Some companies provide a quarterly report of unaudited figures on sales and earnings. Others report profits only quarterly and semiannually, providing more detailed data only annually.

Sometimes, the investor will have difficulty in keeping informed of current changes in the fortunes of an enterprise during the fiscal year. The problems of infrequent reporting and inadequate information are most evident with smaller companies whose securities are not listed, and the problems are uniformly greater with Canadian companies than with American ones. *The Financial Post Corporation Service,*[6] a standard source of information on Canadian companies, usually gives enough information to suggest which companies might be interesting on investigation. More detailed information must then be obtained, if at all, from key executives by means of personal interview.

Supplementary Sources for Utilities and Rails. For regulated industries, such as railroad transportation, the current reports that must be made to the regulatory agencies make it possible for the analyst to get statistical information on a monthly basis. The daily newspaper is the earliest source, but the analyst will probably consult as well the current statistics compiled by one of the standard financial services. Sometimes the analyst can make arrangements to get monthly figures direct from the railroad company. In addition, the investor can have mailed to him monthly statistical bulletins from the Bureau of Transport Economics and Statistics of the Interstate Commerce Commission. Finally, additional information may be available from private statistical sources such as the Association of American Railroads.

The great mass of railway statistics available currently and the uniform accounting system required by regulatory authorities provide adequate information on railroads. A major problem arises, however, because interpretation of statistical trends necessitates computation of ratios and other types of "derived" statistics. The complex

---

[6] Toronto: Maclean-Hunter Publishing Co., Ltd.

character of railroad transportation as a business makes difficult the selection and interpretation of data. For example, one type of derived statistic may indicate a favorable trend at the same time that another indicates just the opposite. The problem is to properly interpret the statistics. While the anual reports to stockholders are frequently helpful, the analyst will sometimes feel the need of a personal interview with executives in order to discover the real explanation of statistical trends. In analyzing rail securities, the investor can easily make a wrong decision with a meager sampling of a few statistical trends.

Monthly financial statistics are available for a good many corporations in the public utility industry, such as electric power companies and communications utilities. Monthly reports will appear in the newspapers and among the current statistics reported by the financial services. Sometimes, the information is based on reports to a regulatory agency, such as the Federal Communications Commission. Also, some electric utilities issue monthly "releases" of statistical information. These are not sent to stockholders, but the analyst may be able to obtain them on request from the company. The trend of earning and output for the industry as a whole can be followed on a monthly basis by subscribing to the Federal Power Commission's loose-leaf service called *Electric Power Statistics.*

Unlike the railroads, most electric power companies issue quarterly reports to stockholders in addition to an annual report. Since the electric utility industry operates under a uniform system of accounts, management has no incentive to withhold information because it must be reported to regulatory agencies in any event. Therefore, reports to stockholders tend to be of good quality. As contrasted with the problems involved in analyzing railroads and some industrials, analysis of a public utility seldom involves major problems of a purely statistical character.

Information on Financial Institutions and Government Securities. The investor interested in banks, insurance companies and investment companies may find basic information on these firms in *Moody's Investment Manuals—Finance.* However, more detailed information is available from other sources. *Best's Insurance Reports* are published annually in two separate editions, a *Fire and Casualty Edition* and *Life Insurance Reports.* These publications provide the most detailed insurance company information available anywhere. In addition, Best's publishes a *Digest of Insurance Stocks* which provides basic data on the technique of analyzing insurance company statements and analyses of the larger stock fire and casualty and life insurance companies. A source of data on the life insurance industry is the *Life Insurance Fact Book*, published by the Institute of Life Insurance.

The annual *Investment Companies*, published by Arthur Wiesenberger and Company, is the best source of information on investment companies. This publication provides an evaluation of investment company performance, financial statements of these companies, and other background data. Unfortunately, this publication is not generally available, but it is usually available to the investor at most brokerage houses.

Merrill Lynch, Pierce, Fenner & Smith Inc. publishes a weekly bulletin on government securities as well as an annual detailed description of U.S. government securities. *The Bond Buyer*, published weekly, is the best source of current information on state and local government bonds. In addition, the same firm publishes the *Daily Bond Buyer*, a source of more detailed information on proposed state and local bond issues.

Various brokerage houses that specialize in commercial bank stocks have available current data on bank stocks. For example, First Boston Corporation publishes a book, *Data on Selected Commercial Banks*. Generally, similar publications available are sources of data on local bank stocks.

INDUSTRY DATA SOURCES

An acquaintance with the industry in which a company operates can contribute much to an interpretation of a corporation's past record and to an intelligent appraisal of its future. The analyst cannot hope to become an expert in all branches of American industry, but he must strive to become as well-informed as possible. He needs two types of information: (1) a knowledge of the basic economic characteristics of the industry, and (2) an acquaintance with the statistics available to measure the major interrelated economic factors and their current trends.

Basic Characteristics

A good first source of industry information, considering its brevity, is the "basic" study offered by Standard and Poor's in its *Industry Surveys*. The basic studies are revised each year. The sources available to build more detailed historical background vary greatly, depending on the industry. To locate books and magazine articles, the investor must use the card file of a good library and the standard guides to periodical literature, such as the *Business Periodicals Index* or the *Public Affairs Information Service Bulletin*. Some of the most valuable information may be found in publications of the United States government: hearings before congressional committees, special studies by independent agencies, such as the Federal Trade Commission; and even the briefs, records, and opinions in court cases involving litigation against one or more important companies in an industry. Some suggestions on use of government publications are offered later in this chapter. Here, we merely note that a good bibliography of sources, both governmental and nongovernmental, can be obtained from the Inquiry Reference Service of the U.S. Department of Commerce. These bibliographies, entitled *Basic Information Sources*, are classified by industry.

One of the best ways of building up a working knowledge of an industry is to read the current issues of trade journals as they become available. This approach to a study of the industry has the added advantage of acquainting the investor with the types of statistics available. A general knowledge of the economic characteristics of an industry is not very useful to a security analyst unless he knows how to *measure* basic economic factors and how to evaluate current trends. A comprehensive list of trade publications can be found in *Business Magazines Classified by Subject*.[7] The list can be brought up to date by consulting the latest annual issue of *Industrial Marketing, Market Data Book Number*,[8] or *Ulrich's Periodicals Directory*.[9]

Trade associations, such as the American Iron and Steel Institute or the Automobile Manufacturers Association, also publish statistics or current periodicals, which are often valuable. Some trade associations, such as the Machinery and Allied Products Institute, do not grant public access to their current periodicals, which are circulated only among member firms of the association. However, a personal interview with the economist or some other executive of a trade association sometimes can advance the investor's knowledge of an industry as much as can months of laborious research. A list of the most important trade associations can be found in *Business Executives of Amer-*

---

[7] Marian C. Manley (Newark, N.J.: Newark Public Library, 1933).

[8] Chicago: Advertising Publications, Inc.

[9] New York: R. R. Bowker.

ica,[10] *National Associations of the United States,*[11] *Directory of National Trade Associations,*[12] and the *Encyclopedia of American Associations.*[13] The National Industrial Conference Board, an association of business firms and other contributing members, publishes very useful information, most of which is available to the public.

Industry Statistics

The well-informed investor will acquire a knowledge of the particular type of statistics available for each industry. The investor does not have to go to the original sources in many cases, because industry statistics are often compiled by service organizations. However, the statistics offered for a fee by such services as the *Dodge Reports,* on construction contract awards,[14] or *Polk's National New Car Service,* on registration statistics,[15] are published elsewhere, perhaps with a time lag or in less detail. The investor's first step is to classify statistics by industry rather than by source and to learn how to use these statistics in order to determine meaningful relationships.

Trade Publications. One of the best methods of getting acquainted with the statistics available in an industry is to consult the annual statistical issue of a trade journal of that industry. Once the investor has learned how to use the information available, he can then consult original sources for a detailed description of each statistical series and proceed to outline the most convenient method of getting current access to the figures. In general, current sources for statistics will be trade journals, financial or trade newspapers, current statistical reports from the government, and specialized services offered for a fee. Considerable data will be available in the current statistical bulletins to supplement the statistical sections of Standard and Poor's trade and securities service.

The annual statistical issues of business periodicals and trade journals generally discuss statistics not only for the particular industry but also for related industries. For this reason, the investor can consult the issues of relatively few publications and obtain an acquaint-

---

10 *Op. cit.*

11 Jay Judkins (Washington, D.C.: U.S. Department of Commerce, 1949).

12 *Ibid.*

13 Detroit: Gale Research Company, 1956.

14 New York: F. W. Dodge Corp.

15 Detroit: R. L. Polk Co.

ance with statistical series relating to a large number of American industries. To obtain a more complete list of annual statistical or review issues of business periodicals, the reader should consult the *Selected List of Annual Statistical and Review Issues of American Business Periodicals*.[16]

It is not meant to suggest that all the analyst's problems will be solved by consulting trade publications. The definition of an industry is not always precise. There are industries within industries. The so-called "building industry," for example, can be broken down into a great many segments, such as the plywood industry, the warm-air furnace industry, and the gypsum industry. Furthermore, many corporations operate in more than one industry. To understand the nature of their markets, the analyst must know where to find detailed statistics on specialized segments of widely separated industries.

Government Publications. The best source of monthly or quarterly statistics on specialized segments of industry is the United States government, the largest statistical agency in the world. *Government Statistics for Business Use*[17] contains an analysis of government statistical series of use to businessmen. It includes chapters on "National Income and Other Business Indicators," by Milton Gilbert; "Transportation and other Public Utilities," by Frank L. Barton; "Money, Credit and Finance," by Edward T. Crowder and others. "Facts for Industry Publications,"[18] provides statistics on thousands of individual commodities, ranging from red cedar shingles to penholders and pen nibs. The investor should consult the *Catalog of United States Census Publications*, available from the Census Bureau, to aid in locating information on particular commodities.

Other useful sources of information are the *Mineral Industry Surveys*.[19] For example, this series includes a monthly report on cement and a quarterly report on gypsum. Periodic surveys of other industries, such as lumber, are found in the "Industry Reports" of the Business and Defense Services Administration. These reports provide a commentary and discussion in addition to statistics. The same is true

---

[16] Harvard University, Graduate School of Business Administration, Baker Library (rev. ed.; Boston: The Library, 1954, Reference List No. 9).

[17] Philip M. Hauser and William R. Leonard (eds.), *Government Statistics for Business Use* (2d ed.; New York: John Wiley & Sons, Inc., 1956).

[18] U.S. Department of Commerce, Bureau of the Census, Industry Division.

[19] U.S. Department of the Interior, Bureau of Mines.

Name of Current Periodical	Title of Annual Statistical Issue	Time of Publication
American Gas Association Monthly	Round-Up of Utility Annual Reports	March or April
American Machinist	Production Planbook and Buyer's Guide Issue	Mid-September
American Petroleum Institute Statistical Bulletin	Review of the Year	March or April
Automotive Industries	Annual Statistical Issue	Second issue in March
Baking Industry	Annual Survey	March
Broadcasting—Telecasting	a) Broadcasting Yearbook	January
	b) Telecasting Yearbook	August
Coal Age	Coal in Review Issue	February
Electrical Merchandising	Annual Statistical and Marketing Issue	January
Electrical World	Annual Statistical and Review Number	Second issue in January
Engineering and Mining Journal	Survey and Outlook Number	February
Engineering News-Record	a) Annual Report and Forecast	Usually second issue
	b) Construction Costs Yearbook	Quarterly reports
Implement and Tractor and Farm Implement News	Annual Statistical Number	November
Fibre Containers and Paperboard Mills	Annual Statistical Review	August
Industrial and Engineering Chemistry	Facts and Figures for the Chemical Process Industries	Biennially in September
Iron Age	Annual Review Issue	First issue in January
Leather and Shoes	Leather and Shoes Blue Book	Biennially in February
Oil and Gas Journal	Annual Number	Last issue in January
Paper Trade Journal	Review Number	Last issue in February
Printing Magazine	Printing Magazine Yearbook	November
Railway Age	Annual Review and Outlook Number	Second issue in January
Rock Products	Annual Directory and Outlook Issue	January
Television Digest	Special Report	Biennially
Textile Organon	Annual Review	February

of the monthly publication of the Business and Defense Services Administration and the Labor Statistics Bureau, *Construction Review*, and the monthly publication of the Agricultural Marketing Service, *The Agricultural Situation*, available from the Superintendent of Documents. The monthly *Survey of Current Business*,[20] also available from the Superintendent of Documents, carries many statistics relating to American industries, but most of these statistics relate to rather broad classifications, such as retail or mining.

Despite the apparent wealth of statistics available from the federal

---

[20] U.S. Department of Commerce, Office of Business Economics.

government, the investor will encounter many problems. He will sometimes find a multiplicity of statistics on one subject but none at all on another subject that he considers of strategic importance. Furthermore, the quality of statistics needs to be improved, as well as the quantity. The analyst should view statistics not necessarily as facts but as estimates of facts. For this reason, he should strive to become acquainted with the reliability of each statistical series he uses. A description of methods used to compute many of the series published by the federal government is available in the annual *Statistical Abstract of the United States*[21] and in the *Statistical Supplement to the Survey of Current Business.*[22]

Because of the need to improve the quality of statistical information, various organizations have made independent investigations of the past historical record. Such studies use a variety of sources but must, of necessity, rely to a large degree on statistics published by the Census Bureau in past years. Their usefulness lies in the long-term historical record of past relationships among industries. They contribute also to an understanding of how the economic system works. A particularly useful book for this purpose is *America's Needs and Resources.*[23] A convenient historical record is available in *Historical Statistics of the United States, Colonial Times to 1957.*[24]

This book is particulary valuable because it includes a description of the statistical material and detailed notes containing original sources of the information.

GENERAL ECONOMIC AND MARKET DATA SOURCES

It is difficult to draw a sharp distinction between statistics relating to industries and those relating to general economic conditions, because one method of following the course of the general economy is to study the economic relationships among industries. Also, statistics of particular industries, such as the output of steel, the volume of freight-car loadings, and the generation of electricity may be used as indicators of business conditions. A number of these indicators will be discussed in Chapter 20.

---

[21] U.S. Department of Commerce, Bureau of the Census, Superintendent of Documents.

[22] U.S. Department of Commerce, Office of Business Economics.

[23] J. Frederic Dewhurst and Associates (New York: Twentieth Century Fund, 1955).

[24] U.S. Department of Commerce, Bureau of the Census.

Basic Economic Data

Business statistics consist of measures of changes in business activity, of changes in income or expenditure flows, of changes in prices, and of changes in the financial situation (money, credit, and the banking system). These measures are available for stated periods of time—a year, a month, a week, or a day.

Some basic economic data may be expressed in relative terms. For example, instead of reporting that the production of steel this year was so many tons, the statistics might state that it was twice as high as in some base year. Generally, the relative for the base year is given as 100, so production twice as high would be given as 200. Suppose one wished to compare the *combined* output of steel, automobiles, and lumber this year relative to some base year in the past. Such a statistic would be known as an index or index number, because mathematical techniques are used in order to combine such diverse measures as *tons* of steel, *number* of automobiles, and *board feet* of lumber.

Business Activity. The aim of certain physical indexes of production or of business activity may be to measure business conditions. The aim implies a measure of the extent to which production or business activity is above or below normal, and this makes it necessary to define "normal." If production this year is 10 percent above a decade ago, it may actually be below normal because the secular trend may be upward, due to growth in population and productive capacity. The statistical index must, therefore, be adjusted for secular trend. Again, if department store sales are higher in one month than in the month before, a complete explanation may be the normal seasonal increase due to the approach of Christmas, or some other factor. Monthly indicators of business activity must be corrected for seasonal variation.

It is not possible to list here all the available business statistics. A few, however, are so well known that there is frequent reference to them in the financial news. Perhaps the best-known physical index of production is the *Federal Reserve Index of Industrial Production.* It is an index published monthly, with the base period defined as 1957–59. Index numbers are available, both adjusted and unadjusted for seasonal variation, to measure output of manufactures and of minerals. A combined index of both is generally the one that receives most public attention as a measure of industrial production. The *Federal Reserve Bulletin* publishes many other Federal Reserve indexes that measure industrial production by broad classes of manufacturing and mining, by industries within these classes, and by certain branches of these industries.

National Income. Another widely used series of statistics is the "National Income Series" of the Department of Commerce. They are value statistics, and seek to measure income and expenditure flows. Measures of personal income are available monthly, but other broad measures appear only quarterly. Detailed breakdowns of annual and quarterly data appear with a time lag of about a year. The monthly and quarterly data are adjusted for seasonal variation. A description of the national income statistics will be found in *National Income,* 1954 edition, a supplement to the *Survey of Current Business,* and in *Personal Income by States Since 1929,* also a supplement to the *Survey of Current Business,* available from the Superintendent of Documents. Current figures are published in the monthly issues of the *Survey of Current Business.*

The statistical concepts used in compilation of the national income estimates are rather complex. To understand national income data fully, the investor may consult other literature, such as *National Income Accounts and Income Analysis.*[25] Table 8–1 shows a statement of the basic relationships of these statistics. The accepted statistical concepts are in parentheses. The accuracy of such a simplified and abbreviated table as presented is only approximate.

Other publications provide current interpretations of business statistics. One can acquire some added knowledge by reading these interpretations in such publications as the *Survey of Current Business* and the *Federal Reserve Bulletin.*[26] Stimulating discussions also appear in the *Monthly Letter,* monthly economic letter of the First National City Bank of New York, the *Monthly Review of Credit Business Conditions* of the Federal Reserve Bank of New York, and the Cleveland Trust Company *Business Bulletin,* issued monthly.

Summary of Basic Data Sources

In addition to daily newspapers, which will be discussed later, the following sources seem to be adequate for the average investor. *The*

---

[25] Richard and Nancy D. Ruggles (2d ed.; New York: McGraw-Hill Book Co., Inc., 1956).

[26] Board of Governors of the Federal Reserve System.

TABLE 8–1

Basic Interrelationships among Items in the National Income Statistics

Total Money Income Spent	Money Value of All Goods and Services Produced	Total Money Income Available for Spending
1. Spent by Business (Gross private domestic investment) *a*) For new construction *b*) For new equipment *c*) For additions to inventories 2. Spent by consumers (Personal consumption expenditures) 3. Spent by government (Government purchases of goods and services)	(Gross National Product)	1. Retained by business *a*) Profits withheld from owners (Undistributed profits) *b*) Not reported as profits (Capital consumption Allowances) 2. Collected by government from business 3. Balance available to persons resulting from their participation *a*) Add payments received from government not related to production (transfer payments, net interest paid, subsidies) 4. Total money income received by individuals (Personal income) *a*) Deduct taxes paid to government 5. Balance available (Disposable income) *a*) Spent for durable and nondurable goods and services (Personal consumption expenditures. See 2.) 6. Balance saved (Personal saving)

Economic Almanac provides general business, national income, and governmental financial information for both the United States and Canada. The *Federal Reserve Bulletin* provides financial and banking statistics as well as other business statistics that can be used to keep up to date the graphic record of the past to be found in the *Federal Reserve Chart Book on Financial and Business Statistics*. The best source of historical financial statistics is the Federal Reserve Board's 1943 volume on *Banking and Monetary Statistics* and various supplements to this volume. The *Survey of Current Business*[27] will provide many monthly time series, while a description of the statistical series can be found in the biennial supplement and in *Historical Statistics of the United States.* The historical book is particularly valuable, because it contains statistics on monthly and quarterly indicators of business conditions for the past years, together with descriptions and an enumeration of sources. The *Statistical Abstract of the United States* provides a wide coverage of government statistics with adequate descriptions, while the annual *Economic Almanac*[28] provides a handy record of annual statistics from many nongovernmental sources as well.

A few other sources provide more current data on business trends. Mostly monthly statistics involve such a time lag in reporting that the investor will not know what is happening currently but only what happened a month or six weeks ago. He will, therefore, want to follow some statistical series that are reported weekly. One of the best sources of weekly statistics is the *Weekly Supplement to the Survey of Current Business,* available to those who subscribe to the *Survey of Current Business.* Another publication that frequently gives a little earlier indication of the probable trend of the *Federal Reserve Index of Industrial Production,* and also provides a useful summary of other major statistical trends, is the monthly *Economic Indicators,*[29] available from the Superintendent of Documents. Also, the trends in manufacturers' new orders, inventories, and production are of such strategic importance that a subscription to the monthly *Industry Survey* would be useful.[30] The Securities and Exchange Commission publishes a "Statistical Series" of their current releases on changes in planned business plant and equipment expenditures.

SOURCES OF INFORMATION ON SOURCES

A few selected publications should aid the investor in locating additional sources of information and in keeping up with new types of statistical information as it becomes available. A book that fills many of the gaps is *Sources of Business Information.*[31] Two works of

---

[27] U.S. Department of Commerce, Office of Business Economics.
[28] National Industrial Conference Board, *op. cit.*
[29] Council of Economic Advisers.
[30] U.S. Department of Commerce, Office of Business Economics.
[31] By Edwin R. Coman, Jr. (Berkeley: University of California Press, 1964).

note are *Business Information; How to Find and Use It*[32] and *Information for Administrators; A guide to Publications and Services for Management in Business and Government.*[33]

The most timely sources of information on United States government publications are the weekly *Business Service Checklist*[34] and the *List of Selected United States Government Publications,*[35] published twice a month. Less timely, but useful, are the *United States Government Publications Monthly Catalog*[36] and the Census Bureau publication, *Catalog of the United States Census Publications,* appearing monthly. Available annually from the Superintendent of Documents are the various price lists of government publications, such as *Price List 36—Government Periodicals,* and *Commerce— Business, Patents, Trademarks and Foreign Trade.* These lists are valuable as a means of locating government publications on particular topics.

For a historical record, some comprehensive bibliographies published in past years may be useful. For example, an *Index to the Publications of the United States Department of Agriculture*[37] was published in 1940 and is supplemented with a *List of Available Publications of the United States Department of Agriculture.* A comprehensive list of Department of Commerce publications appears in *United States Department of Commerce Publications, a Catalog and Index,* and is kept up to date through annual supplements.[38] The investor may also find useful the *Subject Guide to United States Government Publications.*[39] For a guide to the use of private as well as government publications, the reader may wish to consult *Business Information; How to Find and Use It.*

One may be confused by the multiplicity of statistics relating to industries and general business conditions. Part of the confusion results because statistics compiled by an agency may be reproduced in many other publications as well as in the daily newspaper. Some of this confusion may be avoided by consulting a book that provides

---

[32] Marian C. Manley (New York: Harper and Row, 1955).

[33] Paul Wasserman (Cornell University Press, 1956).

[34] U.S. Department of Commerce.

[35] Superintendent of Documents.

[36] Superintendent of Documents.

[37] U.S. Department of Agriculture, Office of Information.

[38] U.S. Government Printing Office, 1952.

[39] Herbert S. Hirshberg and Carl H. Melinat (Chicago: American Library Association, 1947).

an orderly description of statistical series with an indication of the time they become available and in what publications they appear. A good book to consult is *Measures of Business Change; A Baker Library Index,* by Arthur H. Cole with the assistance of Virginia Jenness and Grace V. Lindfors.[40] Another publication that provides a list of statistics available daily, weekly, and monthly is available from the U.S. Department of Commerce. Compiled by Jettie Turner, its title is *Sources of Current Trade Statistics, Market Research Series, Number 13.*[41]

READING THE FINANCIAL PAGE

The News and Stock Prices

The periodic financial news is an unreliable indicator of trends in stock prices, because a newspaper cannot give adequate publicity to all of the complex business and financial factors at work. Some factors will be emphasized to the neglect of others. There is danger in assuming that a cursory reading of a newspaper each day can provide a reliable indication of the current or prospective course of the fortunes of particular enterprises or of general business activity. Certain news items that relate to particular corporations may be very useful to the financial analyst; but he must carefully distinguish between facts, such as earnings reports and unfilled orders, and opinions, such as the views of management or brokers regarding the company's future. News items on a particular company are frequently the work of that company's public relations department, and these opinions are likely to be optimistic.

Reports on trends in various industries published in financial or business newspapers are by no means uniformly optimistic. However, distortions of the probable future course of general business conditions can sometimes be created by the type of industrial news that a newspaper chooses to emphasize. It is unfortunate that the most easily understood news is often misleading, while the most useful statistics often are difficult to interpret.

Security Prices

The financial page is frequently used to see whether the general market or the price of a particular security has gone up or gone down.

---

40 Homewood, Ill.: Richard D. Irwin, Inc., 1952.
41 Bureau of Foreign and Domestic Commerce.

A stock has "gone up on the day" only when its price at the *close* of trading exceeds its *closing* price on the trading day before. The price record of Borg-Warner reproduced here for January 3, 1966, may serve to illustrate how the record is read.

| 54¼ 45⅝ | Borg-Warner | 2.20 | 36 | 49⅞ | 49⅞ | 49½ | 49¾ | +⅛ |

In the first column at the left are shown the high and low price of the stock for the year to date. Following the name of the stock is the dividend. These dividend data are frequently misleading, even when supplemented by a footnote. A better source to use in estimating dividends for the year or the current rate is one of the financial services discussed earlier in this chapter. In the fourth column is the volume of trading, in units of hundred-share lots. The figure 36 thus indicates that 3,600 shares changed hands. In the next columns, reading from left to right, is the price at which the stock opened, next the high for the day, the low, and the close. The final column shows how much the closing price differed from the previous day's close.

To say that the stock market went up (down) on a particular day generally means that the Dow-Jones Industrial Average closed at a higher (lower) level than at the close of trading the day before. There is also a Dow-Jones average of railroad stock prices and another for utility stock prices. The Dow-Jones averages are the best known, but not necessarily the best measure of stock prices. An average price of all three types of stocks—utilities, rails, and industrials—is known as a composite average. Many different types of measures of stock prices, both specialized and composite, are published by the financial services, such as Moody's and Standard and Poor's, and by the Associated Press or the larger daily newspapers, such as the *New York Times* and the *New York Herald-Tribune*. A description and past record of these indices can generally be obtained from the newspaper's financial editor. A detailed record and description of the Dow-Jones averages is available from Dow-Jones Company, Inc. It is possible to compute the yield on the stocks included in a Dow-Jones average. These averages and the yield on these averages should not be a guide to investment timing; the average investor cannot buy all the stocks included in the Dow-Jones Industrial Average, because the purchase of each stock, in small amounts, would result in prohibitively high brokerage commissions.

A newspaper that reports some average measure of stock prices will frequently also publish a chart. The movement of the average, measured against a vertical scale, is depicted by vertical lines, one for each trading day. The top of the line measures the high for the day, and the bottom measures the low. Each line is cut by a short horizontal line drawn across it. This indicates the close. At the bottom of the chart may be found other vertical lines, one for each trading day. The height of these lines measures the volumes of trading (the number of shares traded).

The best financial newspapers and the larger dailies will report not only prices of stocks traded on the New York Stock Exchange but also prices of those traded on the American Stock Exchange and on organized exchanges in other cities, such as the Midwest Stock Exchange. If certain stocks do not sell on a particular day, bid and asked prices will be shown for all such stocks eligible for trading on the New York and American Stock Exchanges. Prices for over-the-counter stocks are quoted on a bid and asked basis, while prices of stocks listed on exchanges outside New York are shown only when sales actually have taken place.

Bond prices are quoted on a basis somewhat different than that used for stock prices. Stock quotations represent the actual number of dollars or points at which a stock sells, plus fractional parts of a dollar as small as a sixteenth. Bond quotations are in percentages of maturity or face value, and a point is 1 percent of face value. A bond with a par value of $1,000.00, quoted at $112\frac{1}{8}$, is priced at $1,121.25. A point represents $10.00 instead of $1.00 in this case, because it is a $1,000.00 bond. The same is true of U.S. Treasury bonds, but fractions of a point are quoted in thirty-seconds rather than in eighths. Thus, a Treasury bond quoted at 100.5 (or 100-5) is priced at $100\frac{5}{32}$ points (approximately $1,001.56). When bid and asked prices are quoted for bonds, the yield at the asked price is sometimes shown also. In other cases, the yield at both bid and asked prices is shown, but the actual prices are omitted. Treasury notes, certificates of indebtedness, and Treasury bills, for example, are quoted in this manner, and the 3 P.M. quotations by dealers in these securities are shown in the newspaper. A quotation such as 1.04@ 0.94 means that someone offered to buy at a price that would yield 1.04 percent but that the only offer to sell was at a higher price, which provided a yield of only 0.94 percent.

Money Rates and the Banking Situation

The daily newspaper is the best current source of information on factors that are likely to affect the availability of credit, the trend of interest rates and yield structure of outstanding obligations, and the inflationary pressures in the economy. The activities of the United States Treasury and the Federal Reserve System influence these trends. A background in monetary and banking theory is helpful in understanding these influences. It may be helpful to the investor to consult *Banking Studies,* by members of the staff of the Board of Governors of the Federal Reserve System.[42] A detailed description of pertinent statistics and their significance will be found in *Banking and Monetary Statistics,* referred to earlier.

Statistics on Bank Reserves. Some very useful statistics on bank reserves and the money market are available in the newspaper. A combined statement of condition of the Federal Reserve banks as of Wednesday each week appears in the following Friday edition of the *Wall Street Journal.* With this statement of condition appears an interpretation of these data, which reviews the change in member-bank reserves that took place during the week and states the amount of excess reserves. The discussion is followed by a statistical explanation of how the change in reserves took place. These statistics are very useful in interpreting changes in the supply and demand for funds. Table 8–2 shows the transactions that cause changes in bank reserves. This table analyzes the effect on reserves only when reserves occur in each of the statistical items. To complete the analysis, one must simply remember that the effect of a decrease will be just the opposite. Increases and decreases are indicated in the newspaper by plus and minus signs.

The *Wall Street Journal* reported that for one particular week member-bank reserves were increased by $71 million. Utilizing the published statistics and referring to Table 8–2, the reasons for this change are shown in Table 8–3. Figures are shown in millions, and increases or decreases are indicated by plus or minus signs. By totaling each column, ignoring plus and minus signs, the gross change in reserves can be calculated.

Banking Condition. Along with the explanation of changes in bank reserve position published each week in the *Wall Street Journal* is a detailed listing of the bank's holdings of securities, classified by type and maturity, and comparisons with a week ago and a year ago. These data provide valuable evidence of central bank policy and its relation to the Treasury's management of the public debt. In the same newspaper will appear a statement of condition relating to member

---

42 Baltimore: Waverly Press, 1941.

TABLE 8–2

Increases in Financial Items that Increase or Decrease Bank Reserves

Changes That Increase Member-Bank Reserves	Changes That Decrease Member-Bank Reserves

1. Increase in "Total Reserve bank credit"
  a) "U.S. government securities (including guaranteed securities)"
  b) "Loans, discounts, and advances"
2. Increase in "Gold stock"
3. Increase in "Treasury currency"
	1. Increase in "Money in circulation"
	
	2. Increase in "Nonmember deposits"
	3. Increase in "Treasury deposits with Federal Reserve banks"
	4. Increase in "Treasury cash"

banks, also of the preceding Wednesday. This statistical sample, however, is not entirely adequate, being limited to weekly reporting member banks only in central reserve cities (New York and Chicago).

Deposit liabilities of the member banks are classified as demand (checking accounts), time (savings), and United States government. The amount of "demand deposits, adjusted" when added to "currency in circulation" will give the analyst an amount roughly equivalent to the money supply—the total quantity of money in existence. Also shown are total debits to demand deposits (volume of checks written), which can be compared with the amount of demand deposits outstanding to estimate the "turnover of money" (debits divided by demand deposits). Lending policy of the banking system in relation to the needs of business and of the United States Treasury can be observed by noting the volume of commercial, industrial, and agricultural loans and the banks' holding of government securities.

TABLE 8–3

Explanation of a Change in Reserves

Changes That Tended to Increase Reserves		Changes That Tended to Decrease Reserves	
U.S. government securities	+16	Other Reserve bank credit	−93
Gold stocks	+ 2		
Loans, discounts, and advances	+56	Treasury currency	− 1
Money in circulation	−33	Total	−94
Treasury cash	− 3		
Treasury deposits with Federal Reserve banks	− 2	Increase in reserves that is to be proved	+71
Nonmember deposits	−53		
Total	165	Total	165

Public Finance

An analysis of money rates and the banking situation is never complete without considering the influence of federal public finance. A convenient current source of information on budget receipts and expenditures is the daily Treasury statement published in most large daily papers. The figures are cumulative, for the current month and for the current fiscal year (ending June 30), and appear with a time lag of only five days. The statement shows the size of the budget deficit or surplus, the total outstanding debt, and amount of the Treasury's working balance, as well as receipts and expenditures by major classifications.

It should be noted that budget receipts and expenditures are not an accurate measure of the actual flow of money from the private economy to the government and from government to the economy. Budget expenditures may be shown that do not involve any cash payments. For example, some government securities bear no interest but rise in redemption value as time passes. The government may budget the accrual of increased redemption value as interest on the federal debt, but no cash payments will be involved.

The monthly *Treasury Bulletin*[43] is useful in showing expenditures and receipts adjusted to indicate actual cash flows, and is a source for a considerable amount of other detailed information on federal finances. Unfortunately, the *Bulletin* is late in reporting these statistics. For example, a November issue may not reach the subscriber until the middle of the month, and that will contain, as latest information, data from the preceding September. Sometimes, a joint use of the *Bulletin* and the daily Treasury statement will permit a rational estimate of the current trend in cash expenditures when the investor knows there is likely to be a significant difference from budget expenditures. For many Department of Defense programs, for example, expenditures are budgeted in the fiscal year prior to the one in which cash expenditures are made.

One method of arriving at a rough estimate of the discrepancy between budget and cash expenditures is to compute the change in the federal debt and in the Treasury's working balance. The Treasury can obviously spend more than its current receipts only if it incurs more debt or draws down its working balance. The discrepancy be-

---

[43] U.S. Treasury Department.

tween budget and cash expenditures can be approximated by comparing the reported budget deficit (based on budget expenditures) with the sum of the increase in the federal debt and the decline in the Treasury balance.

News Articles as Sources of Information. In today's political climate, it is almost impossible to make intelligent investment decisions without a careful reading of at least one metropolitan daily newspaper. Foreign affairs and political action have a profound effect on the prospects of many companies. The investor should acquaint himself with the specialized newspapers, such as the *Wall Street Journal* and the *Journal of Commerce* (especially good for a survey of industry trends), and industrial newspapers, such as the *American Metal Market*. Certain weekly publications also contain a convenient review of selected statistics and are the original source of others. The *Commercial and Financial Chronicle*, for example, along with the Securities and Exchange Commission, is the original source of information on new corporate security issues. *Barron's* publishes its own weekly and monthly index of production and trade, which is very useful because it is prompt. This index of business activity is adjusted both for seasonal variation and for secular trend.

The investor should attempt to check his original sources of data before forming any conclusions based on newspaper stories. It should be kept in mind that bizarre and unusual news items sell newspapers. Therefore, newspapers tend to capitalize on the sensational aspects of any news story in order to make the paper more interesting to the reader. The use of news stories exclusively for making investment decisions will usually result in the investor's "running with the herd," and such action will almost always result in losses.

REVIEW QUESTIONS AND PROBLEMS

1. Indicate the sources of information on the contractual terms of specific stocks and bonds.
2. An investor wishes to locate a member of a financial firm who is likely to know the trend of current earnings of a particular company and to have an informed opinion on its management. How might he proceed?
3. An investor knows that some stock of a particular company is outstanding and held publicly, but he cannot find a discussion of the company in the manuals of the investment services. How would you suggest he obtain information on the company?

4. From the manuals and other publications of the various investment services, or any other sources, prepare the following information for a large industrial corporation.
   a) Capitalization, showing total book values of bonds and preferred stock, and total market value and number of shares of common stock outstanding, as of the most recent date.
   b) A 10-year record of the high and low price of the stock and of earnings and dividends per share.
   c) The latest available record of quarterly earnings and dividends per share of common stock, the current market price, and the estimated yield.
   From a study of the products the company produces and the types of markets in which it sells, choose for the industry a suitable value statistic or physical index of output that can be used to compare the trend of the sales or physical output of the company over the last 10 years.
   From a study of the latest issue of a trade magazine, summarize significant recent trends in the industry which will tend to affect the profit prospects of the company.
   From other sources, summarize all the significant news that has appeared concerning the company since the last annual report to stockholders.

5. The following measures of various kinds of economic activity have been listed as those that lead other statistics in measuring the general level of business activity. Determine the original source and what you consider to be the most convenient source document or publication for the following data.
   a) Total liabilities of industrial and commercial failures.
   b) Industrial common stock price index.
   c) New orders, durable goods industries.
   d) Residential building contracts, floor space.

6. What is a prospectus? How can it be used by the investor?

7. How do the Dow-Jones Averages differ from the Standard and Poor's Stock Price Index and the SEC Index? Which of these indexes do you consider the most representative of the general trend of security prices and which is the most useful in your opinion?

8. What are the significant differences between the method of quoting common stock prices, U.S. government bond prices and the municipal bond prices?

CHAPTER **9**

Investment Mechanics and the Security Markets

Most of the capital needed by our national economy is funneled through our system of security markets. A business firm that needs capital funds may secure these funds by selling securities to the public. The initial or primary marketing of securities is a function performed by investment bankers. They act as middlemen by marketing large security issues to many different investors. However, the corporation may place the securities issue privately with institutional investors. Sometimes, this private placement is accomplished without the services of an investment banker.

If investors were not able to convert back into cash the securities purchased on an initial offering, they would not be inclined to invest. As a consequence, there has developed a secondary market for securities. These markets include the over-the-counter market and the organized security exchanges.

In this chapter, the functions and procedures of investment banking and the primary securities markets, as well as the mechanics of buying and selling in the secondary markets, will be described.

PRIMARY MARKETING OF SECURITIES

The short-term financing needs of the industry are met by the commercial banks and various other sources of funds. As a rule, corporations have neither the experience nor the proper machinery to market the securities necessary to fill their long-term borrowing and equity needs. Very often, corporation meets the need for long-term capital by plowing back a portion of earnings into the business. However, when a corporation must go outside its own resources for financing, it

150

must either offer additional securities to present stockholders or sell securities to the public.

If the amount of money required by the corporation is over $1 million, the services of an investment banker are usually used. The investment banker is usually used whether the security is sold publicly or privately placed. When the investment banker assists with a private placement, he is performing, not as a banker, but as an adviser or broker.

Public Sale of Securities

The primary public sale of large issues of securities usually requires the services of an investment banker. The investment banker performs a banking function in that he puts up capital to underwrite (buy) and market the securities. If, for some reason, he is unable to sell the particular security issue at the offering price, the investment banker sells at the best price he can and sometimes experiences a loss.

Larger security issues require larger amounts of money. The amount needed to underwrite an issue may be in excess of the investment banker's resources. In such a case, more investment bankers will be invited to join in a temporary arrangement called a syndicate. The syndicate as a group underwrites the entire issue of securities and resells it to the public.

The investment banker also advises the corporation on the form the financing should take. As an adviser, he should be in a position to recommend the most favorable time for the issuance of securities. To do this, he must be familiar with the credit standing of the corporation, the current buying patterns of investors, and the money market. This type of relationship between corporation and investment banker would result in a negotiated deal, and the relationship would probably be continuous as long as both parties were satisfied with it.

Sometimes, new issues are sold to the highest bidders under competitive bidding procedures required by the Securities and Exchange Commission for large public utility issues or by the Interstate Commerce Commission for most railroads. Competitive bidding is also typical for new issues of government obligations, including federal, state, and municipal issues. When investment bankers form syndicates to bid competitively against one another for the right to market an issue of securities, the issuer must take on the function of evaluating its own credit standing, the current buying patterns of investors, and the money market. It must decide which form of security best fills the need for its long-term capital requirements.

Underwriting Procedure. The Securities Act of 1933 brought the regulation of securities issued in interstate commerce under the control of the federal government. The law requires that a new security issue must be registered with the Securities and Exchange Commission before public offering of the issue, with the following exceptions: (1) United States government obligations, (2) state and municipal bonds, (3) railroad securities, (4) receivers certificates, (5) securities of savings and loan associations and commercial banks, and (6) certain issues not exceeding $300,000 at the option of the SEC.

The SEC requires a registration and copies of all prospectuses to be used, stating specific information on the company, the industry, and any information that might affect the potential security purchaser's decision. The SEC examines the material filed with it but does not pass on the investment quality of the issue. The SEC may issue a deficiency letter, a stop order, or take no action at all. The deficiency letter probably would be received by the underwriters about 10 days after the filing date. It sets forth deficiencies in the materials filed with the SEC that are judged to be honestly left out. On receipt of the deficiency letter, the registrant has an opportunity to correct the erroneous or misleading statement or supply the needed missing information before the indicated effective date. But if the registration statement includes untrue statements or obvious omission of material facts, stop order proceedings are started immediately. The SEC takes positive action only in a restrictive manner. Inaction on the part of the SEC means they have found no reasons why the registration should not be effective on the effective date, usually 20 days after the original filing date.

Meanwhile, the investment banker who originated the underwriting and who usually will manage the syndicate selects certain other investment bankers and invites them to take part in the underwriting. They then draw up among themselves a legal agreement that is effective until the particular underwriting is completed. At this time, there may be formed a selling group that includes additional firms that do not participate in the underwriting but have requested a selling participation.

After the investment banking firm has accepted a participation in an underwriting, that firm's sales force is notified, and they receive a preliminary prospectus, or red herring, which contains most of the features of the securities being offered. The price and terms, not having been agreed on at this time, do not appear in the red herring. Each customer's man in the various houses involved shows the securities to those institutional and individual accounts which they feel might be interested in the particular type of security being offered and information about the company. The actual offering of the securities is made as soon as possible after the price is agreed on, since this lessens the risk assumed by the underwriters that market conditions will change while they own the securities. The manager of the underwriting group may postpone the offering date beyond the effective date, which is 20 days after the original filing of the registration with the Securities and Exchange Commission, but he cannot offer the issue prior to that date. Toward the end of the waiting period, a final meeting, called the "due diligence meeting," takes place. There, the members of the syndicate are brought up to date concerning recent developments with respect to the issuing corporation.

Finally, the issue day arrives after all clearances have been received from regulatory authorities and the due diligence meeting has been held. The underwriting syndicate may retail—sell to their own customers—a certain portion of the issue and allot the balance to members of the selling group. The selling group members make a smaller profit than do the underwriters. Outside the selling group, firms that are members of the National Association of Securities Dealers may purchase securities at a small discount from the offering price for resale to the public.

An additional issue of securities already outstanding obviously cannot be offered at a price higher than the current market price. Under these conditions, the underwriting syndicate may attempt to temporarily support the market price by maintaining a bid for the security at the offering price or slightly below. Such stabilizing activities must be reported to the SEC and in the prospectus, and the maximum amount of purchases that underwriters will make to attain stability is fixed in the agreement among the underwriters.

When a new issue of securities is not well received, the market price may drop abruptly following termination of such market support. Prices of new issues that have been well received may go above the initial offering price. It is important to the underwriters that securities be well placed in the hands of investors who will hold them for a considerable period of time and not dump them on the market because of nervousness or a free riders' desire to realize a speculative profit.

Underwriters may also establish price support for a new issue by overallotment. For example, the group manager may retain for resale by the underwriters $5 million of a bond issue of $10 million, and may allot $6 million to members of the selling group. This represents an overallotment of 20 percent. In effect, the underwriters are selling short. To cover the overallotment, the group manager on behalf of the underwriting group goes into the market and buys bonds that have already been sold. This tends to support the market price.

The group manager keeps a record of the serial numbers of all securities alloted to each house, and securities repurchased by him in performing his stabilization function are redelivered to the proper house and at the actual cost to the trading account, which is the purchase price plus the buying brokerage commission. The house must then sell the same security for the second time, but it is credited with only one commission less brokerage costs. This penalizes the house for its original failure to place the security well. Sometimes, the group manager may cancel the commission of the house on the original sale and reallot the security to another house that can place it more satisfactorily. Once the securities are placed and paid for, the profits or losses from the underwriting can be divided according to the original underwriting agreement and the syndicate can be terminated.

Private Placements

In recent years, there has been an increasing tendency for corporations to sell securities directly to financial institutions, such as insurance companies, pension funds, and trust companies. As mentioned previously, such private placements are frequently made with the assistance of one or more investment bankers. With a private placement, the investment banker takes no underwriting risks. He acts as a finder for and adviser to the corporation placing the issue. Since there are no understanding risks, the marketing costs are somewhat less because the investment banker's fee is smaller. The advantage of the lower costs to the corporation may be offset to some degree, because a more favorable price and better terms usually must be given to the buyer of a private placement.

TABLE 9-1

Corporate Bonds, New Issues, 1957-64

	Total	Publicly Offered	Privately Placed
1957	9,957	6,118	3,839
1958	9,653	6,332	3,320
1959	7,190	3,557	3,632
1960	8,081	4,806	3,275
1961	9,420	4,700	4.720
1962	8,969	4,440	4,529
1963	10,872	4,714	6,158
1964	10,865	3,623	7,243

Source: *Federal Reserve Bulletin.*

This method of financing has become increasing popular in recent years, as indicated by Table 9-1.

SECONDARY MARKETS FOR SECURITIES

The two types of secondary markets for securities are (1) the organized securities exchanges and (2) the over-the-counter market.

The organized exchanges are often referred to as the "auction" markets, while the over-the-counter market is a "negotiated" market. The exchanges provide a focal point where orders to buy and sell may funnel through a specialist who matches them, thereby creating an auction market. The market is made on the floor of the exchange. There are many focal points for an over-the-counter security, since many investment houses may inventory a security and stand ready to buy or sell it. The individual or institution that wants to sell a security over the counter gives the order to his broker, who seeks out the lowest offer or the highest bidder among the various houses and executes the order there.

The Stock Exchanges

A security to be bought and sold on an organized securities exchange must first be listed, or formally accepted, for trading. The requirements for listing on an organized security exchange limit the number of companies whose securities are traded. Listing a security on an exchange requires the approval of the governing body and the filing of a listing application. The listing application is designed to obtain information as to the history, business, and products of the applicant corporation, its capitalization, management, financial condition and operating results, and other pertinent information essential to an informal evaluation of its securities. Investors who wish to buy or sell a listed security using the facilities of the exchange must do so through one of the exchange members.

Memberships or seats on the stock exchanges allow their owners access to the facilities of a central marketplace for each listed security. A brokerage house that owns a seat will use a floor broker to do the actual buying or selling for its customers on the exchange. Orders to buy and sell are transmitted to telephone clerks on the floor, who then pass the orders to a floor broker designated by the firm. The floor broker takes the order to the trading post where each stock is traded and attempts to execute it.

There are 19 trading posts on the floor; about 75 stocks are assigned to each. Specialists who keep the market on each stock stay at the post assigned to that stock, and each specialist has a definite spot on the outside of the post opposite which all trading in the shares is to take place. A specialist is a member of the exchange who maintains a market in one or more specific issues of stock listed on the exchange.

The specialist enters orders in his book as they are received from floor brokers. The market on a stock then becomes the highest price at which an order is listed in his book to buy (bid) and the lowest price another order is listed for sale (offer). Except the highest bid and the lowest offer, the specialist may not disclose the orders he has on his book.

It is necessary to understand the work of the specialist in order to understand how the stock exchange works. He is the funnel through which all round-lot—usually 100 shares—buy-and-sell orders must go to be executed. It is his job to keep a fair and orderly market in a stock. There is sometimes a gap between supply and demand of a stock. A specialist is not expected to keep a stock from rising or falling quickly, but he is expected to keep an orderly succession of prices in the trading pattern of the stock.

An order to buy or sell an odd lot, 99 shares or less, is given to the odd-lot specialist. He executes the order at the price of the next sale and charges a fee for it. His fee is an eighth of a point on stocks below $40, and a quarter of a point on stocks selling at $40 or more. This is in addition to the regular commission charged by the customer's broker. For example, the market order is to buy 50 shares of Ford Motor Company at the market and the next sale after entering the order is 56. The odd-lot buyer pays $56\frac{1}{4}$, plus his regular commission.

Transactions effected on the floor in round lots are printed on the ticker tape soon after the sale takes place. Reporters are stationed at each trading post. When a transaction takes place, it is the duty of the selling broker to tell the nearest reporter the number of shares sold and the price. The reporter writes this information on a slip of paper and gives the note to a page boy, who carries it to a pneumatic tube sending station. Before he puts the note in the tube connecting the post with the ticker operating room, he calls out the name of the stock and the price for the benefit of the odd-lot specialists who are holding orders to execute. All this takes from 10 seconds to over a minute. The reporter also writes out a quote slip each time the bid-and-asked price changes on the stocks for which he is reporting. These are given to the quotation clerk, who keeps the quotation room informed of changes that can be given to any member firm that calls for an up-to-date market.

The Over-the-Counter Market

All stocks now listed on the various security exchanges were first traded in the over-the-counter market. Securities that trade over the counter include virtually all federal, state, and local government bonds, bank and insurance company common stocks, as well as other corporate bonds and preferred and common stocks. Markets for these unlisted stocks in the over-the-counter market are generally made by dealers who initially sold the security as well as by any other dealers who care to maintain an inventory of the security and to trade it.

As previously mentioned, buy-and-sell orders for listed securities are channeled to a specialist who may maintain a position in the security in order to maintain an orderly market. The specialist is the market for a particular listed security. In contrast, an unlisted issue may have different markets in several geographic locations. The many markets made in any one security operate as if each dealer were a specialist operating his own exchange for that security.

Although each dealer in a security operates his own market, he is always contacting other dealers who maintain a market in the security in order to keep his bid-and-asked prices in line with others.

If a dealer in the security wants to increase or decrease his inventory, he may do so by dealing with another dealer who also makes a market in the stock. And even though buy-and-sell orders from inventory are what trigger the whole over-the-counter market, probably one-half to two-thirds of the transactions made by a dealer are to keep his own inventory in line with market trends. He is risking his capital by taking a position in many issues, and he wants to make a profit by trading. He tries to buy low and sell high, just like all investors.

The dealer is forced to continue trading to remain liquid. He must sell to have money to buy when sell orders come into the market. In this way, he keeps replenishing his inventory. The dealer knows he can accomplish this, because each firm that makes a market must stand ready to buy or sell a minimum unit of stock (usually 100 shares) in which he maintains a market. The dealer must be prepared to honor such orders whenever his customers or other dealers want to do business in the stock.

Many thousands of security issues are bought, sold, and quoted every day in the over-the-counter market. In order to communicate these prices, dealers list their names and the stocks in which they specialize in the daily listing service of the National Quotation Bureau. These lists are referred to as the "pink sheets." A broker who wants to purchase a particular security for a customer refers to the pink sheets in order to see what dealers maintain a market in it. The broker then checks these dealers and executes the order with the dealer that offers the best prices.

Inactive Issues

The markets tend to be regional in industrial issues, and some of these are securities of smaller companies or securities not widely distributed among investors. Inactive issues have some peculiar characteristics. First, houses that make a market in these securities are in such close contact with management that they are likely to know much more about changes in outlook than the average investor, who finds published information very meager. As a result, bids and offers may be subject to very rapid change without apparent reason. For very inactive issues such as these, the spread between bid and asked prices may be quite wide and the size of the market small, thereby reducing marketability. It is futile for the buyer or seller of one of these inactive issues to try to hide the size of his transaction by dividing his business among several dealers, because they are in constant contact with one another. The better course would be to select the most competent dealer and let him handle the whole transaction, trusting that he will handle it discreetly.

Secondary Offerings

The sale of large blocks of securities often cannot be conducted in an orderly manner on the security exchanges. Large transactions are similar in some respects to an underwriting and sale of a new issue of securities. These large blocks of securities outstanding, which would customarily be sold on the floor of the exchange, are sometimes sold in the over-the-counter market. Dealers can handle large blocks of securities more effectively, because there are many more nonmember firms than firms that are members of a security exchange. Participation of nonmember firms in the sale of large blocks of securities provides a bigger system to facilitate distribution and sale. Also, sales efforts are likely to be more aggressive, because profits are larger than those obtained from brokerage commissions.

In the event that some investor wants to dispose of a large block of a listed security, for example, a member firm may get permission from the New York Stock Exchange to have a secondary offering. Nonmember firms may participate in soliciting commitments to buy the security before the date of the offering. The price is quoted net to the buyer with no commission, and the profits of the participating firms depend on the spread between the offering price and the negotiated price at which they obtain the securities from the seller. Secondary offerings of securities are not made on the floor of the exchange and are consummated after the close of trading.

The tendency of secondary offerings to divert transactions in listed securities away from the floor of the exchange has caused member firms to devise the "special offering" as a means of handling large transactions in listed securities. The offering takes place on the floor of the exchange during the trading day and is reported on the stock ticker. It is a brokerage transaction, and only member firms may participate in selling; but sales efforts prior to offering the securities to investors tend to assure disposal of the block at the offering price, because commissions may be higher than usual as a result of negotiation.

TRANSACTIONS ON THE STOCK EXCHANGE

The usual procedure for transacting business with a broker may be illustrated by assuming that an individual is considering a purchase of 100 shares of United States Steel Corporation stock. The first step will be a telephone call to a broker to obtain a quote. The broker may say the stock is "ninety five and five eights—seven eights." This means that the most recent bid for the stock is $95\frac{5}{8}$, while the most recent offer is $95\frac{7}{8}$.

Types of Orders

The customer has a choice concerning the type of order he will give the broker. He may instruct the broker to buy "at the market." This order will be sent immediately to the floor of the exchange, where the floor trader will attempt to buy the stock at the best price obtainable. If the previous bid and offer have not changed, he may try a bid of $95\frac{3}{4}$; but it is more likely that he will take the stock at the offered price of $95\frac{7}{8}$, because any delay involves the risk that someone else may accept the offer and the next offered price might be higher. The customer's broker, after being informed of the transaction from the floor, will probably inform the customer by telephone and will mail a written confirmation of the transaction the same day.

The hazard involved in a market order is that the offered price of the stock may rise before the order is executed, and the customer may find that he has purchased stock at a price higher than he expected. This risk can be eliminated if when he gives a market order he places an upper limit on the price that he will pay. The best brokerage practice is to notify the customer of any substantial rise in the offered price that has occurred since the original quote and to ask the customer to name an upper limit.

The customer may place an order to buy stock at any specific price that he designates. He may choose to name a price between the current bid and asked prices, or even "away from the market," perhaps below the current bid. The one advantage in market orders, as compared with orders naming specific prices, is that the customer is assured of getting stock. For example, if a customer places an order to buy stock at the current bid price there is, no doubt, an order ahead of his. He does not know how much stock is bid for, but it could be a substantial amount. If a stock is attractive for investment, more mistakes are made by investors who strive to avoid paying an extra eighth than by those who place market orders that assure purchase of the stock.

Unless the customer specifies to the contrary, an order expires at the end of the trading day on which it is given. Orders for purchase or sale at prices away from the market may be given to remain in effect until the end of the week in which they are placed, or until the end of the month. G.T.C. orders are "good till canceled," but it is the practice of brokers to confirm them again at the end of each month. Instead of assuming responsibility for possible future execution of orders to buy and sell at prices away from the market, brokers delegate this responsibility to specialists on the floor of the exchange. A specialist devotes all his attention to one or more stocks traded at the same trading post on the floor of the exchange. He keeps a record of all bids and offers relating to those stocks at prices above and below the current market price, and he executes orders when he can match bids and offers. This record is called "the book," and the specialist who has access to it has a considerable advantage in judging probable short-term price behavior of those stocks. He is obligated to trade for his own account in order to provide an orderly market in those stocks discussed earlier.

Stop Orders

Stop orders are examples of orders to buy or sell at prices away from the market. The stop order to sell below current market is the most common and is called a "stop-loss order." An illustration will reveal the reason for its use. Suppose an investor has bought a stock at 30 and has seen it rise to 50. He may feel that it is conservative to take profits, but, at the same time, he realizes that speculative fever could conceivably send the stock to 65. He places a stop-loss order at 48. If the stock moves above 50, he may put in new stop-loss orders at 2 or 3 points under the market and follow the stock upward. If, on the other hand, the stock begins a decline from the orginal price of 50, he will be sure to show some profit, certainly not at a price of 50, but just below it. Stop-loss orders are, therefore, of some use in applying the speculative admonition to "let profits ride but cut losses short."

The stop-loss order is not an assured means of attaining success, however. Assume that, after the stop-loss order was placed at 48, the stock briefly dropped to 48 and then began a climb to 65. The investor would have been sold out as the result of a temporary reaction. Moreover, a stop-loss order at a price of 48 is no assurance that the investor will actually be sold out at that price. His stop-loss order does not become effective until there is an actual sale at 48 or below. At that time, his order becomes a market order to sell at the best price obtainable. If the market is in a rapid decline, the best price might be 45. When the market declines to a price at which, for some reason, a lot of traders have placed stop-loss orders, the execution of these orders will contribute to the rapidity of the decline.

Stop-loss orders are also used for reasons other than the attempt to let profits ride. An investor may be going on a trip, or for some other reason may not be able to carefully watch market behavior. He may hold some common stock quoted at 50 and may feel so sure of its quality that he does not believe the stock could sell as low as 45, unless there were a major decline in general stock prices, in which case the price of the stock could go much lower. If he believes there is some possibility of a major reversal of stock prices, he will put a stop-loss order at 45 and perhaps put in similar orders for other holdings.

Stop orders to buy above the market are used by traders to limit their losses on short sales. For short traders, they have the same limitations as have stop-loss orders for long traders. For example, a trader who has sold a stock short at 50 and wishes to limit his losses may put in a stop-loss order to buy at 53. The stock may rise to 55 and then decline to 40, producing a loss for the trader and precluding any gain from the subsequent decline in price.

Delivery

Delivery of a security by the seller must be made on the fourth business day after the transaction takes place. If there is some reason why delivery cannot be made promptly, arrangements may be made with the broker for delayed delivery before making the offer to sell. Delivery also may be made sooner than the regular way. If an owner of a stock wishes to sell on the day a stock goes ex-dividend but does not want to receive the dividend, perhaps because of tax considerations, he can sell "for cash" and make delivery the same day. This transaction permits the new owner to get his name on the record in time to receive the dividend.

The seller must deliver the security properly endorsed. The broker will supply any additional data, including a guarantee of the seller's signature, if the broker knows the seller personally. An endorsed stock certificate is negotiable; if the seller mails it to his broker, he should register and insure it. The certificate is not negotiable if the name of the buyer appears, but the seller seldom knows who the buyer is. To avoid the necessity of endorsing and mailing stock certificates, some security holders leave their securities with the broker in a street name—that is, the name of the broker appears as the owner. This must be done for margin accounts, which will be discussed later.

Brokerage Commissions

Brokerage commissions are payable by both sellers and buyers of securities listed on the security exchanges, but certain taxes levied by the federal government and by state governments are payable only by the seller.

Brokerage commissions for transactions on the New York Stock Exchange depend on the amount of money involved. Rates for odd lots are less, but the odd-lot fee is involved in the price at which such transactions take place. On transactions amounting to $100 or more, the commission, if the total commission exceeds $6.00, cannot exceed $1.50 a share.

| | | Plus Stated Amount: | |
| | *Percent of* | | *For Less Than* |
Money Involved	*Money Involved*	*For 100 Shares*	*100 Shares*
Under $100		As mutually agreed	
$100 to $399	2%	$ 3*	$ 1*
$400 to $2,399	1	7	5
$2,400 to $4,999	1/2	19	17
$5,000 and over	1/10	39†	37†

* Minimum, $6.00.
† Subject to top commission of $1.50 per share or $75 per single transaction.
To compute the commission on multiples of 100 shares, multiply the 100-share rate by the number of 100's involved.

In addition to commissions, the seller must pay federal transfer taxes and, in a New York transaction, state transfer taxes. The federal transfer tax is imposed at the rate of 4 cents on each $100 (or major fraction thereof) of the actual value of the certificates or shares sold or transferred (a major fraction is an amount greater than $50 but less than $100). The maximum transfer tax that can be imposed is 8 cents on each share. On any sale or transfer, a minimum transfer rate tax of 4 cents will be charged. Taxes levied by New York State depend only on the selling price of the stock, as follows.

Price per Share	*Tax per Share*
Under $5.00	$0.01
$ 5.00 and less than $10	0.02
$10 and less than $20	0.03
$20 and above	0.04

To illustrate the costs of typical transactions, Table 9–2 shows a computation of the total commissions and taxes that would be borne by a seller under several different sets of assumptions. Consideration of the small fee of the Securities and Exchange Commission has been omitted.

TABLE 9–2

Illustrations Showing Commissions and Taxes Payable by a Seller of Stocks on the New York Stock Exchange

Number of shares sold	100	100	25	25
Price per share	$ 10.00	$ 75.00	$ 10.00	$ 75.00
Value of transaction	1,000.00	7,500.00	250.00	1,875.00
Brokerage commission	17.00	46.50	6.00	23.75
Federal tax	0.40	3.00	0.08	0.76
State tax	3.00	4.00	0.75	1.00
Odd-lot fee implicit in price	None	None	3.125	6.25
Total costs	20.40	53.50	9.95	31.76
Total costs as a percentage of value of transaction	2.04%	0.71%	5.23%	1.69%

From the percentage that total costs bear to the value of certain types of transactions, it is obvious that the cost of frequent trading in small dollar amounts is substantial. If a trading profit is sought, the cost of both purchase and sale must be considered. This cost of a "round trip" would be nearly double the costs shown here. The high brokerage costs of buying in small dollar amounts also makes it difficult for small investors to acquire adequate diversification.

For bonds, the unit of trading is $1,000 face value. Although a large part of the trading in bonds takes place in the over-the-counter market, Table 9–3 shows the commission rate charged for bonds traded on the New York Stock Exchange. The federal tax on sale of corporate bonds is 50 cents per $1,000 of principal. No tax is levied on the sale of bonds by New York State.

TABLE 9-3

Commission Rates on Sale of Corporate Bonds
New York Stock Exchange
Price per $1,000 of Principal Amount

Selling at less than 1 ($10) $0.75
Selling at 1 ($10) and above but under 10 ($100) $1.25
Selling at 10 ($100) and above $2.50

The Monthly Investment Plan

The New York Stock Exchange has devised a plan that enables the smaller investor to purchase in relatively small amounts the stock listed on the exchange. The Monthly Investment Plan allows the investor to put as little as $40 per quarter in common stock of a company of his choice. The investor signs an agreement with the broker to invest an amount between a minimum of $40 per quarter of a year and a maximum of $1,000 per month. The purchases are made at the odd-lot price established the day the remittance is credited to the account of the investor. The broker will purchase for the account of the investor as many full and fractional shares (less than one share) as his periodic investment will justify. The investor's option is to have the cash dividends reinvested in the stock or paid to him. This agreement can be terminated at any time either by the broker or the investor. However, the broker normally would not be interested in terminating the arrangement unless the investor has not kept up his payments.

This plan provides a method of regular periodic investment. The only advantages it has over odd-lot purchases of stock on a periodic basis are: (1) by signing the agreement the investor usually invests the agreed-on amount, which he may not have done otherwise; and (2) the plan provides a means of purchasing fractional shares, which cannot be done in the usual odd-lot transaction.

The commissions are the same as the odd-lot commissions discussed earlier. Some typical transactions are shown in Table 9-4.

There are no additional charges nor are there any penalties if the plan is terminated.

Buying on Margin

Buying a security on margin means that the buyer borrows from his broker a portion of the cost of the security. Only listed securities,

TABLE 9-4

Typical Transactions, Monthly Investment Plan

Payment	Amount Invested at Odd-Lot Prices	Commission Amount	Percent
$ 40	$ 37.74	$ 2.26	6.0%
60	56.60	3.40	6.0
80	75.47	4.53	6.0
100	94.34	5.66	6.0
200	194.00	6.00	3.1
300	292.16	7.84	2.7
500	489.11	10.89	2.2
1,000	984.16	15.84	1.6

Source: *The Story of The Monthly Investment Plan*, Merrill Lynch, Pierce, Fenner and Smith, 70 Pine St., New York 5, N.Y.

including unlisted bonds or preferred stocks that are convertible into listed common stocks, can be bought on margin. The amount that may be borrowed is regulated by the Federal Reserve Board of Governors. If the margin requirement fixed by the Federal Reserve Board is 70 percent, let us say, the purchaser may borrow 30 percent of the total cost of acquiring the securities, including commissions. Interest is charged on the loan. When the customer has not borrowed up to the full amount allowable, the broker will frequently add interest, as it is due, to the principal of the customer's debt. Unless the customer pays interest in cash, however, it cannot be deducted as an expense when computing personal income tax liability.

Let us assume for simplicity in calculation that the required margin is 50 percent, and that a customer opens an account by purchasing 100 shares of a stock at 15 and 100 shares of another at 25. The total cost is $4,000. For illustrative purposes, the commissions are excluded from the calculation. The 50 percent required margin is $2,000. The customer decides to be conservative and borrow only $1,800. His equity at the market price of the stock is thus $2,200, or $200 in excess of the margin requirement. This excess is called an excess margin. With it, he can purchase $400 of additional stock without reducing the margin of the whole account below 50 percent.

If, however, the stock he originally bought for 25 declined in market value to 20, the value of his holdings will total only $3,500. Accounts are valued at the closing prices for the securities on the previous trading day. After deducting his debt, his equity is only $1,700, which is $50 lower than the required margin of 50 percent. The account is then said to be undermargined. He could make good the deficiency by putting up $50 in cash or $100 in market value of additional securities. Actually, Federal Reserve Board regulations do not require him to put up any additional margin. Customers with undermargined accounts can even sell securities and withdraw proceeds if the transaction does not increase the deficiency. Likewise, to buy additional securities a margin of 50 percent must be put up, but no additional funds need be posted to reduce the deficiency against other securities.

Accounts that have very thin margins, however, may be subject to controls from other jurisdictions. The rules of the New York Stock Exchange provide for a minimum margin of 25 percent (30 percent in the case of short sales). Even before this limit is reached, the broker may ask the customer to put up additional margin. The danger of buying on margin is that the customer, in the event of a bad break in security prices, may not be able to produce sufficient margin, and the broker will be forced to sell securities at temporarily depressed prices. The potential advantage in buying on margin is that the purchaser can increase the percentage capital gain on his equity. If stock bought on a 50 percent margin appreciates 10 percent, the investor has a 20 percent gain in the value of his equity.

Selling Short

The investor sells a stock short when he sells a stock that he does not own. In order to make delivery, his broker will borrow the stock from someone who does own it and deliver it to the purchaser. The investor hopes that the stock will later decline in price so that he can buy it cheaper than he sold it and thus return the borrowed stock.

According to regulations of the Securities and Exchange Commission, no short sale can be made at market except on an uptick in price. That is, the most recent round-lot sale, which cannot be a short sale, must be at a price at least an eighth higher than the price of the preceding round-lot sale. If the most recent sales were all made at the same price, the investor may go back even into the previous trading day to find the first sale made at a different price. The theory behind this regulation is that a proper function of short selling is to dampen the enthusiasm of investors during periods of rising prices, but not to create an added amount of selling during periods of falling prices.

The customer's broker will borrow the stock for the short seller, perhaps lending stock that is in the margined account of one of his customers, if the customer has given consent. Or the broker may borrow the stock from another broker. It will clarify the procedure to think of the brokers as lending and borrowing the stock. Brokers interested in borrowing or lending stock indicate their intention at the loan desk on the floor of the exchange, or they call other brokers who may have stock to lend.

To illustrate, when an investor sells 100 shares of United States Steel Corporation stock short at 95, he may put up a margin of $9,500 with the broker or a minimum of at least half of the short sale, or $4,750, if margin requirements are 50 percent. The broker for the investor who has sold short borrows the 100 shares of United States Steel stock from another broker who has the stock to lend. The short seller's broker deposits the proceeds of the short sale with the broker who lends the stock, as security for the loan of the stock. The broker who lends the stock frequently pays interest to the short seller on these proceeds of the short sale. Whether or not interest is paid on these funds depends on the supply of stock available for lending and the demand for the stock by short sellers. If the stock is very difficult to borrow, short sellers may have to pay a fee to borrow it.

If the sale of 100 shares of United States Steel at 95 was a margin transaction, the seller deposited $4,750 in his brokerage account to cover the liability that might be incurred if the seller had to buy back the stock in the future at a price higher than 95. In addition, he left the gross proceeds of the sale with the broker. If the price of the U.S. Steel stock should rise to 100, the margin in the customer's account would be less than 50 percent, and the proceeds of the short sale would no longer be equal to the market value of the loaned stock. When a substantial rise in price has taken place, the broker may ask the short seller to put up more funds. Refunds may be made in the event of substantial price declines. The short seller, of course, must pay to the broker the equivalent amount of any dividends paid on the borrowed stock in order that the lender of the stock may receive them.

So long as stock can be borrowed, there is no limit on the length of time a trader may remain short; but remaining short for a long time may involve considerable expense, such as payment of dividends and perhaps premiums on borrowed stock. A successful short sale must be followed by a market price drop for which the seller does not have to wait too long. Short selling also involves other special risks.

The investor who buys stock for $1,000 can lose no more than $1,000. The trader who sells stock short for $1,000 could lose $2,000 if the stock tripled in price. There is also the possibility that a shortage of stock available to borrowers will develop. Owners of the stock may ask for a termination of the loan at any time.

The borrower must return exactly the same class of stock that was borrowed. This makes short sales of stocks of companies in reorganization somewhat dangerous. Borrowed stock must be returned before new securities replace the old stock of the company going through reorganization. The rush of traders to buy stock to cover their short positions before the reorganization is consummated may cause the stock to rise instead of fall in price.

Puts, Calls, Straddles, and Spreads

Dealers offer for sale various types of options that give the buyer of the option the right to buy stock from, or sell stock to, the dealer who sold the option at a price specified in the contract. The dealer who offers the option for sale is known as the maker. The price at which he offers the option, called the premium, is for the privilege of buying or selling a round lot of a specific stock. The privilege expires at the end of a specified period of time, generally 30, 60, or 90 days. The option may grant the privilege of either buying or selling the stock at the market price prevailing at the time the option is made, or it may be at a price above or below that price.

The word "premium" is used to designate the price charged for such an option, because the business of making options is somewhat similar to writing insurance. Options are available for most actively traded stocks, and certain dealers who specialize in these options offer a great variety of options on a long list of stocks. They will lose money on some options, but they rely on the law of averages to return them a profit out of the premiums charged. Investors who use such options also regard their cost as payment for insurance against larger potential losses.

Puts. A put is an option to sell stock to the seller of the option at a specified price. Suppose an investor buys 100 shares of General Motors Corporation stock at its opening price of $113 on October 27, 1965. He believes that over the next three months the stock may go as high as $120 a share. He wants to avoid a chance of a sizable loss. To escape this possibility, he purchases a 90-day option to sell 100 shares at $113 for $525. This is the maximum he can lose. On the other hand, he would not buy this insurance if he felt that General Motors stock would advance only moderately in price. The cost of the put requires that the price of General Motors rise above $118\frac{1}{4}$ before he can break even.

The cost of a put will vary with market conditions, the length of time the option runs, and whether the put is at the market or away from the market. At the time a stock is selling at 50, for example, the cost of a 30-day put at 3 points away from the market—that is, at 47—will be less than the cost of a 90-day put at market, because before the 30-day put can be exercised profitably the stock must decline, and there is less time for the decline to take place. Puts—as well as calls which shall be discussed presently—when quoted away from the market are offered at a constant price of $137.50 for 30 days. Variation in the risk to the dealer is reflected in the variation in number of points away from the market. Puts and calls away from the market for longer periods of time are available only through special negotiations.

Thirty-day puts away from the market can be used instead of short sales by traders who want to limit potential losses to a small amount. Thus, a trader can buy an option to sell a stock at 47 when it is selling at 50, wait until the stock goes to 39, buy the stock, and exercise the put or option to sell. If the stock never declines below 50, he will lose the cost of the put. If the stock declines promptly but goes no lower than 47, he will not exercise the put, but his option will have appreciated in market value, for it is now a put at market for a period only slightly less than 30 days. The important consideration is that he can lose no more than the cost of the put, no matter how high the stock should go above 50.

Calls. A call is the reverse of a put. It is an option to buy stock from a dealer at a specified price. Calls may be at the market price or away from the market. Away from the market, for a call, is above the present market prices. Investors who believe that the price of a stock will rise will buy a call. This takes less capital than buying the stock, even when the account is margined. Calls can also be used to limit losses on short sales. If a stock is sold short at 50, the seller may also buy a call at market, or 50. This will assure him that he will always be able to get stock at 50 to cover his short sale in case the stock advances. If the stock declines to 39, he covers his short sale, and his profits are reduced by the cost of the call, which is not exercised. The call can also be used to freeze a profit on a short sale. If a short sale is made at 50 and the stock declines to 39, a call at market can be bought, and the trader is assured of his profit, less the cost of the call, regardless of what the stock does thereafter. If the price of the stock declines below 39, the trader will, of course, cover at lower prices and not exercise the call.

It should be noted that more than one trade can be made under the protection of a put or a call. Suppose, for example, that a stock is selling at 50. An investor who believes that the stock will advance buys a 30-day call at 53. When the stock advances to 57, he may sell short at this price. He is certain that he can acquire stock at 53 to cover. A reaction then carries the stock down to 50 again. The investor covers by buying stock at this price. If the stock rises again to 56, he can again sell short, knowing that his losses are protected by the call. Such trading may continue during the life of the call; the option may never be exercised. The option merely provides insurance against large losses.

Straddles and Spreads. What has already been said about the use of puts and calls should be enough to explain the reason for the straddle, which is merely a combined put and call at the market. A straddle for a stock selling at 50 is both a call at 50 and a put at 50. The cost is, of course, greater than a put or a call alone. A spread is a combined put and call at prices away from the market. A spread for a stock selling at 50 may be a call on the stock at 53, and a put on the stock at 47. Within the protection that such contracts afford, the trader will hope that frequent trades will accumulate enough profits to offset the cost of the protection.

The high cost of buying insurance against a permanent loss in market value is shown by the premiums demanded for puts and calls running for 90 days, as of October 25, 1965, as shown in Table 9–5, page 172. The options are at market, and the premiums have been expressed as the dollar cost of the put and call options for 90 days. The cost of insurance for a year would be over four times this much.

SUMMARY

The primary market for securities is dominated by the investment banker, a financial middleman who brings together the issues of securities and the investors. The investment banker, like any merchant, places his own capital in new securities, not for investment, but for almost immediate resale at a profit. He may do this by out-

TABLE 9-5

Selected Premiums for 90-day Puts and Calls
October 25, 1965

		Premiums per 100 Shares	
Stock	*Price*	*Puts*	*Calls*
American Telephone & Telegraph ..$ 67		$225	$300
General Motors $111		$525	$650
Standard Oil of New Jersey ....$ 82		$437.50	$487.50

right purchase of new issues by negotiation or competitive bidding. The investment banker may also use his specialized knowledge to assist the corporation in privately placing the securities with a financial institution.

After the initial issuance, securities are then traded in the secondary market. The secondary securities market includes the organized security exchanges and the over-the-counter markets. The organized exchanges provide a single focal point from which to execute brokers' orders for a particular stock for their customers. If the stock is unlisted, it is traded in the over-the-counter market. The over-the-counter market is made up of many different markets provided by the dealers who position the security and stand ready to buy and sell it.

REVIEW QUESTIONS AND PROBLEMS

1. Distinguish between the economic function of the organized security exchange and the investment banker.
2. In a primary offering of securities, what is the difference between a syndicate participation and a selling group participation?
3. What are the differences between a primary offering, a secondary offering, and a special offering?
4. Describe the procedure used in the underwriting of securities.
5. What types of new security issues are exempt from registration with the Securities and Exchange Commission?
6. What are the major differences between the organized security exchanges and the over-the-counter markets? Is it possible for a firm to be a member of an organized security exchange and still participate in the over-the-counter market?
7. Point out the major risks and potential advantages of the following:
   a) Using market orders to purchase stocks.
   b) Limiting losses by stop loss orders.

c) Buying common stock on margin.

d) Selling short.

8. Warrants, rights, and calls all have one common characteristic. What is it? How are they different?

9. In what capacity does a member firm act:

   a) When it executes an order to buy a stock on the exchange?

   b) When it buys a stock for the account of the firm?

10. Could an investor accomplish precisely the same results through voluntary systematic purchases that could be accomplished through the Monthly Investment Plan?

11. Why would an investor ever have any interest in purchasing a straddle?

CHAPTER **10**

Introduction to Security Analysis

The investment policy outlines, in general terms, the investor's objectives and his relative ability or willingness to assume risk. The next step in investment management is selection of media that meet the general investment policy specifications. It is nearly always possible for the investor to find suitable media to meet any realistic investment objectives because of the wide range of investment possibilities.

The types of investment media range all the way from the low-income, stable-value savings deposits of insured commercial banks to the most speculative common stocks. With each investment medium in this wide range, the investor has the problem of value determination. The determination of investment media value is the end product of investment analysis. Most institutional investment media—for example, saving deposits—do not require specific analysis and valuation, because their values fluctuate within such narrow ranges.[1]

DEFINITION OF INVESTMENT ANALYSIS

Investment analysis may be defined to include (1) determination of an investor's needs and (2) selection of the proper media to satisfy these needs. The first step in investment analysis is to determine the investor's objectives. These objectives may vary widely with vastly differing needs for quality of investments, liquidity, income, and income and estate tax position. These factors and their impact on investment analysis were discussed in Chapter 7.

The next step is to determine the security's quality and its value

---

[1] There are exceptions, such as investment company shares. The analysis of the value and risk characteristic of these media is discussed in Chapter 17.

in relation to its price. Emphasis on both quality and value helps the analyst to better select securities that suit the investor's needs as well as to purchase securities that are reasonably priced. That is, a security may be undervalued but not of sufficiently high quality to justify its purchase. The purpose of security analysis, then, is to determine: (1) the quality of the security and (2) whether or not the security is undervalued or overvalued in terms of current market.

APPROACHES TO SECURITY ANALYSIS

Security analysis is a specialized form of economic analysis that focuses attention on the individual firm or company. Anything that may affect the fortunes and prospects of the company is worthy of the analyst's attention.

The analyst must, of course, find some way or approach to efficiently sift out, examine, and weigh these factors if he is to analyze competently. To be worthwhile, an analytical approach must be an analysis of the causative factors that will effect change in the basic value factors of the company, such as sales and profits. In other words, security analysis is a systematic examination of the factors that affect the present value of the security and its quality.

There is a surprising diversity of opinion on which approach is the best to achieve the goal of security value and quality determination. The difference of opinion concerns not so much what factors should be examined as what importance should be attached to each of them. That is, the difference is primarily one of emphasis rather than of substance. The two basic approaches to security value and quality determination are (1) the technical market analysis approach and (2) the appraised or intrinsic value approach.

Market Analysis

Some analysts use market analysis as a means of predicting future levels of specific common stock prices and future levels of the stock market prices in general. There are several different methods or techniques of market analysis, all of which have one thing in common. Each market analysis technique uses a time series of market prices as a basis for valuing common stock. The analyst plots the daily prices and studies the pattern of these prices over a period of time. Various price patterns give the analyst buy signals (the stock is undervalued) and sell signals (the stock is overvalued). Thus, market analysis is used to determine the relative value of common stock. The specific techniques used will be discussed in detail in Chapter 20.

The usefulness of technical market analysis is limited. First, market analysis does not establish the quality of securities. It uses the same pattern of analysis to determine value irrespective of the quality of the securities. It might indicate that a low-grade common stock is a good buy when the investor should have only high-quality securities in his portfolio. Second, market analysis techniques are designed to forecast short-run changes in common stock prices, while the average investor is interested in longer-term commitments. Third, no market analysis technique is available for forecasting bond prices.

The major shortcoming in market analysis techniques is that they tend to oversimplify rather complex economic phenomena. These techniques are superficial in that they assume the best index of a company's financial performance is the market action of its common stock. Therefore, attention is not concentrated on the causative factors, such as sales, earnings, and dividends, but on the end result—market price.

Intrinsic Value Approach

The goal of the intrinsic value approach is to determine from an analysis of the basic factors affecting a company's earnings potential whether or not (1) the securities meet minimum quality standards and needs, and (2) the company's securities are a good buy at present market prices. Ideally, the analyst hopes that his appraisal of the company will result in an independent specific appraised value. That is, the analyst would like to be able to say with confidence, after analysis, that the common stock of company A is worth $28.50 a share. An analyst cannot hope to be that specific and absolute in his estimates with any degree of accuracy. He should say only that the common stock of company A, after an examination and analysis of all pertinent facts, is relatively a good buy at present market prices. That is, the analyst can only hope to evaluate the security in relative terms.

The intrinsic value approach to security analysis involves an examination of both qualitative and quantitative data. Qualitative analysis can best be described as an analysis of factors affecting a company's earning potential which cannot be measured numerically, such as quality of the company's management. Quantitative analysis involves an analysis of definite quantities or actual performance as measured by financial and operating statistics.

Qualitative Analysis

A number of qualitative factors influence the value of a company's securities. The characteristic of a qualitative factor is that it usually deals with something that will happen in the future, and the present estimate of its effect is not definitely measurable.

Many investors rely almost entirely on qualitative developments in making investment decisions. The investor who, in selecting securities, emphasizes these qualitative factors without reference to a company's past performance tends to lose perspective. He is influenced by the news. He tends to sell on bad news and buy on good news. The widespread use of qualitative analysis is indicated by the action of common stock market prices when a company announces a new development that affects its future prospects.

The problem in considering only the qualitative factors is that the analyst does not have a reference point or bench mark. A rational consideration of the effect of prospective new developments on the value of a company's stock often seems to be virtually impossible for many investors. They seem to get swept up in a tide of emotions, which causes them to overcompensate for both favorable and unfavorable developments. They often bid up prices of common stock of some companies to a point that even a superficial analysis of the past financial performance would indicate is not justified.

For example, the common stock of Communications Satellite Corporation was sold in June, 1964, at $20. In the prospectus, it was stated that the company would not have any significant operating revenue before 1967 and might operate at a loss for a number of years after 1967. In addition, the management announced that no dividends would be paid for an indeterminate period. Even with this rather bland and bleak prognosis, investors have bid the stock of Communications Satellite up to as high as $71 a share.

These investors are obviously bidding up the price of Communications Satellite common stock on a purely qualitative basis, since the company has no operating performance. Conversely, investors often get panicked by bad news and sell securities prematurely. To avoid these extremes, the analyst should study the past financial and operating performance of companies in evaluating the news of developments that affect companies.

Quantitative Analysis

To make a complete analysis, the analyst should study past financial and operating performances of the companies, as well as the qualitative factors. The study of financial data is usually referred to as quantitative analysis, because it is an analysis of definite quantities or actual performance as measured by financial and operating statistics. These data include industry statistics, company production, plant and expenditure, and financial data as well as the balance sheet and income statement. The security analyst typically concentrates on the analysis of financial statements, because financial statement data reduce the company's operations to dollars and because these data are almost always available to the investor. Other quantitative data, such as production statistics and plant capacity, are also useful, but they are not always available nor are they uniformly reported.

The primary advantage of financial statement analysis is its objectivity. The analyst is able to concentrate his attention on the key factors in security analysis—profitability and working capital adequacy. However, financial statement analysis should not be used to the exclusion of qualitative analysis unless the analysis assumes that the past performance of the company is indicative of the future.

Importance of Market Price Fluctuations

The future market price of the security is generally a secondary consideration to the income investor. He has established an income goal based on his personal requirements. Short-run market price changes in the security do not concern him so long as they are not a reflection of an impairment of the company's earning power. Otherwise, price changes result only in opportunity losses or gains, providing he is not forced to sell the security. The capital appreciation investor is primarily interested in the future market price of the security. He is, as a matter of admitted policy, interested in capital gain, and he usually confines his commitments to those securities that afford the greatest possible gain, usually common stock.

Use of security analysis and establishment of independent appraised value are of real significance only when they are reflected in the market price of the common stock. It is assumed that the independent value of a common stock will eventually, if not immediately, be recognized by other investors, and the market price will gravitate toward this independent value derived from security analysis. If this is not the case, security analysis is useless to the capital appreciation investor. Indeed, there are investors who suggest that it is useless, because the future market price of a company's stock often does not reflect the optimistic or pessimistic forecasts of the company's performance indicated by security analysis. It is altogether possible that investors collectively (the market for the stock) will fail to recognize the merits, potential, or lack of potential of a particular company or industry. This failure may result in the common stock's not advancing (or declining) in price over a complete market cycle. However, in investment management and analysis, patience is usually rewarded. Consider that International Business Machines common stock has sold as low as $3.50 a share during the last 20 years, and as high as $494 a share in 1964.

Summary

The goals of the intrinsic value approach to security analysis are to determine the relative quality of the security and to decide whether the security is or is not a good buy at current market prices. To achieve these goals, the analyst uses both qualitative and quantitative analysis. The analyst interested in a systematic intensive appraisal of a company and its prospects will find that the use of both qualitative and quantitative analysis is necessary. Analysis of financial statements brings the analyst's knowledge of the company up to the present. At this point, the analyst must decide whether the company's future prospects are better than, worse than, or about the same as its past performance. Since the value of a company's securities are based on its future performance, the analyst must consider the qualitative factors in completing the analysis and in making the valuation of the common stock.

The analyst can eventually test his subjective judgments of these qualitative factors. As time passes, the accuracy of his estimates is reflected by the quantitative data, such as sales, earnings, or changes in capital structure. The final test of the analyst's ability to make sound qualitative decisions is his success in selecting securities that measure up to forecast performance. The purpose of quantitative analysis is to reduce to the absolute minimum the necessary degree of judgment that is unsupported by fact.

SECURITY ANALYSIS PROCEDURE

Security analysis, like any other form of economic analysis, is not a mechanical process. That is, the analyst cannot use a few formulas and ratios to determine the quality and value of securities. It is possible, however, to follow a well-defined procedure in security analysis.

The first step is the preliminary screening or sifting from thousands of investment possibilities specific securities that deserve further consideration. The standards used to select candidates for further analysis are the usual indicators of value, such as earnings and market price. The precise measures used depend on whether the security under consideration is common stock, preferred stock, or bonds.

The next step is an investigation and appraisal of the industry's prospects, because the corporation's earnings potential is tied to the economic prospects of the industry. As a part of this industry analysis, the analyst also should make an estimate of the nation's economic potential, both long term and short range, as these economic segments are closely intertwined.

The third step is the quantitative and qualitative analysis of the firm. This step involves an analysis of the company's financial strength, quality of its management and its earnings potential.

Finally, the analyst must interpret the analysis to make judgments as to the relative quality of the security as well as the earnings potential of the company. Implicit in this process is an examination of the legal characteristics of the security with respect to its claim on the earnings and assets of the corporation. This last step includes the estimate of future earnings as a prelude to making the ultimate decision on whether it is overvalued or undervalued in terms of current market price.

Obviously, the analyst may deviate from the general procedure outlined above if he thinks that certain modifications may enable him to make a more accurate appraisal. He may place more emphasis on one phase of the analysis, such as the qualitative aspects when government regulation is a major factor in value determination. In fact, in the following discussion of the problems and techniques of security analysis the analyses of industrials and the various regulated industries—railroads, public utilities, etc.—are discussed separately, even though the general procedure outlined above will be followed.

Preliminary Screening

The first task confronting the analyst is to select from the securities available those that he is going to analyze in detail. The investor's general needs, as indicated by his investment policy, enable him to narrow his choice somewhat. For example, if the investor's objective is capital gain or appreciation he will be able to eliminate most bonds and preferred stocks. Conversely, if his objective is a stable income the investor should eliminate from consideration those common and preferred stocks that do not pay dividends, or companies whose earnings are so unstable that dividend payments are erratic. Therefore, the analyst eliminates all securities that have contractual characteristics which by their very nature are not suitable for his further consideration.

In addition, the analyst must give consideration to screening of securities that do not meet minimum quality requirements. The investment services, Moody's and Standard and Poor's, give general quality indications. These quality ratings for bonds are based on the relative certainty of payment of interest and principal. The highest rating is awarded to bonds that have ultimate protection as to interest and principal. Similar ratings are awarded to preferred stock, and the basis for the rating is the relative security of dividends as evidenced by overall dividend coverage. Common stock quality ratings combine measures of earnings stability and earnings growth. The highest quality ratings go to stocks that exhibit both stability of earnings over the past eight years and earnings growth.

These quality indications or ratings are valuable and useful in screening. The analyst can save time and effort in using them to eliminate situations that do not meet an investor's minimum quality requirements.

The basic tools for screening securities differ for bonds, preferred stock, and common stock. The analyst should be interested in the following types of data for each type of security.

FIGURE 10–1

TXT[1]   # Textron Inc.   2218

Stock—	Approx. Price	Dividend	Yield
COMMON (NEW)	41⅞	[2]$1.00	[2]2.4%
$1.25 CONV. PREFERRED	90½	1.25	1.4

RECOMMENDATION: Textron has developed an expanding and broadly diversified sales base through acquisitions and an aggressive product development program. Integration of new lines and various cost-reduction programs have produced an improving trend of profit margins. Expanding orders for helicopters, a sharp rise in 1965 earnings and the favorable outlook for 1966 have lifted share prices to new peaks. However, the shares (split 2-for-1) are still worth holding for the growth potential.

** Charted on special comparable scales; values not shown.

SALES (Million $)

Quarter:	1965	1964	1963	1962	1961
March	197.0	165.1	141.7	132.2	98.0
June	205.3	169.5	144.6	139.7	115.3
Sept.	213.1	190.0	139.9	132.1	122.4
Dec.		195.6	160.8	145.5	137.4

Sales for the nine months ended October 2, 1965 rose 17% from those of the like 1964 period to a new interim high. While the sales expansion covered all product groups, an increase in helicopter volume was especially important. The favorable economic climate, growth of new products and increasing efficiency contributed to wider margins. Operating income advanced 23.2%. Depreciation and interest charges were larger, but other expenses declined. Pretax earnings increased 30% and were equal to 6.8% of sales, up from 6.1% a year earlier. After lower taxes at 49.5%, against 50%, net income advanced 31.2%. Earnings were equal to $1.91 a share, up from $1.48, as adjusted for the 2-for-1 split in December, 1965.

[3]COMMON SHARE EARNINGS ($)

Quarter:	1965	1964	1963	1962	1961
March	0.57	0.46	0.40	0.34	0.01
June	0.64	0.49	0.43	0.35	0.16
Sept.	0.70	0.53	0.42	0.35	0.40
Dec.		0.56	0.46	0.44	0.46

PROSPECTS

Near Term—Sales for 1965 are estimated at $830 million, up from $720 million in 1964. Earnings are estimated at around $2.65 a share, up from the $2.04 of 1964, as adjusted for the 2-for-1 split in December, 1965.

A further sales gain of some $100 million is in prospect for 1966 (including $30 million from the acquisition of W. A. Sheaffer Pen Co., scheduled for early 1966). Military orders for UH-1 type helicopters exceed $300 million. New products, expanding capacity and other acquisitions enhance potentials. With wider margins expected, continued earnings improvement is likely in 1966. Dividends have been initiated at $0.25 quarterly on the split shares, up from the equivalent of $0.22½ (adj.) on the presplit shares.

Long Term— Product development through an aggressive research program, expansion of foreign business and further acquisitions should produce continued growth of sales. Plant and equipment improvements and various cost-savings programs should also contribute to earnings growth.

RECENT DEVELOPMENTS

Acquisition of W. A. Sheaffer Pen Co. for some $19.4 million is planned. Sheaffer, a leading maker of writing instruments and electronic hearing aids, earned $590,000 on sales of $15,142,000 in the six months ended August 31, 1965. In late 1965, concerns making hand tools and die forgings were acquired.

DIVIDEND DATA

At January 2, 1965, $51,000,000 of surplus was not restricted. Dividends in the past 12 months were:

Amt. of Div. $	Date Decl.	Ex-divd. Date	Stock of Record	Payment Date
0.45. . .	Feb. 24	Mar. 10	Mar. 15	Apr. 1'65
0.45. . .	May 26	Jun. 10	Jun. 15	Jul. 1'65
0.45. . .	Jul. 28	Sep. 10	Sep. 15	Oct. 1'65
*.	. . . .	Jan. 3	Dec. 17	Dec. 31'65

*2-for-1 split.

        ---Aft. 2-for-1 split---

| 0.25. . . | Oct. 27 | Dec. 14 | Dec. 17 | Jan. 1'66 |

[1]Listed N.Y.S.E., Midwest S.E. & Pacific Coast S.E.; Com. also traded Boston, Detroit & Phila.-Balt.-Wash. S.Es.   [2]Indicated rate.   [3]Adj. for 2-for-1 split in Dec., 1965.

STANDARD LISTED STOCK REPORTS   STANDARD & POOR'S CORP.
© 1966 Standard & Poor's Corp. All rights reserved. Reproduction in whole or in part without written permission is strictly prohibited.
Published at Ephrata, Pa. Editorial & Executive Offices, 345 Hudson St., New York, N. Y. 10014
Vol. 33, No. 1   Monday, January 3, 1966   Sec. 8

FIGURE 10–2

2218 **TEXTRON INCORPORATED**

INCOME STATISTICS (Million $) AND PER SHARE ($) DATA

Year Ended Dec. 31	Net Sales	%Oper. Inc. of Sales	Oper. Inc.	Depr. & Amort.	Net Bef. Taxes	Net Inc.	[1]$1.25 Pfd. Earns.	—[2]Common— Earns.	Divs. Paid	———Price Range——— $1.25 Pfd.	[2]Common	Price-Earns. Ratios HI LO
1966--	-----	---	----	----	----	----	-----	---	0.25	---------	---------	-----
1965--	-----	---	----	----	----	----	-----	---	0.87½	100 -56¼	47¼ -25⅞	-----
1964--	720.21	8.1	58.58	11.70	44.09	22.09	119.70	2.04	0.77½	56¾ -42½	26⅞ -19⅝	13-10
1963--	587.05	7.4	43.69	10.38	32.25	18.05	66.20	1.71	0.68⅛	43 -32	20⅜ -14¾	12- 9
1962--	549.49	8.0	44.14	11.85	26.67	14.77	41.69	1.48	0.62½	36⅝ -26⅝	15⅝ -11¼	11- 8
1961--	473.12	6.9	32.87	11.05	14.45	10.55	29.67	1.03	0.62½	31½ -24⅞	14¾ -10⅜	14-10
1960--	383.19	8.7	33.31	8.62	16.86	14.17	38.43	1.46	0.62½	26½ -22¾	12⅜ - 9⅜	8- 6
1959--	308.20	10.4	31.94	8.09	14.92	14.27	38.74	1.43	0.56¼	31⅞ -23	14⅝ - 9⅞	10- 7
1958--	244.23	9.9	24.12	8.23	10.76	10.76	25.44	1.15	0.50	24 -15¾	10⅞ - 4⅞	10- 4
1957--	254.58	8.6	21.76	8.26	8.70	8.70	20.57	1.12	0.57½	21 -15⅛	10¾ - 5	10- 4
1956--	245.79	7.5	18.48	7.04	6.50	6.50	15.32	0.79	0.80	29⅝ -20⅜	14⅞ -10⅛	19-13
1955--	191.57	8.3	15.86	4.45	5.32	5.50	8.81	0.74	0.30	25¾ -18	12¾ - 6	17- 8

PERTINENT BALANCE SHEET STATISTICS (Million $)

Dec. 31	Gross Prop.	Capital Expend.	Cash Items	Inventories	Receivables	——Current—— Assets	Liabs.	Net Workg. Cap.	Cur. Ratio Assets to Liabs.	Long Term Debt	[2]($) Book Val. Com. Sh.
1964--	140.26	21.00	15.61	125.90	88.30	232.20	107.47	124.73	2.2–1	57.91	14.69
1963--	115.68	18.88	16.34	107.72	74.42	200.49	95.20	105.23	2.1–1	35.56	13.55
1962--	147.64	9.74	16.80	108.32	77.74	204.88	95.83	109.05	2.1–1	73.06	12.28
1961--	151.72	55.34	21.22	94.57	67.88	185.84	71.38	114.46	2.6–1	89.83	11.41
1960--	133.29	14.10	20.18	83.15	49.14	159.39	65.04	94.35	2.5–1	83.52	10.27
1959--	116.92	23.21	14.53	68.03	32.35	120.25	34.35	85.89	3.5–1	62.24	9.66
1958--	132.09	4.32	7.85	56.70	25.21	93.96	33.26	60.70	2.8–1	53.76	8.16
1957--	128.34	6.60	8.87	52.56	22.46	87.23	40.06	47.17	2.2–1	56.52	8.61
1956--	128.94	18.60	10.26	57.08	27.05	98.70	52.88	45.83	1.9–1	58.88	8.06
1955--	109.23	4.58	14.01	41.43	23.84	81.64	38.00	43.65	2.2–1	31.49	7.29

[1]Divs. paid regularly. [2]Adj. for 2-for-1 split in 1965.

Fundamental Position

Textron is a multi-industry company with about 30 divisions in diversified fields. Sales by product groups in mid-1965 were: Agrochemical 12%, Consumer 16%, Defense 35%, Industrial 20%, and Metal Products 17%.

AGROCHEMICAL--Spencer Kellogg chemical products, oilseed products, livestock feeds, corn milling and poultry products.

CONSUMER -- Electronic components; Hall-Mack bathroom accessories; Homelite chain saws, generators, pumps, outboard motors; E-Z-Go electric golf cars; cast aluminum and iron cooking ware, tubular furniture; Shuron eye-glass frames, lenses and optical machinery; Speidel watch bands; Vita-Var paints; Weinbrenner footwear.

DEFENSE--Fluid controls and heat exchange equipment; Bell Aerosystems Agena rocket engines, VTOL aircraft, air cushion vehicles, inertial guidance, automatic landing systems; Bell helicopters; radar antennae, sonar, magnetic detection and microwave systems; nuclear and metallurgical research; electro-optics.

INDUSTRIAL--Ball and roller bearings; cushioning materials, polyurethane foam; gray iron castings; chaplets and chills; environmental test systems; equipment for oil production; auto and appliance trim; gas meters and regulators; underfloor electrical systems and pre-engineered metal buildings.

METAL PRODUCTS--Cold flow parts; Pittsburgh Steel Foundry heavy rolling mills, aluminum and steel foil mills; fasteners and tools; Waterbury cold heading machines, Sendzimir rolling mills, Cleveland hobbing machines, turret lathes, grinders.

Foreign sales, by export or foreign plant, rose 25% in 1964 to $39.5 million. Royalties from international license agreements totaled $892,000 through seven divisions. In 1964, a West German manufacturer of balancing machines was acquired, and in 1965, over 90% of a Belgian machine tool company. Company R & D outlays totaled $10,000,000. Ownership of Textron Electronics was increased to over 97% in 1965.

Dividends, either in cash or stock, have been paid each year since 1942.

Employees: 37,900. Shareholders: 35,000.

Finances

In July, 1961, assets of Spencer Kellogg were acquired for 2,077,642 (adj.) common shares. Sale of Amerotron Textile division for some $45,000,000 in early 1963 was followed by retirement of $33,600,000 debt. Purchase of Parkersburg-Aetna late in 1963 involved $10,040,000; several other acquisitions were also made for cash. In 1964, acquisitions were made for $34,100,000 cash and 88,040 (adj.) shares of common; convertible debentures were called and a $32,000,000 five-year term loan obtained at 4¾%.

CAPITALIZATION

LONG TERM DEBT: $52,782,000.

$1.25 CUM. CONV. PREFERRED STOCK: 130,099 shs. (no par); red. at $26; conv. into 2.157 common shares.

COMMON STOCK: 10,977,254 shares ($0.25)

WARRANTS: To purchase 907,120 com. shs. at $15 each to May 1, 1969, increasing each 5-year period by $2.50 until expir. in 1984.

Incorporated in R.I. in 1928. **Office**—10 Dorrance St., Providence R.I. **Pres**—G. W. Miller. **Treas**—D. L. Grote. **Secy**—R. R. Thurber. **Dirs**—R. C. Thompson, Jr. (Chrmn), J. E. Bierwirth, F. C. Church, G. F. Doriot, H. C. Flower, Jr., H. B. Freeman, N. B. Frost, H. Gaylord, H. E. Goodman, R. L. Huffines, Jr. G. W. Miller. A T. Roth. **Transfer Agents**—Rhode Island Hospital Trust Co., Providence; Bank of America N.T. & S.A., Los Angeles; (Com.) Morgan Guaranty Trust Co., NYC; (Conv. Pfd.) Chase Manhattan Bank, NYC. **Registrars**—Industrial National Bank of Rhode Island; Manufacturers Hanover Trust Co., NYC; Security First National Bank of Los Angeles.

Information has been obtained from sources believed to be reliable, but its accuracy and completeness, and that of the opinions based thereon, are not guaranteed. Printed in U. S. A.

Common Stock	Preferred Stock	Bonds
1. Trend of earnings per share	1. Dividend coverage	1. Interest coverage
2. Dividend yield	2. Dividend yield	2. Yield
3. Price–earnings ratio	3. Special features, call price, conversion, etc.	3. Special features
4. Market price range	4. Market price range	4. Market price range

Computation of these measures would be a burdensome task. Therefore, the analyst should use the readily accessible published data. Several investment services publish basic data on common stocks. Data including the key measures mentioned, such as yield, market price ranges, earnings per share for the last three to four years, and capitalization, are published in monthly digests such as Standard and Poor's Stock Guide.

More detailed data which the analyst may use in the screening task are available in the form of brokerage house analyses: *Standard Stock Reports* on listed stocks, like the one reproduced in Figures 10–1 and 10–2; the data and commentary published in the periodicals of Moody's, Standard and Poor's, and The Value Line investment services.

It is possible for the investor to rely entirely on these sources for investment suggestions. While the use of investment service data in making analyses is feasible, the analyst should never accept these data without question. The analyst should always refer to annual reports, if possible, because the investment services do not normally make some of the necessary refinements in financial statement data, such as examining the financial statements and making adjustments for differences in statistical and accounting methods.

Industry Analysis

Industry analysis is concerned with the conditions and factors that will affect the demand for the industry's production, its cost structure, and its raw material supply. The industry analysis should be accomplished in two phases. First, the analyst should evaluate the long-range economic potential of the national economy. Second, he should appraise the effects on the prospects of the industry of such diverse developments as the regulatory environment, technological change, or shifts in foreign affairs. The wide range of considerations is discussed in Chapter 11.

As a part of the industry analysis, the analyst must evaluate the long-range economic potential of the national economy. The American investor generally assumes that the growth of the American economy has exceeded all others and that it will continue to grow in the future. This assumption does not fit the facts as measured by growth in gross national product.

In the past, investors have been unwilling to invest in foreign countries because of political instability, currency exchange problems, and so on. However, these problems should not be a major barrier to investing in Canada and other rapidly growing countries, which can be classified as stable western economies.

TABLE 10-1

**Index of Gross National Product in Constant Prices,
Selected Countries, Selected Years, 1956–63
1958 = 100**

Country	1963	1962	1961	1960	1959	1958	1957	1956
Argentina	101	106	109	102	94	100	93	88
Australia	122	116	110	108	104	100	93	91
Belgium	122	117	113	108	103	100	101	99
Canada	121	115	108	106	105	100	99	99
China (Taiwan)*	142	133	125	116	107	100	94	88
Denmark	129	126	120	113	106	100	98	93
France*	128	123	116	110	103	100	97	93
Germany (West)*	132	128	123	116	107	100	97	92
Greece	134	124	121	108	104	100	97	89
Ireland*	124	119	116	110	105	100	102	102
Italy	137	130	122	114	107	100	94	89
Japan **	182	162	155	134	117	100	97	90
Netherlands*	126	122	119	115	105	100	101	98
Norway	126	120	117	110	104	100	101	98
Philippines	125	120	115	109	108	100	98	95
Portugal	136	129	121	114	105	100	97	94
Sweden*	124	119	115	109	105	100	99	96
Switzerland*	133	127	121	113	107	100	102	99
Thailand*	147	136	131	126	111	100	96	96
Turkey	123	114	108	107	104	100	89	84
United Kingdom	117	114	112	110	105	100	100	98
United States*	122	118	111	109	107	100	102	100
Venezuela	123	118	111	109	108	100	99	88

* Gross domestic product at market prices.
** Gross national product at market prices.
Source: *Statistical Yearbook of the United Nations.*

Industry Analysis Problems. The specific industry analysis is generally more exact and intensive than analysis of the health and outlook of the national economy. A number of factors influence an industry's prospects. In fact, the influences on an industry's prospects are usually so varied that many of the larger brokerage and investment banking houses have analysts who are industry specialists, because they know it is not possible for an analyst to keep up with developments in a number of industries.

One of the most effective arguments against diversification of holdings, by industries, is the average investor's inability to keep abreast of significant developments in each industry if he spreads his holdings over too many industries. Whether the individual should concentrate his investments in one industry and become a specialist in that industry, or should diversify his holdings, is a personal decision, because it can be argued effectively that either approach is acceptable.

The analyst may reject a particular security as an investment after completing the industry analysis. Even a company with a record of good earnings may be eliminated because it is so heavily committed in an industry whose prospects are so bleak that maintenance of the present level of earnings would be difficult. In the analysis, the analyst would, of necessity, adjust the future earnings of the company to reflect changes in the industry prospects.

Some investors make it a practice to deliberately choose securities in industries that are declining, or to buy at a time when an industry is in disfavor with investors. Reliance is placed on choosing the securities of a company that has an outstanding management to enable it to carry through the period of adversity without significant operating losses or impairment of earning power. In some cases, emphasis is placed on special factors, such as a change in management, or perhaps even a dissolution and distribution of assets, which would result in an eventual capital gain. There is nothing wrong with such an approach, but it requires an extraordinary ability to analyze these special situations, and ability and willingness to assume financial risk.

Generally, the average investor is content to forego the substantial capital gains available from such special situations and to confine his investments to the more conventional investment possibilities where analysis indicates that the industry's prospects are favorable. When the industry's prospects are favorable, the analyst proceeds to the company analysis.

COMPANY QUANTITATIVE ANALYSIS

The company quantitative analysis involves an examination of data indicating financial position, efficiency of operation, and profitability of the firm. Raw material for analysis of these conditions is provided by the company balance sheets and income statements.

To effectively analyze financial statements, various tools must be used. Of these analytical tools, described more completely in Chapter 13, the one most widely used by the analyst is the ratio.

Ratio Analysis

The purpose of ratio analysis is to facilitate the interpretation of financial statements by reducing items on the financial statements to comparable quantities or ratios. A ratio is a numerical relationship between two items on a financial statement. Ratios increase the analyst's comprehension. The absolute dollar amounts on financial statements are not meaningful by themselves. These data must be compared or related to other items on the financial statement in the process of analysis. For example, the company's dollar sales figures become significant only when compared with expenses, earnings, or sales in previous years. It is conceivable that the analyst could interpret financial statements by simply examining the absolute dollar amounts shown on the statements, but comprehension of these data can be increased by computing ratios. For example, the relationship $2,894,222 to $1,447,111 is more easily understood if the relationship is expressed as a 2 to 1 ratio.

The analyst should regard these ratios as tools of analysis rather than as the product of analysis. Almost an infinite number of relationships or ratios may be computed. To use these ratios most effectively in analysis, the analyst must be selective or he will compile such a mass of data and ratios that it will be virtually impossible to interpret it. The analyst must always keep in mind that the objective of the analysis is to make an investment decision. Generally, the analyst will develop over a period of time a regular pattern of analysis which will enable him to strip away and discard excess data and select those particular relationships that are most meaningful to him.

Analytical Reference Standards

Effective interpretation of several ratios may be accomplished only by having something to compare them with, or a reference standard. While reference standards make ratio analysis more useful, the weight assigned to the ratio analysis in the evaluation of securities is a matter of judgment. There is often a tendency to attach too much importance to the comparison of one ratio with another. The inexperienced analyst will attempt to reduce the whole process of security analysis to the calculation of ratios and their comparison with some reference standard.

Four reference standards may be used: (1) the absolute standard, (2) the industry standard, (3) the historical standard, and (4) the limited industry standard. In using the absolute standard, the analyst must assume that certain minimum relationships or ratios are acceptable for all companies. For example, the current ratio, which is the relationship of current assets to current liabilities, is widely used as a test of solvency of a business. Many analysts suggest that a current ratio of above 2 to 1 is acceptable; therefore, for these analysts 2 to 1 is an absolute minimum standard. This standard is not too useful because it suggests that all businesses have similar operating and financial characteristics.

A second and more useful standard is composite industry data. The analyst compares the financial performance of the corporation with the composite performance of other firms in the industry. This standard assumes that all companies within the industry are homogeneous. To some extent, this limits the usefulness of this standard, because every company has unique operational characteristics. However, the companies within an industry, by definition, do have some common products and operating problems which make the industry standard a useful one. In fact, the conventional standard used in security analysis is a type of industry standard. It is not a composite of the financial performance of all companies within the industry, but the comparison of one company with other companies that have similar operating characteristics. This standard is sometimes called a "limited industry" standard. The ratios of company A are compared with the ratios of company B. The analyst may, of course, make the comparison with as many companies within the industry as he wishes. The important thing is that the companies be similar in their operations, product lines, and so on.

Another useful standard is the historical standard—a comparison of the ratio analysis of current financial statements with a similar analysis of past statements. This standard is particularly useful in judging the trend of sales and earnings and the stability of earnings of the corporation. Typically, the analyst compares current financial performance with the financial statements for the past five to ten years. To go back much farther than ten years is usually rather fruitless, because most companies experience so many operational changes that the performance of, say, fifteen years ago is not even roughly comparable with today's performance.

The analyst should use any or all of these standards if he feels that the results will be revealing. Although the limited industry standard is the one conventionally used in security analysis, the analyst should cross-check his results with composite industry financial data. In every situation, the historical standard should be used. A company's performance may fall below either of these industry standards, but a discernible trend in the financial performance of the corporation may be more significant than comparison with composite industry data would indicate.

Comparability of Financial Statement Data

Use of these analytical reference standards assumes that the accounting methods and reporting practices of the companies are comparable. This assumption is warranted when analyzing the financial statements of public utilities and railroads, because these companies have prescribed for them definite accounting rules and account classifications.

Unfortunately, this same comparability of financial statements does not exist for the broad classification of companies engaged in such diverse activities as manufacturing, mining, or service enterprises, arbitrarily called industrials. The companies in the industrial classification use significantly different accounting methods and vary considerably in the completeness and form in their annual reports.

The frequent differences in industrial financial reporting and accounting practices make it necessary for the analyst to inspect financial statements to determine their comparability. Differences in account classifications are obvious from an inspection of the financial statements, and the variance in accounting practice can frequently be established from a study of the footnotes to the financial statements.

These differences in accounting practices which affect the comparability of financial statements can sometimes be corrected by making adjustments. Normally, the analyst's wisest course of action is to select for comparison another company that has similar accounting practices.

The differences in detail of the financial reports and account classification often make analysis of financial statements a tedious undertaking. To relieve this tedium, the analyst may wish to reclassify reported data into standard balance sheet and income statement classification. The nature and significance of these differences in accounting method and practice as well as the process of standardizing financial statements are discussed in detail in Chapter 12.

Importance of Interpretation

The conclusion of the analysis is interpretation of the amassed data and the decision on whether or not to invest in the company's securities. To assist in this final investment decision, the analyst should use various selection measures which relate certain key indicators of profitability to market value measures.

Various measures may be used to indicate the profitability of the firm. The central factors that should be examined include:

1. Sales trend.
2. Earnings trend.
3. Profit margin analysis.
4. Asset utilization analysis.
5. Common stock equity utilization.
6. Sales and earnings stability.

To maintain its profitability, the company must have sufficient working capital. Working-capital inadequacy occurs when the firm does not have enough current funds (assets) both for operations and for servicing current obligations. Working-capital stringency may cause reduced operations and impaired profitability, which would be of primary concern to the common stock investor. To the bond investor, inadequate working capital may be a prelude to an impaired financial position and credit capacity.

In addition to the measures of working capital adequacy, the analyst should examine the company's credit capacity. The company's sources of working capital are the funds generated internally through operations and by external financing, either debt or equity. Generally, there is no working capital stringency if internally generated funds are adequate. Therefore, to cure the problem of working-capital inadequacy external financing is necessary. It is usually desirable that this be debt financing, because of the dilution effect of further equity financing. Of course, if the company's credit capacity is exhausted, the company must then resort to equity financing or reduce its scale of operations.

The major elements in credit capacity are (1) the size of debt in relation to equity and (2) the debt service requirements in relation to income. An important element is not only the size of debt and debt service, but also the contractual provisions of the debt. Sometimes, there are contractual provisions that may prevent future debt financing and make equity financing a necessity.

Finally, the analyst is interested in relating certain value indicators, such as earnings and dividends, to what the investor must pay to participate in the earnings. In other words, he is interested in how much he is getting for each dollar he invests as an aid to making the final investment decisions.

COMPANY QUALITATIVE ANALYSIS

As mentioned before, the qualitative factors are those that would cause the company's future financial performance to depart significantly from its past performance. Since these data are not reported uniformly and are not precisely measurable, the analyst must seek such information from various sources, and sift out and evaluate the reliability and significance of the information. The more important sources of information for qualitative data include technical newspapers and magazines, government publications, management interviews, and interviews with the company's competitiors and customers. The analyst is trying to determine from these information sources the general reputation of the company as well as specific things such as the following:

1. Sales prospects.
2. Competitive situation.
3. New product prospects.
4. Status and condition of production facilities.
5. Adequacy of raw material supplies.
6. Plans for expansion.
7. Research and development activities.
8. Quality of management.
9. Labor relations.[2]

Qualitative Information Sources

The basis for a qualitative appraisal of the company may be interviews of its customers, competitors, and large institutional investors. Competitors are often a particularly good source, since they must

---

2 Joseph M. Galanis, "A Primer for Field Contact Work," in *Readings in Financial Analysis and Investment Management*, ed. Eugene M. Lerner (Homewood, Ill.: Richard D. Irwin, Inc., 1963).

make a realistic evaluation of the company as a matter of survival. The analyst also can get information from the management by personal interview or from their pronouncements in financial newspapers and at annual meetings. Although these bases of company appraisal are highly subjective, they should be used to supplement the management interview.

Corporate management usually builds a good reputation either by increasing earnings or publicizing its exploits, particularly new product developments, or by both. If the management's reputation is based on these factors, the market price of the stock usually already reflects it. Consequently, use of this index of management ability would tend to cause the analyst to compound his optimism or pessimism in his estimate of the future earnings. The net effect would be to value such things as the earnings record and product developments twice, because these factors would tend to be already reflected in the price of the company's common stock.

Management Interview

The analyst may avoid this pitfall by seeking a personal interview with the management or, at least, by asking pertinent questions of the management by mail. Obviously, a personal interview would be more desirable, because both questions and answers can usually be developed more fully. The analyst, when interviewing the management of a firm, cannot help being influenced by the personalities involved. However, in such an interview, he will be able to get a general impression of the management personnel and, in many cases, to get specific answers to important questions.

Most executives are willing to grant interviews. A good many will answer quite frankly all reasonable questions that are asked, and a few are actually anxious to volunteer information. However, the quantitative analysis of the company should precede the personal interview so that the analyst can ask intelligent questions. The questions should be specific and planned in advance. The questions should parallel or be an extension of the analysis of the company's financial statements. If the analyst shows by his questions that he is not familiar with the past financial performance and operations of the company, the executive, even if he wants to cooperate, can hardly be expected to undertake a complete education of the questioner. The net result of the interview, in such cases, will probably be that the analyst will receive a few general replies to his questions, with perhaps a volunteered opinion that the company's stock is a good value. The investor may find that the results of a personal management interview or of questions asked by mail may not be too satisfactory. However, an analyst should operate with the philosophy that if he doesn't ask the questions, he will not have a chance of getting answers.

SUMMARY

Some investors rely almost entirely on quantitative or financial statement analysis, and others emphasize qualitative analysis. Investors who use the qualitative approach do not assign any validity to past performance of the company. If a company develops a new product, it is implicitly assumed that the present market price is a reasonable valuation of past performance. Therefore, favorable news increases the value of the company's securities, and adverse news decreases their value.

The quantitative approach uses past performance almost exclusively as the basis for determining the intrinsic or appraised value of securities. This is a mechanistic approach by which the analyst correlates past earnings, dividends, and other financial data to past market prices of the securities, usually the common stock. The appraised value is determined by simply projecting these relationships into the future.

The integrated approach to security analysis uses both quantitative and qualitative factors derived from an examination of the national economy, the industry, and the company. The quantitative analysis indicates the past financial and operating performance and the effects of changes in national economic activity on the company's sales, costs, and earnings. At this point, the quantitative analysis ends. The analyst must then decide whether the past performance pattern will continue into the future. In general, an examination of industry and company qualitative factors will indicate three possible choices; the past performance pattern will continue, future performance will be better, or future performance will be worse.

It is evident that the analyst is always led back to the evaluation of qualitative information. As indicated earlier, the analyst's judgment is all-important, and the correctness of his appraisals of the value of common stocks is directly dependent on his ability to interpret the quantitative analysis and to evaluate the qualitative factors. Since the validity of the final result—the appraised value—is dependent on the analyst's judgment, the importance of a background in economics, finance, accounting, and monetary and banking theory cannot be overemphasized. Mastery of these disciplines tends to fortify the judgment of the analyst, because it will never be possible in a capitalistic society to reduce security analysis to a simple mechanical process.

REVIEW QUESTIONS AND PROBLEMS

1. Why is the determination of an investor's objectives and needs an integral part of investment analysis?
2. What is the purpose of security analysis?
3. What are the approaches to security value and quality determination?
4. What is the basic assumption underlying technical market analysis techniques?
5. The values of securities established through security analysis are relative values. Why must these values be relative and not absolute?
6. How would you go about screening out investment possibilities that deserve further analysis?
7. What procedure would you use in appraising the quality of a company's management?
8. New companies require a special type of security analysis. Why? How would you proceed to analyze a new company?
9. What are the inherent shortcomings of relying on either quantitative analysis or qualitative analysis exclusively?
10. Why is it necessary to examine the legal characteristics of the outstanding securities of a corporation as a part of the security analysis?
11. Why shouldn't an investor spread his investment funds over as many industries as possible?

CHAPTER **11**

Analysis of Industrial Securities—
The Industry

Each potential investment is a company which is part of a larger economic entity, an industry. As discussed in Chapter 10, analysis of the common stock of the company must include an examination of the secular and cyclical economic characteristic of the industry of which it is a part.

The analysis of the industry is complicated by classification problems. It is customary to classify corporate securities, particularly common stocks, rather arbitrarily as industrial, utilities, railroads, and miscellaneous. Presumably, these classifications separate regulated industries—railroads and public utilities—from nonregulated industries. It is not meant to suggest that all companies in the miscellaneous classification are unregulated, because banks, insurance companies, and other financial institutions are included in this classification and are subject to considerable regulation.

For purposes of this discussion, it is desirable to separate those industries not subject to specific regulation, because they have different operating problems. It is often more difficult, even for well-qualified management, to build earning power in a highly regulated industry than it is in one where such control does not exist. Therefore, in this chapter, our discussion will be confined to the industrial classification. Analysis of regulated industries will be covered in later chapters and will be treated as a special analytical problem.

Even within the broad classification of industrials, the analyst has problems of classification, because the days have passed when company operations were confined to a single industry. Today, the single-product company is disappearing and is being taken over by multi-industry operations known as "corporate pluralists." A single company may produce a wide range of product classifications which

195

are not even roughly similar, in some cases ranging all the way from machine tools to bathing suits. There are even situations in which a company operates in both regulated and nonregulated industries, but such interindustry operations are rather uncommon. For example, Textron, Inc., operates in the regulated transportation industry as well as in several diverse manufacturing classifications, and is a corporate pluralist in every sense of the term (Figure 11-1).

FIGURE 11-1

Textron, Inc.
Percentage Distribution of Product Lines, 1965

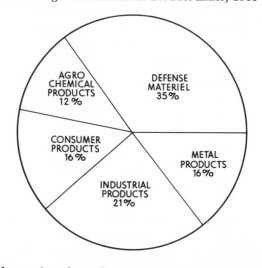

In the analysis of multi-industry procedures, it is necessary to determine the common economic characteristics of growth and cyclical stability of the products produced. It will be evident from the discussion in this chapter that each product has certain economic characteristics which enable one to classify the company as operating primarily in growth industries, moderate growth industries, or declining industries. Similarly, it is possible to establish a pattern of relative cyclical stability for the company. Such patterns of industry prospects and stability cannot be determined until the industry analysis has been completed.

Two major points of emphasis in the investigation of industry prospects and characteristics are of interest to the investor. First, the analyst should be concerned with the secular outlook for the industry. Is it growing? Is it a mature situation? Or have its fortunes begun to decline? The second major point of interest is the responsiveness of the industry to cyclical fluctuations in business conditions. That is, do the sales of the industry's products rise and fall in sympathy with changes in general business conditions? Or do the industry's sales fail to respond to cyclical influences and remain stable? Discussion of these major points in industry economics and factors that influence industry prospects will be concerned first with secular characteristics of the industry and then with the cyclical characteristics of industries.

ECONOMICS OF INDUSTRY GROWTH

Several related factors affect industry growth prospects. Most of these factors are related either to the demand for the industry's products, or the costs of producing them and their price. Evaluation of product demand and growth of the industry requires that we have a measure of output. Several measures of output have been suggested, but the most common measures are those of physical output and dollar volume.[1]

A consideration that, to the investor, is equally as important as growth in product demand is the price competition within the industry. A rapidly growing industry characterized by severe price competition and declining profit margins would not be a desirable investment.

Finally, the third group of considerations are those dealing with cost of production, raw materials supply, and industrial technology. Cost factors are especially important, particularly when higher costs cannot be passed on to consumers. Attempts by the federal government to set wage–price guidelines make it difficult if not impossible to pass costs to the consumer in the form of higher prices. Vulnerability to higher costs may be the result of such things as union activity, changes in technology, and costs of raw materials. Some of these costs may be beyond the ability of the government to control and influence. However, vulnerability of an industry to adverse product demand and cost changes may be offset by research activities, product diversification, and government subsidies.

---

[1] E. B. Alderfer and H. E. Michl, *Economics of American Industry* (3d ed.; New York: McGraw-Hill Book Co., Inc., 1957), p. 14.

STAGES OF INDUSTRY DEVELOPMENT

It is helpful to think of industrial development as going through certain phases which we term a life cycle. Measurement of the industry's development is nearly always in terms of physical output or production, because it is difficult to remove the influence of price changes from other measures of industry development. In industry analysis, the analyst examines the long-run or secular changes in the industry's output. The classical life cycle of an industry is shown in Figure 11–2.

FIGURE 11–2

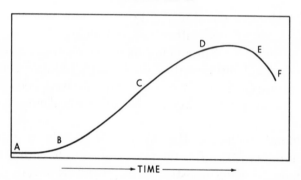

There are four stages to the classical industry life cycle. The first stage, between points A to B, is the pioneering stage of the industry. During this period, the new product or process is being perfected, production techniques are being developed to mass-produce the item, a distribution system is being established, and the product is being advertised to gain user acceptance. Many embryo industries never get out of this stage because of failure to overcome one or more of the production or distribution problems.

The second stage of development, from B to C, is the period of very rapid growth. It is evident that the investor who invests in a company of an industry at this stage may realize considerable appreciation in the value of his investment. However, there are basic hazards for the investor who buys into an industry at this stage of development. First, the investor risks overestimating the extent of future growth if he bases his estimate solely on an appraisal of past performance, or he risks overestimating the speed with which growth will materialize. Second, he can never be sure which companies in the industry will increase in value as a result of the industry's growth, or which companies will survive.

The industry may reach maturity, shown as the points between C and D. The investor may buy stock of a company too late in the industry's development cycle. In many cases, the investor pays inflated prices for the stock of a company because of an excellent past record of growth, only to discover that the company has suddenly stopped growing and has reached maturity. Generally, the companies in the industry at this stage can look forward to relatively stable earnings and sales. The industry may go into a period of actual decline, depicted in Figure 11-2 as the stage from D to E. However, the industry may reach maturity and never actually go into the decline phase $D-E$ because of factors affecting industry prospects.

INDUSTRY GROWTH AND ITS INVESTMENT IMPLICATIONS

Investors frequently become enamored with the prospects of particular industries and bid up the common stocks of companies in these industries, discounting the growth potential at extremely high rates. In other words, the investors overestimate the rate of growth. During the 1961–62 speculative market, this happened in a number of industries, such as book publishing, discount retailing, and electronics.

In some cases where there are prospects of growth in an industry, it is questionable whether this growth will be of much significance to the investor. As was mentioned, industry growth typically is measured in terms of physical output and sometimes in terms of sales. Growth in physical output is meaningful to the investor only when it is accompanied by a growth in profits. An industry characterized by severe competition between companies within the industry may grow very rapidly in terms of physical output, but the growth may not be profitable to the investors. For example, the rapid growth of the television industry was a singularly unprofitable one. With 1935–39 equaling 100, the radio and television industry's index of average sales for the period 1951–55 was 1,860.5. The rate of return on capital declined by 17 percent, and dividend yields on the market value of common stock declined by 29.7 percent during this period.[2] Profits in the exploitation of this technological development by the industry were dissipated by severe price competition. This

---

[2] Sidney Cottle and Tate Whitman, *Corporate Earning Power and Market Valuation, 1935–1955* (Durham, N.C.: Duke University Press, 1959).

competition resulted in such low prices that it was difficult to operate profitably.

Typically, the profitable exploitation of a product or group of products is dependent on some factors that restrain free entry into the industry. Without such influences, the profitable production of the industry is usually short-lived. These restraining influences on freedom of entry into a growth industry are (1) large capital investment required, (2) patents or other government protection, (3) trademarks and customer good will, and (4) control of limited supply of raw materials.

Large Capital Investment as Limiting Factor

In certain industries, the nature of the size of the capital investment required limits freedom of entry into the business. For example, the automobile industry requires tremendous financial resources if a company is to successfully produce and market passenger cars and trucks. No new automobile company has been successfully launched in the last 30 years, even though the long-term growth potential of the industry was obvious. In 1964, about 95 percent of the passenger car business was done by the big three—General Motors, Ford, and Chrysler—with General Motors controlling about 51 percent of the total passenger car market. In addition, five companies accounted for about 97 percent of the truck business in 1964; General Motors again was largest single producer of trucks. Therefore, any technological development or style change by the automobile manufacturing companies may be successfully exploited without fear of market saturation from new entrants.

Patents, Trademarks, and Customer Goodwill

In some cases, the future of an industry and the companies in it is directly dependent on an exclusive right to produce or sell the product. Pitney-Bowes, Inc., held patents on postage meters, letter canceling machines, and similar equipment, which until 1959 gave them a monopoly in that field. Even though their monopoly was broken in 1959 by federal government action, Pitney-Bowes, Inc., continued to dominate this industry because of customer goodwill built up over the years. However, the future profitability of the companies in this industry is directly dependent on their exclusive rights to produce and market this machinery.

In other industries, the outstanding success of the leaders is less a matter of assets or productive efficiency than a matter of successful advertising and sales promotion. If sales promotion is successfully continued, a trademark can be an intangible asset more important than a patent, because it has an unlimited life.

By recalling some of his favorite radio or television programs, the reader could probably list those industries in which the intangible value of trademarks and successful sales promotion is of major importance. The tobacco industry is an outstanding example; others are packaged foods, biscuits, proprietary drugs (patent medicines) and cosmetics, liquor, and soaps and vegetable oils. The analyst may regard the intangible value of a trademark as real, but he will recognize that a sudden lapse in the effectiveness of advertising, or the introduction of new competitive products, could cause this intangible value to disappear.

An example of a trademark's relative value is the Coca-Cola trademark. Coca-Cola was developed as a soft drink and first marketed in 1886. Several cola drinks developed have been competitive with Coca-Cola, but no one has been successful enough to overcome Coca-Cola's leadership in the soft drink market. This has been in the face of Coca-Cola's major competitors who always offer larger-size bottles of cola drinks at a reduced price.

In some of the consumer products industries such as those mentioned before—cosmetics, soap, beer, cereals—the cost of manufacturing the product is incidental to the unit cost of advertising. Advertising is of prime importance in consumer products industries. An outstanding example of advertising's power to produce sales and earnings is the Alberto-Culver Company. In 1963, this company spent 42 percent of its sales on advertising, and has been a major advertiser of its products since its start in 1959. Sales and earnings of Alberto-Culver have shown substantial increases each year, and it has led the industry in profitability and rate of return.

The importance of advertising and its impact on earnings is evident from Figure 11-3, which shows earnings increases for a Standard and Poor's Industrials, Dow-Jones Industrials, and the 100 Leading National Advertisers. This does not mean that the investor has only to select those companies with the largest advertising budgets and invest in them, because in many instances large and expensive advertising campaigns have failed. On the other hand, the leading advertisers apparently are able to better establish their markets and their position in their industries. In addition, continued advertising

FIGURE 11–3

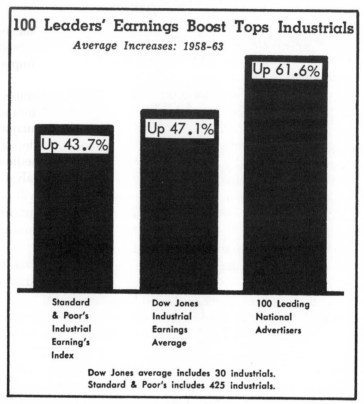

100 Leaders' Earnings Boost Tops Industrials

Average Increases: 1958-63

Up 61.6%

Up 47.1%

Up 43.7%

Standard	Dow Jones	100 Leading
& Poor's	Industrial	National
Industrial	Earnings	Advertisers
Earning's	Average	
Index		

Dow Jones average includes 30 industrials.
Standard & Poor's includes 425 industrials.

Source: *Advertising Age*, August 31, 1964, p. 59.

enables a company to maintain its position in a market even when it is threatened by a new product introduced by a competitor. For example, Gillette's position in the safety razor blade market was threatened by competitors' introduction of stainless steel blades. Gillette was able to retain its position because of the brand image established from its intensive advertising campaigns over the years.

CAUSES OF CHANGE IN INDUSTRY PROSPECTS

It is obvious that the classical life cycle depicted in Figure 11–2 might be altered by any one of several influences. The measurement of industry development is a function of time and physical output. Anything that effects rate of change in physical output either to accelerate or decelerate the change will change the classical life cycle.

The basic causes for change in the rate of growth and/or decline in physical output are:

1. Technological changes.
2. Changes in buying habits of consumers.
3. Population growth and changes in its composition.
4. Competition from new industries and foreign countries.[3]

Technology and Industry Prospects

Changes in technology tend to have a dual effect on industry prospects. A particular change in technology, such as the invention or development of a new product or process, may quite frequently cause sudden and dramatic changes in an industry's prospects. In turn, the change may rejuvenate one industry and cause the decline of another. For example, the development of home television rejuvenated and started the rapid growth of the television and radio industry. This development also started the decline of the motion picture industry.

Technological advances also may be the reason why the decay or decline of an industry may be prolonged beyond original expectations. The coal mining industry is declining partly because of the inroads made on the market by competing fuels and partly because of the rising costs of producing coal. New continuous mining machines have stemmed the tide somewhat, but the slow pace of adopting this machinery has not prevented the decline.[4] The industry's rate of decline has been slowed by more efficient methods of production that reduce costs and make coal a competitively priced fuel. For example, the bituminous coal industry signed a new wage contract in 1964 with the United Mine Workers, calling for wage increases amounting to about $2.00 a day. At one time, an increase of such magnitude would have had a disastrous affect on the industry. It was not expected to significantly effect large producers in 1964, because they had systematically displaced workers by automated mining techniques which have improved worker productivity.

Importance of Research and Development Programs. The development of new products is a major factor in the growth of many industries today. The importance of new product development is clear if one examines Figure 11–4. The dark part of each bar is the share of

---

[3] Alderfer and Michl, *op. cit.*, p. 14.

[4] Daniel Parson, "Long-Term Outlook for Energy," *Commercial and Financial Chronicle*, August 21, 1958.

the growth in sales expected from new products. As may be noted, the growth expected from new products ranges from 30 percent to 100 percent for these industries.

FIGURE 11–4

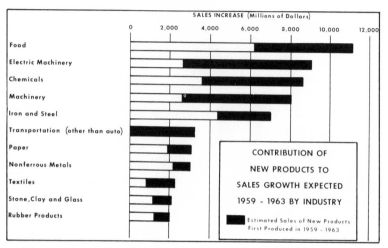

Source: Federal Trade Commission and McGraw-Hill Book Co., Inc.

The importance of continuing research and development programs is obvious when one considers the basic life cycle of new products in relation to their profitability. "A primary conclusion, derived from analyzing the life cycles of numerous products, is that sooner or later every product is preempted by another or else degenerates into profit-less price competition."[5] (See Figure 11–5.) For example, research and development efforts have resulted in the foil fiber, plastic, and aluminum can; the keyless coffee can, the pull-tab beer can; and the rip-off bottle cap. However, saturation of the market for these new products causes price competition and lower profit margins. The rapidity of market saturation for aluminum containers is obvious when one considers that aluminum consumption for can manufacture was 70 percent more in 1963 than in 1962, and in 1964 it is estimated that use of aluminum cans would climb more than 100 percent over 1963 consumption.[6]

---

[5] *Management of New Products* (New York: Booz-Allen & Hamilton, 1960), p. 6.

[6] *Security and Industry Survey, Summer, 1964* (New York: Merrill Lynch, Pierce, Fenner and Smith, Inc., 1964), p. 29.

FIGURE 11-5

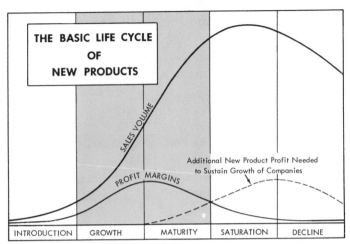

Source: Management Research Department, Booz-Allen & Hamilton.

Changes in Buying Habits of Consumer

Changes in the buying habits of consumers and new consumer products both have a profound effect on industries that produce goods for direct consumption. For example, the consuming public's consciousness of heart disease and weight control has stimulated demand for vegetable oil products and dietetic soft drinks, while reducing demand for dairy products and sugar. Health considerations have had significant effects on a number of industries. For example, the U.S. Surgeon General's report on smoking and health will undoubtedly have an adverse affect on the cigarette manufacturing industry. The same report, for the most part, exonerated cigar and pipe smoking, which tended to change consumer habits and rejuvenate an otherwise dying industry.

The classic illustration of changes in consumer habits and the decline of an industry is the demise of the American woolen industry. Development of better home heating systems and better automobiles caused buying of heavy woolen clothing to begin to decline after World War I.[7] The decline of the woolen industry was rather gradual

---

[7] Seymour Himmelstein, "The Decline of the American Woolen and Worsted Industry," *Analysts Journal*, Vol. 14, No. 1 (February, 1958), p. 85. This article is an excellent one-page discussion of the decline of an industry.

until the development of synthetic textile fibers. Although the government, through tariffs, attempted to forestall the decline in the woolen industry, the price and composition of synthetic fibers and foreign competition made such serious inroads into the consumption and production of domestic woolen goods that the industry has been plagued by heavy financial losses and company liquidations.

Population Characteristics and Industry Growth

The fact that an industry has reached maturity does not mean that it has ceased growing. The mature industry is generally characterized by sufficient productive capacity to saturate the market. The industry may experience additional growth, but its growth will be limited to the population growth as a whole. For example, the major factor in the growth of the shoe manufacturing industry is population growth.[8] The per capita consumption of shoes has been remarkably stable, evidenced by Figure 11–6. The shoe industry has attempted

FIGURE 11–6

Per Capita Consumption of Shoes

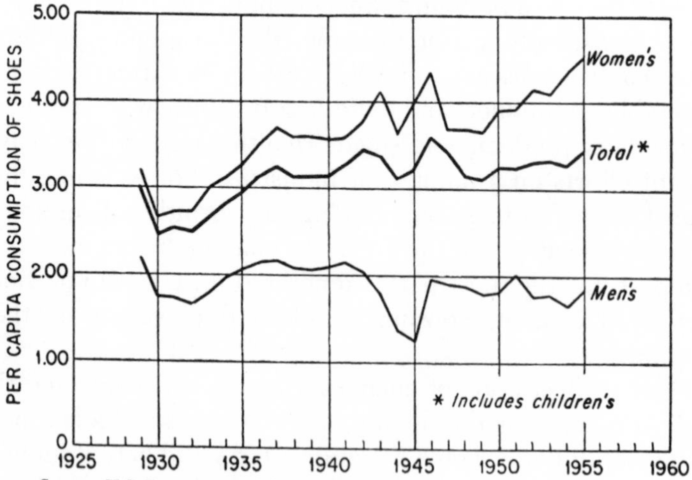

Source: U.S. Department of Commerce.

to stimulate demand for shoes by style changes, and has succeeded with women's shoes to some extent, which accounts for the slight increase in per capita consumption. However, the consumption of

---

[8] Alderfer and Michl, *op. cit.*, p. 478.

shoes has increased at about the same annual average rate as population.

Changes in the population composition tend to accelerate the demand for the products of some industries. For example, the bulge of population in the younger age groups tends to stimulate the demand for school textbooks and beverages of all types. The population increase in the family formation age group (19–25 years of age) tends to increase the demand for such things as housing, furniture, and baby food. For example, the increase in the family formation rate in the decade of the 1960's will cause a gradual increase in new housing starts from an annual level of 1.6 million in 1963 to over 1.8 million in the second half of the decade, thus stimulating demand for building materials and household appliances. These tendencies will be more strongly felt in the Canadian economy, because while the age distribution of the population is about the same as in the United States, Canada has, in addition, an immigration factor that will cause greater demand for housing and similar requirements.[9]

Foreign Competition and Industrial Growth

Competition from foreign producers for domestic markets generally has not been a major concern for most U.S. industries. It has been a major factor for some industries in competing in foreign markets. For example, the cotton textile industry has been priced out of the foreign market by Japanese producers, and the Japanese have made significant inroads into the domestic market.

In some instances, the volume of imports of a product has not been a significant proportion of the total output, but imports constitute a major marginal difference. If domestic industry had had the imported volume, it would have been more profitable. For example, the rising level of steel imports has been a major problem for the steel industry since 1959. Steel imports have risen significantly since 1954 (See Figure 11–7) and have been a major factor in causing the industry to operate at below-capacity rates.

In recent years, industries have tended to seek government intervention if they cannot compete effectively in foreign markets or maintain their positions in domestic markets because of foreign competition. An example of this is the oil import quotas discussed below.

---

[9] "Perspective on Consumer Spending," *Monthly Review, The Bank of Nova Scotia* (Toronto: June, 1964).

FIGURE 11-7

**Comparison of Exports and Imports
Steel Mill Products**

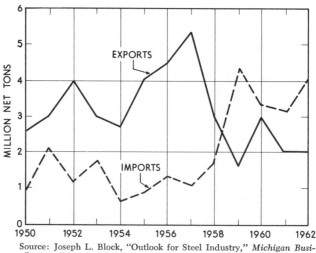

Source: Joseph L. Block, "Outlook for Steel Industry," *Michigan Business Review,* January, 1964.

SPECIAL FACTORS IN INDUSTRY ANALYSIS

Estimating future prosperity for an industry, projecting profits of a company into the future, or anticipating upturns and downturns in earnings is often difficult because of qualitative factors for which there are no precedents. However, an evaluation of the special factors that may affect the earning power of an industry is necessary if the analyst is to appraise the industry's prospects. Special or unusual considerations which are not accurately predictable include such things as (1) governmental attitudes and actions, (2) commodity price fluctuations, and (3) general economic conditions.

Governmental Actions

The motivation for governmental action may be political considerations contrary to the economics of the situation. Traditionally, governmental interference and regulation have been concerned with protecting those in inferior bargaining positions—that is, consumers against a vastly superior economic power. For example, electric utility regulation has as its goal the protection of consumers against exorbitant charges for electric power. However, in recent years, the federal government has tended to interfere in almost any emergency situation, no matter how minor. As a consequence, it is often difficult to predict what one's investment position will be, because the outcome is dependent on the desires and whims of a regulatory agency or functionary.

There also has been a tendency in recent years to use the powers of the federal government for the purpose of preventing some emergency, usually overproduction, in a segment of the economy. Therefore, it is becoming increasingly important for the analyst to have a knowledge of political trends and affairs in appraising industry prospects. For example, the future prospects of domestic crude oil producers were rather dim in 1964. The discovery costs of crude oil in Venezuela and the Middle East were so low that it was cheaper for oil refiners to buy foreign oil and pay transportation costs than to purchase domestic crude oil. The political uncertainty in the Middle East and Venezuela, plus the possibility of increased demand for oil, caused the U.S. government to give domestic crude oil producers special protection in the form of import quotas. These quotas limited the amount of foreign crude oil that could be imported. The net effect of these quotas was to reduce the profitability of the refiner-crude producer, known as an integrated oil company, who depended primarily on foreign crude, and to give a subsidy to the domestic crude producer.

Whether the investor agrees with a particular governmental action is not relevant. The important thing in investment analysis is that he anticipate the effect of this action on an industry in which he is interested. For example, the price support and crop control program of the U.S. Department of Agriculture limits the number of acres a farmer may plant in a certain crop. The net effect of this control has been more intensive cultivation of acreage allotments. Such cultivation has caused an unparalleled demand for fertilizer, which has improved sales of a number of companies in the chemical industry. However, in 1964 the cost of the price support program caused the U.S. Department of Agriculture to remove or lower price supports on many farm products. The futures of the fertilizer and farm equipment industries depend on the future of farm income, which, in turn, depends on action taken on the price-support program.

Commodity Prices as a Factor

In some industries, a change in the margin of profit is dependent on the price of a single commodity. The change in commodity prices is usually beyond the control of the industry affected. Generally, the defense of these companies against price fluctuations is to follow conservative financial practices, such as limiting the amount of debt capital used. These price fluctuations do affect profits and the value of their common stock as an investment. For example, copper prices make a considerable difference in the profits of copper producers, as may be seen in the Table 11–1, showing the estimated earnings per share of seven companies, at copper prices ranging from 25 to 35

TABLE 11–1

Estimated Earnings Per Share of Seven Companies at Different Levels of Copper Prices

Companies	25¢	Copper Prices 27¢	30¢	35¢
		Earnings per Share		
Anaconda	$2.10–2.15	$3.25–3.50	$4.25–4.50	$ 6.25
Copper Range	(loss)	(loss)	2.35	3.20
Inspiration	1.75–2.00	2.50	3.50	5.75
Kennecott	4.00	5.50	7.50	11.00
Magma	(loss)	(loss)	Break-even	8.00
Phelps Dodge	2.60–2.70	3.75	4.50	6.00

cents a pound. In forecasting copper prices, the thing to watch is the course of the index of industrial production because of the relationship of copper consumption to industrial production.

In other industries, a change in the margin of profit is dependent almost entirely on the price of a single commodity. Cigarette manufacturing is a good example. Labor costs are low, and the major costs are for leaf tobacco, which amount to three-fourths of the total manufacturing cost. Because of aging requirements, manufacturers carry a two- to three-year supply, and this inventory is valued at average cost. A decline in the price of leaf tobacco reduces the average cost of the inventory that eventually goes into cigarettes, and the margin of profit is wider because prices of cigarettes are relatively fixed. The analyst of tobacco company securities will, therefore, pay a good deal of attention to the trends in the price of leaf tobacco.

Not all companies value inventories in the way tobacco companies do. The customary accounting procedure is to revalue the total inventory at current market price if it is below the cost of the merchandise shown on the books. This results in recording a loss, which can substantially affect reported earnings in any one year. However, since an analysis covers a number of years, inventory pricing influences tend to balance out. Falling inventory prices may, therefore, impair the reported annual earnings of companies in certain industries, while the profits of cigarettes may actually move counter to the prevailing trend in general business conditions.

An industry vulnerable to inventory losses resulting from price declines is nonferrous metal smelters and refiners. In the case of copper smelters, the thing to watch is the course of scrap prices. These are very sensitive and tend to forecast trends in the primary market. A factor to watch relative to lead prices is the severity of the winter, since more lead storage batteries are replaced in very cold weather, and a major source of demand for lead is manufacture of batteries. Probable changes in tariffs are of importance to both copper and lead prices. Other industries in which there is a risk of inventory loss are meat-packing, because of already narrow profit margins, and broiler growing and packing, which is vulnerable to sharp seasonal price changes and market gluts.

Industry Cyclical Characteristics

In evaluating a company's securities and their suitability for the investor's program, the analyst should examine the vulnerability of the industry to cyclical fluctuations. An industry is generally considered to be vulnerable to cyclical fluctuations when production and/ or earnings fluctuate in sympathy with cyclical variations in general business activity.

The analyst will be more interested in the industry's earning's pattern, because earnings are more closely related to the value of securities, particularly common stock, than is production. However, comparable industry earnings and sales data are not available; therefore, industry production data are usually used in determining the relative vulnerability to cyclical fluctuations. Obviously, in those industries where composite earnings and sales data are available, the analyst should use these data. Generally, the analyst will have to rely on the data and the classification of industrial production used by the Federal Reserve Board of Governors, and for purposes of this discussion these data will be utilized.

Type of Production and Cyclical Variation. The stability of an industry's production is related to the ability of the user of its production to postpone consumption or replacement of the product. For example, the need to replace a consumed loaf of bread is not lessened simply because the wage earner in the family is out of work. Thus, the bakery industry's production is very stable. On the other hand, a railroad can indefinitely postpone replacement of a freight car by spending more on its maintenance or by lengthening the hours it operates. Consequently, the railroad equipment industry is characterized by violent fluctuations in production.

In analyzing the cyclical characteristics of industries, the most important distinction the analyst can make is between durable and nondurable goods industries. Nondurable goods are those destroyed quickly through use and, if essential, must be replaced. The purchase of durable goods, such as railroad equipment, can be deferred for indefinite periods. More significantly, when this deferred demand for durable goods is satisfied later by much greater purchases business activity increases, which tends to increase the amplitude of the fluctuations. The relative differences in the production of durable and nondurable goods and the output of utilities are shown in Figure 11–8. During the recessions of 1954, 1957, and 1959, production of durable goods dropped appreciably more than production of nondurable goods, and there was scarcely a ripple in the output of utilities.

The analyst cannot assume that all durable goods industries have erratic sales and all nondurable goods industries experience stable sales. It is necessary to make a further refinement in the classification. The analyst should determine whether the goods are used by consumers or producers. If the industry's production is used by persons to provide direct satisfaction and comfort, it is classified as a "consumer" goods industry. Products used to aid the production of other goods are called "producers" goods. Both consumer goods and producer goods may be either durable or nondurable. Consumer goods, particularly nondurables, tend to have a more stable demand pattern than the other classifications. The demand for producers goods tends to fluctuate in about the same degree as business activity.

There are often exceptions to these generalizations. For example, cosmetics and toilet articles are nondurable consumer goods, but the industry's production has shown a tendency to fluctuate with changes in business activity. In most cases, however, this general classification can provide the evidence the analyst needs to determine the cyclical stability of an industry. The classic example is the steel industry, a basic producers goods industry. Figure 11–9 shows the index of monthly output of steel from 1945–1965. This industry is very sensitive to cyclical fluctuations, since production dropped in sym-

FIGURE 11-8

Industrial Production, Durable and Nondurable Goods Manufactures and Utilities, Monthly, Seasonally Adjusted

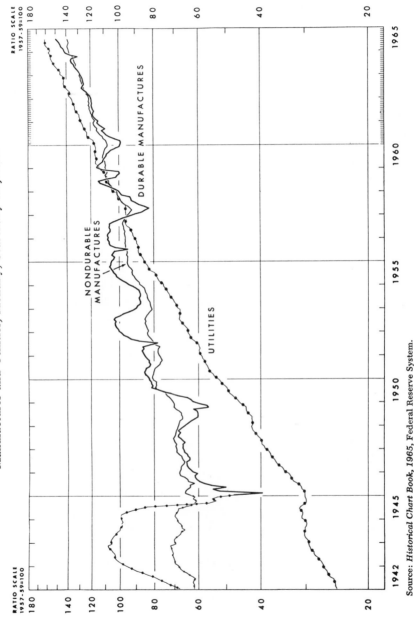

Source: *Historical Chart Book, 1965*, Federal Reserve System.

pathy with every decline in business activity in the last 20 years. However, with the tendency in recent years for companies to diversify their industry interests, it has become increasingly difficult for the analyst to generalize about an industry's cyclical characteristics.

SUMMARY

Appraisal of the relationship of stock market prices to industry prospects is a matter of properly assessing qualitative factors that may affect the industry in the future. Past performance of the industry provides the basis for estimating the future growth of the industry. The preceding discussion may leave one with the impression that the investor should buy securities only in growth industries. The implication is also that the investor should buy the securities of those industries with a favorable outlook and sell the securities of those with an unfavorable outlook. This policy will be successful only if the analyst can recognize changes in industry prospects before these changes are recognized by a lot of other investors, and before they are already reflected in market price.

Recognition of when industry prospects have been discounted by the market is a matter of judgment. Judgments unfettered by emotion are difficult unless the analyst has some measure of the relative appraisal of the industry's prospects by the market. The best method of measuring this is to compare the average prices of a group of common stocks of companies within the industry with some measure of the general level of stock market prices, such as the Dow-Jones averages or Standard and Poor's 500 stock average. These comparisons are usually available in published data. An example of price comparisons is shown in Figure 11–10.

These charts provide a comprehensive picture of the trend of market prices of common stocks by industry groups. Such data as these can provide a checkpoint which should be helpful in deciding the market's appraisal of the industry's prospects.

The basic economic climate of an industry may be favorable to the profitability of companies in the industry. It is necessary to add to this the all-important ingredient of company management. The industry may grow in production, sales, and profits, but it cannot be assumed that every company in the industry profits from this growth. Opportunities for profits may abound. However, if the management of the company does not take advantage of them, the company may

FIGURE 11-9

Monthly Steel Production Index
(1957–59 = 100)

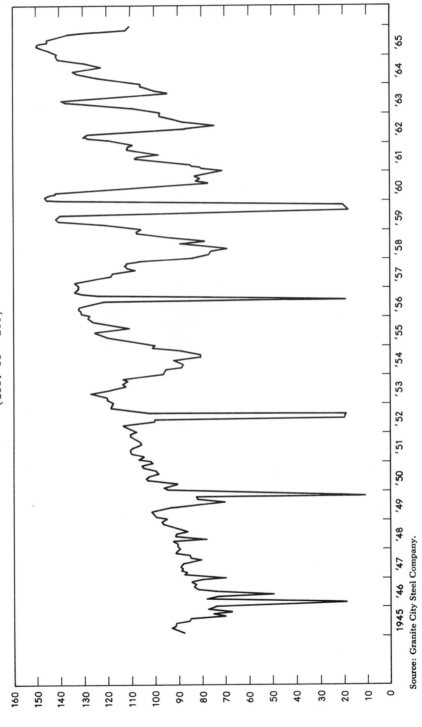

Source: Granite City Steel Company.

FIGURE 11–10

Price Performance of Industry Stock Groups
Relative to General Market
(Rate Scales—1941–43 = 10)

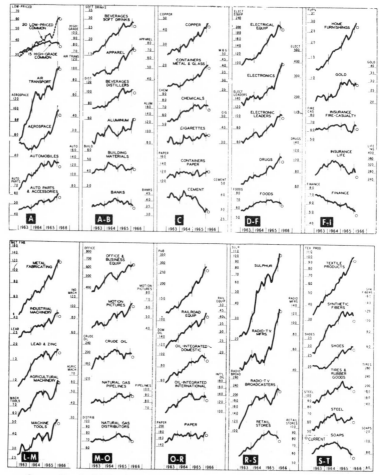

Source: Standard & Poor's Stock Summary.

not prosper. It is often said facetiously that some companies make profit in spite of the management.

There are a number of examples in which the management of a company has failed to capitalize on the opportunities for growth in its industry. One such example is Curtis Publishing Company, which was once a leader in a growing industry. Mismanagement or lack of management by a succession of managements caused the company to slip badly and to experience severe losses from 1960–64. Another example was Studebaker Corporation, which lost its market position in the post-World War II automobile market. After a series of halting recoveries it finally, in 1964, gave up as a domestic producer of automobiles.

In contrast, Inland Steel Corporation has showed a steady increase in sales, profits, and the market price of its stock at a time when the steel industry was plagued with overcapacity, foreign competition, and a wage–price squeeze. Zenith Radio Corporation is another company which has shown an excellent performance, even at times when the radio and television industry was generally unprofitable due to overcapacity and price-cutting.

REVIEW QUESTIONS AND PROBLEMS

1. What are some of the reasons why industries show differing rates of growth?
2. What are some of the reasons why a company may have a certain degree of shelter from competition?
3. Why would a rapid growth in sales not be profitable for an industry?
4. Why is research and development a necessity in such industries as food and electric machinery?
5. Why would the shoe industry almost be guaranteed a moderate growth in sales and production in the next decade?
6. Describe the stages of industry development. Why may an industry depart significantly from this pattern?
7. What industries would be affected significantly by a change in farm prices; a change in oil prices; a change in coal prices?
8. What is meant by the term "corporate pluralist"?
9. What dangers for the investor are inherent in government subsidies to and protection of an industry?
10. What is the important distinction between (a) durable and nondurable goods, (b) consumer and producer goods?
11. If a consumer goods industry reaches maturity, what factors would determine its future rate of growth?

CHAPTER **12**

Analysis of Industrial Securities— Financial Statements

Every serious student of security analysis critically analyzes company financial statements. The data provided by these financial statements—the balance sheet or statement of financial position and the income statement—reduce the performance of the company and its management to a quantitative standard of value, the dollar. Therefore, analysis of these data is helpful in appraising the value of the company's securities, because it places the qualitative estimates of the company's future prospects in better perspective.

INTRODUCTION TO FINANCIAL STATEMENT ANALYSIS

The efficient analysis of financial statements requires that the analyst follow a basic procedure. The financial statement analytical process involves: (1) establishment of the purpose and objectives of the analysis, (2) familiarization with accounting and reporting practices, (3) preparation of the statements for analysis, (4) selection and use of tools of analysis and interpretation of the analysis.

Determination of the objectives and purpose of the analysis is of the utmost importance. If the analyst can decide why he is making the analysis, it will help him in selection of the proper data and tools of analysis. In addition, the standards chosen for judging financial position will tend to be different if the analyst is viewing the business as a creditor, not as a common stock investor or as part of the company's management. For example, when judging the current financial condition of a business, a general impression is the higher current ratio, the better the financial position. From the viewpoint of the creditor, a high current ratio would be a favorable indication of credit worthiness. However, it would not necessarily reflect favorably

218

on the company as a common stock investment, because it may be an indication of an overcautious management, which may have redundant cash balances and poor asset utilization.[1] As a consequence, the efficient analysis of financial statements requires that the analyst carefully determine what his objectives are.

Familiarization with Accounting Practices

The accounting profession has belatedly begun to recognize that there is a sort of double standard in financial reporting.[2] It has been a "generally accepted accounting practice" to allow companies to use different inventory costing techniques, depreciation methods, etc., which yield significantly different financial results for companies with approximately the same operating performance. This tendency limits the usefulness of corporate financial statements generally.

As discussed earlier in Chapter 10, the analyst frequently uses the financial statements of one or two other companies as an analytical reference standard—the limited industry standard. The meaningful comparison of one company's financial statements with those of another assumes that both have followed similar accounting practices. The tendency in present-day accounting practice and techniques is to allow the company to use those procedures that minimize income tax liability. These standards give companies considerable latitude in the choice of accounting techniques and procedures, which may produce widely varying results. The company has conformed to generally accepted standards and the certified public accountant attests this fact. Some of the more important variations will be discussed later in the chapter.

A less important limitation is the completeness of data presented on financial statements. Generally, companies present sufficient data for the analyst to assess the past financial performance of the companies. There are some notable exceptions that frustrate the analyst's attempts to get a good picture of financial condition and earning power. For example, major classifications of expenses on the income statement are sometimes lumped together.

---

[1] Erick A. Helfert, *Techniques of Financial Analysis* (Homewood, Ill.: Richard D. Irwin, Inc., 1963), p. 55.

[2] Leonard M. Savoie, "The Accounting Principles Board," *Financial Analysts Journal*, Vol. XXI, No. 3 (May–June, 1965), p. 39.

Preparation of Statements for Analysis

Details presented on financial statements differ considerably. To facilitate the analytical process and reduce the tedium, it is often helpful to reduce the many different descriptive titles and forms for presenting data on financial statements into a standard form. The product of this procedure is the standard balance sheet and income statement.

After the analyst has become familiar with the accounting practices of the companies being analyzed, the terminology used on the financial statements, and the basis of valuation, he will usually find that it is helpful to reduce all the detail to a standard financial statement, such as the examples of a standard balance sheet and standard income statement shown in Tables 12–1 and 12–2.

TABLE 12–1

Standard Balance Sheet Form

Assets		Liabilities	
Cash	XXX	Short-term debt	XXX
Receivables	XXX	Long-term debt	XXX
Inventories	XXX	Total debt	XXX
Gross plant and equipment . XXX		Preferred stock	XXX
Depreciation . . XXX		Common stock and capital surplus .	XXX
Net plant and equipment	XXX	Retained earnings	XXX
Other assets	XXX	Total	XXX
Total	XXX		

The preparation of standard balance sheets and income statements can become involved if the analyst attempts to be too precise. To do so would be self-defeating, because the process does not have any significance other than to increase comprehension and simplify the analytical process. Sometimes, items presented on the published statements are not clearly identified or explained. In those situations, a more intensive investigation may be indicated. It may be necessary for the analyst to make inquiry of the management of the company as to the nature of the item. Before such an investigation is begun, the test of materiality should be applied. The analyst should ask himself whether the amount in question will make any material or significant difference in the end result. Are the amounts so large that they will tend to have a distorting effect on evaluation of the financial performance of the company? Generally speaking, if the total of questionable items does not amount to more than 5 percent of total assets, income, short-term debt, long-term debt, or net worth, it is not worth spending time on additional investigation.

The income statement or, as it is sometimes called, the profit and loss statement bridges the gap between the balance sheet made up at the beginning of a fiscal period and the ending balance sheet. No uniform order of presentation or content for the income statement has been established by the accounting profession.

TABLE 12–2

Standard Income Statement Form

Net sales		XXX
Cost of goods sold		XXX
Gross income		XXX
Operating expenses:		
Selling and administrative expense	XXX	
Taxes, other than income	XXX	
Other expenses	XXX	
Total operating expenses before depreciation		XXX
Net operating income before depreciation		XXX
Depreciation and depletion expense		XXX
Net operating income		XXX
Interest on debt		XXX
Income before income taxes		XXX
Income taxes		XXX
Net income		XXX

The classification of items shown on this standard income statement should not be regarded as final and definitive. It is a suggested form that might be used by the analyst to facilitate analysis. However, the classification of items should be changed if it would be more meaningful to the analyst.

Choice of Tools of Analysis

Choice of the proper tools of analysis is the first step in effective interpretation of financial statement analysis; proficient interpretation is the basis of security valuation. The novice frequently believes that the more ratios he computes, the better is his analysis. He somehow equates the quality of the analysis with its weight in pounds. The net effect of such a practice is that he gets lost in a morass of data, and interpretation of the data is practically impossible.

The measures discussed in this chapter are believed to be adequate for analysis of most industrial financial statements. Because of some uniqueness in a company's operations, there may be special circumstances that make it necessary to devise or use other tools. The analyst should keep his analysis to bare essentials, because superfluous ratios decrease comprehension and increase the difficulty of interpretation.

Importance of Interpretation

The importance of interpretation of financial statement analyses varies with the type of security being appraised and the basic investment objective of the investor. The quality of high-grade bonds and preferred stocks can be more accurately appraised from past financial performance than can the quality of the common stock. To be rated as high-quality investments, bonds and preferred stock must meet certain standards of quality which are more accurately measurable.

Common stock evaluation places less emphasis on past financial performance. The investor is purchasing a claim to an indeterminable amount of future earnings. Consequently, the analyst will be as interested in the effect of qualitative factors on future earnings as he is in past financial performance. The previous discussion of qualitative versus quantitative factors may have left the impression that there is seldom any relationship between the past and the future. This is not so, because rarely are there dramatic developments that cause a company's earnings to depart significantly from the past pattern.

Sometimes, in common stock valuation the analysis of financial statements is apparently almost useless. For instance, in the valuation of speculative situations where (1) the period of operation has not been long enough to make the financial statements meaningful or (2) future prospects are so outstanding that past performance is apparently in no way indicative of future financial performance. In these situations, the analyst has no way of appraising the probabilities of loss or gain. Such situations are the province of what is popularly called "the speculator." An example of such a situation in 1965 was the common stock for Kalvar Corporation, which manufactures film that can be used in dry process photography. The company was organized in 1956, and by April, 1965, had not shown a profit. The common stock of Kalvar has sold as high at $700 a share, and in 1965 was selling at prices ranging between $55–75 a share. It is possible that future earnings may justify the confidence that investors have had in this company, but an analysis of past financial performance would be of little help in evaluating the situation.

THE BALANCE SHEET

The first step in financial statement analysis is familiarization with the company's accounting practices, and preparation of its statements for analysis. The basic financial statements of the corporation are the balance sheet, or financial position statement, and income statement. The analyst examines each item on these statements as well as the underlying accounting principles used.

The balance sheet shows the financial position of the company at any one point in time. For example, a balance sheet for the year ending December 31, 1965, shows the financial position at that time. Use of this balance sheet in adjudging the financial position of the company at a later time must be done with the implicit assumption that there has been no radical change in the financial position of the company since the issue date.

The analyst should study more than one balance sheet if he is to get some indication of the company's past performance. An intelligent appraisal of financial position and performance must include an examination of the income statements of the company and a number of past balance sheets. Listed on the left side of the balance sheet are the assets, or uses, of corporate resources; on the right side are the claims against these assets by creditors (liabilities) and stockholders (net worth), or the sources of funds. The basis for segregating items on the balance sheet is time. Certain portions of both assets and liabilities are customarily classified as "current." Current assets consist of cash and other assets that will be converted into cash within one year through operations. Current liabilities, called in the following discussion "short-term debt," are debts that must be paid or replaced by other financing within one year. The difference between current assets and short-term debt is the net working capital or that portion of current assets financed by capital funds (long-term debt plus net worth). The remaining assets are generally either the company's plant and equipment or a catchall classification, "other assets."

The purposes in analyzing the balance sheet are to determine: (1) whether a company has sufficient working capital, (2) the present financial position of the corporation and its solvency, and (3) the capital structure of the corporation and the relative claims of its securities.

Current Assets

The major classifications on the left side of the balance sheet are usually current assets, fixed assets or plant and equipment, and other assets. Current assets are those that will be converted into cash within a short period of time, or within one year will be sold, consumed, or otherwise change composition through normal operations of the business. These current assets are usually divided into three broad groups —cash, receivables, and inventories. Sometimes, a balance sheet may show prepaid expenses as a current asset. As an example, the Ralston-Purina Consolidated Balance Sheet of September 30, 1965, shows prepaid expenses as a current asset. These prepaid expenses represent payments to others for services to be received. In one sense, they are an inventory of services. The relatively small size of the prepaid expense item usually does not cause it to be a major factor in preparation of the balance sheet for analysis. However, it is normally included in the other asset classification on the standard balance sheet (see page 220).

Cash and Its Equivalent

The purpose of cash balances is to allow the company to transact business in an orderly manner during periods when cash outflow exceeds cash inflow from operations. Obviously, it is in the best interests of the company to keep its cash balances to a minimum, because they do not yield income to the company. For this reason, many companies tend to hold cash in the form of marketable securities, certificates of deposit, and other short term investments. These highly marketable and liquid assets should be considered as part of the company cash balances. Companies tend to include these liquid current assets as part of the cash balances.[3] For example, the Husky Oil Co. Canada, Limited annual report for 1964 lists the cash items as "cash and short-term investments."

---

[3] *Accounting Trends and Techniques* (18th ed.; New York: American Institute of Certified Public Accountants, Inc., 1964), p. 23.

Large holdings of marketable securities generally cannot be considered as either cash equivalent or current assets. For example, Sinclair Oil Corporation holds as an investment 2,447,162 shares of common stock and $15,294,700 of convertible subordinated debentures of Richfield Oil Corporation. Although these securities are listed on the New York Stock Exchange, it would be unrealistic to assume that this stock could be liquidated in sufficiently short periods to include it as a part of the cash and its equivalent.

Cash earmarked for a specific purpose, or restricted as to use in operations, should not be considered part of the cash balances. Sometimes, certain portions of the cash are designated for construction of a building or for liquidation of long-term debts. For example, Douglas Aircraft Company, Inc., in its 1963 annual report listed an item, "U.S. Treasury Bills held for additional construction at new Space Systems Center." Although these funds were held in a form that would be considered as cash equivalent, they could not be considered as part of the cash available for the normal operations of the business.

Receivables

Receivables consist of credits extended by the company to others. These credits may include: notes receivable, which are formal promises to pay; accounts receivable, which are extensions of credit on open book account; advances to subsidiaries; and receivables arising from unusual transactions, such as sales of capital assets. For purposes of analysis, the advances to subsidiaries and receivables from unusual transactions should be excluded from the receivables classification on the standard balance sheet. The general rules to follow in determining whether or not to include an item in this classification are: (1) will it be collected within the next 12 months; (2) did the receivable arise during the normal operating cycle of the business? If the receivable meets these tests, it should be considered as a part of the receivables and working capital of the company. Companies often segregate receivables that do not meet these criteria. For example, Otis Elevator Company in 1963 showed as noncurrent assets "Notes and Accounts Receivable-Long Term—$4,849,736" and "investments in and Advances to Subsidiaries-Not Consolidated—$19,410,500." Obviously, these receivables do not meet the tests for receivables enumerated above.

Quality of the receivables is important to the analyst. A substantial increase in receivables as a percent of sales may indicate that the company is attempting to improve or sustain sales volume by liberal credit policy. A good example of this tactic was used by the management of J. I. Case Company in 1959. J. I. Case increased sales from $81,579,000 in 1956 to $194,000,000 in 1959, an increase of 286 percent. During the period, net income of J. I. Case also increased at an even more rapid rate. The poor quality of receivables emanating from these sales became evident in 1960 and 1961, when the company had substantial credit losses.

To get indication of receivables quality, the analyst may compute receivables as a percent of sales and number of days' sales represented by receivables. Receivables as a percent of sales is computed by dividing the receivables at year-end by sales for the period. The number of days' sales or collection period analysis is derived as follows:

1. Determine average daily sales:

$$\frac{\text{SALES}}{\text{DAYS}} = \frac{\$7,300}{365} = \$20 \text{ per day.}$$

2. Determine days' sales represented receivables:

$$\frac{\text{RECEIVABLES}}{\text{SALES PER DAY}} = \frac{\$823}{\$20} = 41.1 \text{ days.}$$

This analysis gives a rough indication of the overall quality of receivables. This is particularly true if number of sales represented by receivables is related to the company's terms of sale.

A more specific indicator of quality may be obtained by an "aging" of receivables. Aging is a classification of receivables by due dates—which are current and which are overdue. Since this information is not available to the analyst, he can use the previously explained tools, which would provide warning signals if there are any significant departures from past patterns.

The analyst should pay particular attention to companies that sell goods on long-term credit. These companies include bowling equipment manufacturers, land development companies, farm implement manufacturers, and office equipment manufacturers.

Inventory

A corporation's inventory is the stock of goods and services it has for sale. The inventory, like any current asset, is a direct link between the balance sheet and income statement, because today's inventory, an asset, is tomorrow's cost of goods sold, an expense. Therefore, the inventory valuation method will affect the cost of goods sold figure on future income statements. If the last goods in are charged against current income (LIFO) in a period of rising prices, the value of the inventory on the balance sheet would be less than if the first goods in are charged against current income (FIFO). In the case of rising prices, the LIFO company is also understating profits or net income relative to the FIFO company. A more detailed discussion of the effects of LIFO versus FIFO on corporate net income will be deferred to the discussion of the income statement. For the present, the important factor to recognize is that during periods of rising prices firms using LIFO tend to have inventories that are undervalued relative to firms using FIFO.

The differences in the methods of inventory valuation make it difficult if not impossible to compare financial condition and operating performance of companies that use different methods of inventory valuation. A 1963 survey of the accounting techniques of 600 companies indicated that the "most frequently used method of cost determination" was LIFO.[4] Frequently, the analyst's problem is further complicated because the company may not disclose its method of inventory valuation in its annual report. In the aforementioned survey, it was reported that 185 out of 600 survey companies, or about 30 percent, did not disclose the method of inventory valuation.

An analysis of changing relationships between the various classes of inventory—finished goods, work in process, and raw materials— can sometimes indicate management's effectiveness in forecasting sales and its general overall ability to manage production scheduling. An increasing proportion of raw materials inventory may suggest that management has bought in excess of current needs or that the current sales for the fiscal period did not meet its expectations. An increasing proportion of total inventory and finished goods may suggest that the goods are not being sold so rapidly as before or, perhaps, that obsolete merchandise is not being closed out or written down fast enough. When the balance sheet is drawn up, the usual procedure is to value inventories at original cost or current market price, whichever is lower. If current market is lower, the write-down will produce a loss

---

[4] *Ibid.*, p. 47.

that will reduce stated earnings for the fiscal period. This write-down will permit a lower cost for the goods that are sold in the coming fiscal period, thus improving the future profit margin.

The primary measure of the quality and relative size of inventory is the turnover. The inventory turnover is computed by dividing annual sales by the ending inventory. Ending inventory is used because an unusual buildup in inventory during a fiscal year would be more easily detected than had an average inventory been used. The rate of inventory liquidation can be estimated by using this turnover figure. For example, a turnover of four times a year would indicate that inventory is being completely sold out every 90 days. A declining rate of turnover would indicate either a failure to dispose of obsolete inventory or too much inventory in relation to sales, as mentioned earlier.

Fixed Assets

Fixed assets consist of land, buildings, machinery, and equipment. These items are usually carried as plant and equipment or property, plant, and equipment. For this account, the value usually stated on the balance sheet is the gross dollar amount that was expended or the original cost of these items. To arrive at net amounts, there is usually a depreciation deduction that indicates the amount of gross plant and equipment written off. The amount deducted is usually referred to as the allowance for depreciation or the accumulated depreciation.

It is difficult for the analyst to draw any meaningful conclusions about a company from a study of its fixed asset accounts because of the significant variations in depreciation methods and the differences in cost of plant additions. Depreciation (which will be discussed later in the income statement section) may be accumulated either on an accelerated basis or by use of the straight-line method. The net effect of using one of the accelerated methods is to understate the relative value of the plant and equipment account.

These differences in method in fixed asset accounting are not too important to the analyst, since the tendency is to place emphasis on the earning power of the company rather than on its asset values. However, this item is a significant matter in judging the relative earning capacity of firms, because the depreciation charges using an accelerated method may cause a relative understatement in earnings.

Liabilities

Liabilities are recognized claims of creditors against the assets of the firm. These liabilities have a claim on the assets and earnings of the firm prior to the owner's equity interest, both of which are shown on the right-hand side of the balance sheet. These liabilities may be cash liabilities or service liabilities. Cash liabilities are debts that must be paid in cash, such as bank debt and bonds. Service liabilities are the deferred income or deferred credits that may be liquidated by the delivery of the company's product or the performance of services.

The conventional balance sheet classification of these liabilities is current liabilities and noncurrent liabilities. Generally, current liabilities include short-term borrowings; the long-term indebtedness is presented in the noncurrent liabilities section. A third liability account, deferred income, is used to identify the services liabilities mentioned before. These deferred income accounts may be shown separately, as a current liability or as a deduction from a related asset. For example, unearned discount on notes receivable may be shown on the balance sheet either as a deduction from notes receivable or as a liability. Cash liabilities that are payable or mature within one year are classified, for our purposes, as short-term debt. Cash liabilities that have a maturity of longer than one year will be included in the capitalization or capital funds classification. The capital funds include all permanent or long-term financing of the company, both long-term debt and equity.

Short-Term Debt

The short-term debt, or cash current liabilities, consists of notes and accounts payable to trade creditors, accrued taxes, and wages. Sometimes, corporations will include as short-term debt the portion of long-term debt that matures within the next year.

The significant analytical consideration in the appraisal of short-term debt is the size of the debt. A relatively large short-term debt often foretells the need for additional long-term debt or equity financing. Corporations sometimes use bank loans to finance expanding operations. After the net working capital reaches a low point, they refinance the short-term debt by the issuance of bonds or the sale of additional common stock. For example, Home Oil Company, Ltd., a

Canadian crude oil producer, follows this policy in financing oil exploration and acquisitions with bank loans and refinancing the bank loans with long-term debt. Its net working capital of $1,280,000 at the year-end 1961 declined to net working capital deficiency of $14,890,991 in August, 1964. At that time, the company refinanced the short-term debt by the sale of convertible subordinated debentures which conformed to the company's past pattern of financing.

There are other forms of short-term debt of the service liability type. These service liabilities may be shown on the balance sheet at any one of three places, discussed below.

Deferred Income

Deferred income is used to identify credit balances that will normally be transferred to revenue accounts as they are realized or earned. This deferred income may be shown in three different places on the balance sheet. It may be shown as a deduction from the related asset. For example, Combustion Engineering, Inc., at the end of 1963 showed "Accounts receivable, less unearned billings of $33,-296,831 in 1963 and $30,897,384 in 1962."[5] In other cases, the deferred income account is shown as part of the current liability section or as a separate classification between the noncurrent liabilities and stockholders' equity section. For example, the Meredith Publishing Company, magazine publishers, showed an "Unearned Subscription Liability" of $16,083,623. This service liability will be taken into income as magazines are printed and delivered to fulfill the product and services liability.

The method by which this deferred income is taken into earned income should be investigated by the analyst. This is particularly true where the deferred income represents time charges on installment contracts. The company may take the charges into income on a straight-line basis, on a sum-of-the-year's-digits basis, or some combination of these methods. Use of the straight-line basis would result in a lower earned income than would use of the sum-of-the-year's-digits method.

Long-Term Debt

Cash liabilities of the company often include long-term debt. This classification includes all debt that has a maturity of longer than one

---

[5] *Ibid.*, p. 96.

year. For purposes of our discussion, it will be included in the capital funds classification.

Capital Funds

The capital funds or capitalization includes all long-term or permanent financing, such as the long-term debt and the net worth of the company. Long-term debt is all debt with a maturity longer than one year. Stockholders' equity is the total of preferred stock, common stock, capital surplus, and retained earnings.

The use of debt or preferred stock in financing a company provides capital structure leverage. The advantage to the investor of capital structure leverage is that it tends to increase the earnings available to the common stockholders. For example, a company has assets of $200,000 and earns $20,000 before interest and taxes on these assets, or 10 percent. If the company finances the entire amount with common stock, the return to common stock will also be 10 percent. The use of debt of $100,000 at 4 percent interest to finance the assets, along with $100,000 in common stock, would have the effect of increasing the rate of return on the common stock. To illustrate:

$$\frac{\text{Income before Interest and Taxes } \$20,000}{\text{Total Assets } \$200,000} = 10 \text{ Percent}$$

After the debt is issued, the income statement would read as follows.

```
Income before tax and interest ............$20,000
Less: interest @ 4 percent ................  4,000
Income available to common stock ........$16,000
```

The rate of return on common stock would be increased from 10 to 16 percent.

$$\frac{\text{Income after Taxes and Interest } \$16,000}{\text{Common Stock Equity } \$100,000} = 16 \text{ Percent}$$

Additional funds for a company's expansion may come from (1) internal generation of funds and (2) external financing. Frequently, rapidly growing companies do not internally generate sufficient funds to finance continued growth and expansion. As a consequence, these companies usually must seek funds externally. The form of this financing is of utmost importance to the common stockholder. If a company's expansion is financed by the use of prior claim capital, the growth in earnings per share of common stock is obviously going to be accelerated because of the leverage afforded. That is, all other things being equal, the earnings per share will increase at a more rapid rate than earnings before interest and taxes.

A rapidly expanding company may outrun its ability to finance continued expansion by the use of prior claim capital and internally generated funds. In this case, the company may be faced with the alternative of selling more common stock or curtailing its expansion. Neither of these alternatives may be good for the stockholder. Obviously, curtailment of profitable expansion is not a desirable course of action. If the choice is to finance the expansion by the sale of more common stock, the result may be a dilution in the per share earnings of the present common stockholders. This dilution is caused by the necessity of spreading the total earnings of the company over a larger number of shares of common stock. It does not necessarily follow that *all* new common stock sales will reduce per share earnings of common stock, but in leveraged situations it almost certainly will have that effect. A detailed discussion of the dilution of new common stock issues may be found on page 310.

Analysis of Capital Funds. Analysis of the capital funds of a corporation involves an examination of (1) the coverage of debt service charges, and (2) the leverage position of the company. Leverage tends to magnify the volatility of a company's earnings. For example, Kaiser Steel Corporation has a highly leveraged capital structure, with long-term debt amounting to about 47 percent and preferred stock 13 percent of capital funds. Kaiser Steel has historically used more prior claim capital than steel companies generally, and it is evident from Table 12–3 that Kaiser continues to use proportionately more prior claim capital than does the steel industry. Naturally, this tends to cause a more pronounced fluctuation in the earnings of Kaiser Steel than in those of the industry generally. (See Figure 12–1).

Of greater significance in times of poor business conditions is the relative ability of the corporation to service its long-term debt. Debt service payments include (1) interest on debt, (2) sinking fund payments, and (3) maturing obligations. Tests for coverage of interest payments or fixed charges will be discussed in a later section. The analyst should analyze the amount of required sinking fund payments and maturing obligations as well as the interest charges. The maturity of a large portion of the long-term debt in any one year is inherently dangerous. The dangers arise from two factors. First, the corporation may have to refund the debt at a higher interest rate, which will affect

FIGURE 12–1

Earnings 1953 to 1964—Kaiser Steel and the Steel Industry

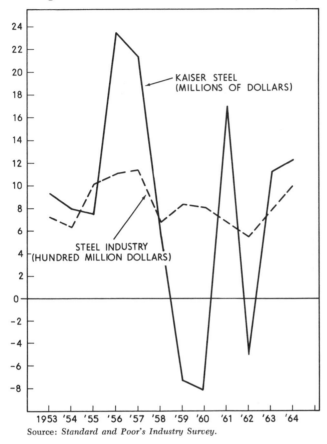

Source: *Standard and Poor's Industry Survey.*

the future profitability of the company. This is particularly significant for public utilities, whose rate of return on assets is limited by regulation. This analysis problem will be discussed in more detail in Chapter 15.

A more serious problem is the possible inability of the corporation to refinance the maturing obligations on any terms, or to have sufficient cash on hand to retire them. This set of circumstances is, of course, the more dangerous of the two, because it almost inevitably results in at least a temporary impairment of the value of the securities, both bonds and stock, of the corporation. Analysts have tended to de-emphasize the importance of this hazard during the last 15 years, because there have not been many cases of loss to investors

TABLE 12-3

Total Liabilities and Net Worth, Year-end 1964,
Kaiser Steel Corporation and Steel Industry

	Kaiser Steel (in thousands)		Industry (in millions)	
	Amount	Percent	Amount	Percent
Liabilities:				
Total Current	$ 47,525	11.4	$ 2,484	14.8
Funded Debt	196,411	47.1	2,689	16.0
Equity:				
Preferred Stock	52,349	12.6	640	3.8
Common Stock	3,317	0.8	2,563	15.2
Capital Surplus	1,754	0.4	919	5.4
Earned Surplus	115,434	27.7	7,544	44.8
Total	$416,790	100.0	$16,840	100.0

Source: *Standard and Poor's Industry Survey.*

from corporate reorganizations and bankruptcy in this period. Although relatively rare among publicly owned corporations, in some cases investors have experienced a total loss. For example, Ludman Corporation was adjudicated a bankrupt in 1960, and the common stock was declared by the court to be worthless. The Ludman Corporation 6 percent debentures, 1968, which sold as high as 105 in 1955, were selling at 38 in May, 1960. This financial difficulty arose from an inability to make sinking fund and interest payments.

Contractual Equity Value Factors

The analyst should investigate the terms and provisions of contracts that have been entered into by the company and their possible effect on the future earnings and value of the common stock. The two most common contractual equity value factors are (1) dividend restrictions in bond indentures and (2) potential equity dilution from the exercise of contractual rights, such as conversion privileges.

Most bond indentures include some restrictive provisions designed to protect bondholders against the dissipation of corporate assets. They usually prohibit payment of dividends if such payment would reduce cash or working capital or retained earnings below a specified dollar amount. For example, Vanadium-Alloys Steel Company has a loan agreement provision "which restricts the payment of dividends other than in shares of stock of the Company. At June 30, 1963, approximately $4,500,000 of accumulated retained earnings was free of this restriction. There is also a requirement that the Company maintain a working capital of $5,000,000."[6] This company would be prohibited from paying cash dividends if working capital drops below $5 million, even if the company has sufficient earnings to justify payment of dividends.

The possible dilution of the equity interest of the corporation through the exercise of conversion privileges, options, or warrants may be quite large. For example, on September 30, 1964, McCrory Corporation had outstanding 5,210,396 shares of common stock exclusive of any treasury stock. McCrory Corporation had reserved 4,139,667 shares of additional common stock to cover stock options, the possible conversion of convertible preferred stock, the exercise of warrants, and employee stock purchase plans. The exercise of all these contingent rights to purchase common stock of McCrory would increase the common stock outstanding by approximately 79.5 percent, and would exert a downward pressure on earnings per share of existing stock. Of course, the exercise of these warrants and options, and the conversion of these bonds, would also either reduce outstanding indebtedness or increase the basic equity of the company. But the common stockholder is in the unfortunate position of having other investors watching to see whether the company's future operations will be profitable and, if they are, participating in these future profits. On the other hand, if the profits do not materialize in the future, the present common stockholders bear the brunt of the poor earnings.

Consolidated Balance Sheets

Much of the growth of companies in the last 10 years has been through acquisitions of other companies by purchase of all or part of the common stock and other securities of these corporations, which become subsidiaries of the parent corporation. In consolidating balance sheets, these corporations, consisting of the parent and subsidiary companies, are treated as though they were essentially one company, despite the fact that each corporation is an individual entity.

The accounting practices of companies vary considerably with respect to consolidating operating results of subsidiaries. A 1963 survey of the practices of firms in consolidating the operating results of

---

[6] *Ibid.*, p. 213.

subsidiaries indicates that of 561 reporting companies with subsidiaries, 238 companies fully consolidated results, "298 companies had some not consolidated, and only 25"[7] reported all subsidiaries as unconsolidated.

A company that does not consolidate all its operating results should be examined carefully to determine whether this is being done to eliminate unprofitable operations from reported operations. The reasons for not consolidating results are usually reported. The principal reasons advanced for the decision to consolidate or not are:

(1) the degree of control by the parent company.
(2) the extent to which the subsidiary is an integral part of the operating group, and
(3) whether the subsidiary is a domestic or a foreign corporation.[8]

THE INCOME STATEMENT

The classification of income statement items appears to vary more widely than does the classification of balance sheet data. These variations tend to complicate the analysis of income statements. The following discussion of the more significant income statement items will indicate the problem areas.

Sales

Sales are generally shown as net sales. In some cases, gross sales may be shown, with deductions for sales allowances (refunds of money to customers), sales returns (returns of merchandise), and freight charges. The net sales figure can vary considerably from gross sales. For example, American Home Products Corporation showed, for fiscal year 1963, gross sales of $575,043,128 and a deduction for returns, allowances, delivery, etc., of $42,638,470. The deduction is roughly 7.3 percent of sales.

Sometimes the information reported by companies on the income statement is rather sparse. For example, in 1963 Electrolux Corporation showed as the initial item on the income statement the operating profit before provision for depreciation. It was not possible in this case for the analyst to determine the amount and nature of the operating expenses or the cost of goods sold. For that matter, the trend of sales, which is important to the analyst, could not be observed

---

[7] *Ibid.*, p. 143.
[8] *Ibid.*, p. 143.

because the sales were not shown. Fortunately, this does not happen frequently. In a survey of the 1963 annual reports of 600 companies, only 6 companies failed to show any sales data.

Cost of Operations

The major divisions of cost of operations for analytical purposes are: (1) cost of goods sold, (2) depreciation, and (3) all other operating expenses. The cost of goods sold section deserves inspection because of possible differences in method of costing inventory in matching costs against revenues or sales to find gross profit mentioned earlier. For example, a company would tend to get an entirely different gross profit if last in, first out (LIFO) method of inventory valuation was used rather than the first in, first out (FIFO) method.

The analyst also has a special problem in dealing with depreciation and other noncash charges against income. The accounting principle involved is that an asset with a relatively long life, i.e., plant and equipment, should be written off as a charge against earnings over the economic life of the asset. In determining taxable income, several methods are permitted in writing off these assets. The more common ones are (1) double declining-balance method, (2) the sum-of-the-year's-digits method, and (3) the straight-line method. As with different inventory costing methods, differences in depreciation method have an effect on earnings balances. Therefore, the analyst is primarily concerned with the differences. The significance of these differences is evident from the discussion that follows.

In analysis of the costs of producing the goods for sale (cost of goods sold), the analyst is interested in the level of costs. The conventional measure of the level of cost of goods sold is the gross profit margin (gross profit, after cost of goods sold, stated as a percentage of sales). The gross profit margin is a good measure of the relative efficiency of the firm's operations. In highly competitive industries, that one company's gross profit margin declines more than that of others during a business recession may indicate that the company's lack of trade status forces it to severely cut prices.

The overall index of operating efficiency and ability to control costs is the operating ratio. This ratio is computed by dividing sales into all operating costs $\left(\dfrac{\text{operating costs}}{\text{sales}}\right)$ exclusive of interest and federal income taxes. The relative inability to control costs is reflected by this ratio, particularly when there is a reduction in sales.

Trends in operating expenses are also significant to the analyst. Although it is not necessary to examine each expense item individually, in some cases a particular classification of costs may loom so large that it deserves special attention—for example, the advertising expenses of consumer products companies, such as razor and cigarette companies. The relationship of sales to these particular expense items should be computed, because examining changes in operating expense items and profit items expressed as a percentage of sales can be helpful in evaluating a company from year to year.

Cost of Goods Sold and Inventories

As mentioned earlier, the inventory valuation method affects the company's cost of goods sold. The differences in inventory valuation methods used complicate the analysis of financial statements. The following discussion shows the effect that use of these various methods has on a corporation's inventory value and profits.

First In, First Out. The first in, first out (FIFO) method of determining cost of goods sold matches the cost of the first goods bought against current revenue. The last goods acquired are assumed to be in inventory and are carried at that cost.

To illustrate how the use of FIFO affects profit margins, it has been assumed that the fiscal period is started with an inventory of 200 units of a commodity, that 200 additional units are purchased, and 200 units are sold. The purchases and sales are spread evenly over the fiscal period, and the final inventory is 200 units. It is also assumed that competitive conditions permit the business to sell at a markup of 5 percent above current wholesale costs.

If wholesale prices have remained stable at $2.00 per unit before the fiscal period began and continue to remain stable until the end of the fiscal period, the computation of gross profit would be as follows.

Sales		$420.00	(200 units @ $2.10)
Initial inventory	$400.00		(200 units @ $2.00)
Add purchases	400.00		(200 units @ $2.00)
	$800.00		
Deduct final inventory	400.00		(200 units @ $2.00)
Cost of goods sold		$400.00	
Gross profit		$ 20.00	

Let us assume that the wholesale prices of the purchases had risen to $3.00 per unit. Then, the selling price would be $3.15. The computation of gross profit would be as follows.

Sales	$630.00	(200 units @ $3.15)
Initial inventory	$ 400.00	(200 units @ $2.00)
Add purchases	600.00	(200 units @ $3.00)
	$1,000.00	
Deduct final inventory	600.00	(200 units @ $3.00)
Cost of goods sold	400.00	
Gross profit	$230.00	

It may be noted that the selling price increased by 50 percent, but profits increased by 1,150 percent.

Various devices have been used to reduce the extreme fluctuations in earnings which FIFO produces during periods of rising and falling prices. One method is to value final inventory at the average cost of goods to be accounted for (initial inventory plus purchases). In the example above, which assumed rising prices, the total cost of 400 units is $1,000, or an average cost of $2.50. The final inventory would be valued at (200 units × $2.50) $500, and the gross profit would be reduced to $130. This method of costing inventory is described fully below.

Last In, First Out. A method of valuing inventories which has become popular in recent years is last in, first out, sometimes called LIFO. The reasons for the popularity of LIFO are: (1) it matches current costs against current revenues, thus giving a better accounting of current operating results; (2) it reduces taxable income in periods of rising prices. LIFO is the opposite of FIFO. Table 12–4 contrasts the LIFO and FIFO methods.

The basic assumptions in this example are: an initial inventory of 200 units; purchase of 500 units at an average cost of $2.50, as prices rise steadily from $2.00 to $3.00; and a final inventory of 200 units. The markup is assumed to be 5 percent above costs, and sales are made shortly after each purchase. The LIFO system obviously reduces gross profits during a period of rising prices, and keeps the inventory value well below the cost at current prices and even below the value under the FIFO method. With the LIFO method in the following example, market prices would have to fall by more than one third before the rule of cost or market, whichever is lower, would force a recording of inventory losses. LIFO accounting tends to eliminate inventory profits during periods of rising prices and, conversely, tends to avoid inventory losses during periods of declining prices.

240 Investment Analysis and Management

TABLE 12-4

Transaction	Amount of Purchase	Amount of Sale	Cost of Goods Sold LIFO	FIFO	Inventory Value LIFO	FIFO
On hand, 200 units @ $2.00 ..					$400	$400
Purchased 100 units @ $2.00 .$ 200					600	600
Sold 100 units @ $2.10		$ 210.00	$ 200	$ 200	400	400
Purchased 100 units @ $2.25 .	225				625	625
Sold 100 units @ $2.36¼		236.25	225	200	400	425
Purchased 100 units @ $2.50 .	250				650	675
Sold 100 units @ $2.62½		262.50	250	200	400	475
Purchased 100 units @ $2.75 .	275				675	750
Sold 100 units @ $2.88¾		288.75	275	225	400	525
Purchased 100 units @ $3.00 .	300				700	825
Sold 100 units @ $3.15		315.00	300	250	400	575
Totals $1,250		$1,312.50	$1,250	$1,075		

Average Cost. Another method of valuing inventories and determining the cost of goods is the average cost procedure. This procedure charges the average of the cost of purchases during the period and the opening inventory to cost of goods sold. In the last part of the example shown previously, if the company had an initial inventory of 200 units at a cost of $2.00 per unit and purchases of 500 units at $2.50 per unit, then the weighted average cost would be as follows.

Initial inventory ....$ 400.00 (200 units @ $2.00)
Add purchases .... 1,250.00 (500 units @ $2.50)
Total ....$1,650.00 (700 units @ $2.357)

The weighted average cost per unit of inventory sold would have been $2.357. Therefore, the computation of gross loss is as follows.

Sales ....$1,312.50 (500 units @ $2.625)
Cost of goods sold 1,178.50
Gross loss ....$ 134.00

Use of the average cost method is a compromise between FIFO and LIFO. It tends to provide an income during periods of rising prices and falling prices somewhere between LIFO and FIFO.

Depreciation Charges

For years, one of the major problems of both accounting and investment analysis has been determination of the amount of a company's building and equipment used up in a year's operations or depreciated in value. The general practice was to estimate the economic life of a building or piece of equipment and charge it off or expense it on a straight-line basis. For example, the company would charge off annually 20 percent of the cost of a building that had an economic life of five years. When straight-line depreciation was used almost exclusively by companies, the analyst felt confident that from one company to another the depreciation expense was roughly comparable.

Since 1954, the analysis of income statements and the depreciation expense has been complicated by a change in the Federal Internal Revenue Code, which allows companies to accelerate the depreciation or write-off of plant and equipment acquired after September 31, 1953. This change allows companies to use any one of three depreciation methods or a combination of them: (1) double declining-balance method, (2) the sum-of-the-year's-digits method, and (3) the straight-line method. In addition, a company may use any other method "which would not give an aggregate depreciation write-off at the end of $\frac{2}{3}$ of the useful life" that would be larger than the write-off under the double declining-balance method.[9]

Each of the three depreciation methods will result in substantially different earnings balances. To illustrate the differences between these methods, Table 12–5 shows a company that has sales of $10,000 each and assumes that the only expense is depreciation. The firm's plant and equipment cost $6,000, and has an estimated economic life of five years. The annual rate of depreciation with the sum-of-the-year's digits method is computed by adding the sum-of-the-year's digits of one through five. The sum-of-the-year's digits is 15, and the firm is allowed to charge off $\frac{5}{15}$ of the gross plant and equipment the first year, $\frac{4}{15}$ the second year, and so forth. The straight-line method allows the firm to charge off $\frac{1}{5}$, or 20 percent of the gross plant and equipment each year. The double declining-balance method enables the company to charge off double the straight-line rate, or 40 percent of the undepreciated balance each year. Table 12–5 shows the effect each of these methods has on the earnings balance.

The comparability of the earnings balances and depreciation expenses between companies is further complicated by the fact that a substantial number of companies do not report to their stockholders the depreciation method used. The survey published in *Accounting Trends and Techniques*, 1964, found that only 86 out of the 600 com-

---

[9] *Ibid.*, pp. 171–72.

panies included in the survey even mentioned the method of depreciation used. Even when the method of depreciation is disclosed, without any supplementary data showing the effects of using these accelerated depreciation methods, the analyst has an almost impossible task in making adjustments for comparability.

TABLE 12-5

Illustration Showing the Effect on Earnings Caused by
Different Methods of Depreciation

	1st Year	2nd Year	3rd Year	4th Year	5th Year
Sum-of-the-Year's Digits Method					
Net sales	$10,000	$10,000	$10,000	$10,000	$10,000
Cost of goods sold	7,000	7,000	7,000	7,000	7,000
Gross income	$ 3,000	$ 3,000	$ 3,000	$ 3,000	$ 3,000
Depreciation	2,000	1,600	1,200	800	400
Income before fixed charges and taxes	$ 1,000	$ 1,400	$ 1,800	$ 2,200	$ 2,600
Double Declining-Balance Method					
Net sales	$10,000	$10,000	$10,000	$10,000	$10,000
Cost of goods sold	7,000	7,000	7,000	7,000	7,000
Gross income	$ 3,000	$ 3,000	$ 3,000	$ 3,000	$ 3,000
Depreciation	2,400	1,440	864	518	311
Income before fixed charges and taxes	$ 600	$ 1,560	$ 2,136	$ 2,482	$ 2,689
Straight-Line Method					
Net sales	$10,000	$10,000	$10,000	$10,000	$10,000
Cost of goods sold	7,000	7,000	7,000	7,000	7,000
Gross income	$ 3,000	$ 3,000	$ 3,000	$ 3,000	$ 3,000
Depreciation	1,200	1,200	1,200	1,200	1,200
Income before fixed charges and taxes	$ 1,800	$ 1,800	$ 1,800	$ 1,800	$ 1,800

The Cash Earnings Concept

A practical way to analyze profit margins and expense levels of companies is to separately analyze the so-called "cash expense" items and treat the "noncash" deductions from revenues as a special analytical problem. The cash earnings are generally defined as sales or revenues less cash expenses or net income plus depreciation and noncash charges.

The disparity between the cash earnings and reported earnings can be quite large. For example, Beaunit Corporation showed in their 1963 annual report earnings per share of common stock of $2.02 and "cash flow" per share of $5.44.[10] The difference was presumably the noncash deductions.

---

[10] *Ibid.*, p. 208.

In such cases as this, noncash deductions can make a mockery of reported net income or earnings in the short run because of accelerated depreciation. It should be noted, however, that the cash earnings figure is not a substitute for the reported earnings. The depreciation of plant and equipment is as much a charge against sales in net income determination as is any other expense.

The net effect of use of accelerated depreciation methods by companies that have recently added new plant and equipment is to understate reported net income for the next few years. This understatement will be followed by a relative overstatement of net income after most of the present plant and equipment has been written off. Since there seems to be no practical way by which the analyst can make adjustments to reflect a "true" earnings estimate, the best course is to use the cash earnings as well as the reported earnings for comparative purposes.

Debt Service Analysis

In analysis of a company's ability to service debt, the analyst is concerned with debt service as a cash drain and with debt service as an expense. Debt service as a cash drain includes payments of interest on debt and repayment of debt at maturity. Debt service as an expense includes interest and amortization of debt discount and expense or fixed charges.

In conventional bond analysis, the coverage of interest and amortized debt discount by earnings before taxes is the main criterion. This measure is significant if for no reason other than its wide use. For example, the valuation manual for securities published by the National Association of Insurance Commissioners uses the earnings test for adjudging the eligibility of bonds for life insurance company investment. This test states that the average fixed charges shall have been covered at least 1½ times by average net earnings available for fixed charges of the last five years.

The tests used by the National Association of Insurance Commissioners are significant to a company, because the largest single source of funds for operating companies is life insurance companies. Failure of a company to meet these minimum standards may be indication of future financial difficulty. This is particularly true if there is considerable debt maturing in the next few years.

The analyst should also analyze cash debt service to determine whether there are any periods when cash payments to service and retire debt will be unusually high. This analysis may be particularly significant to the common stock investor. The analysis may indicate that in some year in the near future there will be a period of working capital stringency because debt service payments are high.

The debt service may be analyzed by an annual summary of cash debt payments that must be made. This cash payment will include, interest, payments on maturing debt, sinking fund payments, and rental payments on long-term leases.

Rental payments on long-term leases are usually not shown as fixed charges on the income statement, nor are they shown as a liability on the balance sheet. These rentals are normally included or carried as operating expenses. However, the analyst probably should consider these payments as fixed charges, because a failure to pay them could cause serious financial difficulty and possible reorganization. Lease payments are not the same as interest payments, because the landlord has included in the payment a depreciation cost. Irrespective of its composition, the payment is a fixed charge, because it cannot be reduced below a certain minimum during a recession.[11]

Extraordinary Items

Extraordinary items appeared in the 1963 annual reports of 203 of 600 companies surveyed by the American Institute of Certified Public Accountants.[12] These items are usually gains or losses of a nonrecurring nature arising from the disposal of assets and similar items. Treatment of these items can be of special significance to the analyst, because they may distort the reported earnings. For example, in their 1963 income statement American Machine & Foundry Company had a special charge that reduced net income from $19,-010,012 to $9,510,102. An extraordinary after-tax charge for potential losses on bowling receivables of $9,500,000 was deducted from income.

---

[11] The American Institute of Certified Public Accountants has recommended that lease payments be shown on the income statement as two items—occupancy cost and interest. See Paul Grady, *Inventory of Generally Accepted Accounting Principles for Business Enterprises* (New York: American Institute of Certified Public Accountants, Inc., 1965), p. 173.

[12] *Accounting Trends and Techniques, op. cit.,* p. 193.

REVIEW QUESTIONS AND PROBLEMS

1. What are some of the limitations in using financial statements in security analysis?
2. What is meant by the term, "a double standard" in financial reporting?
3. What are the steps in the financial statement analytical process?
4. If the basis of common stock value is the earnings power of the issuer, of what practical significance is the analysis of working capital position?
5. Corporation "A" sells $10,000,000 in 20-year bonds and uses the proceeds to build a new plant. Corporation "B" leases its plant with total lease payments totaling $10,000,000 over the life of the 20-year lease. How would these liabilities appear on the respective balance sheets of Corporations "A" and "B"? How would you appraise the capital structures of these companies?
6. Discuss the effects of LIFO and FIFO methods of inventory valuation on the working capital position of corporations.
7. "Accelerated depreciation of corporate fixed assets and the investment credit provisions have made reported earnings of corporations virtually meaningless." Do you agree or disagree with this statement?
8. How does one estimate the quality of receivables?
9. What is the distinction between "cash" and "services" liabilities?
10. Why would a reduction in long-term debt tend to stabilize earnings of a corporation?
11. What is meant by dilution of equity? Is there more than one type of dilution?
12. The book value per share of common stock of Reynolds Metals Company on December 31, 1965 was $32.27 per share. Would the conversion of $4\frac{1}{2}$ percent debentures of this company at $63.00 per share result in dilution?
13. Discuss the possible effects of the consolidated versus the unconsolidated statement on reported earnings of companies.

CHAPTER 13

Analysis of Industrial Securities—Financial Statement Analysis and Interpretation

A major step in the valuation of securities is to relate returns to the cost price of the security. In the case of bonds, this relationship is the yield to maturity discussed earlier in Chapter 5. With common stock, it is the relationship of price to earnings or the price–earnings ratio (market price ÷ earnings). As discussed earlier in Chapter 6, dividend yield or payout is not the key value measure in the valuation of common stock, because the dividend size may be influenced directly by the management of the company. Therefore, the price–earnings ratio is the key value measure, because it includes the chief value determinants—earnings per share of common stock and market price per share.

The next problem is to determine what is the proper price–earnings ratio. This is, of course, the basic investment value decision. Is the common stock of Carrier Corporation selling in May, 1965, at 16.9 times 1964 earnings a better buy than the common stock of Fedders Corporation, selling at 14.2 times earnings? In fact, one might reasonably ask why investors are willing to pay $16.90 for $1.00 of Carrier earnings and $14.20 for $1.00 of Fedders earnings. The answer to this question is a complex one, but expressed simply it would appear that investors believe the future prospects of Carrier appear to be more promising than those of Fedders.

None of this discussion is meant to suggest that the value placed on stock by the market is correct. The security analyst implicitly assumes that the market price is not the correct value. The analyst hopes to establish that a particular stock is or is not a good buy at present market prices. The decision as to whether common stocks generally are good buys at a given level of prices will be discussed later, in Chapter 20.

How do we establish whether company A is relatively a better buy than company B? We analyze both quantitative and qualitative factors in making the ultimate decisions as discussed earlier in Chapter 10. Here we are concerned with the quantitative analysis. We analyze the past performance of the subject companies in order to establish whether the price–earnings ratios are relatively high or low.

The chief factors involved in quantitative analysis are the following.

1. Rate of growth—past sales and earnings trends.
2. Profitability—analysis of profit margins and efficiency of asset utilization.
3. Quality of earnings—earnings stability.
4. Credit capacity and working capital adequacy.
5. Dividend policy.
6. Selection criteria.

To help in the examination of these major value factors, certain key ratios and indexes have been selected to help analyze the earning capacity of the company.

1. Measures of growth.
2. Measures of profitability.
3. Measures of earnings quality.
4. Measures of working capital adequacy and credit capacity.
5. Dividend payout ratio.
6. Market price ratios.

To illustrate this analysis system and procedure, Carrier Corporation and Fedders Corporation have been used. Both of these companies are manufacturers of air conditioning equipment.

MEASURES OF GROWTH

It is highly desirable that a company show growth in sales, net income, and earnings per share. If a company's sales have not grown in the past five to ten years, it is probably an indication that the company is losing its position in the industry. Price increases alone should cause some increase in dollar sales. Therefore, the analyst should be concerned with the rate and trend of growth. The growth should be measured in terms of sales, net income after taxes (available to common stock), and earnings per share. To increase comprehension, these data should be shown as index numbers. The analyst should be careful not to select a recession year as the base period for the index, because it would then appear that the company's rate of growth was greater than it actually was for a longer period. It might be advisable to use a three-year average as the base, but for illustrative purposes the indexes used here have as the base year 1960.

TABLE 13–1

Indexes of Growth, Carrier Corporation and
Fedders Corporation, 1960–64
(1960 = 100)

	1960	1961	1962	1963	1964
Sales					
Carrier	100	104	106	117	127
Fedders	100	86	88	74	83
Net income					
Carrier	100	149	156	164	217
Fedders	100	77	55	37	69
Earnings per share					
Carrier	100	159	168	178	239
Fedders	100	73	49	33	62

These companies were used because of the marked contrast in the rates of growth and profitability. The sales of Carrier increased by 27 percent, while the sales of Fedders declined by 17 percent in this five-year period. More significantly, the increase in sales was accomplished by an even more rapid increase in net income and earnings per share. This greater proportional increase in net profits is primarily the result of the leverage in Carrier's capital structure. (See Table 13–7.)

MEASURES OF PROFITABILITY

The real test of the effectiveness of a company's management is its relative ability to maximize the return on the capital invested in the business. The analyst would be interested in testing the effectiveness of the company's management and operations. A measure of effectiveness and the profitability of the operations is the rate of return on the total assets of the company. This return is computed by dividing earnings before interest and taxes—operating profit—by total assets.

$$(\text{Operating Profit}) \frac{\text{Earnings before Interest and Taxes}}{\text{Total Assets}} = \frac{\text{Rate of Return}}{\text{on Assets}}$$

To further examine the rate of return on assets, the analyst may wish to examine two primary areas of management concern—asset utilization, measured by asset turnover, and cost control, measured by margin of operating profit. These two items are the major components of rate of return.

$$\frac{\text{Operating Profit}}{\text{Sales}} \left(\frac{\text{Margin of}}{\text{Profit}}\right) \times \frac{\text{Sales}}{\text{Assets}} \left(\frac{\text{Asset}}{\text{Turnover}}\right) = \frac{\text{Rate of Return}}{\text{on Assets}}$$

To illustrate these measures, we have shown these data for Carrier and Fedders (Table 13–2).

TABLE 13–2

Operational Effectiveness Ratios, 1960–64
Carrier Corporation and Fedders Corporation

	1960	1961	1962	1963	1964
Asset Turnover					
Carrier	1.11	1.13	1.15	1.20	1.29
Fedders	1.75	1.52	1.22	1.04	1.23
Operating Profit Margin					
Carrier	5.23	7.30	7.57	7.02	8.20
Fedders	14.87	13.10	9.76	9.26	12.45
Asset Rate of Return					
Carrier	5.81	8.25	8.70	8.43	10.59
Fedders	26.02	19.91	11.91	9.64	15.31

The common stock investor is interested in appraising the earning power of his equity interest or ownership investment. The measure of earning power of the ownership interest is the rate of return on common stock equity. This measure is a reflection of not only the operational efficiency of the business but also the effectiveness of the company's financial management.

The earning power ratios for Carrier and Fedders are shown in Table 13–3.

The trend of the rate of return is significant, particularly for corporations that have been expanding their operations. An obsession with growth often causes investors to overlook the relative profitability of growth, particularly to the common stock equity. These data show the effect of increased sales on Carrier's earning power and the depressing effect of the decline in sales on Fedder's earning power.

TABLE 13-3

Earning Power Ratios, 1960-64
Carrier Corporation and Fedders Corporation

	1960	1961	1962	1963	1964
Common equity turnover					
Carrier	2.32	2.34	2.37	2.60	2.64
Fedders	2.97	2.40	2.23	1.92	2.05
Net profit margin					
Carrier	1.95	2.79	2.88	2.73	3.34
Fedders	6.60	5.91	4.15	3.30	5.54
Common equity rate of return					
Carrier	4.53	6.52	6.83	7.11	8.82
Fedders	19.57	14.16	9.25	6.33	11.36

MEASURES OF EARNINGS QUALITY

Analysts commonly refer to the "quality" of corporate earnings. The quality of a corporation's earnings is a reflection of its growth and stability. The measures of growth have been considered earlier. To complete the analysis of earnings quality, the analyst should also appraise the stability of the corporation's earnings. Ideally, a company should have a steady growth in earnings, unmarred by temporary declines during general economic recessions.

The stability of corporate earnings is a relative matter. Judgments of the relative stability can be made only in terms of fluctuations in past earnings. Consequently, the corporation's record of operations must be long enough to include periods of recession. The analyst should keep in mind, however, that each industry has unique economic characteristics which tend to cause its sales and earnings to be affected differently by recessions. These differences in vulnerability to cyclical fluctuations were discussed earlier, in Chapter 11.

Even within industry groups, corporate sales and earnings show considerable variation in the fluctuation of earnings. Therefore, generalizations are not sufficient, and the analyst should use specific measures of relative stability. The analyst is interested in the degree of fluctuation in earnings per common share, coverage of fixed charges, and preferred dividend coverage. Obviously, each of these measures is designed to measure the quality of earnings available to different classes of security holders.

An acceptable method of measuring fluctuations in earnings per share is to determine the percentage decline of the lowest year's earnings from an average of previous earnings for a representative period of years. For example, the earnings of Fedders Corporation for the past five years illustrates a method of measuring earnings, while to get a complete cycle of earnings for Carrier Corporation we must use an eight-year period (Table 13-4).

TABLE 13-4

Stability of Earnings Measures
Carrier Corporation and Fedders Corporation

Year	Carrier	Fedders
1957	$ 2.11	..
1958	2.18	..
1959	2.41	..
1960	1.35–low year	$2.37
1961	2.15	1.74
1962	2.27	1.17
1963	2.40	0.79–low year
1964	3.23	1.47
Total	$18.10 = $2.26	7.54 = $1.50 average
	8 years	5 years

$$\text{Carrier} \dots \frac{\$2.26 - 1.35}{\$2.26} = \frac{\$0.91}{\$2.26} = -40.3\%$$

$$\text{Fedders} \dots \frac{\$1.50 - 0.79}{\$1.50} = \frac{\$0.71}{\$1.50} = -47.3\%$$

Fluctuations in the earnings per share are significant to the common stockholder. The relative stability of earnings, irrespective of what causes the fluctuations, are a major value determinant. In the case of Carrier and Fedders, the relative differences are so slight that they would not seriously affect the investor's choice of the common stock of one company over the other.

MEASURES OF WORKING CAPITAL ADEQUACY

The adequacy of working capital is of major importance to the analyst, because a working capital shortage may require new long-term financing. The measures of credit capacity would give an indication of whether or not the working capital shortage could be relieved by long-term debt financing. If long-term debt financing is not possible, the company would then be faced with additional equity financing, curtailment of operations, or suspension of dividends. Any one of these actions would tend to adversely affect the value and price of the common stock.

The measures of working capital adequacy are (1) the current ratio and (2) net working capital as a percentage of sales. The current ratio is computed by dividing current assets by current liabilities. This ratio indicates the extent to which the company is utilizing short-term credit to meet current operating asset needs. An expanding company with a high current ratio has considerable room for expansion before additional financing will be required. A growth in sales is frequently followed by a declining current ratio and net working capital as a percent of sales to a point where long-term financing is required if expansion is to continue. Conversely, a decline in sales will often result in increases in the current ratio and net working capital percentages as the working capital needs decline with sales. The illustrative material shown in Table 13–5 shows the pattern described; Carrier's current ratio and net working percentages decline with increasing sales (see Table 13–1), and the opposite occurs with Fedders.

TABLE 13–5

Measures of Working Capital Adequacy, 1960–64
Carrier Corporation and Fedders Corporation

	1960	1961	1962	1963	1964
Current ratio					
Carrier	3.68	3.53	3.34	3.06	3.18
Fedders	3.22	3.81	4.21	4.22	5.67
Net working capital as percent of sales					
Carrier	43.0	41.8	39.2	36.8	34.6
Fedders	32.1	38.8	51.5	61.4	55.6

MEASURES OF CREDIT CAPACITY

Long-term financing may be used to alleviate a shortage of working capital or to finance an expansion of plant and equipment. The long-term financing could either be debt or equity financing. Additional equity financing might have the effect of diluting the existing equity interests (see p. 110). Therefore, the corporation would usually like to increase leverage by using long-term debt. However, the corporate management does not always have a free choice in selecting between long-term debt and equity. Purchasers of the corporate debt or lenders will insist that the corporation's present and foreseeable future performances meet certain minimum standards, which may be described as tests of credit capacity. The ability to use long-term debt financing is dependent on the credit capacity of the corporation.

The measures of credit capacity are the relationship of debt to capital funds, the relationship of fixed charges to income available for payment of these charges, and the cash flow of the corporation. These measures are expressed as:

1. Long-term debt as a percent of capital funds (equity test).
2. Fixed charge coverage (earnings basis).
3. Fixed charge coverage (cash basis).

The pledge of assets is generally valuable only in reenforcing the bondholder's bargaining position with other security holders during periods of financial difficulty. The liquidated value of corporate assets would usually be substantially less than the book value of the assets. The equity test is, therefore, not a reliable indicator of credit capacity. The earnings tests or measures—fixed-charge coverage (earnings basis) and fixed-charge coverage (cash basis)—are more frequently used. The fixed-charge coverage (earnings basis) is computed by dividing the total income before fixed charges and taxes by fixed charges. The result is the times-fixed-charges-earned ratio. (See page 285 for a detailed discussion of the computation of these measures.)

Coverage of fixed charges on a cash basis involves adding back the noncash expenses, depreciation, bad debt expense, depletion, etc., to income before fixed charges and taxes. Because of the fluctuations and magnitude of these noncash expenses, the fixed charge coverage on a cash basis tends to give the analyst better perspective in appraising the credit capacity when used along with fixed charge coverage on an earnings basis. This is particularly true since 1954, because accelerated depreciation enables companies to make substantially larger noncash deductions for depreciation, as mentioned earlier. For some industries, such as oil, the coverage computed on an earnings basis is practically meaningless, because the noncash depletion charges are a major expense. For example, the 1965 fixed-charge coverage of Sinclair Oil Corporation on an earnings basis was 5.26 times, but on a cash-basis charges were earned 10.58 times.

The measures of credit capacity for Carrier Corporation and Fedders Corporation are shown in Table 13–6. Previous discussion (see p. 57) indicated that profitability was the first line of defense for bondholders. The fixed-charge coverage of Fedders illustrates the effect of declining profits on the quality of debt.

TABLE 13–6

Fixed-Charge Coverages, 1960–64
Carrier Corporation and Fedders Corporation

	1960	1961	1962	1963	1964
Fixed-charge coverage (earnings basis)					
Carrier	5.39	5.65	5.14	5.47	6.21
Fedders	11.69	8.18	5.89	3.33	5.00
Fixed-charge coverage (cash basis)					
Carrier	7.97	7.60	6.76	7.17	7.81
Fedders	12.94	9.23	6.99	4.11	5.65

It could be argued that the equity test is of no real significance, because the assets of the corporation could not be liquidated at anywhere near their book value. However, the equity test as well as the fixed-charge coverage tests are used by the National Association of Insurance Commissioners in adjudging when bonds are eligible for life insurance company investment. For this reason, use of these measures is significant. The equity tests for Carrier and Fedders are shown in Table 13–7.

TABLE 13–7

Long-Term Debt as a Percent
of Total Capitalization, 1960–64
Carrier Corporation and Fedders Corporation

	1960	1961	1962	1963	1964
Long-term debt as % of total capitalization					
Carrier	32.08	31.09	30.54	32.03	29.64
Fedders	20.90	19.40	31.77	32.41	30.00

The general standards of the National Association of Insurance Commissioners are that fixed charges be covered at least 1½ times by earnings available for fixed charges, and that long-term debt not exceed 50 percent of total capitalization or capital funds.

Both companies meet these tests by substantial margins. Excessive coverage indicates that the company has plenty of room for long-term debt financed expansion.

DIVIDEND PAYOUT RATIO

The payout ratio is the percentage of common stock earnings paid out in dividends. The payout ratio is calculated by dividing common stock earnings into common stock dividends. This ratio is computed by considering only cash dividends paid by the corporation, with no credit given for stock dividends. Stock dividends are not included, because the effect of stock dividends is to give out a larger number of shares for what the stockholder already owns. The concern in this discussion is with cash dividends only.

A high payout ratio is a definite plus factor in selection of common stock investments. That is, all other things being equal, a company with a relatively high payout ratio will have its common stock sell at higher price than the stock of a company whose payout ratio is not so high.[1] When the earnings are paid out in dividends, the investor has the choice of reinvesting in the business by buying more of the company's common stock or of investing elsewhere. Of course, the after-tax results are not the same. The dividend income is subject to the federal personal income tax, while retained earnings left with the corporation are not. The payout ratios for Carrier and Fedders are shown in Table 13–8.

TABLE 13–8

Dividend Payout Ratios, 1960–64
Carrier Corporation and Fedders Corporation

	1960	1961	1962	1963	1964
Dividend payout ratios					
Carrier	64.92%	43.90	41.88	39.94	30.34
Fedders	42.08%	56.58	82.52	126.82	68.00

FINAL SELECTION MEASURES

The historical analysis of growth, profitability, and stability gives the analyst an indication of past and present earning capacity. This historical analysis provides excellent background information, but it is often difficult for the analyst to determine which company's securities are the best investment at current market prices.

To facilitate the decision-making function, it is helpful to relate some of the major value factors—earnings, assets, dividends, and sales—to current market price. The basic market-price ratio is the price–earnings ratio discussed earlier. In addition, the analyst may compute the following measures.

---

[1] For an excellent discussion of this point, see Benjamin Graham, David L. Dodd, and Sidney Cottle, *Security Analysis* (New York: McGraw-Hill Book Co., Inc., 1962), chap. 36.

1. Sales per share dollar, at current market.
2. Earnings per share dollar, at current market.
3. Dividends per share dollar, at current market.
4. Common stock equity per share dollar, at current market.
5. Liquid net worth per share dollar, at current market.

Several other measures can be calculated, relating various balance sheet and income statement items to market price, but those mentioned above are the basic ones.[2] (See Table 13–9.)

Each of the above measures relate the dollar amount of each item per share to the current market price per share. Each measure is stated as X cents per dollar of common stock at market. These measures may be stated as percentages by multiplying the dollar amounts by 100.

All the items have been discussed previously, with the exception of liquid net worth. Liquid net worth is the total current assets less the sum of current liabilities, long-term debt, and preferred stock. The liquid net worth per share at market is a valuable tool in estimating sell-out opportunities. Sometimes, a corporation has not realized its full potential because of extremely conservative or poor management, resulting in low earnings. The poor earnings record of these companies usually causes the price of stock to be low. In some cases, the stock will sell below the liquid net worth per share. Obviously, the liquidated value of the company's stock is greater than the market price. Sometimes, a change in management or sale of the company will result in a higher price for the stock. This type of special situation is outside the course of conventional security analysis; however, this measure will often point up these special situations.

The purpose of all these measures is to help the analyst determine actually what he is buying for each dollar invested at current market. Generally speaking, the analyst should place more emphasis on the earnings, sales, and dividends per share dollar than on the balance sheet items. As indicated in earlier discussion, the "true" value of a company's stock is dependent on the returns or earnings it generates rather than on the book value of its assets. Larger amounts of earnings, assets, and sales per share dollar would indicate that a company should be the best investment unless another company clearly has better prospects.

---

[2] For an interesting article that suggests various measures of this type, see Frederick Amling, "Suggested: An Improved Statistical Unit for Comparison in Investment Analysis," *Analysts Journal*, Vol. 14, No. 4 (August, 1958).

TABLE 13-9

Market Price Ratios, June, 1965, Prices and Year-End, 1964, Financial Data Carrier Corporation and Fedders Corporation

	Carrier	*Fedders*
Sales per share dollar	$ 2.94	$ 1.33
Earnings per share dollar	0.09	0.07
Dividends per share dollar	0.029	0.05
Common equity per share dollar	1.21	0.64
Liquid net worth per share dollar	0.42	0.47
Price-earnings ratio	16.9	14.2

There is a complication in the use of the proper price–earnings ratio when valuing common stock. Despite the fact that market prices may go to extremes, investors should pay some attention to average earnings. If past average earnings are entitled to some consideration as an indication of future average earnings, and the stock deserves to sell at 20 times average earnings, the investor should not expect the stock to sell at 20 times current earnings when current earnings are twice the past average. Stock prices may reflect current earnings to some degree, but the price–earnings ratio will tend to decline as current earnings rise above past average earnings. Conversely, price–earnings ratios will tend to rise as current earnings fall below the average. This notion is supported by the action of Fedders, because the 1964 earnings of $1.47 were above the average of the previous two years, and the current price–current earnings ratio dropped below average price–average earnings ratio for the previous two years. (See Table 13–10.)

TABLE 13-10

Current* and Average 1963 and 1964 Price–Earnings Ratios, Fedders Corporation

	Price Range	Average	Earnings Per Share	Price–Earnings Ratio
1963	15⅛–19⅝	17.37	$1.17	14.85
1964	15⅞–19½	17.69	0.79	22.39
1963–64 average	17.53	..	0.98	17.89
Current	20.00		1.47	13.60

* 1964 earnings and June 22, 1965, closing price.

SUMMARY

Selection of common stock for investment involves the purchase of a bundle of future returns in the form of earnings and dividends. To make an intelligent estimate of the future prospects of a company, the analyst should analyze the past financial performance of the company. This analysis includes measures of growth, profitability, quality of earnings, credit capacity, and dividend payout. Finally, the analyst calculates selection measures in the form of market price ratios, which assist in determining which of the companies under consideration is the best buy.

To illustrate, let us consider the following example. Let us suppose that there are two industrial stocks, each earning $15 a share. One stock sells at 45, or 3 times earnings, while the other sells at 165, or 11 times earnings. It might appear that the stock selling at three times earnings is the better value. This conclusion is not justified if the stocks are those of companies in industries of widely divergent economic characteristics. To illustrate the difficulty of making direct comparisons between stocks representing different industries, an example is presented in Table 13–11.

TABLE 13–11

	Steel Stock	Chemical Stock
Current earnings	$15.00	$15.00
Current dividend	$ 4.00	$ 6.50
Past average earnings (8 years)	$ 4.00	$12.00
Past average dividend (8 years)	$ 2.00	$ 5.00
Current price–earnings ratio	3	11
Current yield	8.89%	3.94%
Price–earnings ratio (average earnings)	11¼	13¾
Yield (average dividend)	4.45%	3.03%

Several confusing considerations are involved in this comparison. The chemical stock, having growth characteristics and being less vulnerable to cyclical fluctuations, is entitled to sell at a higher price–earnings ratio and on a lower yield basis than the steel stock. The question for the analyst to decide is how much higher. The price–earnings ratio for the steel stock is lower in relation to current earnings than it is for the chemical stock. In relation to average earnings, the steel stock is not the value that it appears to be from the current price–earnings ratio. The current earnings of the steel stock are obviously inflated. The steel stock is paying only 26⅔ percent of earnings as dividends, while the chemical stock is paying out 43⅓ percent. The earnings withheld by the chemical company, however, will likely provide future growth in both earnings and dividends, while the earnings withheld by the steel company may permit it to show greater efficiency in the next recession. The second consideration is small comfort, since it is the intent of the investor not to be caught holding the steel stock during any future downturn in business. The much higher yield from the steel stock, however, is a great challenge to the investor, because if the business conditions remain good this additional yield will compensate for at least modest capital losses.

Comparisons of this sort between individual stocks in different industries are not typical of the usual approach in managing a portfolio. The investor should determine which industries to invest in and which industries to avoid in view of his needs and ability to assume risks. Allocations of funds will, of course, be made on the basis of outlook for each industry and the prices at which the securities of several leading companies in each indusry are selling. The price consideration requires that the investor be aware of the price–earnings ratio typical of each industry.

REVIEW QUESTIONS AND PROBLEMS

1. Why is the price-earnings ratio of more value to the analyst in valuing common stock than the current dividend yield?

2. In appraising the growth of a company, which of the three measures, the indexes of (1) sales, (2) net income, or (3) earnings per share, is most valuable?

3. What is the special use that can be made of market-price ratios?

4. Do you believe that a high pay-out ratio is desirable in all cases? What would be some situations where a high pay-out ratio would not add to the value of a common stock?

5. What is the best test of the effectiveness of a management of a business?

6. What would be the significance of rapid growth in sales, a declining net working capital as a percent of sales, and declining current ratio of a company?

7. Is it possible for a company to have recurring losses and still be able to service its debt? If so, why?

8. Of what value is the measure, "Liquid net worth per share dollar, at current market"?

9. Complete the quantitative analysis of Smith Kline & French Laboratories for the fiscal years ended December 31, 1964 and 1965:

Smith Kline & French Laboratories and Subsidiaries
CONSOLIDATED BALANCE SHEET
December 31, 1965 (with comparative figures as of December 31, 1964)

ASSETS	1965	1964
Current assets:		
Cash ....$	9,383,651	$ 9,981,757
Marketable securities, at cost which		
approximate market	49,233,376	63,506,320
Accounts and notes receivable, less provision for		
losses, $262,446 (1964, $343,097)	26,599,396	22,949,741
Inventories—generally at the lower of average cost		
or market		
Finished products	7,773,126	8,733,983
Work in process	5,044,682	3,629,876
Raw materials and supplies	6,918,861	4,609,104
	19,736,669	16,972,963
Prepaid expenses	2,455,054	2,269,677
Total current assets .... $	107,408,146	$115,680,458
Investments in foreign companies, at cost	2,672,793	2,648,793
Unamortized payment of past service pension costs	2,162,457	3,236,649
Plant and equipment, at cost:		
Land	3,282,175	3,149,873
Buildings	48,894,798	44,932,320
Machinery and equipment	30,036,370	23,738,884
	82,213,343	71,821,077
Less accumulated depreciation	28,633,507	25,804,282
	53,579,836	46,016,795
Goodwill, patents and other intangibles	15,586,883	2,489,455
	$181,410,115	$170,072,150

LIABILITIES AND SHAREHOLDERS' EQUITY	1965	1964
Current liabilities:		
Accounts and notes payable ....$	9,250,928	$ 8,787,079
Accrued expenses	10,630,048	8,402,120
Income taxes	27,699,104	27,288,142
Total current liabilities	47,580,080	44,477,341
Provision for pensions, unfunded plans	269,272	750,907
Shareholders' equity:		
Common stock without par value. Authorized		
18,000,000 shares; issued 14,641,504 shares		
at stated value	7,124,290	7,124,290
Earnings retained in the business	132,901,123	117,719,612
	140,025,413	124,843,902
Less common stock held in treasury, at cost—		
82,713 shares	6,464,650	....
Total shareholders' equity	133,560,763	124,843,902
	$181,410,115	$170,072,150

Smith Kline & French Laboratories and Subsidiaries

STATEMENT OF CONSOLIDATED EARNINGS

Year ended December 31, 1965 (with comparative figures for 1964)

CURRENT EARNINGS	*1965*	*1964*
Income:		
Sales	$243,670,433	$218,246,837
Interest and other income	3,328,753	2,963,314
	246,999,186	221,210,151
Costs and expenses:		
Material and manufacturing cost of products sold	55,900,419	51,445,059
Marketing, administrative and general	84,111,588	72,388,868
Research	23,806,166	20,001,644
Income taxes, other than Federal	7,340,000	7,020,000
Other	526,483	568,151
	171,684,656	151,423,722
Earnings before Federal income taxes	75,314,530	69,786,429
Federal income taxes	33,100,000	31,100,000
Net earnings	$ 42,214,530	$ 38,686,429
Net earnings per share—		
1965, 14,620,826 shares (average); 1964, 14,641,504 shares	$2.89	$2.64
Depreciation charged to operations (included above)	$ 4,373,958	$ 3,584,829
EARNINGS RETAINED IN THE BUSINESS		
Balance at beginning of year	$117,719,612	$101,727,514
Net earnings for the year	42,214,530	38,686,429
	159,934,142	140,413,943
Deduct cash dividends paid: per share, $1.85 (1964, $1.55)	27,033,019	22,694,331
Balance at end of year	$132,901,123	$117,719,612

CHAPTER **14**

Analysis of Transportation Securities— Railroads and Airlines

It is not feasible in this treatment of investment analysis to consider the characteristics of each major industry that might be of interest to the investor. However, the transportation industry is considered separately because of its legal status. The companies operating in the transportation industry, known as common carriers, are subject to regulation by both the federal and state governments. Common carriers are defined as transporters of goods and passengers, and are required to serve, without discrimination or undue preference, all shippers who seek service. Federal regulation is the most extensive and has the greatest impact on the operation of these carriers. The investment analysis of common carriers, including the railroads, airlines, barge lines, and oil pipelines, involves a study of some extremely complex operating and pricing problems. Because of the complexity of common carrier operations, the amount of data available to the analyst is overwhelming. The analyst must be selective in choosing data for analysis, or he will get lost in a maze of statistics. This discussion is confined to what are believed to be the more pertinent considerations in selecting securities of companies in the transportation industry.

CHARACTERISTICS OF THE TRANSPORTATION INDUSTRY

There are two segments of the transportation market—freight and passenger. Of the two, the freight transportation market is more important in terms of revenue and capital investment. Major considerations in the choice of means of freight transportation are (1) cost of service, (2) flexibility of service, and (3) speed. Cost of service tends to be the major consideration for most freight traffic. For this reason, the freight transportation market has been and continues to be domi-

262

nated by the railroad industry. However, for certain types of freight, flexibility of service and speed are the most important considerations.

In the passenger transportation market, the three major market considerations are (1) speed, (2) comfort, and (3) cost. The emphasis in this market has been on speed and comfort, with cost of service to the consumer a secondary consideration. For this reason, as will be discussed below the railroad's share of intercity passenger traffic has steadily diminished.

FREIGHT TRANSPORTATION MARKET

Practically everything that is produced and distributed in the United States is transported by common carrier, either as raw materials or finished goods. As a consequence, it is not surprising that the growth in volume of freight transportation has paralleled the overall growth in the economy, as indicated by the index of industrial production. (See Figure 14–1.)

The unit of measure of output of freight transportation is the ton-mile. The ton-mile is equivalent to transporting one ton of freight for one mile. The purpose of combining these two units of measure, tons and miles, into a single unit is to provide a measure of the basic factors that determine the costs and revenues of common carriers. The total ton-miles of freight traffic has increased by 38 percent in the decade 1954–64. The railroad industry has not shared proportionately in the growth in freight traffic, because during this period, 1954–64, the number of ton-miles carried by railroads increased by only 20 percent. In fact, the number of ton-miles of traffic carried by railroads was only slightly more for 1964 than for 1951, as is evident in Figure 14–2.

The railroads have lost volume to the motortruck carriers not only in terms of ton-miles but also in terms of revenue. The bulk of the motortruck traffic gain has been in the high-revenue-yielding but lighter-weight traffic classified as "manufactures and miscellaneous" and "less than carload lot" traffic. The significance of this loss is evident, since these two classes of traffic accounted for less than 30 percent of railway freight tonnage in 1963, but provided in excess of 50 percent of revenues. Since the motortruck industry is most competitive in the hauling of these lightweight costly items where speed of transport is a major factor, motortruck competition has had a greater impact on revenues than has the competition from other carriers, oil pipelines, and barge lines.

In some respects, the competition of oil pipelines and barge lines

FIGURE 14-1

Federal Reserve Board Index of Industrial Production and
Transportation Industry Index of Income
(1957–59 = 100)

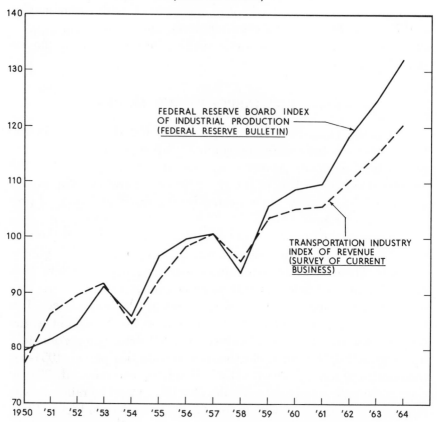

has had a greater effect on the railroads. Railroads are most efficient as carriers of bulky, heavy freight, because with their large investment in fixed facilities they can add volume with a nominal increase in cost. For example, a locomotive pulling 60 cars can add another 60 cars with little added cost in fuel, labor, and depreciation. Between 1940 and 1944, freight traffic increased by 97.5 percent, with an increase of only 4.4 percent in locomotives, 6.7 percent in freight cars, and no increase in road mileage.[1]

The bulkier freight, which includes products of agriculture, mines and forests, and animals, provides about 75 percent of the freight ton-

---

[1] *Standard and Poor's Industry Survey—Railroads.*

FIGURE 14-2

Intercity Ton–Miles

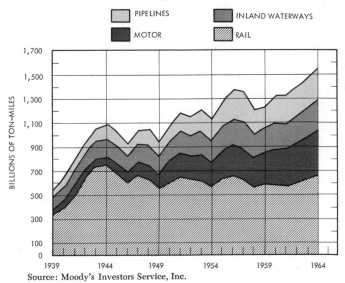

Source: Moody's Investors Service, Inc.

nage of railroads and less than 50 percent of the revenue. The oil pipelines, owned principally by the major oil companies, and the barge lines are competing with the railroads for this traffic. Petroleum products have been diverted to the cheaper oil pipeline transportation, which has affected the freight traffic of western railroads. Because it is a cheaper form of transportation, the barge lines have taken a considerable portion of the bulk freight from the eastern railroads where speed of transport is not important. For example, it has been estimated that barge lines on the inland waterways can transport coal from West Virginia to points on the Mississippi for $1.25 to $1.40 per ton less than by rail.

Even though railroads have appeared to reverse the trend of freight traffic losses with increases in tonnage hauled each year since 1961, the railroad industry could not be classified as a growth industry. However, it would appear that the fortunes of the industry are improving.

PASSENGER TRANSPORTATION MARKET

Intercity passenger traffic has increased by over 300 percent in the period from 1948 to 1964. Technological improvements in automobiles and highways have resulted in most of this increase being carried by private automobiles. In 1963, of the 835 million passenger miles of intercity passenger travel, about 90 percent was by private automobile and the balance, about 10 percent, was by common carriers— airlines, buses, and railroads.

Obviously, the passenger transportation market is one in which there is considerable room for expansion by common carriers. However, the only means of public passenger transportation that has been able to make substantial advances in this market is the airlines. The air transport industry has made substantial gains in the public transportation market primarily at the expense of railroads, and has continued to capture an increasingly larger share of the total market.

These gains by the air transport industry are the result of a number of factors. The airlines have always had the advantage of speed over other carriers. The introduction of jet aircraft has served to increase that advantage. In addition, air travel is generally considered to be more comfortable, and jet aircraft have improved the comfort of flying by lessening vibration and noise fatigue.

The only remaining advantage to bus and railroad passenger carriers is cost. The growing affluence of Americans has made cost of travel a less significant factor in the passenger transportation market. In addition, the economies realized from jet equipment have enabled the airlines to require only moderate increases in fares. Both bus and railroad fares have been substantially increased, thus reducing the wide cost advantage they once held over airlines.

It appears that the private automobile has captured the cost-conscious segment of the passenger traffic market. The increased speed and comfort of air travel at reduced rates have helped the airlines to capture the largest share of the remaining passenger transportation market. The scheduled airlines carried 10 million passenger miles of traffic in 1950, and carried in excess of 68 million passenger miles in 1964.

It is evident from Figure 14–3 that most of the increase in airline traffic has been at the expense of railroads and bus transportation. The railroads' share of passenger traffic has declined every year since 1948. In 1950, railroads carried about 45 percent of all public passenger traffic, buses carried about 38 percent, and airlines and inland waterways carried the balance. By 1963, airlines accounted for about 50 percent of common carrier passenger traffic, buses carried about

FIGURE 14–3

Passenger Miles
Railroad versus Airline and Bus

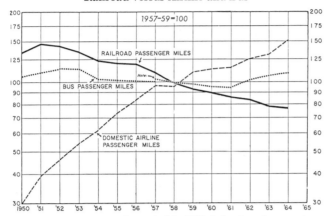

Note: Bus passenger miles revised in 1957. Index for prior years is on 1957 base, and subsequent years are not comparable to earlier figures due to changes in data. Airline passenger miles are for domestic operations of certificated route air carriers—all services.

25 percent, railroads about 22 percent, and inland waterways the balance.[2]

Railroads and Passenger Traffic

The decline in railroad passenger traffic has been a vexing development for the industry, because the railroads have lost money on passenger service in every year since 1946. The largest deficit was in 1957, when the railroads lost over $724 million. Since that time, the passenger deficit has declined steadily, reaching the post-World War II low level of $394 million in 1962, and a slightly larger loss of $399 million in 1963.

Improvement in the size of the deficit from passenger operations is directly related to the Transportation Act of 1958, which enabled the railroads to obtain speedier action on petitions to the Interstate Commerce Commission to abandon unprofitable passenger routes. The railroads have been steadily abandoning passenger service since 1950, and at an accelerated rate since 1958. The total passenger miles of railroads in 1964 were 18 billion—a decrease of 21 percent from

2 *Annual Report of Interstate Commerce Commission, 1964*, p. 34.

1958, and 45 percent below the 1950 total.[3] Passenger revenues of railroads have declined from about 10 percent of total revenues in 1950 to about 6 percent in 1964.

Passenger traffic will continue to decline in importance for most railroads, with the possible exception of those located in the eastern part of the United States. These railroads are under considerable political pressure to continue short-haul commuter traffic. In fact, over 35 percent of the passenger traffic of these roads is unprofitable commuter traffic, which they have little hope of abandoning. However, provisions of the Transportation Act of 1958 did force various state and local governments to offer to railroads some relief of burdensome passenger losses to assure continuance of passenger services. New York reduced property and franchise taxes on railroads by about $15 million, and New Jersey offered some tax relief for commuter roads. In 1964, passenger revenues still accounted for about 34 percent of total revenues of the New York, New Haven, and Hartford Railroad. Although this railroad was granted tax relief by the four states in its service area, the relief was not sufficient to offset the large passenger losses, and the New Haven has been in receivership since 1961. Remedies for the plight of these Eastern railroads with heavy commuter traffic are (1) possible subsidies of passenger services, (2) mergers with other railroads, and (3) further curtailment of unprofitable passenger services.

RAILROAD INDUSTRY

Railroads have certain inherent economic advantages which they are not able to fully exploit because of artificially fostered competition, pricing policies or rate-making policies, and labor contracts. These economic characteristics of railroads are (1) high fixed costs, (2) fixed location, and (3) operational inflexibility because management prerogatives are circumscribed by regulation and union contract.

In recent years, the railroads have been relieved from some of the operational rigidities caused by the slowness of regulatory processes and the reluctance of the labor unions to accept change. Many problems are yet to be solved.

---

[3] *Yearbook of Railroad Facts, 1965 Edition* (Washington, D.C.: Association of American Railroads), p. 27.

Railroads and Their Competitors

Railroads have high fixed costs as a result of their heavy investments in roadway facilities and equipment. These high fixed costs tend to give the railroads substantial operating leverage. Evidence of this leverage is that costs per ton of freight carried decline rapidly as the volume of traffic increases. For this reason, railroads can add substantial traffic with only a nominal increase in cost. In contrast, the competitors of railroads, such as motor carriers, require an increase in equipment, drivers, and fuel with any substantial increase in traffic.

In addition, the railroad's competitors have substantial indirect subsidies from federal, state, and local governments, because they use publicly owned and maintained roads, highways, and waterways. It is estimated that the cost of owning and maintaining their road and other facilities cost railroads about 20 percent of operating revenues in 1964. Motor truck lines, on the other hand, spent only about 4.5 percent of total operating revenues on use taxes for highways, etc.[4]

While the railroads are basically the lowest-cost transportation mode, they often have been placed at a competitive disadvantage due to relatively higher maintainance of rights-of-way costs. This competitive disadvantage has resulted in traffic losses, which served to load higher costs on the remaining traffic in some markets. On the other hand, the railroads have not been able to exploit their advantage in other situations due to the laws and regulation of rates and service.

Regulation of Rail Rates and Service

Competition by other carriers is the most important limiting factor on railroad earnings. To a certain extent, these competitive difficulties result from government regulation of rates and the services the railroad must offer. On the other hand, many of the competing carriers are relatively free from such regulation.

The rates that railroads may charge for their services are regulated by the Interstate Commerce Commission. The services provided must be continued whether they are profitable or not, unless the ICC and/or state regulatory authorities specifically allow them to be abandoned.

---

4 *Standard and Poor's Industry Survey—Railroads.*

Rate Regulation. One frequently hears that railroads are subject to public regulation because they are monopolistic. In 1887 when the Interstate Commerce Act, basis for railroad rate regulations, was passed, the railroads did have a monopoly in the transportation of freight and passengers, for all practical purposes. The major question now is whether the railroads can earn enough to support a healthy and efficient rail transport system in competition with other segments of the transportation industry.

The earnings of railroads are obviously affected by the rates charged for carrying freight and passengers. The rates that the railroads may charge are subject to approval by the Interstate Commerce Commission. Therefore, rate changes require ICC permission. The ICC is often slow in granting permission because of the complex problems involved in such rate changes.

To understand the railroad's pricing problem in relation to earnings, one must distinguish between the rate *structure* and the rate *level.* The rate structure is the whole complex interrelationship between rates and the determination of specific rates for various commodities and hauls. The railroad management may take the initiative to change the rate structure, subject to approval of the ICC.

To institute a rate change, the railroad files a proposal, and may place the new rate in effect unless prior to its effective date the rate change is suspended by the ICC. Suspension may be the result of a complaint from a shipper or competing form of transportation that the rate is unfair or discriminatory. Use of this criteria of fairness rather than cost of service has worked a hardship on railroads. In many cases, railroads are required to keep rates high enough to protect other common carriers from "unfair or destructive" competition. The rates in many cases must be high enough to protect a less efficient form of public transportation.

An amendment to the Interstate Commerce Act sought to eliminate the Interstate Commerce Commission's practice of maintaining rates of railroads in order to protect the competitive position of other forms. However, the amendment still provided that the commission protect other carriers against "unfair or destructive competitive practices."[5] The amendment attempted to remedy some inequities and allow each form of transportation to make rates that would reflect, in each

---

case, the competition from other carriers as well as the cost and type of service. The purpose of the act was to allow the various forms of transportation to offer their services at the lowest possible cost without requiring that the rate structure be designed to protect all competing forms of transportation.

Problems of Rate Level. Problems of rate level, on the other hand, always involve the question of whether the average amount charged for transportation, as a whole, is too high or too low, and whether the railroads are making too much or too little money. Changes in the rate level are always directly approved by the ICC, and it may, of necessity, be slow in granting permission. Any general increases or decreases in the level of rates disrupts the rate structure and nearly always results in thousands of specific rate changes to adjust inequities.

The Interstate Commerce Commission has allowed a number of increases in rate level in the period following World War II. These increases were necessary to allow the railroads to cover their increased costs of operation. In fact, it could be argued that the railroads should be allowed larger increases in rate level.

The solution to the railroad's competitive problem is not to further increase the rate level, which would only cause a further diversion of traffic to competing forms of transportation. The solution appears to be in loading the costs of maintaining their right-of-way on competing forms of transportation, thus removing the cost advantages shared by the motortruck lines and inland waterways. It appears that action will be taken to equalize these costs, either by this method or by direct subsidies to railroads.

Work Rules and Cost of Operation

The railroads have had considerable success in reducing the number of employees needed for operations. The number of employees has been reduced from 1,220,784 in 1950 to 665,017 in 1964, a reduction of nearly 45 percent.[6] In spite this large reduction, railroads have not been able to reduce wage costs as a percent of operating revenues.

The railroads bargain with some of the strongest unions in the nation. That these unions have been able to get substantial wage increases is evident from the fact that the railroads have reduced their number of employees yet have experienced substantially in-

---

[6] *Yearbook of Railroad Facts, 1965 Edition, op. cit.,* p. 74.

FIGURE 14–4

Employment and Compensation
Class I Roads
(1957–59 = 100)

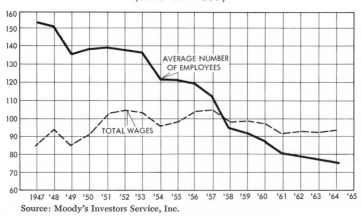

Source: Moody's Investors Service, Inc.

creased wage costs. These wage increases have been forced on the railroads by the strong bargaining position of the unions when the railroads have been faced with intensified competition from alternative modes of transportation. The long-term outlook for the railroads' earning power has become dependent on the outcome of the race between the demands of labor and the ability of the railroads to produce the same amount of transportation service with fewer employees.

This long-run trend toward more efficient use of railway labor has been due to increased investment in more modern and efficient railroad facilities. The degree of latitude that railroad management has in reducing wage costs by improving facilities and equipment is limited by contracts with railroad labor unions. In most cases, the unions have resisted attempts of railroads to reduce manpower needs and wage costs through utilization of various laborsaving devices and techniques. However, the railroads did receive a change in work rules in April, 1964, which allowed them to eliminate most firemen in freight and yard service.

Merger Movement

Considerable attention has been given to the railroad mergers in order to eliminate duplicate facilities and services. This better use of equipment and facilities could enable the railroads to reduce freight rates, and thus regain their competitive position and lost traffic.

It was estimated that if all the proposed railroad mergers contemplated in 1964 were completed they would increase railroad earnings before taxes by about $350 million annually. This earnings increase would represent an increase of about 150 percent in the 1964 pre-tax earnings of $885 million.[7]

Summary

The demand for railroad freight transportation services parallels the index of industrial production. Changes in levels of overall business activity as reflected by the level of industrial production exercise a major influence on the levels at which railroads operate.

Because of rigidities of costs, however, the railroads are not able to reduce their aggregate expenses so much as the decline in revenues during a business recession. During periods of rising business activity, aggregate railroad expenses do not rise so fast as revenues because the railroads can use excess capacity. Although total railroad operating expenses are not so fixed and independent of the traffic level as one might believe, the adjustment of rates to new price levels and the adjustment of operating expenses to new traffic levels takes time. Rapid changes in the level of business activity cause extreme fluctuations in the railroads' operating income.

It would appear, however, the present trend is more favorable for the railroad industry than it has been in the post-World War II period. A more favorable regulatory environment, a breakthrough in union work rules changes, coupled with the merger movement give the industry a more promising investment outlook.

Analysis of Railroad Financial Statements and Operations

The analysis of railroad operations and financial statements may become needlessly complex. This complexity is usually a product of the amount of data available. The uniform accounting system provides relatively comparable financial and operating data of railroads. The reports that the railroads are required to submit to the ICC

---

[7] Pierre R. Bretey, "Merger Progress Slow But Sure," *Financial Analysts Journal,* Vol. XXI, No. 2 (March–April, 1965), p. 65.

provide a fantastic amount of data on their operations. For example, 701 different classifications of data on railroads are published each year by the ICC. This mound of data presents a veritable feast on which many railroad analysts gorge themselves. For the most part, the analysis of minute details is not necessary unless the analyst has a specific reason for investigating a particular operation or cost. As a routine part of the analysis, selectivity in the use of railroad data is even more important than it is in industrial analysis.

Because of the uniform accounting system, the analyst does not have the problems of adjusting railroad statements for comparability which he has in the analysis of industrial statements. However, the ICC regulations pertaining to railroad accounting have not kept pace with the changes in industrial accounting and financial reporting. As a result, there are some differences between industrial and railroad financial statements, particularly the income statement, which require the analyst's special attention.

The Balance Sheet

The magnitude of railroad operations is apparent from the condensed balance of all Class I railroads shown in Table 14–1.

TABLE 14–1

Balance Sheet, All Class I Railroads, 1964
(Millions of Dollars)

Current assets	$ 3,318	Current liabilities	$ 2,154
Investments and special funds	1,126	Long-term debt	9,752
Properties (net)	22,918	Other liabilities and reserves:	
Other assets	306	Preferred stock	1,139
		Common stock	6,105
		Capital surplus	2,161
		Retained earnings	9,357
Total	$30,668	Total	$30,668

Total assets of Class I railroads amounted to more than $30 billion in 1964. About 70 percent of those assets are properties or plant and equipment of the railroad industry.

The heavy plant and equipment investment, including such things as track, terminals, and locomotives, represents the major factor in profitable operation. As can be noted from previous discussion, any utilization of additional capacity makes almost a direct contribution to profit, because cars can be added to a train with a small addition to cost.

This vast investment in plant and equipment has been financed by about 32 percent long-term debt financing, 61 percent equity financing, and the balance in short-term debt. The indebtedness of railroads has been declining steadily since 1946, when long-term debt represented about 40 percent of total financing.

Payment of interest and principal on long-term indebtedness is still a problem for a segment of the railroad industry. For example, on July 7, 1961, the New York, New Haven, and Hartford Railroad filed a petition for reorganization in bankruptcy. The railroad stated that it was "without sufficient funds to pay and discharge its financial obligations." Other railroads have a large amount of long-term debt that must be considered in analysis. The analyst should concern himself with the composition, maturities, and charges associated with the long-term indebtedness as a routine part of his analysis of railroads. The technique for analyzing the ability to service debt will be discussed in a later section.

Limitations of Balance Sheet Data. Railroads sometimes publish consolidated income statements for the whole system, including the results of subsidiaries, but will not consolidate the balance sheets. The balance sheet generally pertains to the parent company only.

Frequently, the balance sheet does not include any financial information on leased lines. The parent company may have assumed the responsibility for the debt of the leased line, but it does not appear on the balance sheet of the parent company as a liability. This failure of balance sheets to reflect assets on lease and liabilities assumed on leased lines is mainly because of the lack of statement consolidation rather than a difference in accounting practice for reflecting leases in balance sheets.

The financial condition of a lessor company can be determined only by studying its balance sheet separately. While the assets and obligations of subsidiary companies are sometimes consolidated with the parent company's balance sheet, the parent company may, with the permission of the Interstate Commerce Commission, list only its own original investment in the securities or in the property of such companies. Investments in companies that are jointly owned with other railways always appear as investments in affiliated companies.

The lack of a consolidated balance sheet is not primarily the fault of either the railways or the Interstate Commerce Commission. Inter-corporate relationships are so complex in the railway industry that a consolidated balance sheet would be difficult to interpret. Such varied legal devices are used to weld a railway system together that it would be difficult to devise a "uniform" system of accounts to correctly reflect the economic facts in each instance. The miles of line, weight of rail, number of locomotives and other rolling stock, and other statistics provide a "physical" measure of assets employed by the whole railway system. The money value at which these assets are carried on the balance sheet is of minor significance.

Measures of Plant and Equipment Utilization

It is obvious from the composite balance sheet (Table 14–1) that railroads have a large investment in plant and equipment in the form of track, right-of-way, equipment, etc. It is apparent from previous discussion that a railroad's profitability is dependent on its ability to utilize its plant and equipment.

The two types of measures of utilization of track and equipment are (1) traffic volume measures and (2) revenue measures. The measures of physical utilization is number of tons of freight and number of passengers or traffic volume moved or carried over the railroad's track.

The unit of measures of railroad traffic are *revenue ton-miles* and *passenger-miles*. A ton-mile was defined earlier as the equivalent of transporting one ton of freight for one mile. This measure of freight traffic combines into a single unit two basic factors—weight and distance—that affect railroad costs and revenue. To combine passenger-miles and ton-miles, the analyst may convert passenger-miles into ton-miles. The conversion factor commonly used is that two passenger-miles are roughly equivalent to one revenue ton-mile.

Traffic Analysis

Railroad freight traffic has certain characteristics that affect the railroad's profitability. These characteristics are (1) traffic density, (2) source of traffic, and (3) type of freight carried.

Traffic density is measured by the revenue ton-miles per mile of track operated. A high traffic density is desirable, because the railroad's roadbed must be maintained irrespective of the usage intensity.

In addition, light traffic roads tend to have difficulty in controlling transportation costs when traffic declines.

The "source" of freight traffic, whether originated by the railroad or traffic from connecting lines, is also an important factor in a railroad's profitability. The originating railroad usually receives a more favorable division of revenue on interline freight traffic than it does on traffic from connecting lines. Rising terminal costs in recent years have tended to make originating and terminating traffic relatively less important, but railroads with this type of traffic are still in a better position than those with mostly connecting or bridging traffic.

A third factor in analyzing a railroad's traffic is the revenue quality of the traffic. Railroads do not receive the same rate for each ton of traffic carried. Therefore, one railroad may have a relatively higher traffic density than another, but still have about the same revenues from the traffic. This may be seen in an analysis of the traffic of the Chesapeake and Ohio Railroad and the Boston and Maine Railroad for 1963. The Chesapeake and Ohio had a revenue freight traffic density of 6,316,212 ton-miles per mile of road, which was about 271 percent higher than the Boston and Maine's traffic density of 1,699,703 ton-miles. The Boston and Maine had a higher quality traffic in that 58.4 percent of its tonnage was in manufactures and miscellaneous, which accounted for 64.7 percent of its revenue. The C. & O. had the bulk of its traffic in lower revenue-yielding freight, because the revenue yield per ton-mile was 1.05 cents for the C. & O. in 1963, while the revenue per ton-mile of the Boston and Maine was 2.00 cents.

The higher revenue yield from the tonnage carried by the Boston and Maine was not sufficient to offset the higher traffic density and origination of the Chesapeake and Ohio. The measure that combines all the three factors—weight, distance, and type of traffic—is operating revenue per track-mile. The C. & O. had operating revenue of $70,189 per track-mile, which is 69 percent higher than $41,540 per track-mile of the Boston and Maine.

Importance of Location. The volume and quality of traffic of a railroad is dependent on the area it serves. The location of a railroad is fixed and immovable. Government regulations and costs of moving prevent railroads from tearing up their tracks and moving to new regions in pursuit of industries that are changing location; within limits, competitors of railroads can change the location of their operations with relative ease.

The railroad's only chance of increasing its traffic is to attract industries to locate along its existing lines. The competitive weapon it uses to influence regional development is the rates it charges. Use of rates to attract industry and increase traffic is limited because the rates for railroad transportation are regulated.

After industries are located along its lines, the railroad will find that in times of low business activity its shippers bring pressure for lower freight rates to help restore their profits. Even in times of normal business activity, the competition that exists between American business firms will be mirrored in the relative pressures brought by shippers for changing the relationship between specific freight rates.

The Income Statement

The railroad income statement differs from the typical industrial income statement in terminology and order of presentation. In railroad accounting, the terminology is different in describing gross income and net income. "Revenue" always means gross income before the deduction of expenses. The word "income" is synonymous with "net income" on the typical industrial income statement. Occasionally, statistical services will refer to "gross revenue," which is redundant.

The other major departure of railroad accounting from conventional accounting is the classification of federal income taxes on the income statement. Federal income taxes are included in the same classification as property and excise taxes. This total tax figure is deducted from income before fixed charges and miscellaneous income and expense.

The data in the operating expense section are invaluable to the analyst in analyzing the railroad's operations and in estimating its future prospects. These data combined with the data on physical operations provide the basis for analysis of the railroad's operation.

Analysis of Operating Expenses

It is obvious that a railroad's profitability is dependent on its ability to carry through its revenue to net operating income after payment of expenses. A railroad's operating expenses can be classified as (1) transportation expenses, (2) maintenance expenses, and (3) general and other expenses. Transportation expenses are those incurred in moving the trains. Maintenance expenses are those amounts spent on the upkeep of the roadway and equipment. These two expense categories account for about 90 percent of the total expenses of most railroads.

The overall measure of a railroad's ability to control operating expenses and to operate efficiently is the operating ratio. The operating ratio is the percentage of revenues eaten up by operating expenses. The largest single item in operating expenses is wages, which in 1963 accounted for more than 60 percent of the total expenses. The balance is made up of depreciation, materials and supplies, fuel, loss and damage claims, etc.

The operating ratio is most affected by the level of revenue. It tends to rise when revenues fall and vice versa. The reason for this characteristic of the operating ratio is the relatively fixed nature of operating expenses alluded to earlier. The fixity of expenses is a product of heavy plant and equipment investment. In addition, permanent changes in operational method are difficult for railroad management to institute, because management prerogatives are circumscribed by regulation and union contracts.

Transportation Expenses. The major expense of railroad operation is the actual cost of moving trains. The measure of the efficiency of train operations is the transportation ratio, which is the percentage of revenues consumed by transportation expense. The level of transportation expenses tends to vary only slightly with changes in the volume handled. As mentioned, the transportation ratio is influenced by the level of revenues. Poor revenues will push up the transportation ratio.

Railroads with a large passenger traffic characteristically have higher transportation ratios. For that reason, the Boston and Maine, which derived 7.9 percent of total revenues from passenger traffic, showed a transportation ratio of 46.3 percent in 1963, which was higher than average for Class I railroads. The Chesapeake and Ohio, with only about 1.5 percent of revenues from passenger service, showed a transportation ratio of 38.1 percent in 1963. Of course, other factors undoubtedly in addition to the passenger service load also account for this difference in the transportation ratios of these two railroads.

The railroads have made significant technological advances in 15 years by converting from steam locomotives to diesels, which reduced fuel and other costs. In addition, the number of transportation employees was significantly reduced, but these economies have tended to be offset by rising wage rates. (See Figure 14–4.) A further reduction in the number of employees by future changes in work rules and nonessential employees will result in further operating economies and a lower transportation ratio.

Maintenance Expense.   Maintenance expenses of a railroad are governed by (1) the volume of traffic, (2) the terrain over which the railroad operates, and (3) management policy. These expenses are of particular interest to the security analyst because they may be varied from year to year at the discretion of the management. Under normal operating conditions, maintenance expenses tend to vary directly with the volume of traffic.[8] These expenditures may be reduced in a year of low revenue by postponing maintenance until traffic picks up. However, for any railroad there is an absolute minimum maintenance expenditure necessary to keep the railroad operating.

Although the management of the railroad, in an effort to stabilize net income by cutting costs during periods of declining revenue, usually begins by reducing maintenance expenditures, its efforts to reduce these expenses are limited. For example, maintenance expenses may be deferred for long periods of time and the railroad can still operate.[9] But if the roadbed and tracks get in too poor a state of repair, the railroad will be required to reduce the speed and weight of trains, thus increasing transportation costs.

The minimum maintenance expenditure is, for the most part, determined by weather conditions and the terrain of the operating territory. The steepness of grades and curvature of tracks affect the wear and tear on both equipment and roadbed. In addition, maintenance of way expenditures may be increased by unusual weather conditions, such as floods or ice storms, and by conditions of the soil on which the roadbed is laid. For example, roadbed laid on solid rock requires less maintenance to meet minimum safety standards at given train speeds than does a roadbed laid on gumbo, loam, or sand.

Railroads with light traffic density tend to spend more on way maintenance than on equipment maintenance. Conversely, a high traffic density road tends to have a high equipment maintenance ratio. For example, the Pittsburgh and Lake Erie Railroad spends nearly

---

[8] Dwight R. Ladd, *Cost Data for the Management of Railroad Passenger Service* (Boston: Harvard University Graduate School of Business, 1957), p. 97.

[9] Ladd recounts the case of a small railroad that deferred maintenance during the 1930's. Then the war started. Materials shortages prevented badly needed repairs, even though revenue was available. Trains were run at greatly reduced speeds. At the end of the war, the railroad "literally fell apart."

twice as much on equipment maintenance as on roadway maintenance, while lightly traveled roads, such as the Maine Central, spend more on road maintenance than on equipment maintenance.[10]

The equipment maintenance ratio also tends to vary with revenues. The level of maintenance necessary to keep the equipment in good working order depends on mileage traveled and age of the equipment. In recent years, large amounts of railroad equipment have been replaced, with the result that in the analysis of most railroads today the age of equipment is not a significant consideration. The equipment maintenance ratio is relatively stable, as mentioned earlier, because as traffic drops the usage of equipment tends to decrease. Also because the need for equipment, particularly cars, is not so great, the management allows the amount of equipment in need of repair to increase. Failure to keep equipment in proper repair will quickly be reflected in the published annual report statistics that measure the physical condition of equipment. Reduction in equipment maintenance is not a serious matter so long as there is enough equipment in good condition to handle the available traffic. If the equipment needed for current operations is in a state of disrepair, the transportation expense as a percent of total revenues or the transportation ratio may rise.

Estimating Normal Standards. Normally, the analyst should not attempt to evaluate the effect on maintenance costs of each operating condition. Therefore, the analyst should use some general maintenance standards in measuring the relative adequacy of a railroad's maintenance. Since it is generally assumed that the physical amount of repair work necessary to maintain equipment varies with the number of cars needed and how intensively they are used, the analyst can compare percentage changes in the physical amount of repair work with percentage changes in total freight and passenger car-miles. Another, and simpler, rule of thumb used in analyzing maintenance is to note that total maintenance for way and structures and equipment "normally" amounts to about 30 percent of total revenues, with maintenance of equipment accounting for slightly more than half. Departures from this norm, however, do not necessarily indicate undermaintenance or overmaintenance. Railways, for example, that own an excess of rolling stock and succeed in augmenting their rev-

---

[10] *Standard and Poor's Industry Surveys, Basic Analysis—Railroads,* July 12, 1962 (Section 2), p. R49.

enues by renting it to other roads may consistently report expenditures for equipment maintenance that are above normal.

The adequacy of expenditures for way and structures is more difficult to determine. Such expenditures, when adjusted for changes in the price level by a combined index of wage and material costs, are "normally" supposed to vary proportionately with changes in ton-miles of traffic. When passenger traffic is important, the analyst will need to add passenger-miles to ton-miles, considering two passenger-miles equal to a ton-mile. This combined measure of both freight and passenger traffic can then be divided by the average mileage operated to arrive at a combined density figure. This facilitates comparison with maintenance expenditures which are frequently available on a per-mile basis.

The rail analyst should be aware of the possible influence of certain factors on maintenance statistics. For example, when maintenance expenditures, adjusted for price changes, are divided by mileage of road operated, one should expect the resulting figure of maintenance per mile to be high for a railway such as the Pennsylvania, which has a substantial amount of second track. This statistical result is explained by the fact that the statistics on mileage operated do not give any weight to additional trackage. To make maintenance statistics on a per-mile basis more nearly comparable between different railroads, the Interstate Commerce Commission divides maintenance of way and structures by "equated track-miles." These include all first main track mileage, 80 percent of additional main track mileage, and half of all other track mileage. The tracks in addition to the first are included at less than actual mileage, because they presumably do not add so much to maintenance needs as would additional main tracks. Statistics of maintenance of way and structures per equated track-mile are usually available in *Moody's Transportation Manual*.

Analysis of Other Income

The "other income" classification on the railroad income statement may be sizable. This is particularly true when the railroad holds stock in other railroads or other nontransportation, income-producing assets. For example, a railroad may own stock of other railroads in order to influence interchange of traffic. In some cases, the stock holdings may be substantial, but the financial reports of the "affiliated" railroad are not reported on a consolidated basis. For example, two income statements are available for the Pennsylvania Railroad, one for the Pennsylvania Railroad Company and another consolidated statement for the Pennsylvania Railroad System, which includes all transportation corporations controlled by, or affiliated with, the Pennsylvania Railroad Company.

When a railroad owns substantial interests in nontransportation assets, the "other income" may be quite large, and the analyst will need to devote a great deal of attention to these sources of income. For example, the total "other income" of the Union Pacific Railroad exceeded net operating income by nearly $5 million. The major portion of this other income was from oil wells and from ownership of Sun Valley Lodge in Idaho. The income from these other sources amounted to over $57 million in 1963.

Analysis of Fixed Charges and Debt

Railroads traditionally have been highly leveraged companies. Railroad debt has been reduced steadily since 1929. These debt reductions have improved the capital of most railroads to such an extent that there is not likely to be a repetition of the rail bankruptcies of the 1930's and 1940's. Some railroads still have a high debt-to-capital ratio, but the percent of debt to capital varies considerably from 8.3 percent for the Union Pacific to 60.3 percent for the Missouri Pacific.

Analysis of Claims of Bonds

Railroads have issued securities with complex provisions that require special knowledge and analysis in order to establish their quality. The complications arise in determining the relative claim of these obligations on income and assets. The types of debt obligations that deserve special attention are (1) guaranteed bonds, (2) mortgage bonds, and (3) equipment obligations.

Guaranteed Bonds. It has been customary for a railroad to lease the property of a branch line and operate it as part of the railroad system. As part of the transaction, the lessee guarantees the indebtedness of the leased railroad. In analyzing guaranteed bonds arising out of leases, two things must be investigated—the independent earning power of the leased properties and the financial strength of the guarantor railway. Sometimes figures are not available to determine results on the basis of separate operation of the leased line. When guaranteed securities arise out of leases of properties that are profitable and strategic, and the guarantor's credit is strong, they can become investment securities of high quality.

Mortgage Bonds. To list all the mortgage bond issues of a railroad in the order of their priority of claim against assets is often a difficult and complex undertaking. In the case of railroads like the Pennsylvania or the New York Central, which have complex debt structures, considerable time would be consumed in such a study. These complications arise because much railway debt is secured by mortgage, and in railway reorganization considerable weight is given to the relative priority of the mortgage and to the character of the property on which it constitutes a lien. Because of railway consolidations in the past, many mortgages constitute liens only on certain divisions or portions of the total railway property. Furthermore, even a consolidated mortgage on the whole property will rank first, second, third, or lower on individual portions of line, depending on the number of liens on those portions already outstanding and undisturbed by reorganization or consolidation.

To simplify the analytical task, organizations supply maps showing the relative claims of the various bond issues on the railroad's properties. Naturally, some sections of a railroad system are more valuable than others. H. H. Copeland and Son publishes traffic density maps which show the freight density (net ton-miles per mile of road) between each two consecutive freight stations.

The basic contribution of the Copeland service in solving some of the problems of the railway bond analyst is that ton-miles of freight traffic are accurately allocated to specific segments of rail property and are classified as to direction of traffic. A bond issue that has a lien on any specific segment of rail property can thus be analyzed relative to the total density of traffic, and its balanced or unbalanced character over that segment of property alone. Copeland also publishes other statistics, one of which is net ton-miles per dollar of debt secured by mortgage against that particular property. Net ton-miles per dollar of debt can be high either because density is high or because debt per mile of line is low. Since a fairly high density is necessary before a railway can show reasonable operating profits (regardless of the size of the debt), the bond analyst will be interested in both density per mile and ton-miles per dollar of debt. The second ratio is computed for a particular bond issue on a cumulative basis, similar to the manner of computing times-earned ratios. For example, to compute ton-miles per dollar of debt for a second mortgage bond, the total debt would be taken to be the sum of the first and second mortgage debt.

Equipment Trust Certificates. Equipment trust certificates are an important class of securities and are used by railroads to finance the purchase of railroad equipment. The amount outstanding represents a significant proportion of the total debt of American railroads. The equipment trust obligations and funded debt of Class I railways as of December 31, 1964, in thousands of dollars, were as follows.

Funded debt (unmatured) $6,704,642
Long-term debt in default 162,626
Equipment trust obligations 2,876,546

Source: Moody's Manual, Railroad Securities.

The principal investment characteristic of railroad equipment trust certificates is low degree of financial risk. This is partly the result of ingenious financial and legal devices used to protect the investor. The particular method of financing is well suited to the purchase of standardized equipment such as locomotives, passenger coaches, and freight cars, which have a long life and meet basic needs. In case of default, the rolling stock can quite readily be sold to some other railway.

Investment experience with equipment trust certificates has been very satisfactory. Actual default has been rare. During the depression of the early thirties, a period of wholesale railroad bankruptcies, there were instances in which maturities were extended, but the certificates were eventually paid off. Serial maturities make them especially desirable for staggering the maturities of institutional investments in bonds.

Analysis of Fixed Charges

A railroad can get into financial difficulty in either of two ways: (1) by failure to meet annual fixed charges, whether these originate from outstanding debt or from rental payments on leased properties; (2) by failure to meet maturity payments on debt that is outstanding. The maturity payments can usually be arranged by refinancing if the earnings coverage of fixed charges appears ample. Hence, ability to pay principal depends more on earnings than on current assets.

The general credit position of a railroad obviously depends on the relationship between fixed charges and the income available for fixed charges. Analysis of these fixed charges is important to the common stock investor as well as the bond investor, because failure to meet fixed charges may result in serious consequences, such as a reorganization that causes both bondholders and common stockholders to suffer losses. These fixed charges not only include the interest on debt, amortization of debt discount, and payments on leases, but also contingent interest on income bonds normally is included. To a certain extent, the inclusion of contingent charges is illogical, because the interest on income bonds is paid only if it is earned in a particular year. However, it is an expense for income tax purposes and is usually included in computing fixed-charge coverage.

Coverage of Fixed Charges. The most commonly used tool for analyzing fixed-charge coverage is the times-interest-earned ratio. This is the number of times that fixed charges are earned. This measure of debt burden was also discussed earlier in Chapter 13. To further illustrate the use of this tool, the skeleton income statement following assumes that the railroad has outstanding first mortgage bonds, second mortgage bonds, and income bonds. It was mentioned earlier that federal income taxes are deducted before other income and expense in the railroad income statement. It is necessary for the analyst to add back income taxes to the balance before fixed charges to arrive at the net income available for fixed charges. This adjustment has been made on the statement.

1.	Railway operating revenues	$100,000,000
2.	Income available for fixed charges, before income taxes	15,000,000
3.	Fixed charges:	
	4. Interest on first mortgage bonds $2,000,000	
	5. Interest on second mortgage bonds . 2,000,000	
	6. Contingent charges 1,000,000	
7.	Total charges	$ 5,000,000
8.	Balance	$ 10,000,000
9.	Income taxes	3,800,000
10.	Net income	$ 6,200,000
11.	Preferred dividends	620,000
12.	Balance available for common	$ 5,580,000

The first mortgage bonds have a prior claim on earnings. The interest on this issue is being earned 7.5 times, computed by dividing income available for charges (item 2) by the interest on the first mortgage bonds (item 4).

The coverage of the second mortgage bonds is computed by adding the sum of the first mortgage interest and second mortgage interest, and dividing the income available (item 2) by this sum, $4,000,000. It is necessary to accumulate the charges of prior claims when computing the times-interest-earned ratio, or the analyst may find that the times-interest-ratio of the junior issue, such as the income bond's contingent charges, is higher than the earnings coverage of the first mortgage bonds. This would suggest that the income bonds are safer than the first mortgage bonds.

To illustrate the effect of this incorrect procedure, the total interest on the first and second mortgage bonds is $4,000,000, which when substracted from the income available leaves a balance of $11,000,000. This is 11 times contingent charges, while the interest on the first mortgage is covered only 7.5 times. The correct way to compute the coverage of contingent charges is to add them to the interest on the first and second mortgage bonds, and divide the income available by this sum ($5,000,000). On this basis, the times-interest-earned ratios are 7.5 times for the first mortgage bonds, 3.75 times on the second mortgage bonds, and 3.0 times on the income bonds.

In analyzing the ability of the railroad to pay debt service charges, it should be kept in mind that debt service includes the debt that is maturing each year as well as the interest and rental payments. This analysis of ability to pay debt service charges requires an analysis of the maturities of outstanding debt. Because of the complexities of the financial structure of railroads, the analysis of the maturities of debt deserves special consideration.

Analysis of Maturities

In approaching the problem of maturities, the analyst should include as debt only the amounts actually outstanding in the hands of the public. From total debt outstanding (both direct obligations of the railway and guaranteed debt of leased lines) should be subtracted from any debt owned by the parent company itself. It also seems desirable to subtract debt of leased lines if that debt is guaranteed only as to payment of interest and not as to principal. While it is conceivable that the parent railway would come to the aid of leased lines in meeting maturities on debt whose principal is not guaranteed by the parent, such action would be logical only if the particular line were profitable. To the extent it is profitable, the lessor would presumably not need the aid of the parent in meeting maturities. The analyst should then construct a table showing total amounts of debt that will mature in each year for a considerable period of time in the future. A concentration of maturities in any one year can be a potential source of difficulty for a railway that is not financially strong.

Criteria for Selection

It is obvious that the analysis of railroad securities involves techniques that are complicated and time-consuming. However, certain specific criteria may be used in the selection of railroad securities. The intelligent investor will not rely exclusively on these criteria, but will make a more detailed analysis to support conclusions drawn from the financial guideposts suggested in the following discussion.

Bonds. The standards for judging bonds are related to the (1) relative claims on assets and (2) fixed-charge coverage. The claim on assets is established by the rather complex analysis suggested earlier. The ultimate purpose of the analysis of claims against assets is to relate debt to the earning power of the property on which it has a lien and its strategic importance to the railroad and its operations.

The second selection criteria is based on adequacy of coverage of fixed charges by earnings. At one time, it was felt a before-income-tax-charge coverage of 2.5 times was sufficient for these bonds to be considered prime investments. The assumption was that the railroads provided a necessary transportation service and that their earnings would be relatively stable. It is now recognized that substantial changes have taken place in the railroads' position in the economy, and that income available for fixed charges tends to fluctuate in sympathy with changes in national economic conditions.

Fixed-Charge Coverage Standard. To provide the analyst with a general indication of adequacy of fixed-charge coverage, the coverage of all Class I railroads is shown in Table 14–2.

The volatility of railroad income is indicated by the fixed-charge coverages in recession years. Coverages have varied from 2.28 times in 1961 to 3.02 times in 1964.

Of course, the analyst will not want to use these composite data as the sole basis for selecting railroad bonds, because there is a wide variation in bond quality. For example, the Union Pacific covered fixed charges 23.27 times in 1963, while the Boston and Maine had a fixed-charge coverage of only 0.59 times.

In addition, the accepted analytical procedure is to assure con-

TABLE 14–2

Fixed-Charge Coverage, All Class I Railroads, 1958–64

Year	(1)	(2)
1964	3.02	2.94
1963	2.98	2.89
1962	2.82	2.67
1961	2.28	2.16
1960	2.49	2.33
1959	2.82	2.68
1958	2.91	2.73

(1) Before federal income taxes.
(2) After federal income taxes.

tinued earnings coverage of fixed charges supported by an analysis of a railroad's operating characteristics, character of traffic, territory, etc.

Common Stock. Proper selection of a railroad common stock must be based on the economic and financial analysis discussed previously. The significant changes in the regulatory environment, the basic changes in work rules and labor contracts, mergers, changes in financial structures, and improvements in operations make qualitative considerations of the utmost importance in railroad common stock selection.

The leverage in the operations and capital structures of railroads make them vulnerable to changes in the level of business activity. The sensitivity of rail earnings to economic fluctuations cause wide price swings in the common stock, making the problem of correct timing almost as important as selection. Thorough analysis obviously will tend to improve the quality of selections, but it is not likely to save the investor from paying potentially large penalties for poor timing.

AIRLINES

The companies in the air transport industry are basically passenger carriers, although freight revenue has increased in importance in recent years. More than 90 percent of the industry's total operating revenues were derived from passenger service in 1964. The air freight business has inceased substantially in the last 10 years. Domestic airlines carried 276 thousand freight ton-miles in 1955, and the amount increased to 798 thousand in 1964—an increase of about 190 percent.

However, the air freight business is not a major factor in the air transport industry.

The airlines are classified by the markets they serve. The domestic trunk airlines provide service to the major cities of the United States. The domestic local service or feeder lines serve the smaller cities, and their routes connect into the major cities. Finally, the international airlines operate between the United States and foreign countries.

The international airline service is provided by Pan American and eight of the eleven domestic trunk airlines. The domestic trunk line market is dominated by the so-called "Big Four"—American Airlines, TWA, Eastern Airlines, and United Airlines. These four carriers account for about 70 percent of the gross operating revenues of the domestic trunk airlines.

The local service airlines are a minor part of the U.S. air transport industry, accounting for only about 6 percent of total gross revenues. The major elements in the U.S. air transport industry are the domestic trunk lines, which accounted for 68.3 percent of gross revenues in 1964, as contrasted to the international airlines, which provided about 25.5 percent.

Financial and Operating Characteristics

The airlines and railroads have quite similar operating and financial characteristics. Both have heavy fixed-asset investments and make liberal use of debt financing. The accounting practices of airlines are regulated in much the same fashion as railroads; therefore, the analyst does not have the problem of standardizing and adjusting airlines' statements for comparability. The individual company financial statements use basically the same account classifications.

Assets

The composition of airline assets is similar to the assets composition of a railroad in that property and equipment account for about 68 percent of total assets. Airlines are not required to make the substantial plant investment required of railroads, since terminal facilities are provided by various governmental units.

In the air transport industry, equipment is the primary competitive weapon. Airlines compete among themselves as well as with other carriers on the basis of speed and comfort. Equipment innovations and changes force the airlines to adopt new equipment if they hope to remain competitive. Existing equipment still may be useful, but obsolete. For example, the conversion from piston engine equipment to jet aircraft has already cost $2.7 billion, and the airline industry has on order equipment valued at $3.7 billion for delivery through 1969.

Capitalization

The heavy expenditures for equipment have been met by funds generated internally and by the use of debt financing. The long-term debt of airlines accounts for about 59 percent of total financing. The introduction of jet equipment placed a severe financial strain on the airlines in 1961–63 which has now been relieved somewhat by internal generation of funds (see Table 14–3).

TABLE 14–3

**Capital Structure, Domestic
Trunk Airlines, 1960–64**
(in thousands)

	1960	*1961*	*1962*	*1963*	*1964*
Long-term debt	$1,069,651	$1,425,231	$1,466,233	$1,330,922	$1,436,105
Capital stock	138,775	162,284	166,637	172,598	180,465
Surplus	600,856	555,403	565,381	623,615	790,617
Total	$1,809,282	$2,142,918	$2,198,251	$2,127,135	$2,407,187
Borrowed capital	59.1%	66.5%	66.7%	62.6%	59.7%
Equity capital	40.9	33.5	33.3	37.4	40.3

Analysis of Operations and Profitability

The airlines are similar to railroads in operating characteristics. Both types of carriers have a large equipment investment and high fixed operating costs. The key to profitable operation is the utilization of equipment and the reduction of fixed costs of operation.

The direct costs, such as wages, per revenue passenger mile have been increasing at a rate of about 3 percent per annum. However, the larger capacity jet aircraft has reduced the wage cost per seat mile, since fewer employees are required to a given volume of traffic. The increased capacity of the jet aircraft results from both a larger number of seats and considerably higher speeds which enable the aircraft to make a greater number of trips over a given period of time.

An intense utilization of equipment also has the effect of reducing costs per revenue passenger mile. The measure of intensity of utilization of equipment is the revenue passenger load factor, which is the number of revenue passenger miles flown as a percent of available seat miles.

The airlines obviously attempt to increase their load factor, since this increased volume tends to reduce costs per passenger mile. For example, an increased volume of traffic tends to reduce fixed costs per seat mile, since these fixed costs are spread over a larger volume of traffic.

The increased volume of traffic available from jet aircraft has had the effect of reducing both direct and fixed costs per revenue passenger mile. The net effect of these economies has been to reduce the airlines' break-even load factor, which is the percent of seats required to be sold to cover passenger operating expenses, including all depreciation. The break-even passenger load factor of domestic trunk lines has declined from 59.5 percent in 1957 to 48.9 percent in

TABLE 14–4

**Break-Even Passenger Load Factor and
Passenger Load Factor, Domestic Operations,
Domestic Trunk Airlines, 1953–65**

	Passenger Load Factor	*Break-Even Load Factor*	*Differential*
1953	64.7%	57.3%	7.4
1954	63.4	56.1	7.3
1955	64.1	56.4	7.4
1956	64.1	58.5	5.6
1957	61.5	59.5	2.0
1958	60.0	55.9	4.1
1959	61.4	57.5	3.9
1960	59.5	58.3	1.2
1961	56.2	56.5	−0.5
1962	53.3	51.3	2.0
1963	53.8	50.3	3.5
1964	55.5	48.9	6.6
1965 est.	54.9	46.8	8.1

Source: Report of Transportation Securities Committee, Investment Bankers Association, 1965 Convention.

1964. (See Table 14–4.) There probably will be further improvements in the break-even load factor of domestic airlines through expanded use of larger jets and substitution of jet equipment for the remaining piston engine equipment on short-haul lines.

Volume tends to reduce unit costs, but to be profitable the volume must generate unit revenues. The revenues per passenger mile have declined slightly in recent years because of the tendency of passengers to shift from first class to coach travel. It appears from the pronouncements of regulatory authorities that there may be additional reductions in unit revenues.

Regulatory Environment

The air transport industry is a regulated industry, as are all common carriers. It is subject to regulation by two federal agencies, the Federal Aviation Agency and the Civil Aeronautics Board. The Federal Aviation Agency has control over navigation aids, safety regulations, construction of airports, and related matters. The Civil Aeronautics Board (CAB) controls the determination of fares and has power to authorize routes for the airlines. Of the two agencies, the actions of the Civil Aeronautics Board are generally most significant.

It appears that airlines are going to feel some CAB pressure to reduce fares. According to guidelines laid down in 1960, the airlines are allowed a fair return on investment. This fair return was determined to be 10.5 percent. In 1965, nine of the eleven domestic trunk airlines earned at the rate of 10.5 percent on investment. As a result, the air transport industry will unquestionably be subjected to more regulatory pressure to reduce fares and improve service than they have felt in the past.

These expected pressures to reduce fares may not be an entirely adverse factor. Apparently, there is considerable elasticity of demand for air travel, and fare reductions may generate sufficient new traffic volume to reduce costs enough to offset the fare reductions.

The Civil Aeronautics Board also has the power to determine the routes that airlines may serve. The airline applies for the right to serve a particular area, and the CAB considers the necessity for the service. If it finds that the new service is necessary, the airline is awarded the route. Awarding the route to the airline does not mean that the airline has a monopoly or exclusive right to service over this route. The CAB may award more than one airline the right to provide service over a given route if it feels that it is necessary to give adequate service to the public and will help in development of the industry. Duplication of service between two cities intensifies the competition between the airlines for available traffic. When a new airline is permitted to service a route already being served by others, the existing airlines must either increase the total amount of traffic on the route or have a less intensive utilization of their equipment. A less intensive use of aircraft or lower load factor tends to reduce the profitability of the airline.

Finally, the CAB sets and administers the subsidies available to airlines that cannot generate sufficient traffic to operate profitably. Most of the local service airlines need a subsidy to break even on particular routes. The subsidy provided is based on the traffic available over a route and the capacity offered by the airline. Low traffic volume over a route naturally would result in a larger subsidy. The local service airlines probably will be faced with declining subsidies in the future, since there have been several proposals for their reduction and elimination.

Airline Growth Prospects

Further increases in airline traffic volume may be expected in the future. A growing population and a large untapped market will make this growth possible. It is estimated that over three-fourths of the population of the U.S. has never flown. As a consequence, it would seem that airlines could expect increased volumes in the future from (1) a larger share of the total passenger transportation market and (2) an expanding passenger market.

It has been estimated by the CAB that domestic trunk airlines could carry 120 billion passenger miles in 1975, up from 42 billion in 1964, if fares are reduced annually by about 1.1 percent. However, if fares must be increased to keep pace with rising costs, the growth would be reduced to an estimated 85 billion passenger miles.

REVIEW QUESTIONS AND PROBLEMS

1. What are the major factors influencing (1) the choice of freight transportation and (2) the choice of passenger transportation by users?
2. What is the position of a railroad with respect to its competitors in the freight transportation market?
3. Explain why economic conditions rather than regulatory restrictions are the major determinant of railroad earnings.
4. Compare the composition of railroad operating costs with those of competitors.

5. What has been the nature of the railroad industry's labor problem and what steps have been taken to solve that problem?
6. What economic advantages would the railroads gain from the current railroad merger movement?
7. What is meant by the term "traffic density"?
8. What factors other than traffic density affect a railroad's profitability?
9. What are the major railroad expense classifications?
10. How is it possible for railroad management to create the illusion of stable earnings through maintenance expenditures?
11. In what respect is the amount of income available for fixed charges inaccurately reported on the railroad income statement?
12. Of what value are the H. H. Copeland and Sons traffic density maps to the analyst in evaluating railroad mortgage bonds?
13. Distinguish between the major types of scheduled airlines.
14. Why is type and age of equipment a more important factor in airline profitability than it is with railroads?

CHAPTER **15**

Analysis of Public Utility Securities

Public utilities have certain special economic and financial characteristics which are of concern to the security analyst. First, these companies have a monopoly to provide an essential service under an exclusive franchise granted by a governmental unit, usually a local governmental unit. The public must encourage and protect the monopoly position of these utilities in order to secure the highest quality of service at the lowest rates.

Second, to prevent exploitation of this monopoly position requires that these utilities be subject to regulation by the state public utility commissions, and the Federal Power Commission in certain instances. These regulatory bodies are concerned with the quality of service offered by the utility, the rates or prices charged for the service, and other miscellaneous matters, such as accounting systems and procedures. Naturally, this characteristic of public utility operation has a profound effect on the earning power of the utility and is of considerable importance to the analyst.

A third characteristic of utility operation is that its production is simultaneous with its use. This is an electric utility characteristic with which we are primarily concerned. That is, electrical energy cannot be stored.

Utilities are also required to meet the demands for service of all users when they require the service and in the amounts that they require. The electric utility must forecast and be prepared to meet demand irrespective of fluctuations. This requirement for continuous service, coupled with the inability to store electrical energy, makes it necessary that the utility have capacity available to meet all demands. These operational characteristics require public utilities, particularly electric utilities, to have a large capital investment per dollar of revenue. This is a key factor in public utility security analysis.

Public utilities are usually defined to include companies that provide such services as electric light and power, natural and manufactured gas, water, local transit, and communications. In one sense, railroads and airlines are public utilities, because companies in the transportation industry have a limited monopoly in the areas they serve and are subject to rate regulation. However, because of regulatory and economic peculiarities, companies in the transportation industry are usually classified apart from other public utilities. For example, the operations of companies classified as public utilities are usually localized and subject to state regulation, while railroads and airlines nearly always operate in interstate commerce and are regulated by a federal agency.

The security analyst is primarily interested in the electric light and power industry, because this industry offers the widest range of investment opportunities. Companies in this industry frequently supply other services, such as gas, and a few engage in local transit. Some utilities in major metropolitan areas distribute gas exclusively; in other areas, the electric utilities distribute gas and produce and distribute electric power. One of the most rapidly growing industries in recent years has been the natural gas transmission and distribution industry.

Although there are a number of privately owned water companies, water service is quite extensively provided by municipalities. There is considerable investor interest in the communications industry. This industry is dominated by a few large companies, such as the American Telephone and Telegraph Company and Western Union Telegraph Company.

PUBLIC UTILITY REGULATION

Public utility regulation is concerned with (1) preventing the utility from making too much profit and (2) insuring that the utility's consumers receive a high-quality service. Most regulation is concerned with reasonable rates and profits, because high quality of service is generally assumed in the absence of specific complaints by users.

Rate-Making

The rates or prices the utility is allowed to charge affect its profitability. The regulatory authorities are concerned with allowing the utility to charge sufficiently high rates (1) to cover its operating expenses, depreciation, and taxes and (2) to allow a reasonable rate of return on the net value of the property used by the utility or the rate base.[1]

An important part of rate regulation is to insure that the utility does not improperly include operating expenses that are not part of the cost of providing the service. To assist in policing the propriety of expenses, the National Association of Railroad and Utilities Commissioners and the Federal Power Commission have devised a uniform accounting system.

Of more concern to the analyst of public utility securities is the process for determining a reasonable rate of return on the rate base. There are two parts to the rate-of-return equation. First, the rate base is net value of the property used and useful, which is usually defined to include the gross plant and equipment account less depreciation plus an allowance for working capital.

The second part of the rate determination problem is establishing the rate of return. The rate of return is the utility earnings before interest on debt, dividends on preferred stock, and earnings for the common stock equity but after allowance for income taxes, expressed as a percentage of rate base.[2]

It really does not make too much difference to the investor how the rate base and the rate of return are derived, because he is interested in the end result of how much earnings are available. For example, he doesn't care whether the regulatory commission allows a 6 percent return on a rate base of $140,000 or a 7 percent return on a $120,000, since the dollar yield is the same in both instances. However, the analyst should be able to recognize the probable effects of changes that will take place.

The problem of determining the rate of return is generally solved by arbitrarily establishing a rate between 6 and 7 percent, depending on the liberality of the state regulatory authorities. The variations in the rate of return are usually the result of changes in interest rates. The rises and falls in the utility's money costs affect the regulatory authority's view of what constitutes a reasonable rate of return. As the general level of interest rates increases, the regulatory bodies tend to allow higher rates of return on the rate base; conversely, as interest

---

[1] Paul J. Garfield and Wallace F. Lovejoy, *Public Utility Economics* (Englewood Cliffs, N.J.: Prentice-Hall, Inc., 1964), pp. 44–45.

[2] *Ibid.*, p. 116.

rates decline the allowed rate of return declines. The problem remaining is to determine the "fair value" of the property.

Rate Base

The two concepts of value in determining the rate base for the public utility are (1) original cost and (2) reproduction cost. Original or historical cost is the cost to originally produce the property; reproduction cost is what it would cost to reproduce the utility property today.

The tendency through the years has been to place more emphasis on original cost in determining the rate base. However, during periods of rising prices and construction costs, the public utilities always press for consideration of reproduction costs as the rate base. Several Supreme Court cases through the years have influenced the valuation of properties for rate-making purposes. The rigid rules outlined in earlier decisions usually were outmoded by changing economic conditions. In recent years, the attitude of the Supreme Court has been to allow state regulatory commissions to establish the rate base by using original cost or reproduction cost or any combination thereof which they choose. In the Hope Natural Gas case,[3] the Court implied that even if a regulatory commission uses faulty methods to arrive at a rate base the action taken will be presumed to be constitutional if the end result is not clearly confiscatory. That is, the return allowed on the rate base of the public utility must be so low that it results in the property of the utility being confiscated through the regulatory process. The burden of proof is on the utility company to show that the end result is confiscatory.

Rate Base and the Investor

The net result of the Hope Natural Gas decision has been that each state has selected its own method of determining a fair return and rate base in conformance with the end-result theory. In 1958, 29 states were classified as original-cost states and 19 as fair-value states. "Fair value" means that the regulatory commission gave consideration to reproduction cost as well as original cost in determining the rate base.[4] Generally, "the market performance of public utility common

---

[3] *Federal Power Commission* v. *Hope Natural Gas Company*, 320 U.S. 591 (1944).

[4] Donald A. Ferguson, "Public Utilities, A Real Growth Industry of the 1950's," *Analysts Journal*, Vol. XV, No. 1 (February, 1959), p. 81.

stocks of 'cost' jurisdictions has not been as favorable as where the 'fair value' rule applies."[5]

The rate base is not the only consideration in the analysis of the regulatory climate of a particular utility. Some state commissions are more zealous champions of the consumers' interest in low rates than are others. The investor must take into account the severity of regulation in the locality. The element of judgment causes the process of fixing a fair rate of return on fair value to vary considerably, because the determining factors can sometimes be trends in local politics or the personal attitudes of regulatory commissioners.

THE ELECTRIC LIGHT AND POWER INDUSTRY

The electric light and power industry has certain fundamental operational and regulatory characteristics of interest to the analyst, most of which were enumerated before. In summary, these characteristics are: (1) the electric utility usually operates as a monopoly in its given area; (2) the electric utility is subject to regulation of its rates and the quality of service it offers; (3) the production of electrical energy and its use are simultaneous, making necessary a large capital investment.

In this discussion of the electric light and power industry, we will be concerned with (1) the basic economic characteristics of the industry and (2) the analysis of electric utility financial statements and operations. Attention in this chapter will be directed to the electric light and power industry.

Industry Growth

The electric light and power industry has shown a remarkable growth. The physical output of the electric utility industry, measured in kilowatt-hours (kwh),[6] has grown from 442.7 billion kilowatt-hours

---

[5] *Ibid.*

[6] "Kilowatts measure the production capacity or capability of electric generators and also the power requirement of electrical appliances and equipment.

"Electric generators range in size from a minute fraction of one kilowatt to a maximum of 260,000 kilowatts. In power stations, the most common sizes are 60,000 kilowatts and 100,000 kilowatts. As new generating installations are made, however, the number of larger-sized generators increases. Kilowatt-hours measure the amount of electricity generated and also the amount consumed or sold.

"As an illustration—a 60,000-kilowatt generator running at full capacity in one

in 1953 to 982.7 billion kilowatt-hours in 1964. The growth of electric power has exceeded the growth of the economy as a whole, measured in terms of overall industrial production. This is in direct contrast to the railroad industry, which has grown at a much slower rate than industrial production.

This growth in electric light and power output is the result of population growth as well as widespread and more intensive use of electric power. In 1953, the average annual use per customer was 2,369 kilowatt-hours. By the end of 1964, this figure had grown to approximately 4,703 kilowatt-hours per customer.

The growth in dollar sales of electric power has almost kept pace with the growth in physical output. The kilowatt-hours of electricity sold have increased from 1953 to 1964 by 222 percent, and dollar revenues of electric utilities by 212 percent. The ability of electric utilities to sell their services at relatively stable prices during a period of generally rising costs is the result of increases in efficiency of operation. For example, the number of pounds of coal required to generate one kilowatt-hour of electricity has declined by nearly 25 percent in the last decade. A large part of these savings from increased efficiency has been passed on to consumers. In fact, the revenue per kilowatt-hour has declined in the last 10 years from 2.74 cents per kilowatt-hour in 1954 to 2.3 cents in 1964.[7]

Regional Growth

The rate of growth in consumption of electric energy has not been uniform for all regions of the United States. Consumption has grown at a slower rate in the Northeastern states and East Central (Middle Atlantic states) than in the rest of the nation. Conversely, consumption in the Southwestern region has grown more rapidly than the national average.

The Federal Power Commission has made studies of estimated regional increases for the next two decades, shown in Figure 15–1.

---

hour's time will generate 60,000 kilowatt-hours of electricity. There are 8,760 hours in the year. If this generator operated continuously at full capacity throughout a year without stopping for inspection or repairs, or for lack of consumer demand for electricity, it would generate 60,000 kilowatts $\times$ 8,760 hours, or 525,600,000 kilowatt-hours in a year." Edison Electric Institute, *About the Electric Industry*, 1958 ed.

[7] *Moody's Public Utility Manual, 1965* (New York: Moody's Investors Service, Inc., 1965), p. 15a.

FIGURE 15–1

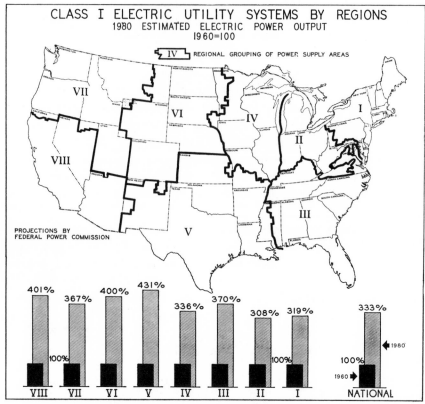

CLASS I ELECTRIC UTILITY SYSTEMS BY REGIONS
1980 ESTIMATED ELECTRIC POWER OUTPUT
1960=100

Source: Standard and Poor's Industry Analysis—Utilities Electric, April 22, 1965.

It appears that electric energy consumption will grow more rapidly in the South Central and West Central regions than in the rest of the nation.

Cyclical Stability and Competition

The electric utility industry has shown remarkable resistance to economic recessions. Indexes of electric power output and sales have shown almost no decline during past economic recessions, because growth in consumption by new customers would compensate for any decrease in electric energy consumption by existing customers. (See Figure 15–1.)

Electric power revenues from each class of customer have grown steadily since 1953. Even industrial sales, which usually reflect any marked change in general business activity because industrial customers are first to cut back consumption during a recession, had only one decline in the period 1953–65. Industrial power sales declined in 1958 due to the general economic recession, but the other customer categories grew sufficiently to offset this decline.

The stable earning power of public utilities can be attributed in part to their monopolistic position. There is very little direct competition between electric utilities in the same locality. The industry is also relatively free of indirect competition, because there are few substitutes for the services the industry provides. This is most apparent in lighting for homes, where the next best substitute is the gasoline or kerosene lamp. In heating or cooking, however, electricity competes with gas. Electric utilities must also offer electricity for industrial use at rates competitive with the cost at which companies can produce their own power or secure it from other sources.

Analysis of Electric Utility Financial Statements and Operations

Analysis of electric utility financial statements is facilitated by the requirement of the Federal Power Commission and the National Association of Railroad and Utilities Commissioners that their financial statements be presented uniformly. As a consequence, the financial statements of these companies not only are presented uniformly throughout the industry, but also are presented in detail.

The objectives of electric utility financial statement analysis are to gauge operating effectiveness and profitability. It should be realized that a utility is not guaranteed the allowed rate of return. In the analysis to help achieve these objectives, the analyst is primarily concerned with:

1. Analysis of the efficiency of asset utilization, which in a utility is primarily plant utilization.
2. Analysis of effectiveness of the utility's financial management.
3. Nature of the utility's operating revenue composition and types of customers.
4. Analysis of its operating costs and efficiency.

It must be recognized that this analysis must be an integrated approach, not unlike the analysis used in industrial securities. The

FIGURE 15-2

Indexes of Electric Power Production and Industrial
Production Seasonally Adjusted
(1957–59 = 100)

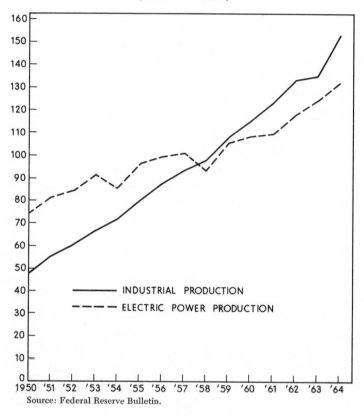

Source: Federal Reserve Bulletin.

profitability equation of margin of profit times turnover of assets is still applicable, only the points of emphasis are different.

The Balance Sheet. It may be noted from the composite balance sheet for the electric utility industry that this industry is characterized by a substantial investment in plant and equipment. Typically, the electric utility's investment in plant and equipment constitutes between 80 and 90 percent of total assets. It may be noted in Table 15–1 that utility plant accounted for 91.7 percent of total assets on an industry-wide basis in 1963. Current assets, in contrast, accounted for only about 6.7 percent of total assets.

This concentration in plant assets reflects the fact that electric utilities have virtually no inventories, because the production and consumption of electric power is simultaneous. The inventories they do have consist of materials and supplies or appliances. Also, since utility customers pay bills promptly, accounts receivable are not large. Because cash and equivalent constitute a large proportion of current assets, the current ratio (current assets divided by current liabilities) will normally be less than two. It is not unusual to find a deficit in working capital (current assets less current liabilities). The deficit is usually due to the temporary increase in current liabilities caused by the inclusion of long-term debt that is reaching maturity.

TABLE 15–1

Electric Utility Industry
Balance Sheet
December 31, 1953 and December 31, 1963

	December 31, 1953		December 31, 1963	
	Amount *(000,000)*	*Percent*	*Amount* *(000,000)*	*Percent*
Assets:				
Electric utility plant	$25,856	95.9	$53,633	104.6
Other utility plant	3,079	11.4	6,228	12.2
Total utility plant	28,935	107.3	59,861	116.8
Less: accumulated provision for depreciation and amortization	5,555	20.6	12,868	25.1
Net utility plant	23,380	86.7	46,993	91.7
Other property and investments	921	3.4	520	1.0
Total current and accrued assets	2,487	9.2	3,426	6.7
Total deferred debits	181	0.7	317	0.6
Total Assets	$26,969	100.0	$51,256	100.0
Liabilities:				
Long-term debt	$12,162	45.1	$23,649	46.1
Common stock	7,240	26.8	12,139	23.7
Retained earnings	1,887	7.0	5,016	9.8
Preferred stock	3,115	11.6	4,507	8.8
Total current liabilities	2,250	8.3	3,726	7.3
Other reserves	94	0.4	395	0.8
Deferred income taxes	..	..	1,548	3.0
Other deferred items	133	0.5	37	..
Other liabilities	88	0.3	239	0.5
Total Liabilities	$26,969	100.0	$51,256	100.0

Source: Edison Electric Institute.

Measures of Efficiency of Plant Utilization. The measures of plant utilization that may be used are (1) the ratio of plant per dollar of revenue and (2) various physical measures of plant utilization. These measures are important, because heavy fixed plant investment not only affects turnover of assets but also has an effect on the operating costs of the utility. That is, the large plant investment causes the utility to have relatively high fixed costs of maintenance, property taxes, etc.

Measure of Plant Turnover. Customarily, in financial statement analysis, asset utilization is measured by a turnover figure (see page 249) computed by dividing the asset item into revenues. Because plant turnover for an electric utility would be less than 1.0, plant utilization is usually measured by the ratio of plant per dollar of revenue. In 1963, the electric utility industry had a plant investment of $4.06 per dollar of revenue. The plant investment is usually lower for a utility that generates its electricity with steam powered facilities than for a utility that uses hydroelectric or water power. For example, Idaho Power Company, which produces all electricity hydraulically, has a plant investment of $6.35 per dollar of revenue, while Central Illinois Public Service, which produces its power with steam generation, has a plant investment of $3.81 per dollar of revenue.

This large investment in plant is necessary because productive capacity must be large enough to meet the peak demands on it, at whatever time the peak occurs during the year. However, during the balance of the year when demand is below the peak, the plant will operate at less than capacity. The profitability of the electric utility is dependent on its ability to utilize excess capacity during off-peak periods. There is a great incentive to utilize this capacity during these periods, because the costs of producing additional power are small. Additional costs consist largely of additional fuel costs if the electric utility uses steam generation as the means of generating electricity, because a large portion of a utility's cost is fixed and does not increase when off-peak power is produced and sold.

The Load Factor. A statistical measure of the degree to which off-peak plant capacity is being utilized is the load factor. To explain the load factor, it must be noted that electricity is energy required to produce work. The rate at which work is demanded is measured by the kilowatt. For example, the rate at which work is demanded by the lighting customer who turns on all his lights at once is measured by the sum of the watts of all his electric light bulbs. Capacity to produce at the time of peak demand at the generating plant is also measured by kilowatts. Output of electricity (the unit for which a charge is made) is the kilowatt-hour, which was defined earlier as "the rate of work demanded (the kilowatt) multiplied by the length of time that this rate is required." Thus, a demand of one kilowatt for one hour is a kilowatt-hour, as is also a demand of one-half kilowatt for two hours. The load factor, which measures how steadily electricity is produced over a period of time, is defined as the ratio of the average demand (called the "average load") to the peak demand, that is, the average demand (say, for a year) divided by the peak demand. Obviously, this ratio is always less than one (less than 100 percent), but the higher it is, the better the utilization of excess capacity at off-peak periods.

To illustrate the method of computing the system load factor, the Allegheny Power System sold 13,724,692,728 kilowatt-hours of electricity in 1964. The average demand for 1964 is computed by dividing the total output (13,724,692,728) by the number of hours in one year (8,760). The average demand for the Allegheny System was 1,556,745 kilowatts. The average demand of 1,566,745 kilowatts divided by the peak demand of 2,278,000 results in a load factor of 68.8 percent.

Capacity Measures. The analyst should be concerned with (1) the adequacy of plant capacity and (2) the average use of capacity. The peak load determines the size of plant investment required for the utility, because the utility must maintain a sufficient capacity to provide for the peak demand of its customers plus a margin of safety. The significance of plant adequacy is that an electric utility operating with a relatively small margin between peak demand and rated capacity will be required to install more generating capacity. The new generating capacity might require additional financing, which, as we shall see from the later discussion, would have a profound effect on common stock earnings.

To illustrate the measures of plant capacity adequacy, the Allegheny System had a net plant capacity of 2,653,100 kilowatts and a peak load of 2,278,000 kilowatts, which leaves a capacity margin of 375,100 kilowatts. This capacity margin or reserve is usually stated as a percent of peak load. For the Allegheny System, the indicated margin of reserves is 16.5 percent of peak load, which is considerably less than the 22.1 percent margin for the electric utility industry as a whole.

The capacity factor, also called the "plant factor" or "plant-utilization factor," is based on the rated capacity of the generating plant rather than on the actual peak load. The plant should normally have a rated capacity somewhat in excess of the peak demand. The capacity factor is computed by dividing the actual output in kilowatt-hours by the theoretical output if the plant were operated at full capacity every hour of the year. Theoretical output is obtained by multiplying the plant's kilowatt capacity by the number of hours in a year. The capacity factor for the Allegheny System was 59 percent for 1964. The system produced 13,724,693,000 kilowatt-hours, with a theoretical capacity of 23,241,156,000 kilowatt-hours (2,653,100 kilowatt capacity times 8,760 hours in one year).

The capacity factor for the electric utility industry has tended to improve in recent years, resulting in a lower plant investment per dollar of revenue. The cause of this tendency is the power interchange program resulting from the interconnection of electric utility systems. This interconnection enables one utility with different peak load requirements to purchase electric power from another and vice versa. It is estimated by the Federal Power Commission that a complete coordination of all electric utility systems would reduce plant investment by $2 billion.[8]

Importance of Financial Management. An important feature of electric utility operation is the substantial proportion of prior claim capital used. The electric utility industry is highly leveraged, and this leverage—the use of prior claim capital—is important to the common stock investor. The composite capital structures of electric utilities for the years ending 1953 and 1963 are shown in Table 15–2. Long-term debt accounts for 52 percent of total capital funds and preferred stock about 10 percent, for a total prior claim capital of 62 percent of total capital funds at the end of 1963.

The common stock earnings are largely dependent on the ability of the utility management to effectively finance expansion. Common stockholders of a utility with growth potential may find that financing the expansion may cause the growth to be a hazard, because (1) debt financing cannot be secured on favorable terms and (2) common stock financing may be required, resulting in short-run dilution of earnings.

As mentioned above, financing expansion can be done most advantageously by selling bonds and preferred stock. For this method

---

[8] *Annual Report, 1964, Federal Power Commission*, p. 47.

TABLE 15–2

Capitalization of Electric Utilities
December 31, 1953 and December 31, 1963

	December 31, 1953		December 31, 1963	
	Amount (000,000)	*Percent*	*Amount (000,000)*	*Percent*
Long-term debt	$12,162	49.8	$23,469	52.0
Preferred stock	3,115	12.8	4,507	10.0
Common stock equity	9,127	37.4	17,155	38.0
Total	$24,404	100.0	$45,131	100.0

Source: Edison Electric Institute.

of financing to be feasible, the "cost of the new money" should be lower than the percentage rate of return the utility is permitted to earn on its rate base. There is a limit to how far a utility may go in financing expansion through the use of debt and preferred stock. If a very high proportion of a company's capitalization consists of prior claim capital, there is a greater danger that even a comparatively small decline in the percentage earned on the rate base will quickly result in inadequate coverage of interest charges or of interest and preferred dividends combined.

Likewise, when senior securities (bonds and preferred stock) comprise a large proportion of total capitalization, variations in earnings on the rate base produce magnified results on earnings per share of common stock. Such stocks become more speculative, because investors are more concerned with probable immediate trends in earnings, which will show magnified results on a per-share basis. Just as in industrial stocks, the conservative investor must proceed with caution when current earnings are inflated above probable long-run average earnings.

There is another reason why a high proportion of senior securities in a public utility's capitalization lowers the quality not only of the senior securities but also of the common stock. A utility with a top-heavy capital structure may be forced to finance future growth in the rate base by the sale of more common stock in order to avoid creating an even more top-heavy structure. The common stockholder, therefore, runs a greater risk that the utility's growth will result in dilution of earning power per share by issue of new common stock on unfavorable terms.

The Nature of Dilution. Additional common stock sales may result in a dilution of (1) voting power, (2) book value, and (3) earnings. We are concerned here with dilution of earning power. The earnings of existing common stockholders are diluted when the sale of new common stock redistributes and changes the proportions of each share of common stock, and thus causes a lower earnings per share. Obviously, the lower earnings per share from the sale of additional common stock should be only a short-run phenomena, because in the long run the expansion should be profitable enough to justify the sale of additional stock.[9]

To illustrate the effects of earnings dilution, let us suppose a utility earns 6 percent on its rate base of $100,000. The utility has the financial structure, shown in Table 15–3, of $50,000 in 4½ percent bonds,

TABLE 15–3

**Effects of Sale of New Common
Stock on Per-Share Earnings**

Capital Structure		
Bonds 4½%	$ 50,000	$ 50,000
Preferred stock 5%	25,000	25,000
Common stock	25,000	50,000
Total	$100,000	$125,000
Earnings per Share Calculations		
Revenue before interest	$ 6,000	$ 7,500
Bond interest	2,250	2,250
Earnings after bond interest	3,750	5,250
Preferred dividends	1,250	1,250
Common stock earnings	$2,500	$4,000
Earnings per share	$2.50	$2.00

$25,000 in common stock equity, with 1,000 shares of common stock outstanding. As shown in the table the earnings are $2.50 per share. The utility plans to expand and finds it prudent not to sell any more bonds or preferred stock. The decision is to sell 1,000 additional shares of common stock for $25,000, increasing the number of shares outstanding to 2,000. The effect on the earnings per share of common stock is shown in the table.

---

[9] Robert F. Vandell, "Effects of New Financing on Common Stockholders' Income," in *Techniques of Financial Analysis*, ed. Erick A. Helfert (Homewood, Ill.: Richard D. Irwin, Inc., 1963), p. 107.

Analysis of the Income Statement. The analyst does not have any major problems in analyzing the income statements of an electric utility as the account classifications are set forth in a uniform manner. There are qualitative differences in some of the items which require further investigation. The items requiring special attention are (1) the analysis of the stability and growth of operating revenues, (2) the analysis of the operating expenses and (3) an examination and analysis of depreciation accounting methods.

Analysis of Operating Revenues. The composition of a utility's customers, sales, and revenues affects the stability of its earnings and intensity of its plant usage. Although the electric utility is selling a single service, types of customers served vary widely. An electric utility's customers are classified into seven major groupings, but only three categories are of any significance to the analyst. These classifications are (1) residential, (2) commercial, and (3) industrial. For purposes of discussion, we will put all others in a catchall "others."

Residential customers are characteristically the most stable segment of an electric utility's load. Their use of electricity is not noticeably reduced during periods of recession, nor does it increase substantially during periods of prosperity. Their demand for electricity has grown at a relatively constant rate. The number of customers has increased, as well as the per-customer usage. The average annual number of kilowatt-hours sold per residential customer has increased from 2,216 kilowatt-hours in 1953 to 4,099 in 1963.

Commercial customers, including stores, restaurants, offices, and others, are also relatively stable consumers of electric power. Their consumption is primarily for lighting and air conditioning, uses that do not change appreciably during recessions. Consumption by this category of customer has tended to grow at a relatively constant but slower rate than residential consumers' consumption.

The most volatile segment of an electric utility's load is the industrial customer. Industrial consumption of electric power tends to vary with changes in economic conditions. During strikes and recessions, use of electricity and revenues from industrial users tend to decline. Industrial consumption is most important to electric companies in the central part of the United States where the large automobile and steel plants are located.

For example, Detroit Edison in 1958 derived about 65 percent of its total sales and about 54 percent of total revenues from commercial and industrial users. During the recession year of 1958, revenues dropped from 1957 by $14.6 million and sales by 840 million-kilowatt-hours. All these declines were the result of a lower commercial and industrial load, because consumption by residential users increased during the same period. The effect of this decline in load was to reduce the earning per share of Detroit Edison stock from $2.62 in 1957 to $2.17 in 1958.

Analysis of Operating Expenses. The real measure of operating efficiency of a firm is its ability to control its expenses. The basic measure of ability to control expenses is a computation of the relationship of operating expenses to operating revenues. The operating ratio computed from the electric utility income statement prepared in accordance with the uniform system of accounts is of limited usefulness to the analyst because of the structure and arrangement of income taxes and depreciation included in the operating expense section, shown in Table 15–4.

Adjusted Operating Ratio. To get a measure of the controllable operating expenses of the electric utility, the analyst should rearrange the operating expenses to exclude those items over which manage-

TABLE 15–4

Electric Utility Industry
Operating Income Statements
for 1953 and 1963

	1953		1963	
	Amount *(000,000)*	*Percent*	*Amount* *(000,000)*	*Percent*
Operating revenues	$5,940	100.0	$11,576	100.0
Direct operating expenses:				
Cost of fuel	1,014	17.0	1,762	15.2
Other production	440	7.4	744	6.5
Transmission and distribution..	643	10.8	975	8.4
Customer service	200	3.4	338	2.9
Sales promotion	101	1.7	209	1.8
Administrative and general	403	6.8	759	6.6
Total direct operating	2,801	47.1	4,787	41.4
Depreciation	565	9.5	1,360	11.7
Taxes other than income	532	9.0	1,195	10.3
Federal income taxes	778	13.1	1,313	11.3
State income taxes	*	...	54	0.5
Deferred income taxes........	29	0.5	130	1.2
Total operating expense	4,705	79.2	8,839	76.4
Operating Income	$1,237	20.8	$2,737	23.6

* Included in "Taxes other than income."
Source: Edison Electric Institute.

ment has no effective control. A reconstructed income statement is shown in Table 15–5.

TABLE 15–5

Electric Utility Industry
Reconstructed Operating Income Statements
for 1953 and 1963

	1953		*1963*	
	Amount (000,000)	*Percent*	*Amount (000,000)*	*Percent*
Operating revenue	$5,940	100.0	$11,576	100.0
Total operating expense	4,705	79.2	8,839	76.4
Less:				
Depreciation	565	9.5	1,360	11.7
Federal income taxes	778	13.1	1,313	11.3
Deferred income taxes	29	0.5	130	1.2
State income taxes	..	..		
Total	1,372	23.1	2,803	24.2
Adjusted operating expenses	$3,333	56.1	$6,036	52.1

The adjusted operating expense figure is related to operating revenue to derive the adjusted operating ratio. The adjusted operating ratio for all electric utilities for the year ending December 31, 1963, was 52.1 percent. The adjusted operating ratio for the industry has declined steadily from 56.1 in 1953 to the present level.

Special Nature of Depreciation. A question might be raised as to why depreciation and income taxes are not included as operating expenses, since both are legitimate operating expenses for rate-making purposes. The reason is that the depreciation charge has been subject to considerable variation from one utility to another in recent years, dependent on their choice of depreciation method. Utilities that select one of the accelerated methods—sum of the year's digits or double declining balance—will usually have a higher depreciation charge than those that use straight-line depreciation.[10]

The real problem for the analyst arises from the income statement treatment of income taxes when liberalized depreciation is used. Obviously, the increased depreciation will reduce taxable income and, as a consequence, the income tax of the utility. State regulatory commissions have split on the proper accounting method for handling these expenses. One group advocates flow-through accounting, stat-

---

[10] For an earlier discussion of these depreciation methods and their effects, see page 242.

ing that only actual income taxes paid by the utility should be deducted. The "normalization" group, on the other hand, requires the utility to deduct an additional income tax equal to the amount by which income taxes were reduced. The operating income of utilities that use flow-through accounting will tend to be much higher than those using the normalization method.

The analyst should always watch for changes in accounting method, because a change from normalization accounting to flow-through would tend to result in a sharp increase in earnings. In addition, utilities that are expanding may get an additional boost to earnings from the investment credit, which allows an offset against income taxes equal to 3 percent of the cost of machinery and equipment purchased and put into service during a year.

Operating Expense Measures. The operating and maintenance expenses should be studied in detail. A complete breakdown according to function of operations is shown in Table 15–6.

TABLE 15–6

Electric Utility Industry
Selected Expense Ratios
1953–63

| | Per Average Customer | | Per KWH Sold | |
Expense	1953	1963	1953	1963
Cost of fuel	20.32¢	28.03¢	.26¢	.19¢
Other production	8.82	11.84	.11	.08
Transmission and distribution	12.89	15.51	.17	.11
Customer service	4.00	5.38	.05	.04
Sales promotion	2.02	3.33	.03	.02
Administrative and general	8.08	12.07	.10	.08
Total direct operating expense	56.13	76.16	.73	.52
Depreciation	11.32	21.64	.15	.15
Taxes other than income	10.66	19.01	.14	.13
Income taxes	15.60	21.75	.20	.15
Deferred income taxes	0.58	2.07	.01	.01
Total Operating Expense ...	94.29¢	140.63¢	1.22¢	0.96¢

	1953	1963
Kilowatt-hours sold*	384,666	921,478
Customers served	49,899,065	62,853,000

* In millions of KWH.
Source: Edison Electric Institute.

Costs of production will vary from one company to another, depending on the source of power. Hydroelectric projects, for example, usually permit generating costs per kilowatt-hour below costs at steam plants, but the investment per kilowatt of capacity is about 60 percent more, and sometimes transmission costs will be greater.

Companies largely dependent on hydroelectricity are exposed to the risk of drought conditions in certain years, which would curtail motive power. However, during periods of price inflation hydroelectric companies are in a better position to control costs than are companies utilizing steam plants, because the hydroelectric companies are not at the mercy of rising prices for coal or other fuels. Fuel cost may account for a large portion of production costs at steam plants— 70 percent on an industry basis in 1963. The highest-cost power, of course, is that purchased at wholesale from other producers. The company that relies largely on this source is essentially a distributor of power and will have a small investment per dollar of gross revenue.

Distribution costs of the electric utility generally are not an important factor in public utility costs. The distribution costs will vary from one company to another, depending on the density of population and physical characteristics of the territory served. In sparsely populated areas, a greater investment in distribution lines per domestic customer served is obviously required.

Expense Ratios. Various expense measures may be calculated which tend to put the level of operating expenses in better perspective. Two of the more meaningful measures are (1) expenses per customer served and (2) expenses per kilowatt-hour sold. Examples of these measures for the electric utility industry are shown in Table 15–6.

Other measures may also be devised for such things as intensity of transmission and distribution systems utilization or customer density. Customer density is measured by the number of customers per mile of transmission line. The customer density of an area has a significant effect on the investment per customer for distribution facilities. Since most public utilities are highly leveraged, as mentioned earlier, the average investment per customer in transmission lines affects the interest costs of the utility and, in turn, earnings available to the common stockholder. The possibility of population growth in a sparsely populated area with low customer density is a highly favorable factor in electric utility analysis, because it usually results in an increase in the number of customers without a proportionate increase in investment in new transmission and distribution facilities.

As suggested earlier, the basis of analysis of the securities of any particular company is a review of the measures of operating efficiency and profitability of that company, and a comparison may be made against certain standards which the analyst devises. Frequently, averages for the industry are used, since they are convenient standards for comparison. The analyst must assume when he uses industry averages that the operating conditions of a particular company are similar to the overall operating conditions of the industry as a whole. In public utility analysis, this assumption is less valid than it is with industrial securities, because each utility is unique in that its market and area of operations are fixed.

SELECTION OF SECURITIES

The selection of public utility securities, like selection of any other type of securities, is a matter of comparing the relative opportunities after a thorough analysis of the companies. The tools used in selection are much the same as those used in selection of industrial securities. The differences in stability of utilities operations and the capital structure of the utility cause the analyst to place different emphasis on various items. For example, the analyst will be interested in the utility's ability to earn its fixed charges, even when the analyst is interested primarily in common stock investment. The reason for this is that a "high leverage" utility will be more vulnerable to adverse developments, such as decline in consumption and rate changes.

Times-Fixed-Charges-Earned Ratio

The basic measure of interest or fixed-charge coverage is the times-fixed-charge ratio. In computing fixed charges earned, the analyst should make certain adjustments to the item "Income before interest charges." First, it would be advisable to add income taxes to the "Income before interest" shown in Table 15–7.

Second, certain adjustments must be made in computing the amount of fixed charges. A catchall classification "income deductions" includes interest, amortized debt discount, and similar charges. In addition, there usually is a credit balance, "interest charged to construction." This amount is the interest on funds borrowed to finance construction in progress. The theory is that since the facility is not yet producing income it should be considered part of the cost of the facility rather than a cost of financing current operations. This item can distort the times-fixed-charges-earned ratio. The material in Table 15–7 shows this item, and it reduces fixed charges by a range of 10 to 16 percent over the years 1960–63. For this reason, the analyst should compute times interest earned before deducting the "Interest charged to construction" credit.

TABLE 15–7

Electric Utility Income Statement
Financial Charges Section, 1960–63 and 1953
(in millions)

	1963	1962	1961	1960	1953
Income before interest charges (after income taxes)	$2,990	$2,852	$2,584	$2,415	$1,337
Income before interest charges and income taxes	4,591	4,436	4,122	3,839	2,202
Interest charges					
Interest on long-term debt ...$	866	$ 834	$ 780	$ 728	$ 357
Interest on short-term debt ...	14	13	20	23	3
Amortization of debt discount expense and premium	3	4	..	..	4
Other interest expense	17	15	14	12	16
Interest charged to construction, credit	(79)	(90)	(86)	(100)	(73)
Total Interest Charges ..$	821	$ 776	$ 728	$ 663	$ 307
Net income ....$	$2,169	$2,076	$1,856	$1,752	$1,030
Preferred dividend charges	208	206	202	191	138
Available for Common Stock	$1,961	$1,870	$1,654	$1,561	$ 892
Common Dividends	1,329	1,284	1,159	1,093	463
Net income after dividends ....$	632	$ 586	$ 495	$ 468	$ 429
Adjusted Times Interest Earned					
Before taxes	5.10X	5.12X	4.76X	5.03X	5.79X
After taxes	3.32X	3.29X	2.98X	3.16X	3.52X

Source: Edison Electric Institute and Federal Power Commission.

To indicate the desired minimum standards of fixed charge coverage, the adjusted times-interest-earned ratio has been computed for the years 1953–63, both before and after taxes. The coverages range from a low of 4.76 times before taxes in 1961 to a high of 5.79 times before taxes in 1953. These standards should be suitable for selection of utility bonds, since the period 1953–63 encompasses two recessions.

Common Stock Selection

In the last edition of this book, it was stated that utility common stocks tend to sell on a "yield basis." For many utilities that operate principally in the Northeastern part of the United States, this generalization is probably true. However, for the electric utility industry as a whole, there is evidence that the investor is now attracted to the growth potential of electric utilities, and pays less attention to dividends and more attention to earnings growth. This tendency is evidenced from the material shown in Table 15–8.

It may be noted that electric utility common stocks tended to sell at a relatively constant yield until about 1957. From that date forward, investors appear to have been attracted by the growth potential of utilities as the price–earnings ratios increased and the yields declined. These yield declines took place in the face of improving yields on other types of investment media. (See page 319.)

Finally, the quality of the earnings that protect the current dividend probably exerts an additional influence. By "quality," we mean the probable stability of earnings per share in the event of a changing volume of operating revenues. If earnings have a high leverage, they can fall rapidly in the event of adversity, even though currently they may appear to constitute adequate protection for the dividend. The degree of leverage is partly the result of the proportion of stock in the capital structure relative to prior fixed-income securities, and is partly dependent on margin of profit before income taxes and fixed charges. The combined effect of the capitalization and the margin of profit before interest and income taxes can be revealed by the percentage of operating revenues brought down to the common stock. The analyst may compute the margin of safety after preferred dividends, as discussed previously. This measure has the virtue of indicating a little more exactly the percentage decline in operating revenues that is sufficient to wipe out common stock earnings, assuming that all costs before income taxes and interest remain fixed.

Summary

The most important factor in public utility security analysis is, of course, the judgment of the analyst, because analysis of utility common stocks is a matter of comparing relative opportunities and selecting the most promising company. In summary, the two basic factors which favor stability and growth in total earning power are: (1) the nature of the territory in which the company operates, technically known as "the physical right to do business," including the attitude of the regulatory commission; (2) the quality of management. Once

TABLE 15–8

Postwar Record of Electric Utility Stocks, 1946–64

Year	Average Price	Earned Per Share	Price Earnings Ratio	Dividends Paid	Average Yield	Dividend Payout
1946 34		$2.19	16	$1.43	4.2%	65%
1947 30		2.16	14	1.56	5.3	72
1948 27		2.22	12	1.60	5.9	72
1949 28		2.36	12	1.66	5.9	70
1950 31		2.62	12	1.76	5.7	67
1951 33		2.44	14	1.88	5.8	77
1952 35		2.62	13	1.91	5.4	73
1953 38		2.78	14	2.01	5.3	72
1954 44		2.94	15	2.13	4.8	72
1955 49		3.21	15	2.21	4.5	69
1956 50		3.35	15	2.32	4.7	69
1957 49		3.41	14	2.43	4.9	71
1958 58		3.63	16	2.50	4.3	69
1959 66		3.82	17	2.61	3.9	68
1960 70		4.12	17	2.68	3.8	65
1961 91		4.33	21	2.81	3.1	65
1962 92		4.73	19	2.97	3.1	60
1963 103		4.99	21	3.21	3.1	64
1964e 104a		5.25	20	3.40	3.3	65

e Estimated.
a As of May 28, 1964.
Source: *Electric Utility Companies, Annual Review, 1964.* Carl M. Loeb, Rhoads & Co.

these factors are given proper weight, the quality of the common stock will further depend on the proportion of the total capitalization it represents. A small equity causes earnings per share to fluctuate more widely, and the percentage of revenues available to the common will be narrower. For this reason, the percentage of average future earnings that will be paid out in dividends may be less than for a more conservative capitalization. The other factor discussed earlier is the risk of diluting the equity by being forced to issue common stock instead of bonds or preferred stock in future financing. For this reason and to finance growth, management may wish to build up the equity by retention of earnings.

REVIEW QUESTIONS AND PROBLEMS

1. Why should the electric light and power industry be viewed as a growth industry?

2. What are the major characteristics of an operating utility?
3. Discuss the impact of differences in customer composition on the cyclical stability of electric utility revenues.
4. Distinguish between (1) original cost, (2) replacement cost, and (3) fair value as public utility rate bases.
5. What was the significance of the Hope Natural Gas decision in public utility rate determination?
6. "The current ratio is virtually meaningless to the electric utility security analyst." Do you agree with this statement? Why?
7. Why are measures of plant utilization of importance in electric utility security analysis? What are the measures that may be used?
8. Contrast the load factor and the capacity factor. Is it possible to have a high capacity factor and a low load factor?
9. What is meant by customer density? How is it measured?
10. What is the composition of electric utility operating costs? What is the most important operating cost?
11. Outline the major factors the analyst should consider in selecting an electric utility common stock.

CHAPTER **16**

Specialized Analytical Techniques— Insurance Companies

The insurance industry is generally divided into two segments: (1) the life insurance industry and (2) property and casualty insurance industry. These companies are in the business of insuring individuals and businesses against loss from a wide range of causes. The life insurance companies confine their coverages to insurance against hazards that may interrupt a person's income flow, such as life insurance, accident and health insurance, and annuities. The property and casualty companies include every type of insurance except life. A property and casualty company may specialize and write only one line, such as automobile insurance or fire and allied insurance. The so-called "multiple-line underwriter" is simply a property and casualty company that writes several different classes of insurance. The range of possible coverages is too wide to enumerate here.

These insurance companies may be organized either as capital stock companies owned by investors or as mutual companies owned by policyholders. Obviously, investors are interested in the capital stock companies, which have common stock available for investment. Common stockholders share in the basic equity of the company and any additions to it through earnings from the insurance business and the investment of policy reserves.

A separate discussion of insurance company common stock as an investment is necessary because of (1) special accounting practices that differ from those customarily used by other businesses, (2) special valuation problems, and (3) regulatory problems.

LIFE INSURANCE COMPANIES

The life insurance industry has grown seven times faster than the population during the past decade. Most life insurance is written by

321

mutual life insurance companies, which are owned by the policy-holders. This growth also has been shared by the investor-owned stock life insurance companies. The common stock of these life companies has offered excellent opportunities for investment. However, life insurance company stocks as investments have not been given much attention by the general investing public. This lack of general interest has been caused by two factors. First, the amount of life insurance company stock outstanding is relatively small and is not listed on the organized security exchanges; therefore, it has not received the publicity of common stocks of industrials and public utilities. Second, and more important, the accounting practices of life insurance companies are so different from those used by other business enterprises that analysis of their earnings potential and investment value appears formidable.[1]

It is possible to understand life insurance company common stock investment analysis by examining: (1) the major points of difference between the accounting practices of life insurance companies and conventional industrial accounting practices; (2) the salient points of life insurance company valuation—earning power, book value, and growth; and (3) the basic nature of life insurance company operation.

Nature of Life Insurance Company Operation

The major sources of life insurance company income are (1) premium income and (2) investment income. The primary source of income to the life insurance company is premiums charged policyholders. The premiums charged for these life insurance policies by the company are based on: (1) the estimated mortality or death rates among policyholders; (2) operating expenses—the cost of doing business; and (3) the assumed rate of return on the reserves built up for each policy.

The other major source of income for life insurance companies in recent years has been the earnings on investments exceeding the as-

---

[1] Because of the inherent complexity of life insurance company common stock valuation, *Best's Digest of Insurance Stocks* does not attempt to value life insurance stocks as they do fire and casualty insurance stocks. However, it is believed that it is possible to provide an approach to life insurance stock valuation which may not result in the precise results that the specialist in life insurance stocks would like, but does provide a basis for the nonspecialist to evaluate these securities.

sumed rates of return on the reserves for policies that have been sold. To understand this source of earnings, it is necessary to understand the mechanics of calculating a life insurance premium. As mentioned above, the insurance company includes an amount in the premium to cover mortality or death claims. Since not all the people will die the first year, the company builds up policy reserves. These reserves are not left as idle balances.

The Source of Policy Reserves

The funds available for investment are the reserves accumulated for the payment of future benefits to policyholders. These reserve accumulations arise because of the nature of the typical life insurance contract and the system of premium payment. Most life insurance contracts are written for the whole life of the insured rather than for a specified term of, for example, one year. If only one-year life insurance policies were written, the investment funds of life insurance companies would be practically nonexistent. The premiums paid into the company would be almost equal to the death benefits and operating expenses. The life insurance company's investments would be confined to relatively short-term, highly liquid investments, because all policies would expire in one year.

However, since most life insurance is written for the entire or whole life of the insured, the company accumulates the premiums in policy reserves to pay future death benefits. For any group of insureds, these accumulations grow into rather substantial amounts. The example in Figure 4–2, on page 48, showed the accumulation of reserves for $1,000 of whole ordinary life insurance on 10,000 people aged twenty, and followed the reserve accumulation premium payments and ultimate disposition of this group's policy reserves. It was noted that with successive declines in premiums paid the policy reserves continue to climb until the group reaches the ages fifty-fifty-nine. Reserves continue to increase because of the interest income from the investment of the reserve accumulations. The amounts shown in the bottom line of Figure 4–2 are the funds available for investment. In this example, the reserve accumulations are invested at $2\frac{1}{2}$ percent, which accounts for the interest income.

Another factor that tends to accelerate the accumulation of reserves is the level-premium plan. To describe the level-premium plan, it is helpful to think first of the way premiums would be calculated and

324 Investment Analysis and Management

paid without it. For a young person, the cost of insurance would be small because the probability of death or mortality risk at early ages is relatively small. Each year the mortality risk would increase, and life insurance would become increasingly expensive until the premiums would be almost prohibitive for persons in the older age groups. Because of these changes in life insurance premiums from early life to late life, the level-premium plan was instituted. With this plan, the premiums on life insurance remain the same throughout the lifetime of the policyholder. During the early years, premiums are relatively greater than the mortality cost, or cost of paying death benefits, while in later years they are much less than the death benefits (see Figure 4–2).

Without the level-premium plan, there would be a relatively small reserve, because premium payments would approximate annual death benefit payments. It is obvious from the material in Figure 4–2 that the level-premium plan results in the accumulation of substantial policy reserves. These reserves, called "the legal reserve," are invested, thus increasing the value of the reserves and reducing the net insurance policy costs.

Life Insurance Company Costs

The costs of life insurance companies are (1) mortality costs, (2) business acquisition, and (3) operation costs. The major cost for a life insurance company is the payment of death claims or payment of the cash values of canceled policies to the insured. These costs are estimated in calculating the premium to be charged on the basis of mortality or death rate tables, which indicate the probability of death at various ages.

As was explained before, there is not a linear relationship between the premium and mortality. There are, as a consequence, two deductions from the income of a life insurance company, both of which bear a relationship to mortality. These deductions are (1) death benefits and (2) reserve increases. A rapidly growing company often will generally show increases in reserves which are substantially greater than death benefits. The reason for this is that a company when writing new business will select good risks or at least, charge premiums and build reserves commensurate with the risks assumed. Eventually, the company will begin to have death benefits exceeding increases in policy reserves, because the risk of death increases with age, and the older maturing policies begin to exceed the newer policies.

The analyst should note the number of policyholders the company has, because a company with a large number of policyholders will come closer to its predicted mortality than a company with a smaller number. The predicted mortality is the number of policyholders of given age that the company predicts will die during a given period of time. If the actual mortality—the number that does die—is less than the predicted mortality, it works to the company's benefit. If the net difference between the predicted and actual mortality is favorable, it permits the company to hold policy reserves for investment for a longer period than anticipated and collect more premiums than anticipated.

Actual mortality greater than predicted mortality is the result of poor selection of risks. New life insurance companies in their eagerness to build volume often will accept poorer risks than will a well-established company. These poor underwriting practices eventually catch up with the company in the form of a poor mortality experience, and will adversely affect the profits of the company.

Acquisition and Operating Costs

Life insurance company operating costs include the expenses of acquiring or selling policies and servicing policies. The ability to control these costs obviously would affect the profitability of the company. These costs vary considerably from one company to another and can best be measured by the ratio of operating expense to total income. The ratio of operating expenses to total income of all life insurance companies has remained fairly constant at around 17 percent of total income.

Of the two groups of costs of operation, the acquisition expenses are generally the larger. These costs include salaries of officers, professional fees, office expenses, and others. Costs may vary widely, depending on type of insurance sold and average size of policy in force. The acquisition or selling costs of a life insurance company are the result of new insurance sold during the year. The company charges off the major commission of the salesman against the current year's income. This is one of the characteristics of life insurance accounting. When a life insurance company sells a policy, it acquires a source of earnings or premium income for the life of the policy-holder, assuming, of course, that he does not cancel the policy. There-fore, the rapidly growing life insurance company shows relatively low earnings or "net gain from operations" in the earlier years when they are selling considerable life insurance, because most of the costs of acquiring the insurance are charged against the current year's in-come. The net effect of this practice is to "understate" the current year's "net gain from operations" and "overstate" the "net gain from operations" in future years.

Net Gain from Operations

The net income of a life insurance company is usually referred to as the "net gain from operations." The Life and Casualty Insurance Company of Tennessee Statement of Income, shown in Table 16–1, is a notable exception. This net gain or profit comes from three sources: (1) return on investment of policyholders' reserves in ex-cess of rate that was assumed in calculating the premium, (2) an actual mortality or death rate that is less than the rate assumed, and (3) savings that may result from operating expenses being lower than assumed in the premium calculation.

During recent years, the life insurance companies have had the benefit of considerable improvement in mortality experience as the result of medical advances which have increased the life expectancy of the American people. The mortality tables now in use by most life insurance companies were prepared in 1941, and the life ex-pectancy of a person at birth has increased from 60.8 years in 1941 to 69.9 years in 1963.[2]

Life insurance company investment income has contributed ma-terially to life company total earnings, because assumed rates on life policies were lowered in the late 1940's from 3–3½ percent to 2–2½ percent. This reduction in the assumed rate in the late 1940's was necessary because the rate of return earned by life insurance com-panies on their investments had been materially lower than the as-sumed rate. The bulk of the life insurance in force for the more rapidly growing companies has been written since 1947 and, as a result, at a lower assumed rate. These companies have also experi-enced a much higher average rate of return on reserves than have

---

[2] *Life Insurance Fact Book, 1965,* p. 97.

some of the older companies, because most of their new premium income has been received and invested during the 1950's, when the general level of interest rates was materially higher than it had been any time during the previous 20 years.

TABLE 16-1

**Life and Casualty Insurance Company of Tennessee
Statement of Income, December 31, 1964
(in thousands)**

Income:
Life insurance premiums $50,405
Accident and health premiums 10,358
Net investment income 16,606
Miscellaneous 1,466
    Total Income $78,915

Deductions:
Benefits, surrender payments, and other benefits paid:
Life benefits $21,936
Accident and health benefits 5,651
    Total Benefits $27,587
Additions of policy reserve 14,607
    Total Insurance Deductions $42,194

Operating Expenses:
Commissions $12,037
General insurance expenses 11,960
Taxes, licenses, and fees 2,193
Dividends to policyholders 409
    Total Deductions $68,793

Net income before income taxes 10,122
Federal taxes on income, estimated 1,827
Net income ....$ 8,295

It is obvious from the earlier discussion of acquisition costs that the life insurance company with the greatest profit potential may well be the one with current operating losses. To make meaningful comparisons of the earnings of life insurance companies, it is necessary for the investor to make an adjustment on the net gain from operations figure.

These adjustments are made by estimating the life insurance company's equity in the existing policies in force. Adjustments constitute the assigning of values to each $1,000 of life insurance in force. The values are as follows.

Ordinary life insurance in force—$15 to $20 per thousand.
Term life insurance in force—$5 to $8 per thousand.

Group life insurance in force—$2 to $5 per thousand.
Industrial life insurance in force—$25 to $30 per thousand.

These adjustments are made to correct the understatement of the current earnings caused by the practice of charging off in the first year the largest portion of the expenses of acquiring new business. These adjustments are made to reflect the estimated contribution the new insurance written would have made to earnings. The value factors and their application are shown below.

Ordinary life and endowment—$218,154,509 × $20.00 per $1000 = $4,363,100.
Term—$154,470,201 × $8.00 per $1000 = $1,235,760.
Group—$64,864,283 × $5.00 per $1000 = $324,320.
Industrial—$129,417,851 × $27.50 = $3,558,995.

For Life and Casualty of Tennessee for the year ending December 31, 1964, the total of these adjustments would add $9,482,175 to the reported net gain from operations of $8,295,000. The adjusted earnings would be $17,777,175, or 114 percent higher than the reported earnings.

Book Value of Stocks of Life Insurance Companies

The book value of life insurance company common stock may be one indicator of approximate "true" value if certain adjustments are made. The book value of the common stock is computed by dividing the stockholders' equity—the capital and surplus—by the number of shares outstanding. Two types of surplus are usually shown in the stockholders' equity section—assigned and unassigned. The assigned surplus is generally (1) a reserve for fluctuation in security values and (2) a reserve for poor mortality experience. Most of these reserves are shown on the Life and Casualty of Tennessee's statement of assets and liabilities as part of stockholders' equity. However, a mandatory reserve for security fluctuation losses is usually listed as a liability, but it is properly a part of the stockholders' equity. Life and Casualty of Tennessee has a stated common stock equity on December 31, 1964, of $61,208,000, but there was also a mandatory security valuation reserve of $8,098,000, which also was part of common stock equity. The total stockholders' equity was $69,306,000. (See Table 16–2.) The book value per share of common stock after this restatement of equity was $11.09 per share.

TABLE 16–2

Life and Casualty Insurance Company of Tennessee
Statement of Assets and Liabilities, December 31, 1964
(in thousands)

Cash	$ 3,175	Policy reserves	$311,716
U.S. government bonds	7,875	Policy claims	3,968
State and municipal bonds	15,824	Policy dividends	1,214
Corporate bonds	68,521	Unearned premiums	1,770
Other bonds	58,749	Taxes accrued	2,722
Total bonds	150,969	Mandatory security reserve	8,098
Common and preferred stocks,		Miscellaneous	1,773
at market	30,391	Total Liabilities	$331,261
Mortgage loans	157,649	Stockholders' equity:	
Real estate	22,088	Common stock	$ 18,900
Policy loans	16,720	Assigned surplus:	
Other assets	11,477	Securities fluctuation reserve	18,000
Total Assets	$392,469	Mortality contingency	
		reserve	16,400
		Unassigned	7,908
		Total equity	$ 61,208
		Total Liabilities and	
		Net Worth	$392,469

Adjusted Book Value

This restatement of book value provides a first approximation of the value of the common stock of this company. The analyst should make some additional adjustments to more correctly state the book value of the common stock of this company.

The major adjustment to book value is the result of life insurance companies' practice, mentioned earlier, of charging off most of the salesman's commission against the current year's income. Life insurance salesmen receive roughly 50 to 60 percent of the first year's premium on all new life insurance policies sold. These commissions are included as a cost of doing business in the calculation of the annual premium charged the policyholder. Therefore, the practice of charging off 50 to 60 percent of the commissions against current income causes the company to have an equity in the policy reserves. This adjustment is similar to one made in the restatement of earnings per share on page 328.

A range of values is given because several variables must be taken into account in the analysis and valuation of a life insurance company common stock. The more important of these variables are (1) differences in the company's lapses or persistency and (2) the volume of participating policies written.

Adjustments and the Lapse Ratio. The assigned values for the life insurance in force used in calculating adjusted book value are based on "average persistency." The persistency of life insurance in force means the extent to which it is not terminated for nonpayment of premiums.

Each life insurance contract may be voluntarily terminated or lapsed at any time by the insured. It is obvious that the life insurance company is not going to recover the acquisition costs that account for its equity in the policy reserves if a high percentage of the insurance in force is terminated or lapsed. A high percentage of lapses or low persistency would necessitate a downward revision in these assigned values. The percentage of lapses is called the "lapse ratio"—the ratio of the number of policies lapsed or surrendered in one year, less reinstatements, to the average number of policies in force.

Lapses tend to run significantly higher for new policies than for older policies. For example, in 1964 the lapse ratio for policies in force two years or more was 3.4 percent, but for all policies in force it was 5.0 percent.[3] The lapse ratio varies considerably among individual life insurance companies. Obviously, a more important factor is the amount of new insurance written in relation to insurance previously in force. Thus, a rapidly growing company will tend to have a higher lapse ratio.

The lapse ratio tends to follow business activity fluctuations. It tends to rise in periods of recession and drop during high levels of economic activity. However, the average annual lapse ratio for all companies has fluctuated between a very narrow range of about 3.2 percent to about 5.7 percent in the last 10 years. A persistency record poorer (higher lapse ratio) than 6 percent would be a signal to the analyst to investigate a company more intensively and adjust the range of assigned values downward.

Adjustments and Participating Policies. In order to compete with mutual life insurance companies for certain types of life insurance business, stock life insurance companies often write participating policies. A participating life insurance policy is one in which the policyholder receives policy dividends from differences between the premium charged and actual cost of the insurance. The actual cost of

---

[3] *Ibid.,* p. 51.

the life insurance is often less than premium charged, because (1) mortality is better than expected and (2) investment returns on policy reserves are greater than calculated. If the policies written by the company are nonparticipating, these insurance cost savings accrue to the life insurance company stockholders, since no dividend is due.

Generally speaking, a company will try to write most policies as nonparticipating and will usually succeed, since the premium per $1,000 of insurance is lower. A company with a substantial portion of its life insurance in force written as participating business will be required to share future savings with policyholders. Such a company would lower values assigned to its business in computing adjusted book value.

Calculation of Adjusted Book Value. From the range of values for life insurance in force, the analyst can usually take the average of values. For example, we assigned values for each $1,000 of life insurance in force for Life and Casualty of Tennessee as follows.

Whole life—$20.00 × $877,161,000 = $17,543,220.
Term life—$8.00 × $487,322,000 = $ 3,898,576.
Group life—$5.00 × $380,380,000 = $ 1,901,900.
Industrial life—$27.50 × $780,884,000 = $21,474,310.

The total value of these adjustments is $44,818,006, or $7.11 per share. The resultant book value would be ($11.09 book value + $7.11 adjustments) $18.20 per share.

Importance of Growth

The life insurance industry is one that has had a considerably better than average growth in the last decade. Life insurance in force has grown from about $186 billion in 1947 to $800 billion in 1964. However, individual companies vary considerably in their rates of growth. To illustrate the differences in rates of growth of two companies that started into business about the same time, Table 16–3 shows increases in life insurance in force of College Life Insurance Company, which began in 1946, and United Home Life Insurance Company, which started business in 1948.

The relative ability of a life insurance company to grow is directly indicative of the size and ability of its agency or sales force. One of the most valuable assets a life insurance company can have, and one

TABLE 16-3

Life Insurance in Force, United Home Life
Insurance Company and College Life Insurance Company, 1952-64
(in thousands)

	United Home Life	College Life
1952	$32,792	$ 60,029
1954	42,035	92,769
1956	51,272	128,199
1958	58,261	183,016
1960	65,835	242,706
1961	68,485	270,761
1962	72,795	304,114
1963	78,078	354,735
1964	81,355	415,659

Source: *Best's Life Insurance Reports, 1959 & 1965.*

that does not show up on its balance sheet, is a well-trained and productive sales force. Continuous production or sale of life insurance is necessary for prolongation of the life of the company, because each year it loses a portion of its business either through death or canceled policies.

The quality of growth in insurance in force is important. It is relatively easy to get insurance in force by intensive sales effort. Sometimes, the insurance is of low quality in that it does not fit the policyholder's needs. In such cases, the company may experience a very high percentage of lapsed or canceled policies or low persistency. This poor-quality business may cause the company to lose money, because most of the first year's premium goes for commissions and other expenses. If a large volume of business is lapsed after it is written, the company may never have the opportunity to recover the acquisition costs on that group of policies.

Summary

In estimating the relative investment value of a life insurance common stock, the major price factors are (1) the price-adjusted earnings or gain-from-operations ratio, (2) the relationship of adjusted book value to price, and (3) the rate of growth of insurance in force. However, the analyst should be careful in making comparisons between rates of growth in life insurance companies, because the growth in total insurance in force may be in lower-value group insurance in one company and more valuable ordinary life in another.

The book value of life insurance company common stock has real meaning to the investor only if he is buying control of the company. Persons that control the company are in position either to liquidate the company or to continue it as a going concern. The minority stockholder must assume that the company will continue to operate.

It is of utmost importance that the investor who is a minority stockholder evaluate management in terms of its ability to market its product, life insurance, because continued growth in insurance in force is necessary if the value of common stock is to increase. The state regulatory authorities require the company to maintain a certain minimum percentage relationship between policyholders' reserves and common stock equity. Ideally, therefore, the rate of growth of life insurance in force should be fairly constant. This constancy enables the company to generate earnings and to add to its equity, thereby preventing a dilution of equity by the sale of additional common stock. Of course, this need for growth assumes that future policies sold will result in a profit for the company, and normally they will, because the company has the profit built into the premium calculation.

Common stocks of life insurance companies generally sell at a price ranging from 85 percent to as high as 350 percent of the adjusted book value. The premium over adjusted book value can be justified only by an estimate of better than average growth potential. For example, Franklin Life Insurance Company common stock has sold at a price roughly 350 percent of book value. To justify that price, the analyst would need to feel that the phenomenal past growth will continue.

PROPERTY AND CASUALTY INSURANCE COMPANIES

The property and casualty insurance companies are in the business of insuring or underwriting uncertain large losses of personal and real property of policyholders. Property and casualty insurance companies are similar to life insurance companies, because they collect from policyholders premiums that are presumed to be sufficient to cover claims against the company. These premiums are accumulated and invested, and the property and casualty insurance company plans to have two sources of profit—underwriting profit and investment income. The underwriting profit—profit from the insurance business— is not so accurately determinable as it is for life insurance companies. The reasons for this difference are discussed below.

A striking difference between a life insurance company and a property and casualty insurance company is in investment policies. Life insurance companies are required by regulatory authorities to invest almost entirely in fixed-income securities, such as bonds and mortgages. Property and casualty insurance companies, however, may invest a greater portion of their assets in common stocks, as will be discussed below. This difference is an important consideration in evaluation of the common stocks of property and casualty companies as an investment, because the common stockholder must rely on the investment income for his return.

Profits of Property and Casualty Companies

As suggested above, these insurance companies have two basic sources of income—premium income and investment income. In computing premiums, the property and casualty insurance company includes costs of acquisition, overhead operating costs, and estimated claims by policyholders over the length of the policy contract, three to five years. The difference between the total cost of these three items and the premiums paid is the amount of the underwriting profit.

The underwriting profits of property and casualty insurance are erratic. (See Table 16–4.) There are two basic reasons for the cyclical character of underwriting profits: (1) poor loss estimation techniques and (2) rate regulation techniques. Failure of a company to properly estimate future losses will result in loss experience for the next two to three years, since insurance policies are forward contracts of that length. In addition, when it is evident that losses are in excess of premium income, there is a time lag before rates can be increased. For this reason, property and casualty companies have not had a satisfactory underwriting profit since 1955.

During this period of poor underwriting experience, the investment gains have been substantial. Rapidly increasing stock prices and improved investment income have more than offset the poor underwriting experience. As a result, the industry has enjoyed a measure of prosperity. It was estimated in 1964 that the total gain from investments (including unrealized appreciation) was nearly $2 billion, which was nearly five times the estimated underwriting loss.

Measures of Underwriting Experience

Due to the lag between changes in insurance rates and changes in claims loss experience, underwriting profits may vary from fairly substantial amounts in one period to losses in another. These variances may be the result of (1) poor selection of risks, (2) higher operating expenses than anticipated, or (3) higher claims expense than planned. Poor selection of risks may increase claims expense, and it is the cause of underwriting losses for some companies. However, there have been periods when the whole industry has experienced underwriting losses. The cause of these industry underwriting losses has not been poor selection of risks by all companies but the result of inflation.

In estimating insurance losses, two factors are involved for any insurance company, whether it is a life company or property and casualty company. One factor is the incidence or frequency of loss occurrence. The other factor is the dollar amount of each occurrence. For example, a property and casualty insurance company may esimate that it will have on a given number of policy contracts 100 claims of $1,000, for a total claim of $100,000, and rates are established accordingly. This loss experience is based on present-day prices. The estimate of incidence may be correct, but the increased price of materials for repairs of houses, automobiles, etc., may increase the value of the losses to, say, $200,000. To compound the loss, the company's operating expenses usually also increase. These, however, may be offset by increased efficiency of operation.

Underwriting loss and increased operating expenses cause the company to request permission from the state to increase rates. The regulatory authority may adjust rates upward or downward in the light of the most recent loss experience so that the property and casualty insurance companies will realize a modest underwriting profit. After an underwriting loss year, the company may request a rate increase. Assuming that it is granted promptly, the company will still suffer an underwriting loss for the next three to four years because it cannot increase the rates on existing policies before expiration. The authorities may grant the rate increase on the first request, but frequently there is a time lag, because the regulatory authorities may require the company to submit further underwriting loss experience before granting the increase. It is possible but not probable that the authorities will grant a rate increase, applicable to new and expiring policies, which would generate sufficient additional income to offset the underwriting losses on the old policies. Therefore, when property and casualty insurance companies, in the aggregate, have an underwriting loss during a year, the analyst can safely conclude that they will have losses for the next two to three years. The material in Table 16–4 supports this conclusion.

The objective of the property and casualty insurance company is to have premiums collected exceed expenses of writing the insurance and payment of losses. The measure of a company's experience in meeting this objective is the underwriting ratio or combined ratio. It is generally referred to as the combined ratio, because it is derived by adding together the expense ratio and the loss ratio. If the combined ratios are less than 100, the company has had an underwriting profit and vice versa.

TABLE 16–4

**Underwriting Ratios, Stock Property and
Casualty Insurance Companies, 1953–63**

	Loss Ratio	Expense Ratio	Combined Ratio
1953	57.2%	35.9%	93.1%
1954	56.9	36.7	93.6
1955	58.2	36.7	94.9
1956	63.4	37.1	100.5
1957	66.2	36.7	102.9
1958	63.7	36.3	100.0
1959	62.5	35.3	97.8
1960	63.6	34.8	98.4
1961	64.4	35.0	99.4
1962	64.5	34.5	99.0
1963	66.3	34.7	101.0
1964	68.0	33.9	101.9

Source: *Best's Insurance Reports, Fire and Casualty, 1965.*

The expense ratio is calculated by relating costs of placing the business on the books to premiums *written*. These expenses include agents' commissions, policy-writing costs, office expense, and others. The loss ratio is computed by relating losses and claims expense to premiums *earned*. The logic in using two different earnings bases for calculation of these ratios is that expenses are closely related to new business written, while losses should be closely related to the premiums as they are earned.

In recent years, property and casualty insurance companies have been able to reduce expenses through reductions in commissions, economies in billing, and other factors. However, as mentioned earlier, poor loss experience has caused companies to have underwriting losses.

Emphasis on Investment Income

Analysts are inclined to place greater emphasis on the income from investments of property and casualty insurance companies than on the underwriting profits. The reason for this is twofold. First, the investment income of these companies tends to exhibit a higher degree of stability than the underwriting profits. Second, it is the usual practice of these companies to pay dividends to stockholders entirely out of investment income. Therefore, it is not uncommon for investment services to compare the market value of property and casualty insurance stock with investment income rather than with total earnings, which would include underwriting profit or loss. This is valid only if a company at least breaks even in the insurance phase of the business. Of course, if the company consistently shows an underwriting profit, it is considered a plus factor because, presumably, future investment incomes on a larger portfolio will be higher with the consistent plowing back of underwriting profits. In addition, the investment income is worth more to the company and the stockholders because it is largely tax-exempt.

Earnings Adjustments

The property and casualty insurance companies handle their acquisition costs in much the same manner that life companies do. The premium when written and paid becomes "deferred income" which is to be prorated over the life of the policy and can be taken into income or become "premium earned" over the life of the policy. All expenses, other than claims, are incurred at the time the policy is written, and the regulatory authorities require the companies to charge these expenses against the premiums earned rather than against premiums written. To calculate the earnings per share, the analyst must make an adjustment similar to the one discussed in the section on life companies. To illustrate the nature of these adjustments, we have used the consolidated income statements of the Continental Insurance Company for the year ending December 31, 1965.

The premiums earned by this company exceeded the premiums written; therefore, there was a decline in the unearned premiums reserve. (See item 2 in Table 16–5.) This means that the company was reducing the volume of insurance in force.

TABLE 16–5

Continental Insurance Company
Consolidated Income Statement
Year Ended December 31, 1965

1. Premiums written		$593,411,602
2. Change in unearned premium reserve		(10,934,528)
3. Premiums earned		582,477,074
4. Losses	$326,441,457	
5. Loss expenses	51,279,740	377,721,197
6. Underwriting expenses		217,450,423
7. Total Losses and Expenses		595,171,620
8. Underwriting profit (loss)		(12,694,546)
9. Interest income:		
Taxable	7,600,828	
10. Tax exempt	8,631,070	16,231,898
11. Dividend income		41,004,236
12. Real estate income, net		979,709
13. Total Investment Income		58,215,843
14. Investment expenses		1,191,477
15. Investment income		57,024,366
16. Other operating income (loss)		(892,439)
17. Operating income		43,437,381
18. Gain from sale of securities, net		10,442,621
19. Total income		53,880,002
20. Income taxes		406,869
21. Net income		$ 53,473,133

Property and casualty insurance companies are required to charge "underwriting expenses" (item 6) incurred against the current year's premium earned. Since the typical policy contract written has a term of from three to five years, the practice of charging all of the acquisition costs against current earnings causes the earnings of a property and casualty company to be understated when premiums written exceed premiums earned. Conversely, the earnings are overstated for the period when premiums earned exceed premiums written. To compensate or adjust for this distortion in earnings, it is the practice to adjust earnings upward for any current increase in the unearned premium reserve and downward for any decrease. The generally accepted formula is to make an adjustment of 35 percent of the change in premium reserve applicable to casualty business and 40 percent to the fire business. Application of this formula to the Continental Insurance Company 1965 results would increase the premium earnings by $4,100,448 ($10,934,528 × .375). An adjustment of 37.5 percent was used, because the fire premiums and casualty premiums were not shown separately. Normally, there would have to be an income tax adjustment of any increase or decrease in earnings from premium reserve adjustments. However, there were no income taxes payable by Continental Insurance, so no adjustment was necessary.

The Balance Sheet

Comparison of a property and casualty company with a life insurance company would show significant differences in their investment policies. The reasons for these differences are (1) the nature of their liabilities and (2) regulatory requirements.

Stability and certainty of current investment income are not important investment requirements, because, unlike life companies, property and casualty companies are not under any obligation to earn fixed minimum amounts on policy reserves. These companies usually plan to receive much of their investment income in the form of capital gains. Therefore, they often take a moderately aggressive position toward financial risk by investing in both bonds and common stocks. That is, most property and casualty companies invest at least a portion of their funds in common and preferred stock and the balance in bonds. The bond portion is usually an amount roughly equivalent to the unearned premium and loss reserves. The balance is invested in equities.

However, there are divergent philosophies on the financial risk position that these companies should take. Those advocating a conservative financial risk position suggest that considerable financial risk is assumed because of the nature of the property and casualty insurance business, and it is not proper for the companies to assume more financial risk in the field of investments. Proponents of a more aggressive financial risk policy point out that the capital funds provide a substantial margin between company assets and liabilities; therefore, they can justify an aggressive financial risk position. It is suggested that a property and casualty company insures against loss from specific events, such as fire, and that the loss may be greater than anticipated when the policy was issued because of increased prices. Therefore, the company must be moderately aggressive to hedge against purchasing power losses.

There is not much difference of opinion over the investment of unearned premium and loss reserves. Most property and casualty company managements hold to the view that the company should take a defensive financial risk position with respect to these funds. The companies tend to invest the funds in high-grade bonds, mostly U.S. government and municipal bonds. This policy tends to make them vulnerable to the interest rate risk. However, liquidity requirements force the holding of relatively short-term obligations, which provides some defense against interest rate losses. The controversy arises over investment of capital funds.

Continental Insurance Company follows the more aggressive financial risk policy. This company had 68.3 percent of its total assets in common stock at the end of 1964. To illustrate the differences in investment policy, the percentage compositions of the Continental Insurance Company and the Western Casualty and Surety Company portfolios are shown in Table 16–6.

TABLE 16–6

Continental Insurance Company and Western Casualty and
Surety Company, Investment Portfolio,
Percentage Composition, December 31, 1964

	Continental	*Western*
U.S. government bonds	2.7%	11.1%
State and local government bonds	3.7	30.6
Government agency bonds	2.8	22.3
Industrial bonds	*	1.5
Common and preferred stocks	90.8	34.5
Total	100.0%	100.0%

* Less than 0.1 percent.

Western's holdings of common stocks amount to about 60 percent of capital and surplus, while Continental has over 100 percent of capital and surplus in common stock.

Liabilities

Property and casualty insurance companies do not have any funded debt, but they do have considerable leverage because of their liabilities to policyholders. The highly leveraged position of casualty insurance companies causes their common stock prices to be rather volatile. Since assets equal the sum of net worth and liabilities, a convenient measure of leverage is the percentage of assets represented by stockholders' equity. The lower the percentage, the greater the leverage, and vice versa. Companies that are highly leveraged tend to hold relatively fewer common stocks. The ratio of stockholders' equity to total assets for selected companies at the end of 1964, listed in Table 16–7, show that insurance companies with a greater degree of leverage tend to invest a smaller proportion of assets in common stocks.

TABLE 16–7

Leverage Ratios for Selected Companies, 1964

Company	Ratios of Stockholders' Equity to Total Assets	Ratio of Common and Preferred Stock Investments to Total Assets
Aetna Casualty and Surety Co.	25.8%	28.9%
Continental Insurance Co.	83.1	74.2
Hartford Fire Insurance Co.	42.9	40.5
Home Insurance Co.	47.0	47.1
Western Casualty and Surety Co.	33.7	22.7

Since liabilities relating to the insurance business take the place of funded debt providing leverage for the common stock equity, it should be noted that the largest item among liabilities is unearned premium reserve. This may be confusing at first, because this account is sometimes referred to as "deferred income." The income used in this definition is before payment of future claims of policyholders and other policy-servicing expenses. The unearned premium reserve may be viewed, in part, as a true liability, though the absolute amount of future claims cannot yet be determined, and, in part, as deferred underwriting income before deduction of acquisition costs.

Another item of substantial amount among liabilities is reserve for claims and claim expense. This represents a liability that is more determinate than the unknown amount in the unearned premium reserve. It is based on claims actually reported, but generally involves as well a considerable amount of estimated claims and expenses that may arise as a result of fires, accidents, and other events that have been reported.

Adjusted Book Value

It is necessary to adjust the book value of the common stock of property and casualty insurance companies if it is to be used as a guide in evaluating these securities. The first adjustment necessary is peculiar to property and casualty insurance companies because of their tendency to invest heavily in common stocks. As mentioned earlier, these common stock investments are usually carried on the books at a value required by regulatory authorities, which is the market value. These security investments are revalued on the books to reflect current market values at the end of the fiscal period, and changes in market value will be reflected in the book value of insurance stocks. Adjustments for changes in market value of the portfolio, however, are ordinarily not made in surplus accounts. Instead, increases in market value are generally recorded as increases in reserve for contingencies, and decreases are charged against this reserve. This reserve should be considered as a part of net worth and should be added to other items when computing book value per share of stock. For example, the consolidated balance sheet (Table 16–8) of the Continental Insurance Company shows a contingency reserve of $125 million, which is included in the total capital and surplus of $1,952,148,258.

The inclusion in book value of a considerable amount of appreciation in the market price of securities makes it necessary to adjust for possible income tax liability. If the insurance company were to liquidate its holdings, a capital gains tax of 25 percent would have to be paid. This adjustment is made by deducting from net worth 25 percent of the amount of unrealized appreciation in security values. On the other hand, it is somewhat unrealistic to assume that an insurance company will be liquidated. The Securities and Exchange Commission has resolved the issue by suggesting that insurance companies show book values in registration statements both ways: (1) before any adjustment for income taxes or capital gains taxes and (2) after such adjustments. For example, the Continental Insurance Company has included in its capital and surplus of $170,359,265 an indeterminate amount of unrealized security appreciation. A statement was made in a footnote to the balance sheet that "provision is not made for capital gains taxes that might be incurred if securities were liquidated," nor was the information provided so that an analyst could adjust for these taxes.

TABLE 16-8

Continental Insurance Company
Consolidated Balance Sheet, December 31, 1965

ASSETS

Cash	$ 32,428,759
Bonds and stocks (market basis)	1,760,906,788
Interest, dividends, and rents accrued	7,491,243
Premiums receivable	63,871,608
Real estate	28,925,733
Mortgage loans	164,363
Other assets	58,359,764
Total Admitted Assets	$1,952,148,258

LIABILITIES, CAPITAL AND SURPLUS

Reserve for unearned premiums	$ 358,405,245
Reserve for losses	340,306,714
Reserve for taxes and expenses	14,771,595
Reserve for reinsurance	16,252,365
Other reserves	50,278,333
Minority interests	1,774,741
Total Liabilities	781,788,993
Capital stock ($5.00 par)	60,000,000
Contingency reserve	125,000,000
Surplus	985,359,265
Total Capital and Surplus (Market Basis)	1,170,359,265
Total Liabilities, Capital and Surplus	$1,952,148,258

The second adjustment is the result of the practice of showing premiums received in advance as reserve for unearned premiums, a liability on the balance sheet, while charging off as a current expense all acquisition costs of selling the policies. The adjustment for this practice was discussed earlier in the section "Earnings Adjustments." It was noted there that the rule of thumb used to compute prepaid acquisition costs was 40 percent of premiums for fire insurance and 35 percent for casualty insurance. This accounting practice results in a hidden asset, which is usually called "equity in unearned premium reserve." The investor should remember that the effect of reporting as income only those portions of premiums earned while recording all acquisition costs as expense is to inflate expenses during periods when increasing amounts of insurance are being sold. This is the method allowed for computing taxable income. Such an inflation of costs provides a temporary tax advantage, because acquisition costs which should properly be charged against income in the future are charged against current income. On the other hand, any underwriting profits which accrue in the future, as unearned premiums become earned, are overstated. Acquisition expenses applicable to these premiums cannot be subtracted from receipts because they have already been deducted at the time the cash outlay was made to cover acquisition costs.Thus, in computing the equity in the unearned premium reserve an allowance should be made for the fact that this equity in the unearned premium reserve will be subject to a 48 percent income tax in the future. Therefore, the analyst should reduce the equity in unearned premiums by 48 percent.

As indicated earlier, it is not possible to separately compute the equity in the unearned premium reserve for the fire and casualty insurance, because the reserves are commingled on the statement. Therefore, in making the adjustment, we assumed that before-tax equity was 37.5 percent of the unearned premium reserve. This equity would be $134,401,967 before taxes and $69,889,023 after taxes.

There is one final adjustment to be made in determining the adjusted book value of property and casualty insurance company common stocks. The item called "reinsurance in nonadmitted companies" is sometimes found among the liabilities. When a property and casualty insurance company reinsures with another company that is not approved for reinsurance, it must be shown as a liability. Reinsurance means that another company is asked to assume for a fee a part of the liability to make good on losses. Since it is not a true liability, however, it should be added to net worth in computing book value per share of stock. The Continental Insurance Company made deductions from assets or increased liabilities at December 31, 1965, in amounts of $23,651,610 for nonadmitted assets and increases in liabilities of $16,252,365 for reinsurance with nonadmitted companies.

In summary one should follow these steps in computing book value.

1. Find the sum of capital, surplus, reserve for contingencies, and reinsurance in nonadmitted companies.
2. Compute the equity in unearned premium reserve before tax adjustment. This is about 40 percent of the unearned premiums for fire insurance and 35 percent for casualty insurance.
3. Deduct 48 percent of the equity in the unearned premium reserve.
4. Deduct 25 percent of unrealized security appreciation.
5. Divide the balance by the number of shares outstanding—the result is the book value after tax adjustments.

It should be kept in mind that these book values are rough indicators of the value of property and casualty insurance company common stock. The common stock of these companies may sell at a premium over or a discount from book value, depending on earnings prospects and the outlook for the industry.

Selection and Adjusted Book Value

During 1964, numerous property and casualty insurers with relatively poor underwriting performance sold at low multiples of investment earnings and at substantial discounts from their book values. In contrast, shares of many companies that had consistent underwriting profits sell at a premium over book value. The apparent reason for this is that the company that consistently shows an underwriting profit will presumably have higher future investment incomes on a larger portfolio from plowing back underwriting profits.

Company common stocks that sell at discounts from adjusted book value will normally improve with improvements in underwriting experience. Therefore, if there is to be a cyclical improvement in underwriting, as was suggested before, the prices of stocks selling at discounts from book value should improve.

REVIEW QUESTIONS AND PROBLEMS

1. What are the major cost factors considered in computing life insurance premiums?

2. Is it possible for the common stock of a life insurance company which has consistently shown net losses from operations to be a better investment than the common stock of a company that has consistently shown earnings? If so, why?

3. In life insurance company common stock analysis, of what significance is the lapse ratio?

4. In calculating the adjusted book value of life insurance company common stock, why is a greater value normally assigned to ordinary life insurance than is assigned to term insurance?

5. At the end of 1965, Life Insurance Company "A" had 1,200,000 shares of common stock outstanding with a stated book value of $134 per share. Life Insurance Company "B" had 1,600,000 shares outstanding with a stated book value of $29.50 per share. The prices of the common stock of "A" are bid-287, ask-293, and the prices of the common stock of "B" are bid-62.00, ask-64.50. Insurance in force, in thousands of dollars, at the end of 1965 was listed as follows:

	"A"	"B"
Ordinary life	$2,812,000	$ 961,000
Term life	331,000	794,000
Group life	5,135,000	2,516,000
Annual accident and health		
premium income	$ 266	$ 122

The five-year average lapse ratio for Company "A" was 4.8 percent for all policies in force and Company "B" was 3.2 percent of all policies in force. If both companies have had similar growth and operating characteristics other than those mentioned, which company's common stock would you buy?

6. Why is it more difficult to estimate underwriting results for a property and casualty company than it is for a life insurance company?

7. What are the measures of property and casualty underwriting experience?

8. Why are the investment experiences of a property and casualty insurance company usually more important to the common stock investor than the underwriting experience?

9. On what basis are the investments of property and casualty insurance companies valued? What effect would this have on their investment policy?

10. Property and casualty insurance company "A" lists the following items, in thousands of dollars, on their financial statement:

    Capital—$2,500
    Surplus—$14,426
    Reserve for contingencies—$254
    Unearned premiums—fire—$8,194
    Unearned premiums—casualty—$9,815
    Unrealized security appreciation—$485

The company has 500,000 shares of common stock outstanding. What is the adjusted book value per share?

CHAPTER **17**

Specialized Analytical Techniques— Investment Companies

An investment company is a corporation that sells its own shares and invests the proceeds. The justification for the investment company or trust is that it enables small investors, through a pooling of funds, to obtain professional management of a diversified portfolio of investments. There are some distinctive differences in investment companies. These differences are found in (1) form of organization, (2) capital structure, (3) investment objectives and policy, (4) acquisition and sale costs, (5) systematic purchase plans, and (6) management performance.

One of the most notable developments in investment companies during the past 20 years has been the growth of the open-end investment company, or mutual fund. The National Association of Investment Companies has estimated that the total net assets of investment companies have increased from $2,162,517,000 in 1946 to $31,405,-588,000 at the end of 1964. Most of this growth in total investment company assets has been the result of the unusually large increase in assets of the open-end investment company. During this period, the total open-end investment company assets increased from $1,311,-108,000 in 1946 to $29,116,254,000 at the end of 1964.

NATURE OF INVESTMENT COMPANIES

An examination of the nature of investment companies, such as form of organization and costs of acquisition, is meaningful only in relation to the effectiveness of management as evidenced by past performance of the investment company. However, evaluation of performance presupposes a knowledge of the basic characteristics of investment companies.

Differences in Form of Organization

The investment company may be formed either as a trust or as a corporation. The earlier investment companies were formed by execution of a declaration of trust between investors and trustees. The investors received certificates of beneficial interest in the fund. The trustee usually was given considerable latitude in the administration and investment of the trust funds. The trustees were usually self-perpetuating and were able to appoint their successors.

Although some of the larger investment companies in existence today are trust organizations, the modern trend is to form investment companies as corporations. In such cases, the shareholders have the right to elect directors and participate in the management as other types of stockholders do.

Of the 38 open-end investment companies organized between 1952 and 1958 included in the Wharton School of Commerce and Finance report, only two were organized as trusts.[1] The probable reason for diminution in use of the trust form in the organization of open-end investment companies is the requirement, under the Investment Company Act of 1940, that officers be elected by the voting securities. Under the "true" trust, the officer group would be self-perpetuating, and it would not qualify.

Whether the investment company is formed as a trust or corporation is usually not of any practical significance. The real distinction of practical import is between the open-end and closed-end investment companies. It should be mentioned, however, that the closed-end investment company is always formed as a corporation, while the open-end company, or mutual fund, may or may not be organized in the corporate form.

The closed-end investment company is a corporation formed for the purpose of investing principally in securities. This type of investment company sells all its stock in one offering, or in two or perhaps three offerings. It has, therefore, a fixed number of shares outstanding equal to the number offered at the time of formation of the company. In some cases, there may be additional offerings of stock, but there is no regular offering. These shares are bought and

---

[1] *A Study of Mutual Funds* (Report of the House of Representatives Committee on Interstate and Foreign Commerce, prepared for the Securities and Exchange Commission by Wharton School of Commerce and Finance) (Washington, D.C.: 1963), p. 45.

sold in the over-the-counter markets and on organized stock exchanges. The owner of closed-end shares can dispose of them by contacting a broker who will find a buyer in the securities markets as he would if he were buying or selling stocks of industrials or public utilities.

Open-end investment companies are formed for the same basic purpose as closed-end companies. They are corporations, or sometimes trusts, which pool the funds of many individual investors and reinvest them in the securities of other enterprises. These open-end companies, in contrast to the closed-end companies, continuously sell new shares to the public and will repurchase or redeem their shares at any time and in any amounts. Usually, the shares are sold at asset value plus a certain percentage of the asset value. This premium above asset value is often called the "load," which will be discussed in a later section. Basically, this premium represents the selling costs plus a margin of profit. The usual practice is for the investment company to repurchase its shares at net asset value per share, although in some cases a small discount (usually not more than 1 percent) is charged for the privilege of redemption.

Differences in Capital Structure

Generally, open-end investment companies issue only common stock. In some cases, closed-end investment companies have used prior claim capital (bonds and preferred stock) in addition to the common stock outstanding. Most of the closed-end companies do not use prior claim capital and therefore are not leveraged; however, one of the largest closed-end companies, Tri-Continental Corporation, is leveraged. The capitalization of Tri-Continental Corporation at the end of 1964 was as follows.

Long-term debt	$ 20,000,000
Preferred stock	37,637,000
Common equity	487,146,558
Total Capital Funds	$544,783,558

The leverage advantage of Tri-Continental has declined over the years as the value of the company's assets has increased. The total capital funds, valuing assets at market, of Tri-Continental in 1957 were $209,421,247, and it had about 39 cents of prior claim capital for each $1.00 of common stock equity. As can be seen above, the value of Tri-Continental's capital funds has increased to $544,783,558 with the increase in the market value holdings. During this time, the prior claim capital has declined slightly, and the prior claim capital for each $1.00 of common stock equity has declined to 10.6 cents.

This decline in leverage advantage tends to cause a reduction in volatility of the price of Tri-Continental's shares. The reason for this is that the effect of leverage for a closed-end investment company is to cause the price of the common stock to rise faster than the general market averages during periods of rising prices and almost always to decline faster during periods of falling prices.

Differences in Investment Objectives and Policy

Fully managed investment companies have considerable latitude in the types of investments they select for their portfolios. The only limitations on securities selection are those outlined in the offering circular or prospectus of the investment company or in the corporate charter and bylaws of the closed-end company.

The types of securities held by investment companies vary widely. One may hold entirely common stock, another may hold only municipal or tax-free bonds, and so forth. That is, there are many combinations and permutations of investment media held by various investment companies. The investor, however, should select an investment company in terms of what it is trying to do with respect to the broad investment objectives of current income and capital appreciation, instead in terms of type of securities held. Irrespective of the type of media held, investment companies tend to manage their assets with either growth, capital appreciation, or income as a primary objective. The investment objective of the company provides the basis for the investment policy and types of media that may be used to attain the announced objective.

Management may be limited to some extent in the types of investment media it may select. This limitation is usually self-imposed, because management selects the investment policy and objective for the investment company at the time of formation.

These limitations are not too stringent. The objectives are usually stated in terms of types of media rather than income or growth. The managements of most open-end investment companies currently operate with relatively broad powers as to investment policy. The charters of most companies permit investment in all types of securities. However, the type of media indicated in the announced policy objective usually provides the basis for classifying the investment company as a growth or income company.

Prospective investors in investment company shares have available a wide range of choices, as may be noted from Figure 17–1. From these many objectives, it is possible to satisfy almost any investment objective. Most investment company portfolios are diversified holdings of common stock or a balanced portfolio of bonds, and preferred and common stocks. These two classifications accounted for more than 75 percent of investment company assets on December 31, 1964.

FIGURE 17–1

**Investment Company Assets by Type of Funds
December 31, 1964**

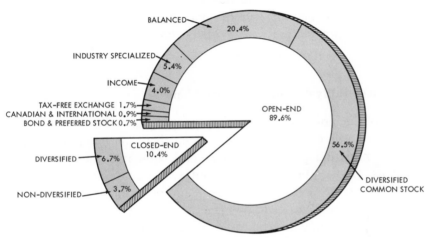

Source: *Investment Companies, 1965 Edition,* Arthur Wiesenberger and Co., p. 20.

An investment company may as a matter of announced policy deviate from the general policy of diversification and concentrate its commitments in one industry or a specific class of risks. For example, an investment company may concentrate its investments in specific industries, as does Petroleum Corporation, a closed-end investment company that has over 90 percent of its investments in the oil and oil equipment industries. Other companies may concentrate their investments in special situations with emphasis on long-term capital gains, as does Atlas Corporation, a closed-end company, or Value Line Special Situation Fund.

Most companies are under no rigid restrictions in their choice of such common stocks. In some cases, a company may have an "approved list" or a "reserve list," and investments must be made from these lists. In general, however, these lists are very broad and very flexible. Some companies limit their common stock investments to companies that have been in business for at least three years. Other restrictions imposed by some companies are that no single commitment should exceed 5 percent of total assets, or that no investment will be made that would give the companies more than a 10 percent ownership of the issuing company. The charters of some companies prohibit them from buying on margin or from selling short.

In recent years, the diversified common stock funds have become more popular. In 1957, open-end investment companies with this objective accounted for about 42 percent of investment company assets, and in 1964 they held in excess of 56 percent of investment company assets. The increase in popularity of these funds indicates the capital appreciation and inflation consciousness of the average investor.

Differences in Systematic Purchase Plans

One of the more controversial aspects of open-end investment companies and sale of their shares has been their "periodic investment" or "accumulation plans." The open-end companies offer two types of plans. One is the so-called voluntary accumulation plan, which differs from the regular purchase of mutual fund shares in that it (1) enables the investor to buy fractional shares from his agreed-on periodic payment, which he could not normally do, and (2) provides for reinvestment of all dividends and capital gains distributions. The sales commission is the same and is charged in the same manner as it would be with a regular purchase. These level-charge voluntary payment plans have no specific duration. The investor may discontinue this type of plan without penalty at any time.

The other type accumulation plan is the prepaid or contractual plan. This type plan has a fixed duration, and the investor is penalized if he does not complete it. The investor signs a contract in which he agrees to invest a predetermined amount periodically for a specified number of years. The penalty for early withdrawal arises from the manner in which the sales commission or load charge is levied. The sales commission for the entire investment is taken from the first payments made by the investor. For example, if the investor agrees to invest $50 a month for five years, the sales commission is calculated as a percentage of the entire $3,000 investment that would be made under the plan. The largest portion of this sales commission is then deducted from the earlier payments. If the investor does not complete the plan, the sale commission paid is deducted and retained, and he is thus penalized. In one such plan offered by the Dreyfus Corporation, an investor who undertakes their "Systematic Accumulation Program" with regular $25 monthly payments finds that "if the Program is terminated after six months or one year, deductions amount to 53.00% and if terminated after two years, the deductions are 30.88%."[2]

If the investor does enter into one of these prepaid plans, he should consider his ability to continue the plan because of the probable penalties of an early withdrawal. If an investor has the alternative of a voluntary level-charge plan or the contractual prepaid plan, it would appear to be to his advantage to select the voluntary plan. Proponents of the contractual plan point out that the cost of the two plans is roughly the same. However, they do not take into consideration the effects of losing the advantage of capital gains, if any, and income, or simply the inverse compounding of the early sales commission deduction. The effects of inverse compounding will be discussed in the section on selection of investment company shares.

Purchasing and Closing Costs

Investment companies, particularly open-end companies, have many of the characteristics of a cooperative venture. However, it should be recognized that the possibility of deriving compensation for services rendered motivates individuals to form and operate these companies. In addition, the salesman who informs the investor of opportunities afforded by investment company shares will not "sell" these shares without compensation.

Of these two costs, the sales commission or load charge is of most immediate concern to the investor. The selling premium or load charge on open-end investment company shares ordinarily runs from 6 to 9 percent of asset value, with a sliding scale to lower rates on larger orders.

This load charge, or selling premium above asset value, has been

---

2 The Dreyfus Investment Program Prospectus, August 30, 1963.

the subject of considerable controversy and misunderstanding. The fact many investors overlook is that in making any type of investment an acquisition cost or commission is usually involved. Since most open-end investment companies redeem their shares at asset value without charge, the selling premium represents the entire cost of buying and selling the investment.[3] The selling premium compares favorably to the commissions charged by brokers in both purchase and sale of relatively small investments in closed-end shares and other securities. The purchase of $100 of closed-end shares costs $6.00, or 6 percent of the value of the transaction. Of course, the normal New York Stock Exchange commissions decline as a percentage of total investment as the dollar amount of the investment increases. For example, the commission for a transaction involving 100 shares of stock costing $25,000 is $63, or considerably less than 1 percent of the value of the transaction. The open-end companies also usually reduce the selling premium on larger orders. However, the reduction normally is not so great as the decline in New York Stock Exchange commissions. The selling charges for $25,000 invested in 1,000 shares of a typical open-end investment company are as follows.

Amount of Purchase	Applicable Percentage of Offering Price
Less than $25,000	7.5%
$ 25,000 but less than $ 50,000	5.5
$ 50,000 but less than $100,000	4.0
$100,000 but less than $250,000	3.0
$250,000 or more	2.5

Commissions on the sale of common stock of a closed-end investment company listed on the New York Stock Exchange are in Table 17–1.

TABLE 17–1

Minimum Commission per Transaction

Money Involved	Percent of Money Involved	For 100 Shares	For Less than 100 Shares
$100 to $399	2 %	$ 3*	$ 1*
$400 to $2,399	1	7	5
$2,400 to $4,999	½	19	17
Over $5,000	$\frac{1}{10}$	39	37

* Minimum, $6.00.

---

[3] There are some notable exceptions, such as de Vegh Mutual Fund and Eaton & Howard Balanced Fund, which levy a redemption charge.

The dollar cost of 1,000 closed-end company shares at $25 a share would be $390 plus $25, or $415, while the dollar cost of purchasing a like number of shares of the typical open-end investment company at $25 a share would be $1,375. Even if one considers the costs of both purchase and sale of a closed-end investment company's shares, the larger investor's costs are lower than they usually are for the typical open-end company.

These acquisition costs can be avoided by buying shares in open-end investment companies that do not have a load charge. A few investment counseling organizations have in recent years established their own investment companies to service the needs of clients whose funds have been less than the minimum requirements for an investment counseling account. Because the shares in these companies are not intended to be sold aggressively, the selling premium has either been eliminated or fixed at a very low rate. For example, Stein, Roe and Farnham, an investment counseling firm, organized the Stein, Roe and Farnham Balanced Fund in 1949, and the Stein, Roe and Farnham Stock Fund in 1958. These open-end companies do not include a selling premium in the offering price of their shares. Since there is no selling premium, there is no incentive for brokers and dealers to sell it. As a result, the Balanced Fund has grown less rapidly than others for which a selling effort has been made. However, at the end of 1964, 16 years after formation, the assets of Stein, Roe and Farnham Balanced Fund amounted to over $100 million.

To a degree, an investor's attention may be diverted by the controversy over acquisition costs. These costs do have an effect on the relative gain available to the investor. However, the acquisition cost is only one of several selection considerations.

SELECTION CONSIDERATIONS

The investor who purchases investment company shares is primarily interested in shifting the responsibility for management of his common stock portfolio to someone more expert than himself. Second, he may be interested in getting a greater diversification than he would be able to achieve himself. Any investment company that has been in existence for any length of time and has had a moderate rate of growth will have generally achieved the desired diversification. There are notable exceptions, such as the specialized funds mentioned earlier.

In any event, the investor's initial task is to screen out or eliminate from consideration those investment companies whose announced investment policy is in conflict with the investor's own requirements and policy. The investor can determine this policy by reading the management's statement of investment policy in the prospectus or offering circular, or in the closed-end company's annual report.

In the selection of investment company shares, the investor's primary analytical problem is evaluation of the quality of management. The management quality should be judged only in terms of results or performance. In comparing one investment company with another, the only denominator that provides any reasonable basis for selection is increases in value in terms of capital gains and/or income over a period of years.

Management Appraisal—Open-End Investment Companies

The analyst of open-end company shares should be careful to analyze the company only in terms of its announced investment objective. If the objective of the company is income, the investor should not expect capital appreciation, and vice versa. The length of time the company has been in existence is of importance to the analyst. Generally speaking, open-end companies that have been in existence for short periods of time—less than five years—should be screened out in the preliminary selection process. There may be, of course, exceptions to any such generalization. There are instances in which the excellence of management has been established by performance in other investment activities. However, new open-end companies in which the management is stated to have an outstanding reputation should be viewed critically, because the reputation might be the result of a carefully planned sales promotion program.

One method of evaluating performance has been devised by Arthur Wiesenberger and Company, and is used each year to evaluate the performance of the larger investment companies in the annual publication, *Investment Companies.* The technique used is the calculation of a performance index or "relative." The method of computing this performance index involves relating the increases in net asset value from one year to the next.

The Wiesenberger method for calculating performance relatives evaluates performance in terms of gross gains for a particular period. These gross gains (losses) are (1) increase in net asset value, (2) capital gains distributions, and (3) dividend distributions. The capital gains distributions and dividend distributions for the period are added to the net asset value at the end of the period. The total is then divided by the net asset value at the beginning of the period. The result is a percentage increase.

To illustrate the method of calculation, the performance indexes have been calculated for Stein, Roe and Farnham Balanced Fund and the Putnam (George) Fund of Boston (Table 17-2). At the year

TABLE 17-2

**Stein, Roe and Farnham Balanced Fund and Putnam
Fund of Boston, Performance Index Computations,
1958–64**

Year- End	Net Asset Value Per Share		Shares Owned		Dividends Per Share		Capital Gain Per Share	
	Stein	Putnam	Stein	Putnam	Stein	Putnam	Stein	Putnam
1964	..... $41.76	$16.03	39.09	103.75	$1.01	$0.45	$0.44	$0.54
1963	..... 38.93	15.31	37.78	97.72	0.94	0.435	0.65	0.48
1962	..... 35.70	14.44	36.30	92.21	0.92	0.43	1.96	0.17
1961	..... 41.22	17.05	33.59	88.53	1.02	0.43	2.02	0.62
1960	..... 37.54	14.57	31.28	83.39	1.04	0.43	2.28	0.55
1959	..... 38.62	14.30	28.74	78.13	0.90	0.42	0.71	0.52
1958	..... 36.25	13.64	27.59	73.31	..	..	..	..

ended December 31, 1958, Stein, Roe and Farnham Balanced Fund had a net asset value of $36.25 per share. For ease in computation, we assumed an investment of $1,000 was made in 27.59 shares, and that all distributions were invested in additional shares.[4] In addition, the investor purchased 73.31 shares of the Putnam Fund at $13.64 a share. At the end of the six-year period, 1959–64, the value of the investment in Stein, Roe and Farnham had increased from $1,000 to $1,632 at the end of 1964, and the value of the investment in Putnam Fund had increased to $1,663. The performance index reduces the measurement of performance to a common basis. If there is no gross gain, the performance index is 100. A gain would be shown by an increase over 100 and a loss by the decrease below 100. To illustrate, the performance index of these two companies is as follows.

---

[4] For some inexplicable reason, Wiesenberger assumes that only the dividend income is taken in cash and capital gains distribution in new shares. See Arthur Wiesenberger & Co., *Investment Companies, 1962 Edition* (New York, 1962), p. 48.

Stein, Roe and Farnham

$$\frac{\text{VALUE OF INVESTMENT, DECEMBER 31, 1964}}{\text{VALUE OF INVESTMENT, DECEMBER 31, 1958}} = \frac{\$1,632}{\$1,000} = 163.2.$$

Putnam Fund of Boston

$$\frac{\text{VALUE OF INVESTMENT, DECEMBER 31, 1964}}{\text{VALUE OF INVESTMENT, DECEMBER 31, 1958}} = \frac{\$1,663}{\$1,000} = 166.3.$$

In evaluating the performance of mutual funds, performance indexes may be calculated for longer or shorter periods of time. It is worthwhile to examine the performance during a period in which there has been an economic recession to get an idea of how well the management is timing purchases and sales of securities. Poor timing of commitments will show up in relatively larger losses in net asset value during periods of economic recession.

Evaluation of Management Performance in Closed-End Companies

In the computation of performance relatives for closed-end investment companies, the investor also has the problem of making the capital gains adjustment. The analyst cannot make "the capital gains taken in additional shares" assumption, because the market value of closed-end company shares may be at a premium or discount from per-share asset values. "Moreover, changes in per-share asset values are at times influenced by factors other than management performance."[5] These factors are leverage in the capital structure and changes in the capital structure, such as retirement and issuance of new securities by the investment company.

When evaluating management effectiveness in a closed-end company, the influences of leverage and capital structure may be compensated by using total assets as the base in calculating the performance index and adjusting for capital structure changes during the year. There is no completely satisfactory way to eliminate the capital gains problem other than by computing the performance relative as a series of annual changes.

To compute the annual performance relative, the analyst must make adjustments to asset value for all payments made to various classes of security holders. This adjustment involves adding back to assets all interest on long-term debt and dividends on preferred stock and common stock. In addition, adjustments are required if there

---

[5] *Ibid.*, p. 49.

have been any changes in the company's capital structure during the year. For example, if an additional $100 in bonds were sold during the year, the net assets at the end of the year would have increased by $100. This increase would not be because of investment management effectiveness, but because of additional capital contributions. The simplest way to make this adjustment is to average the change in net asset value due to additional contributions of capital. This is done by deducting one half of the new capital from the net assets at the end of the current year and adding it to the net assets of the previous year.

To illustrate the method of calculating performance of closed-end companies, the performance index for Tri-Continental Corporation, a leveraged company, is calculated as follows.

Tri-Continental Corporation

Net assets, December 31, 1964	$549,105,133
Plus: Dividends on preferred stock	1,881,850
Dividends on common stock	12,533,905
Interest on debt	831,251
	$564,352,139
Less: One half of increase in capital structure	4,766,651
Total adjusted asset value, December 31, 1964	$559,585,488
Net assets, December 31, 1963	$494,326,058
Plus: One half of increase in capital structure	4,766,651
Total adjusted asset value, December 31, 1963	$499,092,709

1964 Adjusted net asset value $559,585,488
1963 Adjusted net asset value $499,092,709
Performance index = 112.1

The Tri-Continental Corporation has an increase in net asset value of 12.1 percent during 1964. In calculating this performance, an adjustment was made for an increase in the common stock and capital surplus of $9,533,302 during 1964, which represents the proceeds from common stock warrants that were exercised. To eliminate any possible performance index distortion from this capital addition, one half of the increase in the common equity was added to the net assets for the year ending December 31, 1963, and one half was deducted from the 1964 net assets.

Investor's Experience Indexes

Calculation of these performance indexes, indicating the effectiveness of the management would enable the investor to narrow the choices to a few investment companies. He may then want to evaluate these companies in terms of their relative past effectiveness from the investor's point of view.[6]

Analysis of these investment companies from the investor's viewpoint should involve the calculation of a performance relative that would consider the effects of (1) purchasing and closing costs and (2) the differential federal income tax treatment of long-term capital gains and ordinary income. The purpose of this more refined analysis is to evaluate performance measured in terms of returns or gains net of charges and taxes. It does little good to decide that management performance in investment company A is better than the performance in investment company B measured by the gross gains but the end result or net gains to a particular investor are smaller with company A than with company B.

Effect of Purchasing and Closing Costs

The performance index or relative previously discussed assumes that the investor has invested equal amounts in the companies being compared. However, this assumption may not be correct because of differences in sales commission or load charge. For example, a comparison of Stein, Roe and Farnham Balanced Fund, a no-load-charge fund, with Putnam Fund of Boston, which allows brokers 8 percent sales or load charges, would yield entirely different end investment results, although the management performance relative of these funds have been remarkably similar for the years 1959–1964. The gross gain increase of Stein, Roe and Farham Balanced Fund was 63.2 percent and the Putnam Fund increased 66.3 percent. (See page 358.) However, the investor's experience index for these funds would have been substantially different for the same period of time because of the adverse weighting of the Putnam Fund load charge.

Assuming a cash outlay of $1,000, the net initial investment in the Stein, Roe and Farnham Balanced Fund would be the full $1,000, while it would be only $920 for the Putnam Fund. The effect of this initial charge on the final results is evident in Table 17–3. The final value of the investment was $1,632 for Stein, Roe and Farnham, and $1,524 for Putnam Fund. It again should be noted that we have

---

[6] Wayne P. Hochmuth and Arthur S. Bowes, Jr., "Investment Companies: Performance vs. Charges," *Financial Analysts Journal*, Vol. 17, No. 1 (January–February, 1961), p. 43.

TABLE 17-3

**Stein, Roe and Farnham Balanced Fund and Putnam
Fund of Boston, Investor's Experience Index Based
on Actual Cash Investment, 1959–64**

Year-End	Per Share Net Asset Value		Shares Owned		Dividends Per Share		Capital Gain Per Share	
	Stein	*Putnam*	*Stein*	*Putnam*	*Stein*	*Putnam*	*Stein*	*Putnam*
1964	$41.76	$16.03	39.09	95.43	$1.01	$0.45	$0.44	$0.54
1963	38.93	15.31	37.78	89.88	0.94	0.435	0.65	0.48
1962	35.70	14.44	36.30	84.81	0.92	0.43	1.96	0.17
1961	41.22	17.05	33.59	81.43	1.02	0.43	2.02	0.62
1960	37.54	14.57	31.28	76.71	1.04	0.43	2.28	0.55
1959	38.62	14.30	28.74	71.88	0.90	0.42	0.71	0.52
1958	36.25	13.64	27.59	67.45	..	..	..	..

assumed that all distributions were reinvested in new shares. The Wiesenberger method of calculating performance relatives assumes only the reinvestment of capital gains distributions, as mentioned earlier.

The impact of the load charge on the investor's experience diminishes as the period of time the investment is held lengthens. The effect of period of time held is obvious when one considers that at the end of 1959 the value of the Putnam Fund investor's holding was only about $1,028, while the value of the Stein, Roe investment was $1,110. At the end of 1964, the value of the Putnam holdings was $1,524, and Stein, Roe and Farnham holdings were $1,632, as mentioned before.

The impact of one dollar of closing costs or redemption charges is not so great as the effect of one dollar of acquisition costs. The difference in impact is caused by deprivation of one dollar of investment for the period when it is acquisition costs. For this reason, many of the comparisons of the "round trip" acquisition and closing costs of open-end and closed-end investment companies are not accurate. They fail to take into account the inverse compounding effect discussed earlier.

Effect of Federal Individual Income Taxes

A further refinement in the investor's experience index would be to adjust for the differential income tax treatment of capital gains and ordinary income distributions. If an adjustment is not made for federal income taxes paid on investment company distributions, the investor is not only reinvesting his distributions but also is making an incremental or new cash investment equal to the income taxes paid.[7] In addition, one cannot give equal weight to the federal income taxes paid on these distributions—what is done when no adjustment is made—because this undifferentiated tax treatment injects a bias in the investor's experience index. Failure to make an adjustment ignores that a dollar of capital gains distribution is worth more than a dollar of dividend income distribution. The capital gains dollar, of course, becomes more valuable with each successive increase in the investor's marginal income tax rate.

To illustrate the effect of these adjustments, the investor's experience index is computed for an investor in a marginal individual income tax bracket of 50 percent. The investor's experience unadjusted for the six-year period 1959–64 showed a net increase in investment value of 63.2 percent with the Stein, Roe and Farnham Balanced Fund, and 66.3 percent with the Putnam Fund (Table 17–4).

TABLE 17–4

Stein, Roe and Farnham Balanced Fund and Putnam
Fund of Boston, Tax Adjusted Investor Experience
Index, Investor in 50 Percent Tax Bracket, 1959–64

Year-End	Per Share Net Asset Value		Shares Owned		Tax Adjusted Dividends Per Share		Tax Adjusted Capital Gain Per Share	
	Stein	*Putnam*	*Stein*	*Putnam*	*Stein*	*Putnam*	*Stein*	*Putnam*
1964	$41.76	$16.03	34.64	92.86	$0.505	$0.225	$0.33	$0.41
1963	38.93	15.31	33.96	88.03	0.47	0.22	0.49	0.36
1962	35.70	14.44	33.14	84.82	0.46	0.215	1.47	0.128
1961	41.22	17.05	31.44	82.87	0.51	0.215	1.51	0.465
1960	37.54	14.57	29.97	79.69	0.52	0.215	1.71	0.41
1959	38.62	14.30	28.29	76.39	0.45	0.21	0.53	0.39
1958	36.25	13.64	27.59	73.31	..	..	..	..

At the end of the six-year period, Stein, Roe and Farnham showed a smaller tax adjusted increase in the value of investment. The value of the Stein, Roe investment had increased from $1,000 to $1,447, or an increase of 44.7 percent, while the Putnam Fund investment increased from $1,000 to $1,489, or an increase of 48.9 percent. These

---

[7] Hochmuth and Bowes, *op. cit.*, p. 45.

tax adjusted gains in the value of the investment are much smaller than the unadjusted gains, and more accurately reflect the investor's actual past experience.

Summary

A comparison of the management performance relative—the unadjusted investor's experience index for an investor in a 50 percent marginal tax bracket—is shown below. These refinements indicate that superior management performance, as shown by the Putnam Fund, can compensate for or overcome the load-charge factors. However, the investor should compute the investor's experience index to show exactly how he would have come out, considering income taxes, acquisition costs, and closing costs, if any, as well as management performance. The comparative analysis in Table 17–5 shows

TABLE 17–5

Stein, Roe and Farnham and Putnam Fund of Boston Management Performance and Investor's Experience Indexes, 1958–64
(1958 = 100)

	Management Performance		Investor's Experience		Investor's Experience Tax Adjusted	
	Stein	*Putnam*	*Stein*	*Putnam*	*Stein*	*Putnam*
1964	163.2	166.3	163.2	151.4	144.6	148.8
1963	147.1	149.6	147.1	137.6	132.2	134.8
1962	129.6	133.1	129.6	122.5	118.3	122.5
1961	138.4	150.9	138.4	138.8	129.6	141.3
1960	117.4	121.5	117.4	111.8	112.5	116.1
1959	111.0	111.7	111.0	102.8	109.2	109.2
1958	100.0	100.0	100.0	92.0*	100.0	100.0

* This assumes that the investor has paid 8 percent at the beginning in the form of a load charge. To show the relative effect of this, the base index has been dropped to 92.

the differences in results from the different methods of computing these measures. It should always be remembered that these relatives or indexes indicate past performance, and provide no assurance that this performance will be repeated.

In addition, there are other important selection considerations. The prospective buyer of investment company shares should have very clear in his mind what his investment objective or objectives are.

If his primary objective is capital gain, the proper vehicle may be a leverage closed-end investment company or one of the investment companies that devotes its major attention to special situations. In this case, current income will be of minor importance, and the investor may be required to exercise considerable patience before his objective is attained. If the investor places considerable emphasis on marketability, he will probably be well advised to confine himself to open-end companies or listed closed-end companies. The investor who is primarily interested in income and stability of principal will lean toward an investment company that has a balanced portfolio or a portfolio of fixed-income securities.

The investor pays the net asset value plus the selling premium, if any, for open-end company shares. Closed-end investment company shares, on the other hand, have during some periods sold at a discount from net asset value. It seems logical that the existence of closed-end shares selling at a discount would cause investors to buy those shares in preference to open-end company shares. Other things being equal, this would be true. However, if these shares are selling at a discount, it is generally a reflection of investor's attitudes toward the management, inherent risks, or a result of a thin market. In some cases, there seems to be no reason for these shares to be selling at a discount except the popular attitude at the time toward the particular company. Market price should not be the dominant consideration when purchasing these shares. Reference should be to the suitability of the company's shares for the investor, the investor's needs, and the company's performance.

REVIEW QUESTIONS AND PROBLEMS

1. Describe the basic similarities and differences between open-end and closed-end investment companies.
2. Tri-Continental Corporation is a leveraged closed-end investment company while Lehman Corporation is a non-leveraged closed-end investment company. What effect would the differences in capital structure tend to have on the earnings and price action of the common stock of these companies?
3. Distinguish between a balanced fund, a common stock fund, and a specialized fund.
4. Mutual Fund "A" offers you a plan which provides for periodic investments of $30 per month for nine years and eleven months, with an initial

investment of $60 which is the first payment in a ten-year plan. The charges under this plan would be an initial charge of $30 deducted from this first payment of $60 and a sales charge of $15 per month deducted from each of the next eleven payments. An annual charge is made after the first year of $10 per year for custodian fees. Mutual Fund "B" offers you a plan which provides for a periodic investment of $30 per month for nine years and eleven months with an initial investment of $60 the first month. An all-inclusive level charge of 8.5 percent would be deducted from each payment.

Assuming the performance of both funds were identical, which plan would you choose? Would your decision be different if you were required to drop the plan at the end of the first year?

5. Under what conditions might a very small investment company, one with assets under $10 million, be a more attractive investment vehicle than a very large one?

6. Evaluate the performance of these two investment companies by computing performance indexes:

	Company A	Company B
Net asset value per share, December 31, 1960	$10.00	$ 9.12
Net asset value per share, December 31, 1965	14.50	11.17
Capital gains distributions:		
1961	$ 0.05	$ 0.44
1962	1.25	0.69
1963	..	0.33
1964	0.72	0.05
1965	0.33	0.15
Dividends from income:		
1961	$ 0.30	$ 0.23
1962	0.65	0.12
1963	0.39	0.21
1964	0.48	0.19
1965	0.42	0.20

7. Which of the above investment companies would you have selected if you were in the 50 percent income tax bracket?

8. How do the costs of purchasing the shares of a closed-end investment company compare with the costs of purchasing open-end investment company shares?

9. Why are open-end investment company shares generally unsuitable for short-term investment?

CHAPTER **18**

Specialized Analytical Techniques—
Banks and Finance Companies

In addition to the transportation and public utility industries, certain financial institutions are subjected to federal or state regulation, thus requiring application of specialized techniques for purposes of analysis. Among these institutions are fire and casualty insurance companies, life insurance companies, and commercial banks; as custodians of public and private funds, all are regulated by appropriate authority to assure that they will be able to meet such claims as may, from time to time, be made against them.

Insurance companies are chartered, regulated, and supervised by state governments. Banks may operate under either state or federal charter, and may be supervised and examined by the authority that grants the charter. In practice, national banks are examined by national bank examiners; state banks that are members of the Federal Reserve System are examined by state and Federal Reserve examiners. State banks that are not members of the Federal Reserve but are members of the Federal Deposit Insurance Corporation are examined by state and FDIC examiners.

Finance companies are not custodians of funds. They are, nonetheless, subject to supervision and regulation by the states that grant their charters. The purpose of this supervision and regulation is to protect borrowers against various practices which might be indulged in by lenders due to their superior economic position. State regulation is basically concerned with the rate of charge and size of loan that may be made.

COMMERCIAL BANKS

Commercial banks provide a number of different services under a charter granted by the federal or state government. As a financial

366

intermediary, they act as a depository for funds by accepting deposits, both demand and time. They perform services for their demand depositors by allowing them to draw against their accounts by check, thus providing a convenient means of payment. For this service, the bank usually makes a charge.

Another source of funds that has become increasingly important is savings deposits. At the present time, savings deposits provide about one third of total commercial bank deposits. The bank usually pays the saver interest on his deposit as inducement for him to save. A major cause for increase in the importance of savings deposits in recent years has been the increase to $5\frac{1}{2}$ percent as the maximum interest rate that banks may pay on time and savings deposits.

The primary source of bank earnings is the income from lending and investing these deposits. It would be possible for banks to build up unlimited leverage if, without the restraint of basic capital requirements imposed by regulatory authorities, they were able to attract and accept unlimited deposits and invest these funds.[1] This, of course, is not possible because of the necessity of keeping cash to meet the withdrawals of depositors and for other day-to-day operations, the reserves required by regulatory authorities, and the maintenance of some minimum ratio of capital to deposit liabilities. These factors limit the earnings potential of the bank.

The Balance Sheet

The assets of a commercial bank may be divided into two groups—nonrisk assets of cash and U.S. government securities, and risk assets, making up the balance of assets. The statements of condition of the Bankers Trust Company of New York City and Mellon National Bank for the year-end 1964 are shown in Table 18–1. These two banks were selected because they provide considerable contrast in operating policies. It may be noted that Bankers Trust Company had 48.8 percent of its assets in loans, while Mellon National had only 41.5 percent in loans at the end of 1964. The relatively smaller proportion of assets in loans by Mellon National is a serious indictment of bank's management, since loans are the best income-yielding asset of a commercial bank. To compensate for the apparently sluggish loan demand, Mellon National since 1961 has adopted a policy of heavy

---

1 An excellent article dealing with this limit on the expansion of deposits is Leonard W. Ascher, "Practical Limits to Bank Expansion," *Financial Analysts Journal*, Vol. 17, No. 3 (May–June, 1961), p. 23.

investment in public or municipal securities. This change in policy has improved the risk asset position of Mellon National and has improved after-tax earnings. In contrast, Bankers Trust has steadily increased its loan portfolio over the years. Bankers Trust has also increased its holdings of municipals, but not to the extent that Mellon National has.

Obviously, the relative size of the asset classification "cash and due from banks" affects the earnings of the bank. The commercial banker has a dilemma. First, the bank manager must have enough cash to meet all demands of depositors, and, second, he wants to maximize the earnings of his bank. The natural tendency would be to maximize earnings by keeping in nonearning assets only the amount of funds that is absolutely necessary. However, the bank manager does not have a free hand in determining the amounts of funds in the various asset accounts, because they are subject to perodic examination by the various state and/or federal regulatory authorities. These authorities may influence the amounts of funds invested in earning assets. If the supervising authority considers that the bank is exceeding limits of safety by investing too much in earning assets, it will suggest that the bank managers reduce their loans and investments. Such advice is usually heeded. However, supervisory authorities in recent years have been more interested in quality of earning assets than they have been in relative amounts and composition of these assets.

Capital Structure

A major factor in the profitable operation of commercial banks is the leverage afforded them. This leverage results because deposits are debts of the bank. Therefore, the higher the ratio of deposits to capital, the more profitable the bank should be. The measure of a bank's leverage position is its capital ratio—the relationship of total capital accounts, common stock, surplus, and undivided profits expressed as a percent of total assets. The lower the capital ratio, the more heavily leveraged the bank is. There are practical limits on this leverage position of a bank, because when deposits get too large relative to capital, "moral suasion" by the regulatory authorities may force the bank to take remedial action and increase capital.

A new commercial banking development that has enabled some banks to supplement capital without the dilutive effects of the sale of

TABLE 18–1

**Statements of Condition,
December 31, 1964**
(in millions)

	Bankers Trust		Mellon National	
	Amount	Percent of Total	Amount	Percent of Total
ASSETS				
Cash	$1,007	22.3%	$ 535	16.5%
U.S. government securities .	579	12.8	372	11.5
Loans and discounts	2,209	48.8	1,340	41.5
Public securities	435	9.6	914	28.3
Other	295	6.5	72	2.2
Total	$4,525	100.0	$3,233	100.0
LIABILITIES AND CAPITAL ACCOUNTS				
Deposits	$3,900	86.2%	$2,689	83.2%
Other liabilities	181	4.0	195	6.0
Total	4,081	90.2	2,884	89.2
Capital notes	96	2.1	..	..
Capital stock	91	2.0	67	2.1
Surplus	200	4.4	233	7.2
Undivided profits	57	1.3	49	1.5
Total	$4,525	100.0	$3,233	100.0

more common stock is the sale of subordinated debentures. These debentures increase the capital cushion of the bank and, at the same time, increase its leverage.[2] The debenture seems to be an ingenious solution to a problem that has bothered banking authorities for some time —that is, the relatively inadequacy of the capital cushion.

Bankers Trust Company sold $100 million of the subordinated notes in 1963. This increase in the capital base will provide the means for further expansion of deposits. Relatively, Mellon National has the problem of being overcapitalized, as evidenced by the capital ratios of the two banks (Table 18–2).

The capital ratios of large city banks tend to be lower than those of medium-sized and smaller banks, which is another way of saying that the large city banks are more highly leveraged. To make these ratios more meaningful, the analyst should compare the commercial bank under consideration with other banks in its size group. The

---

[2] Paul S. Nadler, "Pitfalls as well as Profits Seen in Capital Debentures for Banks," *American Banker*, December 24, 1963, p. 3.

370 *Investment Analysis and Management*

TABLE 18–2

Bankers Trust Company and Mellon National Bank,
Capital Ratios, 1957–64

	Bankers Trust	Mellon National
1957	8.82%	12.82%
1958	8.57	12.94
1959	9.08	14.01
1960	8.45	13.50
1961	8.06	13.11
1962	8.20	12.76
1963	9.50	11.27
1964	9.81	10.79

composite data by size group is provided in the Annual Report of the Federal Deposit Insurance Corporation.

Capital–Risk Asset Ratio

A commercial bank may be well leveraged, but the management may not use the leverage to advantage. The advantage of a low capital ratio may be offset by heavy investment in nonrisk assets—cash and U.S. government securities. The major earning risk assets are loans and public or municipal securities investments. If a bank management is maximizing earnings potential, it has a low capital ratio and a low capital–risk asset ratio—capital expressed as a percentage of risk assets. This percentage will indicate how large a loss in risk assets can be absorbed by capital. For example, Bankers Trust may have a decline of risk assets of about 14 percent and still cover all liabilities once (Table 18–3).

The lower the capital-risk asset ratio, the more aggressive the bank is in management of its assets. Of the two illustrative banks, Mellon National with a higher capital ratio and lower capital–risk asset ratio has considerably improved its profit potential in recent years.

Loan–Deposit Ratio

A further refinement in evaluation of a commercial bank's earnings potential is measurement of the relationship of loans to deposits expressed as a percentage of deposits. A bank that keeps a substantial proportion of its funds invested in loans is generally able to earn more than one that invests in U.S. government bonds. Of course, it is

TABLE 18–3

Bankers Trust Company and Mellon National Bank,
Capital–Risk Asset Ratio, 1957–64

	Bankers Trust	Mellon National
1957	16.24%	21.12%
1958	16.83	22.42
1959	15.50	22.19
1960	13.87	22.45
1961	14.95	22.75
1962	13.89	19.19
1963	17.06	16.46
1964	16.79	15.46

not only a question of being willing to accept loans, but also a matter of the demand for loans by the bank's customers. When loan demand drops, the bank has no clear choice but investment in bonds or other marketable debt instruments.

It is not unusual for large city banks to have 70 percent of deposits out in loans.[3] The material in Table 18–4 indicates that both Bankers Trust and Mellon National follow a policy more conservative than the average large city bank, since these two banks have about 45 to 50 percent of deposits outstanding in loans.

TABLE 18–4

Bankers Trust Company and Mellon National Bank,
Loan–Deposit Ratio, 1957–64

	Bankers Trust	Mellon National
1957	56.66%	57.79%
1958	50.05	52.83
1959	58.47	59.84
1960	51.68	56.90
1961	50.03	48.82
1962	52.50	45.47
1963	54.10	44.46
1964	56.63	49.83

Profitability Analysis

The profitability of a bank is dependent on (1) the yield on its loans and investments, (2) its operating efficiency as reflected by its ability to control operating expenses, and (3) the leverage factor discussed earlier.

---

[3] Ascher, *op. cit.*, p. 27.

Yield Analysis. The yield on loans and investments is a major factor in bank profitability. The yield realized on loans is usually much higher than the yield on investments, as discussed earlier. For example, the yield on loans for Bankers Trust Company for the 12 months ended October 13, 1965, was 5.20 percent, while the yield on investments was only 3.12 percent.[4] This yield factor is calculated by dividing income from loans and investments by the gross income derived from each type of assets.

Analysis of Operating Costs. In evaluation of the management of a bank, the ability to control costs is obviously as important as the ability to employ funds at a high yield. The ability to control operating expenses can be measured by a break-even yield analysis. The break-even yield is calculated by dividing total costs before taxes by total loans and investments. This break-even yield is the yield needed on loans and investments to just cover operating costs $\left(\frac{\text{loans and investments}}{\text{operating expenses}}\right)$. The break-even yield for Bankers Trust Company for the year ending December 31, 1964, was 3.57 percent, and for Mellon National Bank it was 2.94 percent.

In analyzing operating costs, the analyst should pay particular attention to two major cost items: (1) wages and salaries, (2) interest costs.

Wage and Salary Costs. Wage and salary costs are a major cost item in bank operations. It will be usually about 25 to 30 percent of total operating expenses.

In some cases, the investor is handicapped by the failure of banks to give breakdown of operating expenses in their annual reports.

Banks that have a relatively high proportion of their earning assets in loans will tend to have higher operating expenses, particularly wage and salary expenses, than will banks that rely to a greater extent on security investments as earnings assets. For example, as mentioned earlier, Bankers Trust has a larger percentage of total assets in loans than has Mellon National. The slightly smaller margin of profit of Bankers Trust is probably the result of higher wage costs associated with the relatively larger loan portfolio. (See Table 18–5.)

Failure to keep labor costs in check may result in impaired earnings. However, abnormally low labor costs are not always an indica-

---

4 "How Banks are Doing," *Bank Stock Quarterly*, December, 1965, p. 10. The quarterly is published by M. A. Schapiro & Co., Inc., One Chase Manhattan Plaza, New York, N.Y.

tion of operating efficiency. It may be an indication of low wage and salary scale. The apparent efficiency of operation reflected in total costs gained by low wage and salary levels may be temporary because of the possible loss of competent employees. To check the relative adequacy of wage and salary levels, the investor may use as a supplementary measure the number of bank employees. In some cases, number of employees has been used as an index of operating efficiency.

TABLE 18–5

COMPARATIVE INCOME STATEMENTS
Bankers Trust Company and Mellon National Bank,
Year Ending December 31, 1964
(In 000)

| | *Bankers Trust* | | *Mellon National* | |
	Amount	*Percent of Total Operating Income*	*Amount*	*Percent of Total Operating Income*
Operating Income:				
From loans	$102,510	59.3%	$ 58,884	49.8%
From securities	30,357	17.5	40,620	34.4
From other income	40,021	23.2	18,624	15.8
Total	$172,888	100.0	$118,128	100.0
Operating Expense:				
Interest expense	40,546	23.5	40,326	34.1
Salaries and wages	46,996	27.2	21,296	18.0
Other operating	27,535	15.9	15,437	13.1
Total	$115,077	66.6	$77,059	65.2
Net Operating Income:				
Before taxes	57,811	33.4	41,069	34.8
Federal and other income taxes	23,235	13.4	8,983*	7.6
Net income	$ 34,576	20.0	$37,086	27.2

* Includes miscellaneous taxes in addition to federal income tax.

Interest Expense. Commercial banks have been allowed to pay a higher rate of interest of up to 4 percent on savings deposit and up to $5\frac{1}{2}$ percent on time deposits. The net effect of this increase in the maximum permissible rate of interest on deposits has been to increase the costs of funds to the banks.

In many cases, banks have been forced to increase the rate of interest simply to maintain their present level of deposits; in others, it has resulted in an increase in deposits. It is obvious that it has not been an unmixed blessing to the banks. In recent years, the interest expense as a percent of gross earnings has increased for Mellon National from 13.5 percent in 1960 to 34.1 percent in 1964.

Gains and Losses on Securities

The item relating to net profit on securities in the income statements of commercial banks requires the investor's special attention. Capital gains or losses arising from the sale of securities are shown separately on the bank income statement, because these profits or losses are not properly a part of current earnings. Gains and losses on securities are recorded only when realized. Securities held by the bank as "investments" are not adjusted for changes in market value, but are carried on the books at cost. These gains and losses are recorded only when realized or when the securities are sold.

The bank that shows losses on securities, particularly during a period of rising interest rates, may be a better-managed bank than one that does not show losses, because realized losses can be taken as deductions from ordinary income in computation of the bank's income tax liability. Consequently, a well-managed bank will often take large security losses, when they are available, by selling securities on which it has losses. It then shifts the funds into comparable issues to maintain current income. These securities, held until loan volume and interest rates decline, may be sold at a profit that will be subject to a smaller capital gains tax rate. Although this technique is generally known, some banks avoid using it because management is unwilling to penalize the statement of current earnings in a particular year. To some extent, a bank's earning power strength may be judged by its willingness to take security losses when conditions permit so that it may realize this tax savings.

Summary

Book value per share is a valuable bench mark in selecting bank common stock investments. Although we know that the market value of any common stock reflects the earnings potential and not its book value, the nature of banking and bank assets makes the relationship between book value and potential earnings power a relatively direct one. A bank that is fully "loaned up" with a high loan–deposit ratio and a low capital ratio is nearer its optimum earnings potential, just as Bankers Trust is nearer than Mellon National, which still has room for expansion of both deposits and loans without dilution of the equity interests through the sale of stock. Of course, if the management of a bank with room for expansion does nothing to exploit its advantage, the potential increase in profits is of little value.

Sometimes, failure of a bank's management to exploit its potential is a result of the bank's location. Many of the larger banks are located in the centers of metropolitan areas. Their growth often is limited because population and the local economy are moving away from the central city. As a consequence, in states where branch banking is prohibited the common stocks of commercial banks located in growth areas of the city should be examined by the investor, because the deposit growth of a bank is basically a function of area economics and population trends, as well as the quality of its management.

FINANCE COMPANIES

A finance company is a relatively simple business. The companies borrow money from wholesalers of credit, commercial banks, life insurance companies, and others, and lend to their customers. The basis for profitable finance company operation is to lend the money at a higher rate of charge than it pays for it, and then collect from the customer at maturity.

The finance industry serves a varied clientele. It is helpful to break the finance industry into two parts—commercial financing and consumer financing. The commercial finance company makes loans to business customers. These loans are relatively large, and are usually secured by the pledge of collateral such as inventory, receivables, or equipment.

Consumer credit is extended in two basic forms: (1) sales installment credit, which is the deferment of payment for goods and services purchased; (2) cash installment credit, which is direct cash lending to consumers. Sales finance companies extend credit by purchasing consumer installment contracts, which the seller accepts as the consideration in the sale of an item such as an automobile. Consumer finance or small-loan companies make cash loans directly to the borrower from an office the company has established exclusively for that purpose. These consumer finance or small-loan companies make cash loans to individuals repayable in installments. The lending activities of these companies are usually subject to regulation by state authorities. State laws regulate a number of facets of the consumer finance business. Usually, the more important aspects include regulation of (1) the maximum rate of charge, (2) the method by which the maximum charge may be computed, and (3) the maximum size of loan that may be made to any one borrower. The rate of charge is generally from 2½ to 3½ percent per month and is an all inclusive charge.[5] Since small loan companies are regulated by the states, there is considerable variation in the rates of charges allowed. In recent years, the trend has been toward less specialization in the finance business. For example, General Contract Finance Corporation was originally a sales finance company, but it now operates in the commercial and consumer finance areas as well. Since the various types of finance companies are essentially the same except for the differences cited, the analytical techniques used are generally applicable to all types.

Investment Characteristics

All three forms of finance companies described above have certain common financial characteristics. First, the typical finance company is highly leveraged, which permits them to earn a higher rate of return on their common stock equity than would be the case with a more conventional financial structure. Second, the major earning asset of any finance company is its notes receivable, because basically their business is lending money to their customers at retail prices while borrowing from other sources at wholesale prices. Since they are all basically lenders of money, any differences in finance companies are not in the type of operation but in the customers to whom they lend money and in their rates of charge. Consumer finance or small loan companies generally charge between 25 and 40 percent per annum for their loans, while sales finance companies get between 10 and 18 percent per annum on their paper. Commercial finance company charges run between 9 and 22 percent. The differences in the rates of charge among the various finance companies is caused by differences in (1) the average size of loan, (2) the overhead cost

---

[5] An all-inclusive charge is supposed to include all charges plus interest that could be levied for a loan. The original basis for small-loan laws was that the borrower would be charged one "all-inclusive charge on the unpaid balance." This has been modified in recent years by pre-computation of charges and an allowance of the sale of credit life insurance. The modern tendency is to allow pre-computation.

per loan, and (3) the risk features of the loan. For example, small-loan companies, on the average, make smaller-sized loans, so their average overhead cost per loan is higher, thus justifying their higher average rate of charge.

Analysis of a finance company involves examination of several factors: (1) quality and liquidity of notes receivable, (2) method and costs of financing, and (3) yield of notes receivable and costs of operation. Much of the data necessary to complete this analysis is in the published financial statements that are generally available to public. However, the analyst should try to obtain the audited financial statements and the direct cash lending questionnaire normally provided to the finance company's lenders.

Although there are significant differences in types of finance company customers, as mentioned previously, the basic operation of these companies is essentially the same. In order to simplify the presentation of analytical techniques, we will use the analysis of companies primarily in the sales and consumer finance business to illustrate these techniques.

The Financial Statements

The striking features of a finance company balance sheet to an analyst familiar with balance sheets of manufacturing companies are (1) the composition of assets and (2) the capital structure.

It may be noted from the comparisons of asset composition of two major finance companies, Liberty Loan Corporation and Interstate Finance Corporation, shown in Table 18–6, that current assets consisting almost entirely of receivables constitute the major assets of these companies. Notes receivable constitute the inventory of the finance company and are their primary earning asset, accounting for between 83 and 91 percent of total assets.

Use of any significant amount of its assets in noncurrent applications is often the forerunner of declining earnings. A finance company, many times, will defer the development costs of opening new offices in order to shore up current earnings. This practice is a legitimate one; however, these deferred costs will be charges against future earnings. Poor management control of investment in non-income-producing assets, such as fixtures or real estate, will also adversely affect earnings. As a general rule, when noncurrent assets begin to represent more than 20 percent of total assets and continue to rise as a percentage of the total, it is usually an indication the company is having difficulty in maintaining earnings.

Of equal importance to the analyst is the amount of unearned discount and provision for losses as a percentage of notes receivable. To understand the importance of these measures, it is necessary to understand how the unearned discount and provision for losses arise.

Unearned Income. Unearned discount or income indicates that the charges for the loan have been precomputed and added in or added on to the face amount of the loan. For example, on an $100, 12-month loan, a 12 percent charge means that the charges are $12, and this amount is added on to the face amount of the note. The borrower signs a note for $112, payable in 12 monthly installments. The yield on this loan would be in excess of 12 percent (21.46 percent), because it is an installment loan and the borrower does not have the use of $100 over the 12-month period.

The method by which a company takes its unearned discount into earnings has an effect on the levels of past, current, and future earnings. There are several methods of taking unearned charges into current gross income, but two methods are in general use.[6] One is the so-called "rule of 78ths" or the sum-of-the-digits method.[7] With the sum-of-the-digits method, the company takes in $12/78$ of the unearned charge at the end of the first month of a 12-month loan, $11/78$ the second month, and so forth. The other method is "level-income." In this case, the company takes in $1/12$ of the unearned charges each month. Since the company has a larger amount of funds outstanding in the early months of a loan, the level-income method understates gross income in the early months and overstates it in the later months.

The distortion in gross income can be significant if one realizes that the sum-of-the-digits method causes about 72 percent of unearned charges the first 6 months of a 12-month loan, while the level-income plan takes in only 50 percent. The distortion becomes more pronounced as company rate of growth increases. Therefore, when making comparisons it is essential that the analyst know which methods the companies are using.

A finance company may accelerate the amortization of unearned

---

[6] H. A. Finney, *Problems in Profits* (Hartford, Conn.: Resolute Insurance Company).

[7] The term "rule of 78ths" is derived from the fact that the sum of the digits for a year or 12 months is 78. However, a more accurately descriptive term is "the sum of the digits."

TABLE 18–6

Balance Sheets, Liberty Loan Corporation and Interstate Finance Corporation, Year Ending December 31, 1964
(in thousands)

ASSETS		*Liberty*		*Interstate*	
Cash and U.S. government securities ...		$ 13,170	5.92%	$ 9,104	7.57%
Installment notes receivable	$229,351			$118,811	
Less: Unearned discount ...	20,438			15,216	
Reserve for losses	6,267			3,153	
Net notes receivable .		202,646	91.14	100,443	83.55
Miscellaneous current assets		3,499	1.57	5,081*	4.23
Total current assets		219,315	98.63	114,628	95.35
Furniture, equipment, etc., net		1,350	0.61	685	0.57
Deferred charges		1,695	0.76	4,908	4.08
Total		$222,360	100.00	$120,221	100.00
LIABILITIES AND NET WORTH					
Notes payable	77,555		34.88	$ 58,905	49.00
Long-term debt (current portion) .	2,750		1.23	2,650	2.20
Miscellaneous current assets	10,000		4.50	4,256	3.54
Total Current Liabilities ...		90,305	40.61	65,811	54.74
Senior long-term debt	56,010		25.19	17,200	14.31
Subordinated debt ..	37,130		16.70	14,456	12.02
Long-term debt (subsidiaries)	..		..	2,404	2.00
Total Long-Term Debt		93,140	41.89	34,060	28.33
Preferred stock	5,794		2.60	6,167	5.13
Common stock	2,185		0.98	1,037	0.86
Paid-in surplus	15,002		6.75	4,249	3.54
Retained earnings ...	15,934		7.17	8,897	7.40
Total Net Worth		38,915	17.50	20,350	16.93
Total		$222,360	100.00	$120,221	100.00

* Includes investment in subsidiaries of $4,471,368.

discount in order to increase reported earnings. The analyst can usually establish that the company is following this practice by computing the relationship of unearned discount to gross notes receivable that are discounted or precomputed. The unearned discount for Liberty Loan Corporation and Interstate Finance Corporation ranges between 8.9 percent for Liberty and 12.8 percent for Interstate. The differential in the relationship between unearned discount and notes receivable may also be accounted for by the fact that a company may have a substantial portion of its loans on an interest-bearing basis. That is, compared with Interstate, Liberty Loan operates in more states that require that the charges be computed each month on the unpaid balance. For this reason, the unearned discount bears a percentage relationship to gross notes receivable smaller for Liberty Loan than for Interstate.

Provision for Losses. The provision for losses or bad debts is the reserve established for bad debts. This reserve is usually an amount the company regards as a reasonable estimate of future losses. Generally, this reserve is maintained at between 3 to 4 percent of gross notes receivable. Again, a company that is attempting to maintain earnings may deplete its provision for losses. However, this practice is not a common one.

The general quality of receivables usually cannot be determined by relating the reserve for losses to receivables outstanding. An appraisal of receivables quality can be made only after an aging of the accounts. These data are not normally available to the average investor but are often made available to the finance company's lenders in a semiannual detailed audit. The discriminating analyst would insist on examining this audit to determine on what percentage of the firm's accounts there had been no payments received for 60 to 89 days, and no payments for 90 days or more. Composite data published by the First National Bank of Chicago indicates that $3\frac{1}{2}$ to 4 percent of the receivables are past due for periods longer than 60 days.

Capital Structure. Capital management—the acquisition of funds —is a major and continuous problem with a finance company. It is obvious from the Liberty Loan and Interstate Finance balance sheets that the capitalization of a typical finance company provides substantial leverage for the common stock. Analysis of the finance company's capital structure is of prime importance, since it's composition may have a profound effect on the earnings available to common stockholders. Rapidly expanding finance companies may find that they have reached the limits of their borrowing capacity. Stockholders of these companies are then faced with the prospect of either

(1) a slackening in the rate of increase in earnings per share or (2) dilution of the present common stock equity and/or earnings. (See discussion on p. 310 of dilution and earnings per share.)

The borrowing capacity of finance companies has been increased considerably in the last 15 years by use of subordinated debt. Commercial banks and life insurance companies have been primary suppliers of debt capital and, usually, have been willing to consider subordinated debt as the equivalent of net worth. It is obvious from Table 18-6 that the use of subordinated debt has enhanced the leverage of finance companies. Generally, senior debt will constitute about 65 to 70 percent of total liabilities and net worth. The subordinated debt is usually about 15 percent of the total credit items.

It may be observed from the comparative balance sheets of Liberty Loan and Interstate Finance that Liberty uses less short-term debt than does Interstate. Typically, small loan companies go through a growth pattern that is reflected in their capitalization. During the early years of rapid growth, these companies rely heavily on bank borrowing. When the rate of growth slows, the company typically shifts its financing to long-term obligations as money market conditions permit. Use of long-term debt is a more desirable means of financing than use of bank borrowing, because it tends to stabilize interest costs and the overall financing of the company.

Analysis of Operations

The earnings available to common stockholders of a consumer finance company represent the difference between the charges or gross income received on loans and the costs of operating loan offices, losses on loans, and interest paid for borrowed funds. An analysis of the profitability of a finance company's operation would include an examination of (1) gross income from loans, (2) operating costs, (3) loss experience, and (4) cost of borrowed funds.

Gross Income. The gross income of a consumer finance company includes the interest or charges on loans, income from the sale of credit life or other insurance to borrowers, recoveries on loans previously charged off as uncollectible, and miscellaneous income. Although the sale of credit insurance—life and accident and health— has become an increasingly important part of finance company gross income, the major sources of revenue are the charges made for loans. The gross income level is significant only when related to installment notes receivable to determine the yield of the notes. The yield is the relationship of the company's gross income to its average installment notes outstanding. The gross yield is found by computing the average of the total notes receivable outstanding at the beginning and at the end of the year, and dividing this amount into the gross income for the year. The level of the gross yield is a function of (1) the method by which unearned discount is amortized and (2) the maximum legal rates of charge allowed by the various states in which the company operates.

Costs of Operation. The major costs of finance company operation are (1) general operating expenses, (2) bad debt expenses, and (3) cost of money. Table 18–7 shows the costs of operation as a percent of gross income for Liberty Loan and Interstate Finance.

TABLE 18–7

Income Statements, Liberty Loan Corporation
and Interstate Finance Corporation,
Year Ending December 31, 1964
(in thousands)

		Liberty		*Interstate*
Gross income		$44,770	100.00%	$18,629	100.00%
Operating expenses	$22,995		$9,804	
Provision for losses	5,123		1,721	
Amortization of				
acquisition costs	463		300	
Deferred developmental				
expense	(147)		24	
Total Expenses		28,434	63.51	11,849	63.60
Net income before interest				
and income taxes		16,336	36.49	6,780	36.39
Interest expense		8,217	18.35	4,296	23.06
Income before income taxes		8,119	18.14	2,484	13.33
Income taxes		3,114	6.96	1,043	5.60
Net income		5,005	11.18	1,441*	7.73

* Does not include income of $692,638 from nonconsolidated subsidiary.

It is obvious that the major cost of operation is general operating expenses. The measure of overall operating efficiency is the operating costs per account. Management ability to service more customer accounts with the same number of employees will tend to reduce the operating costs in relation to gross income, because salaries and wages are a major expense item. A companion measure of operating efficiency is the number of accounts per employee.

The operating costs per account and number of accounts per employee will usually tend to be higher for the expanding finance company. This is particularly true if much of the company's expansion is by opening new offices, because initial costs in opening offices are high. The cost of investigating and acquiring loans is a major part of the total cost. Once each loan office has reached a minimum volume of business to cover overhead, operating expenses per account will tend to vary with loan volume. Naturally, operating expenses per dollar of loans outstanding and profit expectations will improve substantially if there is a trend toward average larger-size loans.

Bad Debt Expenses. The amount of notes receivable outstanding or loans written off as bad debts is strictly a matter of management's judgment as to what constitutes a bad debt. The item in the income statement, "provision for losses," is the provision for a bad debt reserve. It does not bear any direct relationship to the amount of loans written off, because the finance company may make a deduction for provision for losses as large as the Internal Revenue Service will allow, thus reducing taxable income. The more significant figures in analysis of bad debt losses are the net write-offs. The net write-off, or charge-off, is the gross charge-off of receivables less the recoveries or collections from bad debts previously written off. The gross charge-off is the total amount of accounts considered by the management to be uncollectible bad debts.

The provision for losses on the income statement is usually about equal to the net charge-off for the year. This is true if there has not been a significant increase in notes receivable, because the company's deduction for losses will be just sufficient to maintain provision for losses at about 3 percent of gross notes receivable.

Costs of Money. The cost of borrowed funds represents a major cost of finance company operation because of the leverage the companies have in their capital structure. For Liberty Loan and Interstate, these money costs are 18 to 23 percent of gross income.

Money costs cannot be so easily controlled by the management of the company as can internally derived costs such as bad debt losses and operating expenses. Changes in market rates of interest can produce significant changes in the cost of money for a finance company. The impact of an increase in the market cost of borrowing varies with the amount of short-term borrowings. That is, a finance company can stabilize its cost of money to some extent by the use of long-term financing.

Other Expenses. The major other expense item is the amortization of deferred loan development expense. This expense arises from the opening of new offices by a finance company. A new loan office will usually show a loss for the first year. Therefore, a rapidly expanding finance company would understate its earnings if it matched the losses of new offices against income in the year in which they occur. As a consequence, it is the practice to defer these costs and write them off against income over a period of, usually, about five years.

Selection Measures

Three market value measures may be used in the final selection of finance company common stock. These measures are (1) price–earnings ratio, (2) dividend yield, and (3) market price as a percentage of book value.

The first two of these measures have been discussed at length in earlier chapters. As a selection measure, market price as a percentage of book value deserves special comment, because it is generally held, in most instances, that there is no discernible relationship to the earning capacity of a firm. However, since practically all of a finance company's assets are cash and receivables, the net worth is usually indicative of a minimum investment value. A company whose stock is selling at or near its book value usually has little downside risk unless the quality of receivables is seriously impaired.

Naturally, the basic factor in selecting a finance common stock is its earnings potential in relation to the price of the common stock. In this connection, a company that is not so highly leveraged should sell at a higher price–earnings ratio. In such a company, there is a possibility of expansion without dilution of earnings through the sale of common stock. The common stock of a low-leverage company with the possibility of growth should sell at a higher price—earnings ratio than that of a company with a highly leveraged capital structure.

In the selection of finance company stocks, importance of the growth factor cannot be overemphasized. The development costs of opening new offices (while growth is taking place) may reduce earnings to such extent that future appreciation possibilities are obscured. The interested investor should examine and analyze the smaller as well as the better-known and larger companies in selecting a suitable investment in this industry.

REVIEW QUESTIONS AND PROBLEMS

1. How does the nature of a commercial bank's liabilities limit the potential return on earning assets?
2. What are the basic measures of a bank's earnings potential?
3. What are the distinguishing features of a commercial bank?
4. Under what conditions would book value per share of bank common stock be the primary factor in the valuation of bank common stock?
5. How does the use of subordinated debt improve the leverage position of commercial banks?
6. The interest that commercial banks have been allowed to pay on time and savings deposits has increased in recent years. What has been the impact of this increase on commercial bank operations?
7. What are the significant considerations in the evaluation of a finance company?
8. Distinguish between the purposes of commercial bank and small loan company regulation?
9. The control of operating expenses is generally of more importance in the profitable operation of small loan companies than it is in other industries. Why is this true?
10. Small loan Company A has a debt to equity ratio of 1 to 1 and Company B a ratio of 3 to 1. Other things being equal, which of these companies has the greatest profit potential and why?
11. What are the relative effects on profits of financing a small loan company by short-term as versus long-term indebtedness?

CHAPTER **19**

Government and Foreign Securities

In recent years, services provided by the federal, state, and local governments have increased substantially. These new services have resulted in substantial increases in government revenues, expenditures, and debts. Therefore, the debt of governmental units has become a major investment medium. Since the debt is issued by governmental units, the techniques used in analysis of private corporate debt are not applicable. Thus, the investor must use special analytical techniques in appraising and evaluating the relative risks and income of the bonds.

Bonds are issued by both the federal government and the state and local governments. Bonds of state and local governments are commonly lumped together in one classification and called "municipal" or "public" bonds. The bonds issued by the federal government and its instrumentalities are commonly referred to as "governments" or "government bonds." Some bonds issued by quasi-governmental agencies, such as the Federal Land Banks, are not guaranteed in any way by the federal government. These agency bonds are not government bonds, in the strictest sense, but are agency bonds and are identified by reference to the issuer—for example, "Land Bank bonds."

In the last section of this chapter, there is a discussion of some problems and techniques in analyzing foreign securities. It seems logical to include a discussion of foreign securities in this chapter, because the major factor in valuation of foreign securities is the actions of government in the country in which they operate.

MUNICIPAL BONDS

Municipal bonds are obligations of the various units of the state and local governments. These bonds are sold to finance permanent improvements, such as streets, schools, hospitals, sewage systems, and parks. Private business corporations and large governmental units, such as the federal government and some state governments, are sometimes able to finance their capital improvements from current and accumulated revenues. Most state and local government units cannot finance capital outlays from current revenues because of the smallness of annual revenues in relation to the cost of most major projects. Any attempt to accumulate governmental surpluses to finance such projects would be met with a cry from the taxpayers for a tax reduction. Therefore, almost any improvement by a state or local government that requires a substantial capital outlay involves the sale of bonds.

The amount of state and local debt outstanding has increased substantially in recent years as individuals have demanded more and better services from state and local governments. The total gross amount of state and local government indebtedness outstanding has increased from $20,246 million in 1946 to about $91.3 billion in 1964. This upward trend in state and local government debt outstanding is evident from the data in Figure 19–1.

General Characteristics

There are two classifications of municipal bonds, segregated by type of security. The first and most common type is the tax-secured or full-faith-and-credit obligation. These bonds are direct obligations of a political entity and are supported by the proceeds of taxation of all resources within the boundaries of the issuer.

The second type is revenue-secured bonds or revenue bonds secured by a pledge of revenues from specific earning assets of a state or local government enterprise, such as a toll road, electric utility, or waterworks. The issuing body agrees to operate the properties and to use the receipts from operations to service the debt, but it does not agree to levy taxes or make appropriations from the general fund if the pledged revenues are insufficient.

Some bonds are both revenue and tax-secured bonds, because the bond contract provides that if there are deficiencies in pledged revenues then the governmental unit agrees to make up the deficiency from general tax revenues. From the investor's point of view, these bonds are tax-secured bonds.

FIGURE 19-1

State and Local Government Bonds Outstanding
Year-End, 1920-64

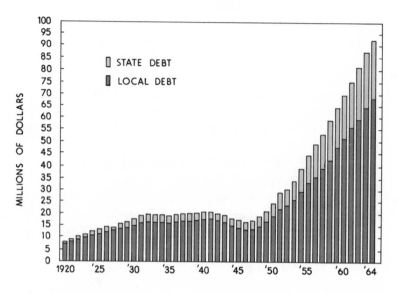

Source: *Moody's Municipal and Government Manual, 1965.*

Investment Characteristics

Certain characteristics of municipal bonds make them unique forms of investment media. The most important investment characteristic of municipal bonds is that the interest income is exempt from federal income tax. Also, most states do not tax interest income from bonds issued by the state and the local government units within the state.[1]

This tax exemption feature makes the bonds a very attractive form of investment to investors in the higher income tax brackets. The average annual yield of high-grade municipal bonds in 1964 was 3.30 percent. The tax exempt interest income makes the effective yield of these bonds considerably higher than the stated yield. The effective yield is the equivalent yield one would have to receive on a fully taxable investment to warrant the purchase of that investment. For

---

[1] The following states tax interest income on all municipal bonds: Colorado, Idaho, Indiana, Iowa, Kansas, Massachusetts, Montana, Oklahoma, Oregon, and Wisconsin.

TABLE 19–1

Privately Held Municipal Bonds, by Type of Holder,
December 31, 1964

Type of Holder	Percent of Total	(Billions)
Individuals, partnerships, etc.	39.4	$33.5
Commercial banks	37.0	31.5
Mutual savings banks	0.4	0.4
Insurance companies	17.9	15.2
Other corporations	3.2	2.7
Miscellaneous investors	2.1	1.8
Total	100.0	$85.1

Source: *Moody's Municipal and Government Manual, 1965.*

example, a couple filing a joint return in the $28,000 to $32,000 net taxable income bracket must find a taxable investment with a return of 6.56 percent to equal a tax-free municipal bond with a return of 4 percent in 1965.[2] (See Table 19–2.)

Municipals generally are suitable media for individual investors in the higher tax brackets and for financial institutions such as commercial banks, mutual savings banks, and insurance companies. Although individuals, partnerships, etc., are the largest single holders of municipal bonds, commercial banks and insurance companies are the largest institutional holders. (See Table 19–1.)

The obvious advantage of municipal bonds to these financial institutions is that the effective yield on high-quality municipals is higher than it is on U.S. government bonds of comparable maturity. For example, the tax-exempt yield on state of New Hampshire bonds due 1985 was 3.20 percent on September 20, 1965. These bonds carried Moody's highest quality rating of Aaa. U.S. Treasury bonds, $3\frac{1}{4}$'s of 1985 were selling to yield 4.29 percent. A commercial bank in the highest corporate income tax bracket could purchase these state of New Hampshire bonds and have a yield advantage 1.86 percent. For the investor with a moderate income, the effective yield of municipals is not high enough to justify their purchase. With each reduction in federal income tax rates, municipals become relatively less attractive for investors. When the yields are roughly comparable, municipal

---

[2] It is assumed in this example and Table 19–2 that the investor is computing the effect of the federal income tax on each dollar of additional income over and above his present income.

bonds are usually investments with limited marketability. In some cases, they are of questionable quality.

Marketability of Municipal Bonds

Municipal bonds generally have limited marketability. Practically all municipal bonds are traded in the over-the-counter market. The degree of marketability depends primarily on the size of the issue. There are daily trading and published quotations of some larger bond issues. Smaller local government issues have a very limited market and may be traded only by one or two local municipal bond dealers. Sometimes, it is difficult to find buyers for smaller issues; consequently, the investor who foresees a need for his funds before maturity of the bonds should invest only in the issues of the larger and better-known governmental units and public authorities.

Municipal bonds are usually quoted and traded on a yield basis. The yield quoted indicates the rate of return to maturity. For example, if a $1,000 bond carrying a $4\frac{1}{4}$ percent coupon rate is offered to the investor on a 3.90 basis, the bond would cost him $1,016.40.

Analysis of Municipal Bonds

The analysis of full-faith-and-credit municipal bonds or general obligations involves basically an analysis of the ability of the governmental unit to pay the interest and repay the principal amount of the bonds. The first step in analysis of ability to pay is a study of the general economic characteristics of the area and the relative debt burden of the municipality. The general economic background analysis is supplemented with specific measures of ability to pay, which relate various economic factors to the revenue and tax burden. In addition, the investor should also concern himself with the questions of legality of the bond issue and, in some cases, with the willingness of the taxpayers to pay taxes to provide revenue for debt service.

Legality

To be valid obligations, municipal bonds must be issued in accordance with the requirements imposed by law. The governmental unit must comply with a host of legal requirements before selling a bond issue. For example, the state law may prohibit a municipality

TABLE 19–2

Yields of Tax-Exempt Securities
(Taxable income in thousands)

JOINT RETURN	$8 to $12	$12 to $16	$16 to $20	$20 to $24	$24 to $28	$28 to $32	$32 to $36	$36 to $40	$40 to $44	$44 to $52	$52 to $64	$64 to $76	$76 to $88	$88 to $100	$100 to $120	$120 to $140	$140 to $160	$160 to $180	$180 to $200	Over $200
SINGLE RETURN	$4 to $6	$6 to $8	$8 to $10	$10 to $12	$12 to $14	$14 to $16	$16 to $18	$18 to $20	$20 to $22	$22 to $26	$26 to $32	$32 to $38	$38 to $44	$44 to $50	$50 to $60	$60 to $70	$70 to $80	$80 to $90	$90 to $100	Over $100
% Tax Bracket	22	25	28	32	36	39	42	45	48	50	53	55	58	60	62	64	66	68	69	70

TAX EXEMPT YIELDS																					
1.00%	1.28	1.33	1.39	1.47	1.56	1.64	1.72	1.82	1.92	2.00	2.13	2.22	2.38	2.50	2.63	2.78	2.94	3.13	3.23	3.33	1.00%
1.25	1.60	1.67	1.74	1.84	1.95	2.05	2.16	2.27	2.40	2.50	2.66	2.78	2.98	3.13	3.29	3.47	3.68	3.91	4.03	4.17	1.25
1.50	1.92	2.00	2.08	2.21	2.34	2.46	2.59	2.73	2.88	3.00	3.19	3.33	3.57	3.75	3.95	4.17	4.41	4.69	4.84	5.00	1.50
1.75	2.24	2.33	2.43	2.57	2.73	2.87	3.02	3.18	3.37	3.50	3.72	3.89	4.17	4.38	4.61	4.86	5.15	5.47	5.65	5.83	1.75
2.00	2.56	2.67	2.78	2.94	3.13	3.28	3.45	3.64	3.85	4.00	4.26	4.44	4.76	5.00	5.26	5.56	5.88	6.25	6.45	6.67	2.00
2.10	2.69	2.80	2.92	3.09	3.28	3.44	3.62	3.82	4.04	4.20	4.47	4.67	5.00	5.25	5.53	5.83	6.18	6.56	6.77	7.00	2.10
2.25	2.88	3.00	3.13	3.31	3.52	3.69	3.88	4.09	4.33	4.50	4.79	5.00	5.36	5.63	5.92	6.25	6.62	7.03	7.26	7.50	2.25
2.40	3.08	3.20	3.33	3.53	3.75	3.93	4.14	4.36	4.62	4.80	5.11	5.33	5.71	6.00	6.32	6.67	7.06	7.50	7.74	8.00	2.40
2.50	3.21	3.33	3.47	3.68	3.91	4.10	4.31	4.55	4.81	5.00	5.32	5.56	5.95	6.25	6.58	6.94	7.35	7.81	8.06	8.33	2.50
2.60	3.33	3.47	3.61	3.82	4.06	4.26	4.48	4.73	5.00	5.20	5.53	5.78	6.19	6.50	6.84	7.22	7.65	8.13	8.39	8.67	2.60
2.75	3.53	3.67	3.82	4.04	4.30	4.51	4.74	5.00	5.29	5.50	5.85	6.11	6.55	6.88	7.24	7.64	8.09	8.59	8.87	9.17	2.75
2.80	3.59	3.73	3.89	4.12	4.38	4.59	4.83	5.09	5.38	5.60	5.96	6.22	6.67	7.00	7.37	7.78	8.24	8.75	9.03	9.33	2.80
2.90	3.72	3.87	4.03	4.26	4.53	4.75	5.00	5.27	5.58	5.80	6.17	6.44	6.90	7.25	7.63	8.06	8.53	9.06	9.35	9.67	2.90
3.00	3.85	4.00	4.17	4.41	4.69	4.92	5.17	5.45	5.77	6.00	6.38	6.67	7.14	7.50	7.89	8.33	8.82	9.38	9.68	10.00	3.00
3.10	3.97	4.13	4.31	4.56	4.84	5.08	5.34	5.64	5.96	6.20	6.60	6.89	7.38	7.75	8.16	8.61	9.12	9.69	10.00	10.33	3.10
3.25	4.17	4.33	4.51	4.78	5.08	5.33	5.60	5.91	6.25	6.50	6.91	7.22	7.74	8.13	8.55	9.03	9.56	10.16	10.48	10.83	3.25
3.40	4.36	4.53	4.72	5.00	5.31	5.57	5.86	6.18	6.54	6.80	7.23	7.56	8.10	8.50	8.95	9.44	10.00	10.63	10.97	11.33	3.40
3.50	4.49	4.67	4.86	5.15	5.47	5.74	6.03	6.36	6.73	7.00	7.45	7.78	8.33	8.75	9.21	9.72	10.29	10.94	11.29	11.67	3.50
3.60	4.62	4.80	5.00	5.29	5.63	5.90	6.21	6.55	6.92	7.20	7.66	8.00	8.57	9.00	9.47	10.00	10.59	11.25	11.61	12.00	3.60
3.75	4.81	5.00	5.21	5.51	5.86	6.15	6.47	6.82	7.21	7.50	7.98	8.33	8.93	9.38	9.87	10.42	11.03	11.72	12.10	12.50	3.75
3.80	4.87	5.07	5.28	5.59	5.94	6.23	6.55	6.91	7.31	7.60	8.09	8.44	9.05	9.50	10.00	10.56	11.18	11.88	12.26	12.67	3.80
3.90	5.00	5.20	5.42	5.74	6.09	6.39	6.72	7.09	7.50	7.80	8.30	8.67	9.29	9.75	10.26	10.83	11.47	12.19	12.58	13.00	3.90
4.00	5.13	5.33	5.56	5.88	6.25	6.56	6.90	7.27	7.69	8.00	8.51	8.89	9.52	10.00	10.53	11.11	11.76	12.50	12.90	13.33	4.00
4.10	5.26	5.47	5.69	6.03	6.41	6.72	7.07	7.45	7.88	8.20	8.72	9.11	9.76	10.25	10.79	11.39	12.06	12.81	13.23	13.67	4.10
4.25	5.45	5.67	5.90	6.25	6.64	6.97	7.33	7.73	8.17	8.50	9.04	9.44	10.12	10.63	11.18	11.81	12.50	13.28	13.71	14.17	4.25
4.40	5.64	5.87	6.11	6.47	6.88	7.21	7.59	8.00	8.46	8.80	9.36	9.78	10.48	11.00	11.58	12.22	12.94	13.75	14.19	14.67	4.40
4.50	5.77	6.00	6.25	6.62	7.03	7.38	7.76	8.18	8.65	9.00	9.57	10.00	10.71	11.25	11.84	12.50	13.24	14.06	14.52	15.00	4.50
4.60	5.90	6.13	6.39	6.76	7.19	7.54	7.93	8.36	8.85	9.20	9.79	10.22	10.95	11.50	12.11	12.78	13.53	14.38	14.84	15.33	4.60
4.75	6.09	6.33	6.60	6.99	7.42	7.79	8.19	8.64	9.13	9.50	10.11	10.56	11.31	11.88	12.50	13.19	13.97	14.84	15.32	15.83	4.75
4.80	6.15	6.40	6.67	7.06	7.50	7.87	8.28	8.73	9.23	9.60	10.21	10.67	11.43	12.00	12.63	13.33	14.12	15.00	15.48	16.00	4.80
4.90	6.28	6.53	6.81	7.21	7.66	8.03	8.45	8.91	9.42	9.80	10.43	10.89	11.67	12.25	12.89	13.61	14.41	15.31	15.81	16.33	4.90
5.00	6.41	6.67	6.94	7.35	7.81	8.20	8.62	9.09	9.62	10.00	10.64	11.11	11.90	12.50	13.16	13.89	14.71	15.63	16.13	16.67	5.00
5.10	6.54	6.80	7.08	7.50	7.97	8.36	8.79	9.27	9.81	10.20	10.85	11.33	12.14	12.75	13.42	14.17	15.00	15.94	16.45	17.00	5.10
5.25	6.73	7.00	7.29	7.72	8.20	8.61	9.05	9.55	10.10	10.50	11.17	11.67	12.50	13.13	13.82	14.58	15.44	16.41	16.94	17.50	5.25
5.40	6.92	7.20	7.50	7.94	8.44	8.85	9.31	9.82	10.38	10.80	11.49	12.00	12.86	13.50	14.21	15.00	15.88	16.88	17.42	18.00	5.40
5.50	7.05	7.33	7.64	8.09	8.59	9.02	9.48	10.00	10.58	11.00	11.70	12.22	13.10	13.75	14.47	15.28	16.18	17.19	17.74	18.33	5.50
5.75	7.37	7.67	7.99	8.46	8.98	9.43	9.91	10.45	11.06	11.50	12.23	12.78	13.69	14.38	15.13	15.97	16.91	17.97	18.55	19.17	5.75
6.00	7.69	8.00	8.33	8.82	9.38	9.84	10.34	10.91	11.54	12.00	12.77	13.33	14.29	15.00	15.79	16.67	17.65	18.75	19.35	20.00	6.00

Source: Wayne Hummer & Co., Chicago, Ill.

from having total debt that exceeds a certain percentage of the assessed valuation of property.

The individual investor is not in any position to make an independent analysis of legality. He must rely on the reputation of the law firm that offers an opinion as to the legality of the issue. Significantly, in the last 50 years no municipal bond issue of any size has been declared invalid because of the bonds being issued without compliance with the state law.

Measures of Ability to Pay

The quality of a municipal bond is dependent on the ability of the governmental unit to pay the debt. Sometimes, analysts refer to an intangible factor called "willingness to pay," but in most cases of default on municipal bonds the governmental officials were unwilling to pay only because the relative ability to pay was impaired.

Debt to Property Ratio. The basic measure of ability to pay indebtedness is a matter of relating the total debt burden to some measure of taxable wealth. One of the conventional measures is the ratio of net tax-supported debt to assessed valuation of the property within the confines of the municipality.

It is necessary for the analyst to make certain adjustments when calculating the debt to property ratio. First, because of the wide differences in assessment practices, the analyst must make an adjustment in the assessed valuation of real property so that it will reflect true value. One local government may assess property at 60 percent of its "true" value, while another may assess property at 90 percent. For example, Bureau of Census data showed that the ratio of assessed values to sales price of nonfarm residential property varied from 5.9 percent in South Carolina to 66.2 percent in Rhode Island.[3] The basis of assessment is usually announced by the governmental officials. When it is not announced, the basis for assessment is available in Dun and Bradstreet's *Municipal Service Reports.*

To calculate total debt, the analyst must add to the direct obligations, including funded debt and floating (unfunded) debt, the debt of political subivisions that overlap or are coterminous with the municipality. This adjustment is necessary because other political subdivisions may have debt outstanding that is supported by revenues from the same sources. For example, an area may have a county government, a city government, and some school districts, all of which may have debt outstanding. If the analyst were appraising the quality of the county's bonds, it would be necessary to include the debt of the city and the school districts as well as the debt of the county in determining the total debt burden of the area. Where political subdivisions partially overlap, the indebtedness can be apportioned on the basis of total population.

The value of the debt to property ratio as a measure of ability to pay is dependent on the nature of the governmental unit's revenue sources. This measure assumes that debt is to be repaid from property taxes. However, in recent years, there has been a shift from property taxes as the primary source of revenue. In 1963, property taxes provided about 30 percent of the revenue of state and local governments. Consequently, it is necessary to use some other supplementary measure of ability to pay when property taxes are a relatively unimportant source of revenue.

---

[3] *Economic Almanac, 1964,* p. 448.

Debt to Area Income Ratio. When property taxes are not the primary source of revenue, state and local governments most often rely on taxes that are directly related to the income of the area. A measure of debt-paying ability in this case would be to relate the debt to the total income of the area—that is, the ratio of tax-supported debt to annual community income. Estimates of individual income receipts for the states are available in the *Survey of Current Business.* Estimates of "effective buying income" are available for smaller areas, such as cities and counties, as well as for states in *Sales Management* magazine's *Annual Survey of Buying Power.*

Ratio of Debt Service Charges to Total Revenues. In municipal bond analysis, the ratio that is roughly analogous to the coverage of fixed charges in industrial bond analysis is the ratio of debt service to total revenues. Debt service includes payments of principal as well as interest. A large municipal debt is not in itself burdensome. It is repayment of the principal component of the debt service that usually causes defaults. Skilled debt management of the maturity dates on outstanding debt can limit the impact of a given amount of debt. The analyst may note that a state or local government may have a concentration of debt maturing in a particular year. In such instances, the likelihood of financial stringency is greatly increased.

Importance of Efficient Fiscal Management

It is fully as important in municipal bond analysis as it is in industrial bond analysis to appraise management quality. The relative efficiency in handling an ever-growing list of municipal functions is difficult to judge. The most practical way to get a general impression of local officials is to read the local newspapers. Scandals and poor administration sometimes receive considerable publicity in the press.

State authorities are a good source of information on local fiscal administration in states that have laws to provide for state supervision of local fiscal practices and accounts. For example, in Indiana the State Board of Accounts conducts periodic audits of local accounts and makes the reports available to the public. Findings of poor fiscal administration and malfeasance are usually reflected in these reports.

Economic Characteristics of the Area

The analyst should investigate the general economic characteristics of the area. This investigation is particularly important when the community is relatively small or is a single-industry city.

Appraisal of the economic characteristics of a community involves an analysis of the types of economic activity that support the community and the effect of cyclical fluctuations on these industries. It is particularly desirable that the community have diversified sources of income, because if the community's economic well-being is primarily dependent on one industry or type of economic activity, the local government's ability to pay indebtedness will tend to fluctuate with the fortunes of that industry. For example, holders of the municipal bonds of the city of Cisco, Texas, suffered a substantial loss, because the city's growth was the direct result of the oil boom in Eastland County, Texas, in 1917. The population of the city tripled from 1910 to 1920. Bonds were sold to finance improvements in the rapidly growing city. The boom collapsed in 1921 with the decline in crude oil prices and depletion of the oil field. The area reverted to its previous rural economy, and defaulted on its bonds in 1934 and again in 1941. Municipal bondholders who purchased the bonds in 1920 and held them until 1955 lost approximately 85 percent of their original investment.[4]

Revenue Bonds

Revenue bonds are used to finance construction of toll roads, bridges, tunnels, waterworks, sewers, electric power plants, and similar projects. They are secured by a pledge of revenues from specific earning assets. As mentioned earlier, this category is limited to bonds in which the issuer agrees to operate the properties and agrees to use the receipts from operations to service the debt, but does not agree to levy taxes or make appropriations from the general fund if the pledged revenues prove insufficient.

There has been a significant increase in the amount of revenue-secured bonds outstanding in recent years. More than 30 percent of the total municipal bonds sold in the last five years have been revenue-secured bonds. The revenue bonds comprised an estimated 10 percent of all municipal bonds outstanding in 1948; the amount increased to about 25 percent in 1958 and about 35 percent in 1964.[5] The reasons for increased volume are: (1) the increasing expenditures for local

---

[4] E. H. Davis, *Of The People, By The People, For the People, An Informal Analysis of Public Bonds* (Chicago: John H. Nuveen & Co., 1958), pp. 31–32.

[5] *Moody's Municipal and Government Manual, 1965*, p. 18.

public works, due to increased demands for public services, and the increase in population; (2) the fact that revenue bonds are not subject to statutory debt limitations.

Analysis of Revenue Bonds. Revenue bonds issued by various authorities require an analysis somewhat different from the analysis of general obligations, since they are usually not a liability of the municipality but are secured solely by the revenues pledged against them. Here, the problem is the same, in essence, as analyzing an analogous private enterprise. Although a municipal enterprise sometimes enjoys a position of at least partial monopoly, indirect competition with alternative services or commodities can sometimes impose rigorous limits on earning power. For example, privately owned buses and automobiles may so injure the competitive position of a municipally owned trolley system that earnings may disappear. Any attempt to assure a profit by raising trolley fares might actually reduce revenues still further by driving customers to competing forms of transportation.

An example of analysis of an electric utility revenue bond issue is shown in Table 19–3. It is obvious that the measures and tools of analysis are quite similar to those used in the analysis of private utilities.

Limited Analogy to Analysis of Industrials. The safety of a revenue bond obviously depends on the adequacy of revenues from the earning assets. This test is similar to that used for an industrial bond, but the analogy is not perfect. First, coverage of a revenue bond will be computed on the basis of combined interest requirements and principal payments (sinking-fund payments, serial maturities, etc.). Second, the analyst may conclude that a revenue bond is safe even though debt service is being covered by a narrow margin. This may be true, for example, for the bonds of a publicly owned electric utility being operated to provide the lowest rates rather than profits. In such a case, the analyst must decide whether additional revenue could be obtained by raising rates. Higher prices will not always increase revenues, however, as is shown by the history of local traction enterprises.

In the case of revenue bonds already outstanding, the investor may utilize the historical record to estimate coverage. In analyzing new issues, however, the project may not yet be constructed and the investor will be forced to rely on an estimate of future earning power published by a firm of engineers. The reputation of this firm will be a matter of importance. But more than this is involved. Even if a firm

TABLE 19–3

P.U.D. No. 1 of Snohomish County
Comparative Balance Sheet, December 31

ASSETS	($000,000) 1949	1957
Utility plant (at cost)	$16.8	$27.4
Bond fund	.8	.8
Special funds (including construction)	1.3	.0
Current assets	1.2	2.0
Other assets	.0	.1
Deferred debits	.9	.3
Total Assets	$20.7	$30.6

LIABILITIES	($000,000) 1949	1957
Total bonds and notes	$19.6	$16.4
Current liabilities	.8	.9
Reserve for depreciation and amortization	.1	1.7
Surplus	.1	11.5
Total Liabilities	$20.7	$30.6

RATIOS	1949	1957
Depreciation reserve to total utility plant	.6%	6.2%
Current assets to current liabilities	150.0	222.0
Total bonds and notes to total utility plant	116.7	59.9
Operating revenues to total plant	20.2	29.7
Net income to total plant	4.6	8.6

Comparative Operating Data, Years Ended December 31

	1950*	1951	1952	1953	1954	1955	1956	1957	Total Cash Pro-duction
Number of customers, end of year	41,451	42,336	44,129	46,162	48,650	51,851	53,409	54,589	
Kilowatt-hour sales to average domestic customer (kwh)	3,857	4,344	4,837	5,253	6,031	7,036	7,746	8,329	
Average cost per kwh to domestic customers	1.41c	1.36c	1.31c	1.28c	1.22c	1.14c	1.09c	1.08c	
					(Add $000)				
Total revenues†	$3,959	$4,350	$4,854	$5,299	$6,057	$6,880	$7,726	$8,186	
Operating expense and maintenance	1,912	2,046	2,190	2,430	2,732	3,234	3,635	4,017	
Taxes	220	242	279	303	334	395	437	487	
Total	$2,132	$2,288	$2,469	$2,733	$3,076	$3,629	$4,072	$4,504	
Net revenues	$1,827	$2,062	$2,385	$2,566	$2,981	$3,251	$3,555	$3,681	
Depreciation charges	420	420	516	516	564	823	903	943	$ 5,105
Balance	$1,407	$1,642	$1,869	$2,050	$2,417	$2,428	$2,652	$2,730	
Fixed charges	637	637	637	632	556	415	401	381	‡176
Net income	$ 769	$1,005	$1,232	$1,418	$1,861	$2,013	$2,251	$2,357	$12,906
									$18,187

* First year of operation.
† Includes nominal other income.
‡ Debt Discount.

Source: E. H. Davis, *Of the People, By the People, For the People* (Chicago: John H. Nuveen & Co., 1958), p. 112. Reproduced by permission.

is capable, the reliability of an estimate of future earnings will vary with the nature of the project.

The investor may well choose to question any estimate of future earnings when it is obvious that a dependable forecast is extremely difficult. An estimate of future earnings of an electric utility might be quite dependable; one concerning a proposed convention hall might be highly tentative. Possible competition must be given due weight. A toll road or a bridge will be subject to competition, for example, and the investor must determine that the project is soundly conceived. Another factor of major importance is whether the city proposes to have an equity in the project or to finance the total costs by a bond issue.

Defaults on revenue bonds are usually the result of factors quite similar to defaults on industrial bonds. These factors include overestimates of revenues, underestimates of construction costs of the project, and poor management. A recent example of default is the $133 million West Virginia Turnpike Revenue Bond issue. This issue defaulted on payment of interest in 1958. The revenues have never covered more than 60 percent of the bond interest. On December 31, 1964, the West Virginia Turnpike Commission was $13,778,000 in arrears on interest payments on the bond issue. The default was a direct result of the two factors mentioned previously. The revenue estimate was too high and the project costs were underestimated.

Terms of the Issue. The indenture should provide for a segregation of revenues from other municipal funds, and for the proper allocation of these revenues so that the properties are maintained well and operating expenses are paid. Maintenance is important because if the investors ever need to take possession of the property, they will not want to be faced with the necessity of providing money for rehabilitation. The indenture should also provide for the segregation and application of revenues to meet the debt service, including a debt service reserve and an operating reserve, and for the payment of all surplus revenues into a surplus fund to be applied to specific lawful purposes or for accelerated debt retirement.

Sometimes, the indenture will have provisions that may make a particular revenue bond more attractive to the investor. For example, the city or state may agree to pay out of general funds the expense of maintaining a bridge or a highway. This will assure that virtually no operating expenses of the project need be covered by revenues from tolls.

The life of an issue of revenue bonds should be well within the life expectancy of the property it finances. The investor should also expect periodic retirement of portions of the debt by serial maturities or sinking funds. For projects with a stable earning power, sinking-fund provisions should call for fixed periodic payments. For projects with a more cyclical earnings characteristic, only a portion of the sinking fund need be fixed with an additional amount contingent on earnings.

Management. Management is an important factor to consider in choosing revenue bonds. Some indentures provide for a separate agency or authority to operate the property. The Port of New York Authority is a well-known agency of this sort. The advantage of having a project managed by a special agency is obvious, but the investor should also investigate the character of the municipal government that has ultimate control power. It may be difficult, at best, for any management to resist the demands of a hostile administration. It is also of some comfort to the investor if he can find a provision to the effect that the government may not interfere with the discretion of the separate agency in the matter of fixing rates, or a provision that requires that rates be fixed to provide adequate revenues to cover maintenance, operations, and debt service.

Other Types of Municipals

There are a great many other types of municipal obligations, but a specific enumeration does not seem to be desirable because they arise out of the great variety of combinations of the following factors from which a bond may take its name: (1) the purpose of the issue; (2) the local government unit that issues the bond; (3) the pledge, or failure to pledge, full faith and credit; and (4) the pledge of specific revenues.

One other type of municipal obligation may be worth mentioning. Special assessment obligations are issued to finance improvements such as streets, sewers, and sidewalks. These improvements, which presumably raise the value of adjacent private property, generally involve a special assessment on the property owners. Special assessment bonds provide that the proceeds from the tax will be earmarked for service of the debt.

U.S. GOVERNMENT SECURITIES

The investor in U.S. government bonds does not normally think in terms of risk assumption. It is true that these securities are considered to be practically devoid of financial risk. However, some government bond issues fluctuate in price in sympathy with the general level of interest rates, and the investor is exposed to the interest rate risk. The U.S. government debt may be classified as marketable obligations and nonmarketable obligations. Most of the debt is in marketable obligations, but the Treasury in the last 20 years has succeeded in selling a substantial portion of nonmarketable debt.

The U.S. government had outstanding in July, 1965, $316 billion in direct obligations. Of this amount, more than $209 billion was in marketable issues, $50 billion in nonmarketable issues (see Table 19–5), and the balance in special issues—bonds issued by the Treasury for special government trust and agency account funds. These special issues are not available to the public; therefore, they will not be discussed.

Marketable Direct Obligations

There are four different types of marketable government securities. The distinguishing characteristic of each issue is the length of time to maturity. There are some other differences in these issues, such as differences in method of paying interest, their eligibility for commercial bank investment, and tax status. Marketable direct obligations are (1) bills, (2) certificates of indebtedness, (3) notes, and (4) bonds.

Treasury Bills. Treasury bills are offered on a regular weekly basis. They are offered on a discount basis and are noninterest bearing—that is, investors derive their income from the difference between the purchase price and the maturity value. Treasury bills were generally issued with a maturity of 90 to 92 days until December, 1958. Since 1958, bills also have been issued with a maturity of six months. In addition, tax anticipation bills are issued to provide corporations with a vehicle for investing funds set aside for payment of income taxes. Most of the Treasury bills are purchased by commercial banks and by corporations that invest idle funds for short periods.

Certificates of Indebtedness. Treasury certificates are also short-term obligations with maturities of less than one year. In recent years, most of the regular issues have had maturities of 11 to 12 months. The Treasury has also sold some tax anticipation certificates that have had varying maturity dates, depending on the length of time from the date of issue until the next income tax payment date. How-

TABLE 19-4

**Marketable Government Securities
June 30, 1965
(Millions of Dollars)**

Issue	Amount
Treasury bills	$ 53,665
Certificates of indebtedness	...
Treasury notes	52,549
Treasury bonds	102,481
Total marketable securities	$208,695

Source: *U.S. Treasury Bulletin*, July, 1965.

ever, in 1965, the Treasury stopped selling certificates. (See Table 19-4.)

The basic difference between a Treasury bill and a certificate is the method of paying interest. Certificates were sold at face or par value, and interest was paid either with or without coupons. The last issues of certificates had coupons attached. These certificates were marketable and tended to fluctuate more in value because of the longer maturities.

Treasury Notes. Treasury notes have maturities ranging from one to five years and are interest-bearing securities sold at face value. They fill the gap in Treasury financing operations between the short-term bills and certificates and the longer-term Treasury bonds. Commercial banks and other financial institutions buy most of these notes. They enable the financial institutions to stagger the maturities of their investments to meet possible requirements for funds.

Treasury Bonds. Treasury bonds are issued in varying maturities in excess of five years. The length of time to maturity of these bonds depends on the conditions of the money market at that particular time. In recent years, bonds have been sold with maturities as short as six years and as long as forty years. These bonds are available either in coupon or registered form. The income from Treasury bonds is fully taxable. In recent years, the Treasury has included in some issues of government bonds a provision that states when the issue is part of an estate, the bonds are redeemable at par plus accrued interest to pay federal estate taxes.

Treasury bonds sometimes have a call date as well as a maturity date. For example, a Treasury bond may be described as 2½-1964-69. This description means that the issue pays 2½ percent interest on the face value, is callable at the option of the Treasury in 1964, and matures in 1969. The Treasury exercises the call option if the general level of interest rates is below the coupon rate. It will let the bond run to maturity if the general level of interest rates is above the coupon rate. The issue mentioned above—$2\frac{1}{2}$ of 1964–69—was callable in June, 1964, but the Treasury took no action; consequently, they probably will run to maturity or until they are called.

Nonmarketable Securities

The two types of nonmarketable government securities are savings bonds and some special issues not available to the public, such as depositary bonds and the investment series of Treasury bonds. The special nonmarketable securities currently being issued are depositary bonds, issued to designated depositaries and financial agents of the Treasury, and certain special issues, issued directly to various government agencies and trust funds. Since these securities are not available to private investors, our discussion will be confined to nonmarketable savings bonds.

Savings Bonds. Two different series of U.S. savings bonds are available to investors, Series E and Series H. These bonds are nonmarketable obligations issued to investors other than commercial banks. The bonds are described in detail on pp. 51–54.

TABLE 19–5

Nonmarketable Government Securities
June 30, 1965
(Millions of Dollars)

Issue	Amount
Savings bonds	$ 50,043
Treasury bonds, investment series	3,256
Depositary bonds	59
Other	2,410
Special issues	48,650
Total nonmarketable securities	$104,418

Source: *U.S. Treasury Bulletin*, July, 1965.

Bonds of Government Corporations and Agencies

A relatively small amount of bonds outstanding are obligations of government corporations and agencies and the International Bank for Reconstruction and Development. Amounts outstanding are shown in Table 19–6.

TABLE 19–6

Securities of United States Government Agencies
June 30, 1965
(Millions of Dollars)

Issuer	Amount
Banks for Cooperatives	$ 686
Federal Home Loan Banks	4,757
Federal Intermediate Credit Banks	2,462
Federal Land Banks	3,532
Federal National Mortgage Association	1,797
Tennessee Valley Authority	225
Total	$13,459

Source: Federal Reserve Bank of St. Louis.

Only the bonds of the Federal Housing Administration are fully guaranteed by the United States government. Bonds of the International Bank are, in effect, guaranteed, because the bank can call on the United States to the extent of $5.7 billion to meet its obligations. The bonds of the remaining agencies are not guaranteed. However, the U.S. government probably would come to the rescue of any issue that encountered difficulty, because these agencies are intimately related to governmental functions and are subject to public supervision. The market makes some distinctions, however, between direct government obligations and obligations of government agencies, as shown by the following comparisons of yields.

Issue	Yield to Maturity
Federal Land Bank 4⅜'s 4/10/69	4.37
Treasury 4's 10/1/69	4.30
Federal National Mortgage Association 4½'s 1977	4.50
Treasury notes 4's 1980	4.27

The yield comparisons are shown for both long and short maturities, as of October 19, 1965.

Risks of Government Securities

As mentioned before, all direct obligations are practically devoid of financial risk. There has never been a default on the interest or principal of a U.S. government obligation, and there is no prospect that there ever will be. Government obligations, like all fixed-income securities, are subject to the interest rate risk. The almost complete absence of financial risk makes U.S. government securities especially sensitive to changes in the general level of interest rates. These changes in interest rates, as mentioned before, tend to cause the prices of government bonds to fluctuate.

The analyst of government bonds is primarily concerned with the factors that influence the supply and demand for money and, in turn, interest rates. The supply of funds is influenced by the rate of savings, and the demand is affected by the businessman's prospects for the productive employment of these funds. Often, actions of the Board of Governors of the Federal Reserve System and the debt management policies of the Treasury tip the balance between scarcity and plenty in the credit and capital funds markets. It is not feasible to describe and discuss all the Federal Reserve actions that may affect the prices of government bonds. However, the material in Figure 19-2 shows the prices of two representative treasury bond issues and the yields on Treasury bills for the years 1962 and 1963 and the first quarter of 1964, with Federal Reserve actions and Treasury offerings during this period. The effect of Federal Reserve actions on government bond prices is rather obvious after examining this illustration.[6] For example, the Federal Reserve began credit-easing actions in March, 1962, in the form of open-market operations, lowering the rediscount rate, and reducing reserve requirements. These actions are described in step 3 in Table 19-7.

FOREIGN SECURITIES

In recent years, considerable attention has been given to investment in foreign securities. The 1960 political campaign stimulated interest in foreign investment when U.S. economic growth became a campaign issue. Democrats stimulated interest in foreign companies by comparing the growth rates of European economies with the growth rate of the U.S. economy.[7]

The American investor interested in foreign investment faces some problems. First, financial information available on foreign companies is limited. These companies are not required by their governments to report to stockholders in the full and complete way to which the

---

[6] For a discussion of the money market and Federal Reserve policy, see Carl A. Dauten and Merle T. Welshans, *Principles of Finance* (2d ed.; Cincinnati: Southwestern Publishing Co., 1958), chaps. 26, 27, 28, 29, and 30.

[7] Gerald Krefitz and Ruth Morossi, *Investing Abroad, A Guide to Financial Europe* (New York: Harper & Row, 1965), p. 5.

FIGURE 19-2

Principal Credit Policy Actions of the Federal Reserve System and Treasury Offerings of New Securities (Except Bills) Prices of 3½'s February, 1990, Yields on Treasury Bills, Discount Rate, Net Reserves* and Index of Production (Range of closing bid prices)

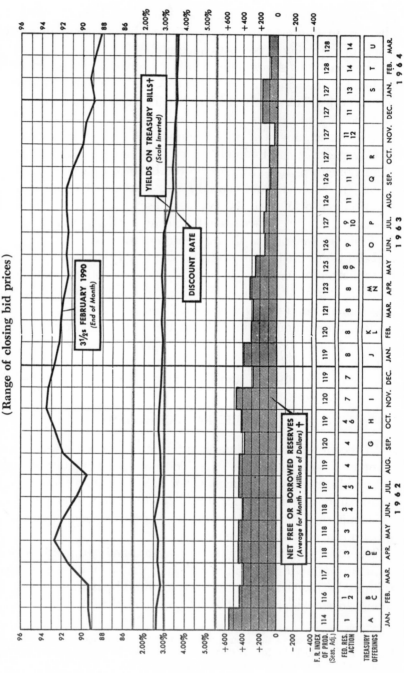

* Member banks' excess reserves less borrowings. † Average bid for new 3-month issue, end of month.

American investor is accustomed.[8] In some countries, it is the practice to report earnings equal to the dividend payout. Messages from management on company prospects and products are rare. As a consequence, it is difficult to analyze these companies' securities as prospective investments.

Political Stability and Government Regulation

In foreign investments one must always be concerned with government attitude toward foreign investment and investors in the country with which he is dealing. The attitudes range from Sweden's virtual prohibition to Canada's active encouragement of foreign investment.

In addition, there is often a tendency for foreign governments to change their attitudes toward foreign investment if it becomes a

TABLE 19-7

Federal Reserve Action

1. January–February, 1962—Reduced system holdings by about $500 million.
2. February, 1962—Authorized transactions in foreign securities.
3. March–June, 1962—Increased system holdings by about $1.3 billion.
4. June–October, 1962—Increased system holdings by about $200 million.
5. July, 1962—Reduced margin requirements from 70 to 50 percent.
6. October, 1962—Reduced reserve requirements against time deposits from 5 to 4 percent.
7. October–December, 1962—Increased system holdings by about $1.0 billion.
8. January–May, 1963—Reduced, then increased system holdings by net of about $470 million.
9. May–July, 1963—Increased system holdings by nearly $1.2 billion.
10. July, 1963—Raised the discount rate from 3 to 3½ percent. Raised maximum rates payable on time deposits to 3½ and 4 percent.
11. July–December, 1963—Increased system holdings by about $1.1 billion.
12. November, 1963—Raised margin requirements from 50 to 70 percent.
13. January, 1964—Reduced system holdings by about $860 million.
14. February–March, 1964—Increased system holdings by about $630 million.

---

[8] Adolph E. Grunewald, "West German Investments," *Financial Analysts Journal,* Vol. XVI, No. 5 (September–October, 1960), p. 37.

406   *Investment Analysis and Management*

Treasury Offerings*

	Books opened	Issued	Term	Issue	Due
A.	Jan. 15, 1962	Oct. 1, 1957	7 yr. 8½ mo.	4% Bond	Oct. 1, 1969
B.	Feb. 5, 1962	Feb. 15, 1962	1 yr.	3½% Ctf.	Feb. 15, 1963
	Feb. 5, 1962	Feb. 15, 1962	4 yr. 6 mo.	4% Note	Aug. 15, 1960
C.	Feb. 19, 1962	Mar. 1, 1962	9 yr. 5½ mo.	4% Bond	Aug. 15, 1971
	Feb. 19, 1962	Jan. 23, 1959	17 yr. 11½ mo.	4% Bond	Feb. 15, 1980
	Feb. 19, 1962	Feb. 14, 1958	27 yr. 11½ mo.	3½% Bond	Feb. 15, 1990
	Feb. 19, 1962	Oct. 3, 1960	36 yr. 8½ mo.	3½% Bond	Nov. 15, 1998
D.	Apr. 9, 1962	Apr. 18, 1962	6 yr. 4 mo.	3¾% Bond	Aug. 15, 1968
E.	Apr. 30, 1962	May 15, 1962	1 yr.	3¼% Ctf.	May 15, 1963
	Apr. 30, 1962	May 15, 1962	3 yr. 9 mo.	3⅝% Note	Feb. 15, 1966
	Apr. 30, 1962	May 15, 1962	9 yr. 6 mo.	3⅞% Bond	Nov. 15, 1971
F.	July 30, 1962	Aug. 15, 1962	1 yr.	3½% Ctf.	Aug. 15, 1963
	July 30, 1962	Aug. 15, 1962	6 yr. 6 mo.	4% Bond	Feb. 15, 1969
	July 30, 1962	Aug. 15, 1962	30 yr.	4¼% Bond	Aug. 15, 1987–92
G.	Sept. 10, 1962	Sept. 15, 1962	4 yr. 11 mo.	3¾% Note	Aug. 15, 1967
	Sept. 10, 1962	Sept. 15, 1962	9 yr. 11 mo.	4% Bond	Aug. 15, 1972
H.	Oct. 29, 1962	Nov. 15, 1962	1 yr.	3⅛% Ctf.	Nov. 15, 1963
	Oct. 29, 1962	Nov. 15, 1962	3 yr.	3½% Note	Nov. 15, 1965
	Oct. 29, 1962	Nov. 15, 1962	9 yr. 3 mo.	4% Bond	Feb. 15, 1972
I.	Nov. 19, 1962	May 15, 1962	8 yr. 11 mo.	3⅞% Bond	Nov. 15, 1971
	Nov. 19, 1962	Jan. 23, 1959	17 yr. 2 mo.	4% Bond	Feb. 15, 1980
J.	Jan. 8, 1963	Jan. 17, 1963	30 yr. 1 mo.	4% Bond	Feb. 15, 1988–93
K.	Feb. 4, 1963	Feb. 15, 1963	1 yr.	3¼% Ctf.	Feb. 15, 1964
	Feb. 4, 1963	Apr. 18, 1962	5 yr. 6 mo.	3¾% Bond	Aug. 15, 1968
L.	Feb. 25, 1963	Mar. 15, 1963	3 yr. 11 mo.	3⅝% Note	Feb. 15, 1967
	Feb. 25, 1963	May 15, 1962	8 yr. 8 mo.	3⅞% Bond	Nov. 15, 1971
	Feb. 25, 1963	Dec. 2, 1957	11 yr. 8 mo.	3⅞% Bond	Nov. 15, 1974
	Feb. 25, 1963	Jan. 23, 1959	16 yr. 11 mo.	4% Bond	Feb. 15, 1980
M.	Apr. 9, 1963	Apr. 18, 1963	31 yr. 1 mo.	4⅛% Bond	May 15, 1989–94
N.	Apr. 29, 1963	May 15, 1963	1 yr.	3¼% Ctf.	May 15, 1964
	Apr. 29, 1963	May 15, 1962	2 yr. 9 mo.	3⅝% Note	Feb. 15, 1966
O.	June 11, 1963	June 20, 1963	7 yr. 2 mo·	4% Bond	Aug. 15, 1970
P.	July 29, 1963	Aug. 15, 1963	1 yr. 3 mo.	3¾% Note	Nov. 15, 1964
Q.	Sept. 9, 1963	Sept. 15, 1963	5 yr. 2 mo.	3⅞% Bond	Nov. 15, 1968
	Sept. 9, 1963	Sept. 15, 1963	9 yr. 11 mo.	4% Bond	Aug. 15, 1973
	Sept. 9, 1963	Apr. 18, 1963	30 yr. 8. mo.	4⅛% Bond	May 15, 1989–94
R.	Oct. 28, 1963	Nov. 15, 1963	1 yr. 6 mo.	3⅞% Note	May 15, 1965
S.	Jan. 13, 1964	June 20, 1963	6 yr. 7 mo.	4% Bond	Aug. 15, 1970
	Jan. 13, 1964	Apr. 5, 1960	21 yr. 4 mo.	4¼% Bond	May 15, 1975–85
T.	Feb. 3, 1964	Feb. 15, 1964	1 yr. 6 mo.	3⅞% Note	Aug. 13, 1965
	Feb. 3, 1964	Feb. 15, 1962	2 yr. 6 mo.	4% Note	Aug. 15, 1966
U.	Mar. 31, 1964	Feb. 15, 1964	1 yr. 4½ mo.	3⅞% Note	Aug. 13, 1965

* Not including 5-year 1½ percent notes issued in exchange for 2¾'s 1975–80.
   Source: *Securities of the United States Government* (21st ed.; Boston, Mass.: First Boston Corporation, 1964). Reproduced by permission.

dominant factor in the economy. For example, a sizable U.S. investment in a country may lead to charges of imperialism and colonialism, and a campaign promise to expropriate American assets.

Transfer Problems

The prospective investor in foreign securities should be aware of the hazards in direct purchase of foreign securities. The typical equity instrument in most European countries is the *bearer share*.[9] Bearer shares have coupons that must be clipped and sent to the corporate home office in order to receive dividends. The investor is paid his dividend in foreign currency, which then must be converted into dollars. This process is a rather involved and often tricky one. Furthermore, the investor may have to send his shares to the foreign country if he wishes to sell them, unless someone has made market in them in this country.

To eliminate these rather involved dividend collections and stock transfer problems, in 1927 the Guaranty Trust Company of New York developed American Depository Receipts, or ADR's.[10] This device eliminates most of the transfer and related problems that the investor faces.

The ADR is a certificate that is evidence that there is on deposit with a leading domestic international bank a specified number of shares of bearer stock. The ADR is then bought and sold like any other domestic security. Holders of ADR's are kept posted on company developments, financial position, and related matters by the issuer of the ADR's. In addition, the bank issuer will collect the dividends, convert them into dollars, and pass them on to holders of the ADR's.

These receipts are a valuable tool to the U.S. investor, but will limit the range of his foreign investment. It is estimated that only about 200 companies have ADR's outstanding, which is just a fraction of the number of foreign companies. For example, over 10,000 companies are listed on the London Stock Exchange alone.[11] However, it would not seem to be advisable for an investor to venture into foreign security markets without considerable study.

REVIEW QUESTIONS AND PROBLEMS

1. What are the basic classifications of municipal bonds? What is the major difference between them?

---

[9] Krefitz, *op. cit.*, p. 285.
[10] *Ibid.*, p. 286.
[11] *Ibid.*, p. 289.

2. Would an investor in the 70 percent marginal income tax bracket have a better after-tax yield from a 9 percent corporate bond than a 3 percent municipal bond?

3. Why is there a limited market for many municipal bond issues?

4. What are the major considerations in evaluating the investment quality of municipal bonds?

5. What are the relative merits of the debt to property and debt to area income ratios?

6. In what respects is the analysis of revenue bonds comparable to industrial bond analysis?

7. Discuss the noneconomic considerations that should be evaluated in revenue bond analysis.

8. What is the primary difference between a special assessment bond and a revenue bond?

9. What are the different types of marketable U.S. Government securities? In what major respects do they differ?

10. Why do Federal Land Bank bonds consistently sell to yield a higher return than Federal Housing Administration bonds?

11. "U.S. Government bonds are virtually a riskless investment. They cannot decline in price and the money is always available to the investor after the investor has held them for a short time." What type of government bonds did the writer have reference to? What are the risks associated with the ownership of government bonds?

12. What are the major considerations when analyzing and evaluating foreign securities?

13. Discuss the possible Federal Reserve and U.S. Treasury actions which might influence marketable U.S. Government bond prices.

CHAPTER **20**

The Problem of Timing Investments

Investment management involves three phases, or steps: determine what you need, what to buy, and when to buy it. Earlier, we discussed the determination of investment needs or policy and investment selection. In this chapter, we will discuss approaches to investment timing, or when to buy. Investment management must be a more or less continuous process. That timing is discussed as a separate problem in investment management suggests that there is a proper time to make an investment in any security.

The timing problem is usually associated with common stock investments, because the prices of common stocks tend to fluctuate much more than the prices of bonds. Therefore, the timing problem in common stock investment is usually a more serious one than it is in bond investment. However, it is apparent from the discussion of investment risks in Chapter 3 that the bond investor is also faced with a timing problem, because the general level of interest rates tends to affect bond prices and makes one time more propitious than another to purchase bonds. Attention here, however, will be concentrated on common stock investment, because the amplitude and frequency of fluctuations in common stock prices are far greater and of more significance to the average investor than are fluctuations in bond prices.

Obviously, the best time to buy any security is when the price is low, and the best time to sell it is when the price is high. However, in a dynamic economy the determination of when these times occur is the very nature of the problem to be discussed. Sometimes, investors ignore the whole problem of timing if commitments are made as long-term holdings. The investor determines through security analysis that the particular security is a good investment at its present price. If he plans to hold the security for a long period of time, he feels that future price levels for common stocks as a whole are not of particular significance to him. His analysis of the security will tend to show him that this particular investment is a reasonable value at its present price. If at a later date he plans to sell the security, it will be subjected to further analysis to determine whether or not the price at that time is justified.

This intrinsic value approach suggests that a particular security is a good buy or good value at any point in time. That is, the price of a specific security in relation to its intrinsic value is of the essence in determining whether or not a security is a good buy. The time of purchase may be when the general level of stock prices is relatively high. Even though the security is a good buy at present prices, timing analysis may enable the investor to realize additional gains from cyclical price appreciation. Therefore, to maximize gains the analyst should use one of the approaches to timing in determining the best time to buy the security.

However, the investor, as contrasted with the speculator or trader, places emphasis on the relationship of value to present price and casts the timing problem in a secondary role. The trader or speculator, on the other hand, is only incidentally concerned with the intrinsic value of the security, and then usually only with a rather superficial analysis of the security. He places primary emphasis on timing and short-term stock price changes.

APPROACHES TO PROBLEM OF TIMING

There are three approaches to the problem of timing: (1) forecasting and the use of major economic trends, (2) the use of technical stock market analysis, and (3) the use of formula plans.

The timing of common stock purchases, using as a basis the forecasting of major economic trends and changes in business conditions, assumes that there is a definite relationship between stock market prices and the general level of business conditions. It further assumes that major economic trends can be predicted with some degree of success. Predictions of future economic conditions are difficult and require an excellent background in basic economics, as well as an understanding and knowledge of monetary theory and the banking system.

Technical market analysis when used as a basis for timing common stock purchases assumes that the best indicator of changes in economic conditions and stock market prices is the stock prices themselves. The technical market analyst studies the pattern of present prices of particular stocks and the general level of stock market prices and uses these patterns as a basis for predicting what the prices of common stocks will be in the future.

The formula plan user decides that common stock prices cannot be predicted with any degree of accuracy or that he does not want to put in the time necessary to predict them, because formula planning is not a timing device. It is a technique that may be used to avoid the timing problem. It is a mechanistic approach to solving the timing problem by simply predetermining the amount of common stocks to be bought or sold at particular times without regard to the present or future level of securities prices. Formula planning is predicated on the idea that the average investor is swept up in a tide of emotion when he attempts to use either of the other two approaches. This device forces action when stock prices, as indicated by a recognized index, attain various levels in both up and down cyclical price movements. The investor does not have the opportunity to reap the gains possible if he timed his commitments by attempting either to forecast major economic trends or to determine the future level of stock prices by technical market analysis. Conversely, he would conceivably suffer losses if he used the other two techniques. The various formula-planning techniques and examples of formula plans will be discussed in more detail later in this chapter.

FORECASTING MAJOR ECONOMIC TRENDS

The investor who wants to time his stock purchases by forecasting business conditions has an initial problem of developing or finding suitable forecasts. He may wish, if he has suitable education and experience, to develop his own forecasts. The investor may make use of published forecasts, which may be free forecasts provided by various financial services and financial institutions throughout the country. Of course, these published forecasts have the disadvantage of being common knowledge, and are often too late for the investor to gain any timing advantage. Economic forecasts made by forecasting services are available to the investor on a subscription basis. These forecasts are generally more timely and complete than the published forecasts. However, the most satisfactory arrangement is for the investor to do his own forecasting if possible.

The techniques of forecasting and the causes of cyclical fluctuations in business conditions are too complex for exhaustive treatment here. If the investor wants to acquire a knowledge of forecasting in order to make his own forecasts of major economic trends, he should take courses in economics, particularly money and banking, and forecasting techniques.

Use of Business Indicators in Forecasting

The study of economics and forecasting techniques will undoubtedly provide the investor with a knowledge of time series of various types of economic data that may serve as indicators or business barometers. The investor should examine and study the National Bureau of Economic Research publications on the nature of business cycles and business indicators, described below.

Some years ago, the National Bureau of Economic Research made a study of various time series of economic data to determine whether or not any one of the many series of economic data published monthly and quarterly indicated when the general level of economic activity was going to pass from one phase of the cycle to another, i.e., recession to recovery. After completing a monumental study of over five hundred different series of data, the NBER determined that certain series of data or indicators "lead" the upturn in business activity, others are "coincident" to it, and still others "lag" behind the changes. The leading business indicators give notice that the direction of business activity is going to change, the coincident business indicators suggest that the turning point has been reached, and the lagging series confirm the new phase of the cycle.[1]

A recent National Bureau of Economic Research study indicates that there are 26 indicators. There are 12 leading, 9 coincident, and 5 lagging indicators. These series are classified in Table 20–1. Each series of indicators has some common characteristics. The leading indicators are economic time series that relate to the future, such as new orders, construction contracts, and hiring rates. The coincident indicators are measures of what is currently happening in the economy. The lagging indicators, on the other hand, do not have any such common characteristics, except that they represent either decisions

---

[1] Henry M. Platt, *Economic Indicators* (Hanover, N.H.: Dartmouth College, Amos Tuck School of Business Administration, under a grant from the Alfred P. Sloan Foundation).

TABLE 20-1

Statistical Business Indicators

Leaders	Coincident	Lagging
Average workweek, manufacturing	Employees in nonagricultural establishments, number of	Business expenditures on new plant and equipment, total
Accession rate, manufacturing	Unemployment rate	Wage and salary cost per unit of output, total manufacturing
Layoff rate, manufacturing	Index of industrial production	Manufacturing inventories, book value
New orders, value manufacturers durable goods	Gross national product in 1954 dollars	Consumer installment debt
Commercial and industrial construction contracts, floor space	Bank debits outside New York City, 343 centers	Bank rates on short-term business loans, 19 cities
Private permanent nonfarm housing starts	Personal income	
Net changes in business population, operating businesses	Sales of retail stores	
Current liabilities of business failures	Index of whole prices, all commodities other than farm products and foods	
Corporate profits after taxes	Gross national product in current dollars	
Index of prices of 500 common stocks, Standard and Poor's		
Change in business inventories, farm and nonfarm, after valuation adjustment		
Index of industrial materials prices		

Source: Julius Shishkin, *Signals of Recession and Recovery* (NBER Occasional Paper No. 77, 1961), pp. 18–22.

or actions taken late in the cycle or "reflect processes of accumulation or liquidation," such as manufacturing inventories and consumer installment debt.[2]

Of course, there are additional meaningful business cycle time series that the serious student may wish to study. Shishkin suggests that one use 25 series to supplement the 26 suggested by the NBER.[3] However, the investor would have difficulty in comprehending 97 different time series with business cycle significance that are published monthly by the U.S. Department of Commerce in *Business*

---

[2] Julius Shishkin, *Signals of Recession and Recovery* (National Bureau of Economic Research Occasional Paper No. 77, 1961), pp. 4–5.

[3] *Ibid.*, p. 25.

Cycle Developments. From this group, the investor should select the measures that are meaningful and useful to him.

Selection of indicators and their use are always dependent on good judgment. It is necessary for the investor to acquire what forecasters would call a feel for the various materials available for forecasting. The use of selected business indicators has some advantages in this respect in that the forecasters, or investor, who does not have a large staff or time to engage in exhaustive studies of the data available is able to make his own forecasts. This feel for the material may represent the subconscious distillation of the lessons of many years of past experience. It is not necessary that one have this experience, because it is possible for the investor to be astute enough in the process of acquiring valuable experience to grasp the significance of various indicators and their relationship to the total economic picture.

Eight leading indicators along with eight coincident indicators that might be used in attempts to forecast the level of business activity and stock prices are shown in Table 20–2. One of the prerequisites to their use is that they be used as a group in attempts to make forecasts, because no one indicator invariably reaches its turning point in precisely the same manner as it did in the past.

Limitations of Data

For the investor, the use of economic indicators in forecasting changes in stock market prices has some limitations. One limitation is the time lag in reporting some statistics. This limitation is not so serious as it once was, because most of the indicators are now reported monthly in *Business Cycle Developments.*[4] Publication of these indicators is scheduled around the twenty-second of the month following the month of the data. The only time lag now is because some of the important indicators are available only on a quarterly basis.

A more serious problem is that one significant leading indicator is industrial stock prices. Therefore, it is necessary to select indicators that tend to reflect changes in the cycle before industrial stock prices. It is evident from examination of selected indicators (Table 20–2) over the last three cycles that no indicator leads industrial stock prices with sufficient consistency to be used for stock price forecasting.

---

[4] *Business Cycle Developments Monthly,* U.S. Department of Commerce, Bureau of Census.

TABLE 20-2

**Selected National Bureau of Economic Research Business Indicators,
Leads (−) and Lags (+) in Months of Peaks and Troughs of
Three Recent Recessions**

	1953–54		1957–58		1960–61	
	Peak July, 1953	*Trough August, 1954*	*Peak July, 1957*	*Trough April, 1958*	*Peak May, 1960*	*Trough February, 1961*
Eight Leading Indicators						
Average workweek of production workers, manufacturing	−9	−3	−20	0	−12	−2
Construction contracts awarded for commercial and industrial buildings	✽	✽	−16	+2	✽	✽
Number of new business incorporations	✽	✽	−17	−5	−12	−1
Price per unit of labor, cost index	−30	−8	−21	0	−12	0
Index of stock prices, 500 stocks	−6	−11	−12	−4	−10	−4
Index of industrial material prices	−29	−6	−19	0	−6	−2
Value of manufacturers' new orders, machinery and equipment industries	−29	−7	−8	−2	−5	−3
Index of new private housing units, building permits issued	N.A.	N.A.	−29	−2	−18	−2
Eight Coincident Indicators						
Number of employees in nonagricultural establishments	−1	−1	0	0	+2	0
Unemployment rate, total (inverted)	−2	+1	−4	+4	−3	+3
Index of industrial production	0	−5	−5	0	−4	−1
Gross national product in current dollars (Q)	−2	−3	+1	−2	0	0
Gross national product in 1954 dollars (Q)	−2	−3	+1	−2	0	0
Personal income	+3	−5	+1	−2	+5	✽
Labor income in mining manufacturing and construction	0	0	0	0	0	0
Sales of retail stores	0	−7	0	−1	−1	−1

Source: Julius Shiskin, *Signals of Recession and Recovery* (National Bureau of Economic Research, Occasional Paper No. 77, 1961); and *Business Cycle Developments*, April, 1964, U.S. Department of Commerce.

These indicators may be used with considerable success for forecasting changes in the level of business activity and stock prices if the investor exercises good judgment. As with the use of any data, interpretation of these data is as important as their construction and derivation. Therefore, one prerequisite is that they be used as a group, because no one indicator invariably reaches its turning point in precisely the same manner as it did in the past.

TECHNICAL MARKET ANALYSIS

Some maintain that the stock market is its own best forecaster and frequently leads the turns in business conditions. The previous discussion indicated that certainly there are few statistical series that lead the major turns in business conditions by a period of time longer than the trend of stock prices. Therefore, one could conclude that use of business indicators as a means of forecasting future business conditions and timing stock purchases is futile. Many technical market analysts maintain that forecasting future business conditions and using these forecasts as a means of timing stock sales and purchases is of very little value, since the stock market is itself the best indicator of what stock prices will do in the future. They maintain that the course of business conditions and the so-called "technical" position of the stock market are separable problems. Therefore, the technical market analyst pays particular attention to the patterns of stock market prices.

In the short run, the market analyst pays attention to conditions that may result in a particular stock's being oversold because of liquidation of an estate or a struggle for control of a corporation, or a condition that may result in a particular stock's being overbought or oversold because of changes in the volume of liquid funds available for investment in the hands of wealthy individuals or business firms. In the long run, the market analyst follows and analyzes the general pattern of stock prices. The technical market analyst maintains that an objective study of stock prices without any subjective appraisal of values or forecast of business conditions is the most effective way to time purchases and sales of common stock. The emphasis is on present and probable future prices rather than on investment values.

The market analyst bases his forecast of turns in stock market prices on the average behavior of stock prices in the past. He assumes that stock prices have momentum. That is, once they start to rise, they tend to continue to rise, once they turn down, they tend to continue down. Technical analysis does not undertake to state that stock prices are high or low, or to predict how much higher or lower they will go. The technician's only contribution to the solution of the timing problem is to determine when stock prices turn or are about to turn.

His approach to the problem of forecasting stock market prices is a mechanistic one. He usually uses a system that provides signals concerning when to buy stocks and when to sell. One difficulty with most of these methods is that there is always the possibility of getting whipsawed because the momentum of the market may not be so great as the system seems to indicate. Stock prices are fluctuating constantly, and the pattern may not be a typical one as suggested by the analysis.

Security analysis and business forecasting study the basic causes that affect values. Values, combined with investment sentiment and other strictly technical factors, in turn influence prices. The technical market analyst recognizes that security stock movements are mere symptoms of more basic causal forces, but he will maintain that forecasting of business conditions is so complex and unreliable that his particular system or method of technical analysis will yield better results, recognizing that technical analysis confines its attention to the symptoms alone.

There is almost unanimity of opinion on the goals of technical market analysis, but many different methods or techniques of analysis have been developed. An interesting compilation of the techniques of market analysis is *A Strategy of Daily Stock Market Timing for Maximum Profit*, by Joseph E. Granville.[5] Granville classifies stock price indicators or market analysis action into three groups: (1) day-to-day indicators, (2) intermediate-term indicators, and (3) long-term or "grand strategy" indicators. The proliferation of these indicators is evident from the fact that Granville lists 55 separate day-to-day indicators.

Since it its not possible to discuss each separate technique or theory of technical market analysis, only the more common techniques will be discussed, such as the Dow theory, the odd-lot index, the confidence index, the short-interest ratio, and the advance-decline line.

---

[5] Joseph E. Granville, *A Strategy of Daily Stock Market Timing for Maximum Profit* (Englewood Cliffs, N.J.: Prentice-Hall, Inc., 1960).

The Dow Theory

One system for forecasting turns in stock prices is probably best known as the "Dow theory." Charles H. Dow, founder of the Dow-Jones financial news service and of the *Wall Street Journal*, advanced the theory in editorials written for that newspaper from 1901 until his death in 1902. S. A. Nelson, in his book on stock speculation, first applied the name "Dow theory" to the ideas contained in Mr. Dow's editorials. It remained for William Peter Hamilton to give the Dow theory wide publicity in his book, *The Stock Market Barometer*.

The theory relies on the Dow-Jones index of 30 industrial stocks and the index of 20 railroad stocks as representative of the general trend of the market as a whole. In order for the Dow theory to work well, movements of the Dow-Jones averages must exhibit enough momentum and amplitude so that it is likely that these averages will be roughly representative of the trend of stock prices as a whole. The significant prices for the Dow theory are the closing prices of the industrial and rail averages at the end of each trading day.

Simply put, the Dow theory holds that a bull market changes to a bear market when the low point in a decline penetrates or breaks through the lowest point reached in the last previous decline. Both Dow-Jones Industrial Average and Railroad Average must perform in this manner to confirm a major change in the stock price trend. Conversely, when a decline stops short of giving such a signal, the subsequent recovery and penetration of both averages on up through the level of the last previous highs indicate a primary bull market, and the upward direction of prices will continue. There are variations of the Dow theory based on selection of time periods for measurement. The pattern these closing prices follow may be viewed as being composed of three different time periods.

First, there are the minor day-to-day trends from which only the floor trader could attempt to profit. Second, there are the intermediate or secondary trends, measured in terms of months. Third, there is the major trend—the bear market or bull market that may endure for one or more years. Assuming that one can distinguish between major trends and secondary trends—not always easy to do —turns in both types of trends are defined by the Dow theorist. An upturn in the general level of stock market prices is evident when the closing price at the end of a trading day exceeds the previous high.

A downturn is established when the closing price is lower than a previous low. A trend, once established, is assumed to continue until a turn in the opposite direction is apparent. Finally, a change of trend is never certain until it has been established by both industrial and rail averages, though they need not simultaneously confirm it.

This basic statement of the Dow theory is deceptively simple. As a practical matter, the task of distinguishing between intermediate and primary trends is sometimes difficult, if not impossible. However, the Dow theorist attempts to define only turns in the major trend; they are difficult to distinguish from an intermediate trend in an index of stock prices such as the Dow-Jones averages. Consequently, waiting for a Dow theory signal to buy or sell may get the investor in or out of the market too late, when the momentum of the market has already been spent. The major danger in using the Dow theory as the basis for timing is that when momentum in stock market prices does not develop as anticipated, whatever capital gains are attained may be so small after paying commissions to the broker that they are not worthwhile.

The Dow theory is not so objective and automatic as it might appear to be. In addition to the problem of distinguishing between intermediate and major trends in stock prices, there are other problems of interpretation. For example, how far should the closing price of the Dow-Jones averages penetrate the previous highs or lows to define a turn? There is also the question of whether the Dow-Jones averages are indicative of the general trend in stock market prices, since they represent only a relatively small sample of the securities traded and are generally classified as high quality.

There are many varieties of the Dow theory. These different variations have been developed by technical analysts who sell their interpretations or forecasts of stock market prices based on application of the Dow theory. Some Dow theorists, for example, see no rational basis for requiring that the rail average be used in addition to the industrial average to indicate turning points. There is some logic in this variation in that railroad securities are not such an important medium for investment as they were when the Dow theory was first formulated.

The Odd-Lot Theory

The study of daily odd-lot statistics is another technique used by technical market analysts. Interpretation of these statistics rests on a unique theory popularly referred to as the "theory of contrary opinion." As mentioned in the chapter on investment mechanics, the usual unit of trading in common stocks is the hundred-share lot, called the "round lot." It is obvious that only larger investors have sufficient funds to buy and sell in such quantities. The volume of odd-lot purchases and sales is indicative of the types of investment decisions being made by small investors who must, of necessity, deal in odd lots of less than one hundred shares. The general thesis of the theory of contrary opinion is that the collective decisions of small investors are usually wrong, and the successful investor should attempt to act contrary to the opinions of the small investor.

Application of the technique, however, is not so simple as it sounds. The small investor exhibits some essentially sound philosophy in his trading. He tends to buy more stocks when prices fall and to buy less when prices rise. When the market is trendless and fluctuates up and down in a relatively narrow range, the small investor tends to stay out of it. Consequently, the volume of odd-lot trading tends to decrease. The general public loses interest, and fluctuations in stock market prices tend to receive less publicity in the press. However, when stock prices move with considerable momentum, the small investor typically tends to buy too soon in a declining market and tends to sell too soon in a rising market. Likewise, the small investor who buys increasingly less stock as prices rise may suddenly become infected with optimism and begin to buy increased amounts of stock near the top of the bull market.[6]

During these periods, the theory of contrary opinion becomes most useful, according to its advocates. It is pointed out that the small investor in a rising or falling market ultimately allows his enthusiasm or pessimism to run rampant. He is swept up in an emotional tide, and studying his actions gives a clear indication that there is about to be a major turn in stock market prices.

Application of the theory of contrary opinion requires that the technician watch the trend of odd-lot purchases and sales relative to changes in stock prices themselves. He can then note how the small investor is reacting to changes in market price. The absolute levels of odd-lot buying and selling are not of so much significance as sudden changes in the ratio of sales to purchases—the odd-lot index. This

---

[6] "Are Market Turns Predictable?" *Forbes*, Vol. LXXXII, No. 2 (July 15, 1958), p. 13.

index is computed by dividing daily odd-lot sales by daily odd-lot purchases. For example, the total odd-lot sales for the week of August 20, 1965, was 1,810,252 shares, and the odd-lot purchases were 1,692,-928 shares. The daily average odd-lot sales (total weekly sales divided by 5) were 362,050, and daily average odd-lot purchases were 338,586. By dividing daily odd-lot sales by odd-lot purchases, we find the index is 106.09. This index is plotted against the closing Dow-Jones Industrial Index or some other market index, such as the SEC Common Stock Index.

The technical market analyst who uses this system looks for differences in directions of the odd-lot index and the stock price index. These divergences provide the analyst's buy signals and sell signals. If the Dow-Jones average is rising and the odd-lot index is falling, the odd-lot system analyst feels that it is time to sell because there is about to be a turn in the general trend of stock market prices.

The odd-lot index and the Standard and Poor's Combined Index of 500 stocks are shown in Figure 20–1 for the period 1960 through October, 1965. This period was selected because there was a significant drop in stock market prices during the time. It is apparent from this sample that the average investor's timing, shown here by the odd-lot index, was poor. He was buying more than he was selling before the downturn in the Dow-Jones averages and was selling heavily during May, 1962. During January, 1963, he reacted as a rational investor and showed excellent timing. However, he began making errors in timing from then on. He was selling more heavily than he was buying during much of the early phases of the 1964–65 bull market. The odd-lot market analyst, of course, gets a buy signal when the market averages are falling and the odd-lot index is rising. It suggests to him that the market downtrend is about to end and that it is now time to go into the market.

The number of odd-lot shares bought and sold daily has been compiled by the Securities and Exchange Commission since March, 1936. These statistics are available currently through the Dow-Jones news service and are published with a short time lag in the *Wall Street Journal.* Statistics on odd-lot short sales have been available since June, 1939. Sometimes, the odd-lot analyst will plot odd-lot short sales or prepare an odd-lot short sales index to confirm the buy and sell signals he receives from use of the odd-lot index. It has been suggested that the small-scale speculator who sells short exhibits, perhaps, an even greater degree of perverse timing than the usual odd-lot trader. *Forbes Magazine of Business and Finance* has prepared what it calls "do-it-yourself" instructions for calculating the two major odd-lot indexes. A very interesting article describing these indexes is published in the July 15, 1958, issue of *Forbes*.

The major shortcoming of this technique is the one common to most stock market analytical techniques—determining when there has actually been a major turn in market prices. Also, as mentioned earlier, even assuming that one can forecast with some degree of accuracy changes in the general level of stock market prices, the investor has no assurance that the individual stocks in which he has an interest will be affected by the change. Unquestionably, the odd-lot index, as other stock market systems, is a useful tool in timing purchases and sales of common stocks, assuming that there is not a blind reliance on it. No system or mechanistic approach to economic or stock market analysis can be substituted for good judgment.

The Confidence Index

An indicator that seemingly has been reasonably accurate in predicting movement of stock market prices is the "confidence index." This index, published by *Barron's*, a financial weekly, attempts to measure the confidence of investors. The index is the ratio between average yield of 10 high-quality corporate bonds selected by Barron's and average yield of Dow-Jones 40 bonds. A high ratio indicates that investors have confidence in the future, since they buy lower-quality bonds. When they are pessimistic, investors buy high-quality bonds, causing the index to fall. This index has been a fairly reliable indicator of the amplitude and timing of stock price advances and declines.[7]

Advocates of this index maintain that it leads stock market prices by two to four months. That is, a decline in the confidence index foretells that a decline in stock prices will take place in two to four months, and vice versa.

The problem in using this index is in determining when it has reached the bottom and the top. As with other such devices, confidence index advocates have developed a series of patterns that are buy and sell signals. For example, a decline in stock market prices is indicated "when the confidence index makes a sharp weekly up-

---

[7] Joseph H. Granville, "Market Forecaster," *Barron's*, Vol. XXXIX, No. 36 (September 7, 1959), p. 9.

FIGURE 20-1

Odd Lot Index and Standard and Poor's Combined Index of 500 Stocks, 1960–October, 1965

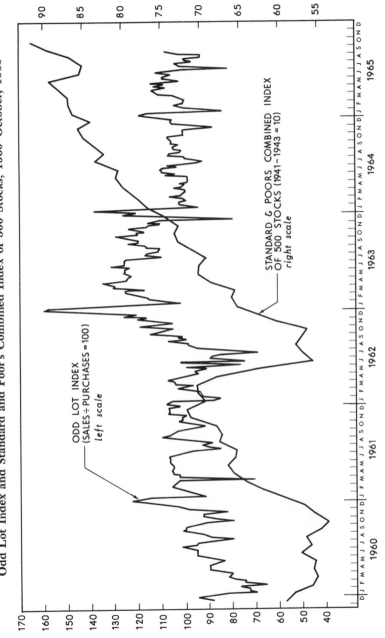

swing to a new high and then retreats immediately the following week."[8]

Most of the writers who advocate technical market analysis as a means of timing stock purchases emphasize the element of judgment in its use. Application of the confidence index also requires that the analyst use some judgment in interpreting it. It does have an advantage over other market analysis techniques in its simplicity. The analyst has only to relate the confidence index to some index of stock prices in order to test its efficiency and to acquire experience in its use. This is in contrast to some other market analysis techniques, which are so complex that the skeptic sometimes wonders if the interpretations are a reflection of the analyst's experience or an actual interpretation of the patterns of stock prices.

The Advance-Decline Line

The Dow-Jones Industrial Average often continues to move up long after the general level of the market. The reason for this movement is that this average is composed of 30 high-quality stocks, and good news affecting two or three of these 30 stocks may carry the average upward even as the general tone of the market has changed.

Proponents of the advance-decline line claim that this indicator will lead stock market prices as indicated by the Dow-Jones Industrial Averages. This line is formulated by tabulating daily the cumulative advances and cumulative declines in stocks listed on the New York Stock Exchange. The differential is plotted along with the Dow-Jones Industrial Average. To illustrate, we started an advance-decline line on May 28, 1964, and carried it through June 11, 1964 (Table 20-3).

The advance-decline line cumulative differential supposedly anticipates changes in the Dow-Jones Industrial Average by three or four days. For example, the increase in the Dow-Jones Industrial Average from 800.31 on June 8, 1964, to 811.25 on June 11, 1964, should have been anticipated by an excess of advances over declines for three or four days before the Dow-Jones Industrial Average began its rise. It may be noted that fluctuations in the cumulative differential between advances and declines seems to coincide with fluctuations in the Dow-Jones Industrial Average in this example.

---

[8] *Ibid.*

TABLE 20-3

Advance-Decline Line and Dow-Jones Industrial Averages, May 28–June 11, 1964

Date	Advances	Declines	Cumulative Advances	Cumulative Declines	Cumulative Differential	Dow-Jones Industrial
5/28/64	590	476	590	476	114	
6/ 1/64	460	609	1050	1085	− 35	818.56
6/ 2/64	346	735	1396	1820	− 424	813.78
6/ 3/64	424	618	1820	2438	− 618	811.79
6/ 4/64	242	883	2062	3321	−1259	802.48
6/ 5/64	634	421	2696	3742	−1046	806.03
6/ 8/64	385	676	3081	4418	−1337	800.31
6/ 9/64	646	461	3727	4879	−1152	805.54
6/10/64	679	367	4406	5246	− 840	807.53
6/11/64	596	444	5002	5690	− 688	811.25

Summary

The appraisal of a common stock, its earnings outlook, asset value, and the trend of the industry and its prospects are the basis for the selection of common stocks. Appraisal, however, is only half of the problem that the investor faces. The investor also has the problem of determining the best time to buy. He is also concerned with how the market will appraise these factors and how these collective appraisals will result in increases or decreases in stock prices through the interaction of supply and demand.

As was suggested earlier, there have been a number of methods devised for timing purchases and sales of common stock. Technical market analysis is one of three basic approaches. This approach to timing purchases and sales uses only the past and current action of stock market prices for judging or forecasting the probable future course of stock market prices. The technical market analyst maintains that security analysis may be a useful tool to the investor, but that it does not measure the attitudes of the thousands of investors in the market. According to technical market analysts, this blind spot makes it necessary for the sophisticated investor to devise some means of measuring the psychology of the market. Differences in temperament, wealth, income, and so forth, cause investors to react differently to given market situations and to given sets of facts. Therefore, it is necessary to analyze changes in market psychology as reflected in stock market prices themselves. The technical market analyst will maintain that it is possible to time stock market prices through business forecasting, but that the investor will achieve a greater degree of accuracy and will certainly simplify his problem by using one of the methods of market analysis.

Technical market analysis is unquestionably a valuable tool to the investor if he can spend the time to use it intelligently. The problem is that the investor cannot attempt to do his own market analysis without spending a considerable amount of time at the task, which might exclude any possibility of using security analysis because adequate market analysis is a time-consuming undertaking. There is nothing necessarily incompatible or contradictory in using both approaches in investment management. One is a matter of quality determination, and the other is a matter of timing purchases and sales of securities.

THE FORMULA PLANS

The difficulty in application and the time involved in using the economic forecasting approach or the technical market analysis approach to timing purchases and sales of common stocks have resulted in development of mechanical methods of timing which minimize the need for subjective judgment by the investor.

The tendency of the average investor to buy when prices are rising and to sell when stock prices are falling was indicated by the discussion of the theory of contrary opinion. To solve this problem, mechanical methods of forcing investment decisions, known as "formula plans," have been determined. These plans have sought to eliminate the necessity for business forecasting and technical market analysis while at the same time, enabling the investor to profit from fluctuations in stock prices.

There are two types of formula planning. The equalizing plan assumes that the investor has an existing capital fund. The plan provides that the investor maintain some constant relationship between the value of bonds or other fixed-income investments in his portfolio and the value of common stocks. The dollar-averaging formula plan assumes that the investor is creating a capital fund by saving systematically.

Both these types of formula plans tend to eliminate the need for business forecasting or technical market analysis, and they remove the influence of emotion in making decisions on the proportion of an investment fund to be invested at a particular time. That is, these plans are essentially designed to avoid adverse timing. This is done by setting up some objective in advance to determine when the investment in common stocks is to be increased and when it is to be decreased, so that when the time for action comes the investor will not be influenced by his emotions or by his own attempts to forecast either business conditions or stock prices. These plans are not a substitute for careful selection of securities based on security analysis. On the basis of his analysis, the investor may change from less desirable securities at any time as long as the proportion of the fund invested in stocks is not changed contrary to the formula. This is particularly true of the equalizing plans, in which the proportions between stocks and bonds must be maintained at all times.

The Equalizing Formula Plans

There are three formula plans of the equalizing type: (1) the constant dollar value of stocks plan, (2) the constant stock-bond ratio plan, (3) the variable stock-bond ratio plan. Each of these equalizing plans is designed to eliminate buying during periods of rising stock prices and to delay selling during periods of falling stock prices. The basic objective is the same for all three. Differences are in application of the basic concept of formula planning.

The Constant Dollar Value of Stocks Plan. The constant dollar value of stocks formula plan is the simplest in basic concept in that it attempts to keep constant the market value of the investment in stocks. To the extent that the market value of stockholdings decreases in sympathy with the decline in the general market, the investor will be forced to buy enough stocks at lower prices to maintain the dollar value of the investment, obtaining the money with which to buy stocks by selling securities from the bond section of the fund. The general effect of this formula is to force the investor to buy common stocks as prices fall and to sell them when stock market prices begin to rise without regard to his own analysis of business conditions or the stock market.

The simplicity of this formula plan is deceptive. Obviously, the investor cannot buy or sell common stocks at every change in value of the common stocks in the fund. If he did so, he would be buying and selling common stocks daily, and only the brokers would make any money. This problem has been solved by limiting action to certain specified dates, such as midyear or end of the year, or by providing for equalization of the value of the common stocks in the fund on a certain specified percentage decline or advance in stock market prices or in value of the stocks. It is generally wisest to use the percentage change in value goal, because the best opportunities to buy stocks cheaply or to sell stocks at a profit might not occur on such specific dates. It is therefore best to provide that action will be taken when the stock index or market value of the stocks declines by a specific percentage, or when the stock index or market value of the stocks increases by a certain percentage.

To illustrate the constant dollar value of stocks formula plan, it has been assumed in Table 20–4 that the investor begins using this plan by investing half of a $1,000 fund in common stock and the other $500 in bonds. The predetermined point of action is decided to be when the index of stock prices show a 20-point gain or loss from the point at which the last action was taken. Assuming that the level of stock prices declines as soon as he begins a formula plan, he will take action when the stock index declines 20 points. At that time he will use $200 from the bond fund to buy stocks, raising the value of his stocks to the constant dollar value of $500. He will have to draw on his bond fund again if stock prices decline still further and reduce the stock index by another 20 points. If stock prices recover and the stock index advances 20 points from the last action taken, he will sell stocks and buy bonds with the proceeds to bring the stock fund back to the $500 level.

Application of this plan as shown in Table 20–4 assumes that the investor begins his formula plan by purchasing 10 shares of common stock at an average price of $50 per share and placing the other $500 in bonds. It is also assumed that the average market price of the investor's holdings of common stock moves in exact proportion to the general level of stock prices, whereas the market prices of his bond holdings do not change. The result is that despite a decline in stock prices of 20 points immediately after initiation of the formula plan, a recovery of somewhat less than the initial level of prices enables the investor to break even. The reason is that the investor takes advantage of the downward movement in market prices to reduce his average cost per share of stock. His average cost at the beginning of the plan is $50 a share. After he has purchased 6.67 additional shares at $30 a share, his total investment in 16.67 shares is $700, or an average of $41.99. Therefore, it is possible for the investor to break

TABLE 20-4

An Illustration of Constant Dollar Value of Stocks Plan

Transaction Number	Index of Stock Prices	Market Value of Unmanaged Fund	Market Value of Fund under Formula			Action Taken	Amounts Spent for Stocks	Amounts Realized from Sales	Total Shares Held	Average Cost Per Share
			Total	Bonds	Stocks					
1	50	$1,000	$1,000	$500	$500	Plan initiated	$500	. . .	10.00	$50.00
	40	800	900	500	400		. . .	. . .	10.00	50.00
	30	600	800	500	300		. . .	. . .	10.00	50.00
2	30	600	800	300	500	Purchased 6.67 shares at $30	200	. . .	16.67	41.99
	20	400	633	300	333		. . .	. . .	16.67	41.99
	30	600	800	300	500		. . .	. . .	16.67	41.99
	40	800	967	300	667		. . .	. . .	16.67	41.99
	50	1,000	1,134	300	834		. . .	. . .	16.67	41.99
3	50	1,000	1,134	634	500	Sold 6.67 shares at $50	. . .	$334	10.00	41.99
	60	1,200	1,234	634	600		. . .	. . .	10.00	41.99
	70	1,400	1,334	634	700		. . .	. . .	10.00	41.99
4	70	1,400	1,334	834	500	Sold 2.86 shares at $70	. . .	200	7.14	41.99
	80	1,600	1,405	834	571		. . .	. . .	7.14	41.99
	70	1,400	1,334	834	500		. . .	. . .	7.14	41.99
	60	1,200	1,262	834	428		. . .	. . .	7.14	41.99
	50	1,000	1,191	834	357		. . .	. . .	7.14	41.99
5	50	1,000	1,191	691	500	Purchased 2.86 shares at $50	143	. . .	10.00	44.28

even when the market price of his stock recovers to about $42. If the investor had been content to hold 10 shares of stock irrespective of the market price and to keep his bond portfolio intact, his total fund at the $42 price level would have shown a value of $920 ($425 in stock and $500 in bonds).

Adoption of this formula plan involves an implicit forecast that the average future behavior of any stock prices will not involve any wide swings in stock prices. It is possible, with this formula plan, for the investor to be trapped with no bond funds when stock market prices are still declining. For example, if the index dropped from a level of 100, if action was taken with every 20-point drop in the stock price index, and if the index dropped to a level of below 20, no action could be taken because the bond fund would be exhausted. Therefore, it would have been necessary for the investor to foresee that stock prices could drop this low so that he would be able to provide a larger bond fund or to make his action points farther apart. It is evident that setting up the plan initially implies a forecast concerning the lowest levels that stock prices are likely to reach.

The Constant Stock–Bond Ratio Plan. The constant stock–bond ratio plan, another equalizing formula plan, was designed to keep the market value of common stocks at a fixed percentage of the total fund. In this plan, no matter how low stock prices go there will always be some funds available from the sale of bonds to buy common stocks. The dollar amounts spent for additional common stocks will, of course, become less if the total fund declines in value. Table 20–5 illustrates this plan, providing that 50 percent of the market value of the fund be invested in common stocks. Investment action is taken in this illustration whenever the percentage of the fund represented by stocks declines or advances by roughly 10 percentage points from 50 percent. That is, stocks are purchased when the stock section of the total fund declines in market value to about 40 percent of the total value of the fund, and stocks are sold when the value of the stock section rises to roughly 60 percent of the total value of the fund.

The same pattern of stock prices is assumed in this illustration as was assumed in the constant dollar value of stocks plan in order to permit comparisons between the two plans. If one makes these comparisons, it will be noted that the constant dollar value of stocks plan buys stocks more aggressively as stock prices decline and spends the same amount for stocks as prices continue their decline to lower levels. The constant stock–bond ratio plan, however, buys most

TABLE 20-5

Illustration of Constant Stock-Bond Ratio Plan

(Assume action taken whenever percentage of fund represented by stock declines or advances by roughly 10 percentage points from a 50 percent level.)

Transaction Number	Index of Stock Prices	Total Fund	Market Value Bonds	Stocks	Value of Stocks as a Percentage of Fund	Action Taken	Amounts Spent for Stocks	Amounts Realized from Sales	Total Shares Held	Average Cost Per Share
1	50	$1,000	$500	$500	50.0%	Plan initiated	$500	‥	10.00	$50.00
	50	900	500	400	44.4		‥	‥	10.00	50.00
	34	840	500	340	40.5		‥	‥	10.00	50.00
2	34	840	420	420	50.0	Purchased 2.35 shares at $34	80	‥	12.35	46.96
	30	790	420	370	46.8		‥	‥	12.35	46.96
	23	704	420	284	40.3		‥	‥	12.35	46.96
3	23	704	352	352	50.0	Purchased 2.96 shares at $23	68	‥	15.31	42.32
	20	658	352	306	46.5		‥	‥	15.31	42.32
	30	811	352	459	56.6		‥	‥	15.31	42.32
	35	888	352	536	60.4		‥	‥	15.31	42.32
4	35	888	444	444	50.0	Sold 2.63 shares at $35	‥	$ 92	12.68	42.32
	40	951	444	507	53.3		‥	‥	12.68	42.32
	50	1,078	444	634	58.8		‥	‥	12.68	42.32
	53	1,116	444	672	60.2		‥	‥	12.68	42.32
5	53	1,116	558	558	50.0	Sold 2.15 shares at $53	‥	114	10.53	42.32
	60	1,190	558	632	53.1		‥	‥	10.53	42.32
	70	1,295	558	737	56.9		‥	‥	10.53	42.32
	80	1,400	558	842	60.1		‥	‥	10.53	42.32
6	80	1,400	700	700	50.0	Sold 1.78 shares at $80	‥	142	8.75	42.32
	70	1,312	700	612	46.6		‥	‥	8.75	42.32
	60	1,225	700	525	42.9		‥	‥	8.75	42.32
	53	1,164	700	464	39.9		‥	‥	8.75	42.32
7	53	1,164	582	582	50.0	Purchased 2.23 shares at $53	118	‥	10.98	44.17
	50	1,131	582	549	48.5		‥	‥	10.98	44.17

aggressively in the early phases of the price decline and spends progressively less as stocks go to still lower levels. This feature is a distinct disadvantage of the constant stock–bond ratio plan if the average behavior of stock market prices is characterized by long, uninterrupted swings. But the plan does overcome the major disadvantage of the constant dollar value of stocks plan by assuring that some stocks can be purchased no matter how low the market goes. It should be noted, however, that although the constant stock–bond ratio plan promotes less aggressive purchase of common stock on a decline in price, it also takes profits less aggressively on a rise in price. Therefore, it is conceivable that the constant stock–bond ratio plan user might have more favorable results than he would with the constant dollar value of stock plan.

The Variable Stock–Bond Ratio Plan. The variable stock–bond ratio plan is a refinement of the constant stock–bond ratio plan. This more refined equalizing plan overcomes the constant stock–bond ratio plan disadvantage, mentioned before, of buying more aggressively in the early phases of a stock market price decline and spending progressively less as stock prices go to still lower levels. This variable plan assures more aggressive purchase of common stocks as common stock prices decline by increasing the proportion of the fund invested in common stocks as the general level of stock market prices goes down. In other words, a smaller percentage of the market value of a variable stock–bond ratio fund is invested in common stock when stock prices are high than when they are low. It is obviously a sound principle to buy more stocks when prices are low than when they are high. But it implies that the investor can determine absolutely when stock prices are high or low. The investor is faced with the problem of forecasting what the general level of stock prices will be in the future and of selecting a normal or median price. This normal or median level of stock prices must be forecast by the investor when the formula plan is initiated.

Naturally, in making this median-level stock price forecast the investor is subjected to the same hazards that were mentioned in connection with technical market analysis and major economic cycle forecasting as bases for timing common stock purchases. There is the possibility that the investor will allow his emotions to influence his judgment, thus defeating the very purpose for which formula planning was designed. Even when the forecast of the average level of future prices is wrong, it is possible to achieve some success with this formula plan, but the investor might not achieve maximum gains.

To illustrate the operation of this variable ratio plan, it has been assumed in Table 20–6 that initially 50 percent of the fund will be invested in common stocks at a median price of 50 as indicated by a stock market price index. In this illustration, it was assumed that with each 20-point increase in the stock price index the proportion of the total value of the fund invested in common stock would be reduced to 30 percent of the total; conversely, with a 20-point decrease the value of common stock holdings would be increased to 70 percent of the total. In other words, it was assumed that action would be taken to adjust values as follows.

Index of Stock Prices	*Percent of Fund in Stocks*
70	30%
50	50
30	70

It can be observed from this illustration that the plan results in expenditure of moderately smaller amounts for common stock as stock prices decline, and realization of moderately larger amounts from the sale of stocks as the general level of stock prices rises. If the results of this plan are compared with the illustrations of the other two equalization formula plans, it may be noted that better results are obtained with the variable ratio plan with the assumed level of prices.

Some variable ratio plans, in effect, follow a rule that no stocks ever will be purchased above a certain level or sold below it. Such a rule is desirable only when the investor's forecast of average future market behavior is correct. An example of such a variable ratio plan is the so-called "Vassar plan." Vassar College uses it in timing its purchases and sales of securities, and will have experienced very poor results if it has not changed its original forecast of average future market behavior. Under the provision of the Vassar plan, no stocks are to be sold below the 135 level of the Dow-Jones Industrial Average. From the point at which the Dow-Jones averages are 135 down to approximately 100, bonds are sold and stocks are bought and when the industrial average reaches 100, the fund is 100 percent in stocks. From the 135 level of the Dow-Jones averages up to about 200, stocks are sold and bonds are purchased, and when the Dow-Jones averages reach 200, the fund is 100 percent in bonds. This plan assumes that the Dow-Jones averages are not likely to go far beyond the 200 mark. If Vassar College has followed this plan in the

TABLE 20-6

Illustration of Variable Stock–Bond Ratio Plan
(Median Stock Prices = 50)

Transaction Numbers	Index of Stock Prices	Total Fund	Market Value Bonds	Stocks	Value of Stocks as a Percentage of Fund	Action Taken	Amounts Spent for Stocks	Amounts Realized from Sales	Total Shares Held	Average Cost Per Share
1	50	$1,000	$500	$500	50.0%	Plan initiated	$500	...	10.00	$50.00
	40	900	500	400	44.4		...	...	10.00	50.00
	30	800	500	300	37.5		...	...	10.00	50.00
2	30	800	240	560	70.0	Purchased 8.67 shares at $30	260	...	18.67	40.71
	20	613	240	373	60.8		...	...	18.67	40.71
	30	800	240	560	70.0		...	...	18.67	40.71
	40	987	240	747	75.7		...	...	18.67	40.71
	50	1,174	240	934	79.6		...	...	18.67	40.71
3	50	1,174	587	587	50.0	Sold 6.94 shares at $50	...	$347	11.73	40.71
	60	1,291	587	704	54.5		...	...	11.73	40.71
	70	1,408	587	821	58.3		...	...	11.73	40.71
4	70	1,408	986	422	30.0	Sold 5.70 shares at $70	...	399	6.03	40.71
	80	1,468	986	482	32.2		...	...	6.03	40.71
	70	1,408	986	422	30.0		...	...	6.03	40.71
	60	1,348	986	362	26.8		...	...	6.03	40.71
	50	1,288	986	302	23.4		...	...	6.03	40.71
5	50	1,288	644	644	50.0	Purchased 6.84 shares at $50	342	...	12.87	45.65

last few years, it has lost the benefit of the protracted increase in the Dow-Jones averages to approximately the 850 to 975 level, and has sustained a substantial purchasing power loss because its funds have been invested entirely in bonds during this period of time.

The Dollar-Averaging Formula Plan

The average investor does not have a capital fund in the earlier years of his life income cycle. He must accumulate such a fund before he can effectively utilize one of the equalization plans, such as the variable stock–bond ratio plan. A relatively simple formula plan that can be kept by the individual willing to pursue a program of planned savings in order to accumulate a capital fund is the dollar-averaging plan. The dollar-averaging formula is based on the simple statistical fact that if the same amount of money is invested in common stocks at periodic intervals more shares will be purchased when the price is low than when the price is high. The result is that the average cost per share of common stock of the investor's ultimate holdings will be lower than had the same number of shares been bought at each price level. If such a program is pursued over a long period of time, the investor's cost per share will be below the past average level of stock prices, assuming, of course, that he continues the plan over a complete cycle of stock market prices.

The following example will illustrate the results of a dollar-averaging plan carried out over a complete cycle in stock market prices. In this illustration, it was assumed that the investor was able to invest $100 per quarter. The price of the stock at the beginning of the plan was $50 per share. The price dropped eventually to $20 a share, then rose to $80 per share, and fell back to 50 a share. It should be noted from the illustration that in Table 20–7 more shares of stock were bought as prices declined and fewer shares were bought as the price rose to $80 per share. At the end of the complete cycle of prices, the investor owned 30.11 shares of stock at an average cost of $43.17 a share, while the average market price per share was $50. The investor's total investment was $1,300 at the end of the period, but the market value of the investment was $1,505.50. Application of this weighted-average principle, which is the basis of the dollar-averaging formula plan, enables him to show a profit with a rather moderate price recovery. In this illustration, the fund shows a profit when the price has recovered to $40 per share after its decline from the initial price of $50 per share to $20 per share. This example, like the other examples, is oversimplified, because the costs do not include brokerage fees and other costs. On the other hand, it also does not include dividends that probably would have been received during the course of the program.

TABLE 20–7

Illustration of Dollar-Averaging Formula Plan

Regular Payment	Price	Shares Purchased	Total Shares Invested	Total Amount Purchased	Total Value of Investment
$100	$50	2.0	2.0	$ 100.00	$ 100.00
100	40	2.5	4.5	200.00	180.00
100	30	3.33	7.83	300.00	235.00
100	20	5.0	12.83	400.00	256.70
100	30	3.33	16.16	500.00	485.00
100	40	2.5	18.66	600.00	746.70
100	50	2.0	20.66	700.00	1,033.40
100	60	1.67	22.33	800.00	1,339.80
100	70	1.43	23.76	900.00	1,661.20
100	80	1.25	25.01	1,000.00	2,000.80
100	70	1.43	26.44	1,100.00	1,850.80
100	60	1.67	28.11	1,200.00	1,686.60
100	50	2.00	30.11	1,300.00	1,505.50
				Net Gain =	$205.50

Source: Prepared by Merle T. Welshans (St. Louis, Mo.: Washington University).

Before an investor begins a dollar-averaging plan, he should make certain that he is able to continue the plan until it is successfully concluded. That is, he should take into account the possible effects of changes in economic conditions on his income and savings pattern. The investor should not in any circumstances undertake this program if he anticipates a possible need for the funds invested in the plan, necessitating a forced liquidation of his holdings at a time when stock market prices are depressed.

The other limitation of the dollar-averaging plan is that as the fund grows larger, each purchase of additional shares constitutes a smaller percentage addition to the number of shares already held. It is obvious that the purchase of additional stock at a price that is below the average costs of holdings prior to that purchase always reduces the average cost of the shares purchased. But the reduction of average cost is very rapid when the fund is small and very slow when the fund is large. Conversely, the fact that the same number of shares is a greater percentage addition to a small fund than to a large fund has a favorable aspect. As can be noticed in the illustration, it permits the investor to buy stock at high prices with only a negligible increase in his average cost.

The worst time to start a dollar-averaging program is just before a rapid rise in common stock prices, because average costs will rise rapidly and any decline in stock prices occurring later when the fund is larger will reduce average costs less rapidly. Of course, this assumes that the investor is able to forecast peak stock prices. Forecasting stock prices is precisely the problem the investor is trying to avoid in using the dollar-averaging plan. Consequently, he will be wise to ignore the general level of stock prices at the inception of the plan, because he still will be better off to accumulate common stock on a systematic basis. Irrespective of when he begins such a plan, the average investor generally will fare much better in using an averaging plan than in attempting to forecast stock market prices.

In any case, the investor's average cost will always be lower than the past average of stock prices. Because of the disadvantages of a very large dollar-averaging fund, mentioned previously, a dollar-averaging program should not get too large. When the investor has built a large capital fund, he should switch to one of the equalizing plans mentioned earlier and start a new dollar-averaging plan. In some cases as their incomes rise over their life income cycles, investors have had as many as two and three dollar-averaging plans operating simultaneously. In some cases, the dollar-averaging plan may be modified by providing for taking profits when the market price of the stock held shows a predetermined percentage capital gain above average cost. If prices rise consistently during the earlier years of the program, capital gains may be taken on a more modest percentage gain than if prices first decline and then recover in later years. In any case, a plan calling for saving as much as $1,000 a year should probably be stopped in about 10 years, provided that some predeterminated percentage gain is available. In some cases, if the investor's major aim is to attain future income when his savings program is complete, he may never liquidate his holdings. However, future maintenance of considerable stability in market value is important the formula plan should contain some rule for liquidating whenever market price shows a predetermined gain above the investor's average cost.

Summary

Formula plans are designed to avoid adverse timing. Since the timing of common stock purchases is predetermined by formula, the investor will be able to avoid capital losses in the long run and will generally do much better than if he has attempted to forecast either business conditions or stock prices as a basis for timing stock purchases. The strongest argument in favor of formula plans is that they eliminate the influence of emotion and possible serious errors in judgment in deciding what proportion of an investment fund should be put into common stocks. The basic argument against formula plans is that objective tests, devised today to apply to future decisions on when to purchase common stocks, rule out, by implication, any rational analysis of prevailing conditions as time passes. Some will argue that adopting a formula plan may eliminate one of the basic advantages of common stock purchase—maximum long-term capital gains—because these plans tend to average capital gains.

A formula plan should not be followed blindly. It is not a substitute for careful selection of securities based on security analysis. The investor still is faced with this problem of selection and switching from less desirable to more desirable common stocks when his analysis indicates that changes must be made.

REVIEW QUESTIONS AND PROBLEMS

1. Explain why investment management implicitly involves business forecasting.
2. Why not solve the problem of timing by purchasing common stocks when business is bad and selling them when business is good?
3. What are some of the more serious limitations of using statistical business indicators as the basis for timing common stock purchases?
4. What is the rational basis, if any, for technical market analysis?
5. Is there a close correlation between stock yields and bond yields? Why?
6. In early 1966, common stock yields were generally lower than bond yields. How could you justify this on the basis of the relative risk factors?
7. If an investor uses both technical market analysis and security analysis, is there any contradiction in the use of both analytical methods?

8. What is the rationale of the Confidence Index? The odd-lot theory?
9. Do constant value of stock plans, constant stock-bond ratio plans, or variable stock-bond plans automatically settle the question of when the investor should take action? What are their limitations?
10. In what sense does any formula plan involve a forecast of the future?
11. What are the significant differences between the constant value of stock plan and the constant stock-bond ratio plan?
12. What is the essential difference between dollar averaging plans and other types of formula plans?
13. What are the major shortcomings of dollar averaging?
14. Why is the average cost of shares purchased lower than the average market price of shares when a dollar averaging plan is used?

CHAPTER **21**

Alternatives for the Investor—
Portfolio Administration

The formulation or setting up of the investment portfolio is preceded by a number of steps discussed in earlier chapters. First, the investor must work out a personal financial plan from which evolve his investment requirements. These investment requirements are to provide for the future financial contingencies of premature death, disability, retirement and other minor contingencies. It was determined in Chapter 2 that insurance is the most efficient way to handle the premature death and disability requirements. The remaining major requirement to be considered is retirement.

It was decided that the best way to satisfy the retirement requirment is through a savings program. A portion of this requirement may be covered by one of several involuntary savings programs, such as company pension plans and social security. It was determined, however, that these programs meet only minimal needs, and the investor should have a voluntary savings and investment program.

The investor should formulate various investment policy objectives and specifications for his investment program. Finally, the investor has the task of choosing investment media that meet his investment policy objectives and program specifications. In addition, the investment portfolio requires constant supervision and administration, because both the investment policy objectives and the investment media characteristics change.

Portfolio administration involves (1) portfolio acquisition and (2) portfolio supervision. These two facets of portfolio administration are not inseparable, because many of the same factors that influence initial acquisition of the portfolio will be present also in its continuing supervision.

PORTFOLIO ACQUISITION

Acquisition of investment media that conform to the investment program specifications starts after the investor has decided which media best fit the needs—the selection problem—and the best time to buy or acquire the media—the timing problem. Hopefully, the investor will be able to make a perfect selection and have perfect timing in making the selection.

It is often thought more important to decide when to buy than to decide what to buy. It has often been suggested that this is not the case. Proper selection should be given precedence over proper timing. The relative importance attached to selection is indicated by the time and space given in this book to security analysis, which is the basis for intelligent selection.

A study published in *Investment Companies, 1958* supports the contention that proper selection is more important than proper timing in portfolio administration. This study, made by Hugh W. Long and Company, involved two investors, Mr. A and Mr. B. These men started their investment programs in 1915 with $100. Mr. A moved in and out of the market, and managed to show perfect timing. Mr. B stayed in the market continuously from 1915 through 1957, but he followed the portfolio strategy of attempting perfect selection. The results of Mr. A's efforts are shown in Table 21–1, and the results of Mr. B's in Table 21–2. Mr. B fared much better with his policy of perfect selection, since he ended the period with over $4 billion. Mr. A, on the other hand, built his portfolio up to a value of only $211,321.

These examples portray obvious impossibilities, because no investor could ever hope to achieve such perfect selection or timing. However, these examples do support the general contention that intelligent selection is much more important than correct timing. Both perfect selection and correct timing are obviously desirable goals, but selection takes precedence as an investment goal.

Media Selection

The major investment policy factors that must be met in media selection are: (1) financial risk factors, or quality of media; (2) type of income needed—capital gain or current income; (3) need for liquidity; and (4) avoidance of income taxes. The ideal portfolio is one that perfectly meets the investment program needs. A failure to

TABLE 21-1

Perfect Market Timing since 1915

		Bought				Sold	
Date	Number of Shares	Price*	Amount Invested	Date		Price	Amount Received
Jan. 1915	1¾	$ 54.63	$ 100	Nov. 1916		$110.15	$ 193
Dec. 1917	3	65.95	198	Nov. 1919		119.62	359
Aug. 1921	5½	63.90	351	Mar. 1923		105.38	580
Oct. 1923	6¾	85.76	579	Sept. 1929		381.17	2,573
July 1932	62	41.22	2,556	Mar. 1937		194.40	12,053
Mar. 1938	122	98.95	12,072	Nov. 1938		158.41	19,326
Apr. 1939	159	121.44	19,309	Sept. 1939		155.92	24,791
Apr. 1942	266	92.92	24,717	May 1946		212.50	56,525
June 1949	349	161.60	56,398	Jan. 1953		293.79	102,533
Sept. 1953	403	254.36	102,507	Apr. 1956		524.37	211,321

* Dow-Jones Industrial Average is used as price of shares. Figures based on a study by Hugh W. Long and Company.

Source: *Investment Companies*, 1958 Edition, Arthur Wiesenberger and Co., p. 27.

meet policy objectives is nearly always costly. For example, failure to provide adequate liquidity in the portfolio may result in a forced liquidation of common stock at considerable loss when the market is depressed. On the other hand, maintenance of too much liquidity is expensive, because it is almost always purchased at the cost of gains in the form of either income or capital appreciation. Therefore, to avoid penalties the investor should neither ignore investment policy objectives nor overcompensate for them.

Media Quality

The quality of investments to be included in the portfolio is, for the most part, separate and distinct from other policy objectives. That is, if there is a need for high-quality investments because the investor's policy objectives are such that he can not tolerate even the smallest capital loss then avoidance of financial risk is paramount. An investor may make selection errors with respect to other policy objectives, but these errors usually are not so costly as failure to meet minimum quality standards. For example, the investor may find that he has failed to meet his liquidity needs with his portfolio selections. He can usually correct this error by selling securities and putting the proceeds into savings deposits or similar dollar contracts. However, if he purchases low-quality or speculative securities and makes a selection error then the loss of capital often will be quite severe.

TABLE 21–2

Perfect Industry Selection since 1915*

| | | Bought | | | | Sold | |
Date	Number of Shares	Industry	Price	Amount Received	Date	Price	Amount Received
1/15	37	Automobile	3 $	100	1/16	14 $	514
1/16	4	Steel	107	428	6/17	156	622
6/17	35	Automobile	17	606	11/19	57	2,002
11/19	43	Dep't Stores	46	1,982	11/22	69	2,963
11/22	40	Util. Hold.	72	2,892	12/24	134	5,364
12/24	148	Automobile	36	5,343	10/25	75	11,144
10/25	320	Agric. Mach.	35	11,136	12/27	91	29,184
12/27	291	Mail Order	100	29,129	11/28	273	79,356
11/28	207	Util. Hold.	382	78,991	9/29	763	157,962
9/29	5,283	Gold	30	157,962	6/32	43	227,697
6/32	17,515	Metals	13	227,695	6/33	83	1,451,994
6/33	27,293	Auto. Acc.	53	1,451,988	11/35	117	3,182,364
11/35	43,121	Copper	74	3,182,330	1/37	160	6,885,424
1/37	59,009	Aviat. Mfrs.	117	6,886,350	11/38	134	7,901,305
11/38	68,409	Air Trans.	116	7,901,240	1/40	174	11,930,530
1/40	123,249	Cement	97	11,930,503	7/41	102	12,509,774
7/41	89,100	Air Trans.	140	12,509,640	7/43	308	27,424,980
7/43	166,212	Tire & Rubber	165	27,424,980	7/44	194	32,261,749
7/44	275,505	Dep't Stores	117	32,261,636	12/45	254	70,033,371
12/45	454,467	Cement	154	70,033,365	6/46	192	87,076,877
6/46	633,226	Oil	163	87,075,806	12/47	170	90,061,871
12/47	892,585	Util. Hold.	101	90,061,827	5/49	128	114,250,880
5/49	641,138	Tire & Rubber	178	114,250,792	10/51	450	288,768,555
10/51	2,289,996	Finance	126	288,786,496	12/52	169	387,009,324
12/52	2,205,181	Machine Tools	175	387,009,265	12/53	217	478,965,313
12/53	2,007,399	Aircraft	238	478,965,306	1/55	607	1,218,290,210
1/55	1,836,987	Aluminum	663	1,218,290,176	12/55	1,178	2,163,787,987
12/55	3,842,633	Office & Bus. Eq.	563	2,163,786,980	7/56	917	3,523,694,461
7/56	14,682,060	Drugs	24	3,523,694,400	12/57	29	4,257,797,400

* Cowles Commission and Standard & Poor's Indexes are used as prices of shares. Figures prior to 1953 based on a study by Hugh W. Long and Company.
Source: *Investment Companies, 1958 Edition,* Arthur Wiesenberger and Co., p. 28.

The income investor often determines his retirement income needs and finds that the current yields of high- and medium-grade fixed-dollar contracts and high-grade common stocks are such that it is not possible to receive the income he wants from media of such quality at current yields. The temptation is to increase income by downgrading media quality. Of course, such action will have the desired immediate effect of increasing income, but the long-run effect will tend to be losses of income and value of the fund.

The investor's quest for quality obviously stems from the investment policy objective to minimize financial risk. Reduction in financial risk exposure also should not be carried to an absurd point. For example, the investor could purchase U.S. government bonds, which would eliminate virtually all financial risk. However, the investor who follows such a conservative course will be sacrificing income and will have undue exposure to the purchasing power risk and the interest rate risk. In other words, this policy of taking an extremely defensive position toward financial risk exposes the investor to other risks. The investor should be moderate in selection of investment media to meet minimum quality standards.

Quality and Financial Risk. Proper management of financial risk will enable the investor to meet his investment objectives with securities of lower quality. This can be done by (1) careful analysis of securities and constant portfolio supervision and (2) diversification.

The investor's security analysis will enable him to become sufficiently familiar with the company and its prospects. If the investor does his own analysis, he can recognize, with constant supervision, any changes in quality of the security. Constant supervision and scrutiny reduce the quality margins needed to meet minimum financial risk standards. If the investor relies on the work of others in judging quality of securities, he must leave himself a margin of safety, because a deterioration in quality may not be communicated to him in sufficient time to prevent large loss.

Quality, Financial Risk, and Diversification. It is obvious that financial risk can be reduced by careful analysis and selection of securities. However, the investor may reduce the quality of his securities and meet the minimum standards of financial risk by diversifying his holdings.

Diversification is application of the law of probability to investment management. Spreading funds over a large number of commitments reduces the probability of loss, because it is unlikely that all of a large number of corporations will fail or get into serious financial difficulty at any one time. Conversely, by diversifying the investor increases the possibility of some loss, but decreases the possibility of large or total loss.

The concept of diversification assumes that investments are of nearly equal quality. For example, the amount of risk assumed with a single commitment in American Telephone and Telegraph Company stock would be much less than the risk with investments in 20 marginal copper or uranium mining companies. Diversification does not reduce the risks of poor-quality investments, but it provides the investor with a means of spreading these risks and reducing the probability of large loss.

Investments may be diversified in any one of several ways. One may diversify holdings by investing in several companies within the same industry. This process may be carried further by diversifying holdings by industry. For example, the investor may conclude that he wants to invest in the growth of demand for energy in this country. Since there are several energy sources and industries such as coal, oil, gas, and uranium, he may want to commit some of his funds in each of these industries to assure that he has an investment in the industry that will be the primary source of energy in the future.

Another means of diversification is by geographical area. This form of diversification has been most significant for the transportation and service industries, because the fortunes of these businesses are usually tied up with the economic well-being of the particular areas they serve. The investor may attempt to minimize the risks of the economic decline in one of these areas by investing in firms that serve more than one area.

The evolution of global wars produces a facet to geographical diversification that has not been considered before. The possibility of destruction of one-plant companies by bombing might be considered as an unusual hazard, but one could not help being impressed by the possibility of substantial losses due to the ravages of war if he had seen the devastation in Europe after World War II. Long-range missiles and the atomic bomb have made such destruction a possibility for this country in the event of another war. Therefore, some consideration should possibly be given to investing in firms or assets that are outside major metropolitan areas or are not large, single-plant operations.

Overdiversification. Practical problems arise in application of the concept of diversification. Primary consideration in investment selection is quality. As we have noted, quality can be determined only after careful analysis and valuation. In their efforts to minimize the possibility of large loss, many investors tend to select too many different investments for intelligent management. They do so particularly when they invest in securities. It is difficult to maintain any degree of expertness on more than one or two industries and companies within these industries because of the amount of time necessary to keep analyses current. Overdiversification may make the problem of analyzing each situation and passing judgment on quality of each investment so complex that overall quality of the portfolio may deteriorate.

Quantitative Measures of Quality. The investor can think in terms of high-grade, medium-grade, or low-grade common stocks and preferred stocks and bonds, but the process of matching these vague classifications of security quality with the investor's needs is a frustrating task. For this reason, there have been attempts to reduce quality and investment objectives to quantitative terms. One such attempt is the *Value Line Survey* system. This system grades each of 1,100 common stocks. Each of these common stocks is rated; the quality range is A+, A, A—, B+, B, B—, C+, C, C—. The highest quality stock is rated A+, and the lowest quality has a rating of C—. The system is based entirely on past performances, as are most rating systems. This ignores the dynamic nature of security analysis, but it has the advantage of measuring the quality consideration in quantitative terms and it provides a checkpoint for the investor's own conclusions. The purpose of the *Value Line* system is "to introduce a rational discipline into the field of stock evaluation."

The investor may develop his own qualitative measures. For example, he may, as a general rule, invest only in corporations whose earnings in any one year have not deviated from the average of the last five years' earnings by more than 20 percent. This rough rule of quality will enable the investor to eliminate prospects for analysis during the preliminary phases of his analysis. The investor may decide that he will classify all common stock by (1) using numerical ratings and (2) in terms of percentage deviation of any one year's earning from the average of the last five years' earnings. Such a system might be used as follows.

Deviation of Percent of Average Earnings	*Numerical Rating*
0– 20%	6
20– 30%	5
30– 50%	4
50– 75%	3
75–100%	2
Deficit	1

Such a system of numerical ratings is not a substitute for analysis and subjective judgment, because the analyst may decide that the future earnings' prospects are such that a rating system based on past performances does not accurately reflect the quality of the common stock.

The numerical ratings of 6 and 5 indicate high-quality common stock; 4 and 3, medium-quality common stock; and 2 and 1, low-quality common stock. These systems have the advantage of simplicity and the disadvantage of not recognizing differences in accounting practices, industry prospects, and other dynamic features of security analysis. The danger in using rating systems is that the investor frequently substitutes for his own judgment ratings based on past performances. This may not be bad in all cases, because, obviously, if the investor's judgment is generally poor he is better off using a rating system.

Capital Appreciation versus Current Income

Usually, the question of whether capital appreciation or current income is the most suitable investment program objective is clearly indicated. An investor usually will be interested in capital appreciation during his working years, and after retirement his policy will switch abruptly to current income.

The investor who is primarily interested in income has the alternative of high-grade common stocks or fixed-dollar contracts, usually in the form of bonds. Normally, the individual investor is not too interested in bond investments, because the yield is not sufficiently large to provide an adequate income. If the income yield from a bond portfolio is sufficient for the investor's needs, one can effectively argue that the investor will fare better by investing his funds in the fixed-dollar contracts of a financial institution, such as a savings and loan association, or in annuities provided by life insurance companies. The costs and trouble of supervising a bond portfolio more than offset, in most cases, the increase in income that would be derived from direct investment in bonds.

Another problem in using common stock as the primary vehicle for income investment is that in recent years the dividend yield has been low. For example, at the end of January, 1966, annual dividend yield for the stocks that make up the Dow-Jones Industrial Average was 2.87 percent. Of course, if the investor had bought these stocks a number of years before, his yield on his original investment might be considerably higher. However, this type of reasoning begs the question. The fact remains that a higher yield is available to the investor on other types of investment media. Therefore, the investor should consider switching to fixed dollar contracts after retirement to maximize the yield on his portfolio.

The yield on common stocks normally provides sufficient incentive to justify such investment by the individual investor. There are exceptions, such as in 1965 when stock yields were so low that it is questionable whether the income investor could afford to provide the continuous supervision and assume the necessary risk of investment in a portfolio of common stocks.

The income common stock is typically one that has provided a stable and reasonable dividend over a long period of time. The outstanding example of the so-called "income stock" is the common stock of the American Telephone and Telegraph Company, which has paid a regular dividend of in excess of $3.00 a share a year since 1881. Characteristically, the income common stock must also be of better-than-average quality so that the investor will be assured of reasonable income stability in the future. A record of continuous dividends often is the primary investment characteristic of the income common stock. If the company has such a record, the investor sometimes feels that the same intensive analysis required for more volatile growth stocks is not necessary. The investor may be lulled into a sense of complacency and will not continuously supervise and reevaluate his portfolio. Such a course of action can be dangerous, and can result in losses of income and capital funds. For example, United Fruit Company paid an uninterrupted dividend of $3.00 from 1899 until 1959. In 1959, the company's management decided to reduce the dividend to 62½ cents for the year. The possibility of a dividend reduction did not come without warning, because the company was having labor troubles and governmental interference with its operation of banana plantations in Latin America.

Capital Gains and the Portfolio

It seems obvious that the capital gains investor can not attain his objective by investing in fixed-dollar contracts, such as saving accounts, cash values of life insurance, and bonds. However, these institutions keep alive the illusion of capital gains through compound interest on dollar savings. Such capital gains are illusory because, first, the interest income is immediately subject to income tax and, second, the dollar gains are nearly always dissipated by inflation, as discussed earlier in Chapter 7. The financial institutions' claims of the possibilities of growth in the value of an individual's investment fund through the power of compounding only serve to confuse the issue. It has been statistically demonstrated that the capital gains investor would almost always have been at an advantage by purchasing common stock, even ignoring the tax and purchasing power considerations. First evidence of this contention was provided by Edgar Lawrence Smith's *Common Stocks as Long Term Investments*,[1] which publicized the so-called "common stock theory." More recent evidence of the merits of common stock as investments for the capital gains investor is provided by a study, *A Re-Examination of Common Stocks as Long Term Investments*, which is an attempt to bring Mr. Smith's work up to date. The substance of this common stock theory is that a diversified portfolio of common stocks will, over the long run, show more increase in both principal value and income than will the same investment in bonds. The Walker study concluded that despite the events of the periods studied, "our tests have turned out highly favorable to stocks." The average results, compared with the movement of the Dow-Jones Industrial Average, are shown below.[2]

Period	*Average Movement Dow-Jones Ind. Average*	*Average Percent Advantage Stocks over Bonds*
1923–51	+170	+455
1929–51	− 30	+ 87
1937–48	No change	+ 42
1937–51	+ 34	+131

The stocks and bonds included in the tests were selected on a rather arbitrary basis. There was no attempt to analyze common stocks and to select those that had outstanding growth possibilities. An investor interested in capital gains could probably improve on this selection of common stocks of companies that have prospects of steady increases in earnings and price, commonly referred to as "growth stocks."

Growth Stocks and Capital Gains

The investor in growth stocks has a long-range timing problem. He may realize gains in the value of his portfolio if he holds growth stocks, but the period of time over which the appreciation in value will be realized may be too long for his purposes. The investor lives only a limited number of years, and his productive and independent life is generally less than 45 years; therefore, this appreciation in value

---

[1] Edgar Lawrence Smith, *Common Stocks as Long Term Investments* (New York: Macmillan Co., 1924).

[2] Winthrop B. Walker, *A Re-examination of Common Stocks as Long Term Investments* (Portland, Me.: Anthoensen Press, 1954), p. 38.

must be realized over a reasonable period of time. In most cases, the gains must be realized in a shorter period, because the investor wants to fulfill his investment requirements. The demands of these requirements are often shorter term than Mr. Smith and Mr. Walker had in mind.

The second problem in the purchase of growth stocks, which is related to the first, is determination of growth stocks value. It seems that investors sometimes lose their perspective in evaluating growth stocks and are willing to pay far more for the stocks than future earnings seem to justify. In other words, the investor buys romance rather than growth, or what growth there is in the situation is fully discounted when bought. As discussed earlier, common stocks are usually valued on the basis of relationship of price to earnings and price to dividend or dividend yield. Generally, a company's common stock should sell at somewhere between 10 and 30 times earnings and should yield in excess of 4.5 percent. The only justification for buying a stock that sells at 30 to 50 times earnings and yields 2 to 3 percent or less is that it will grow in the future. The difference between yield on the growth stock and yields available from other common stocks is the premium the investor pays for a prospect of better-than-average growth in the future.

Income Taxes and the Portfolio

The objective of investment management is to maximize returns on the portfolio after payment of income taxes. As discussed earlier, income tax avoidance may be the dominant investment policy objective not simply to avoid taxes as an end but to achieve the desired result of maximizing returns.

In the highest marginal income tax brackets, the most suitable investment media are state and local government tax-exempt bonds. To illustrate, the material in Table 21–3 shows the yield or return an investor must get on a fully taxable obligation in order to equal tax-exempt yields of 3, 3½, and 4 percent.

The tax-exempt yields become even more attractive in the higher tax brackets. For example, a couple filing a joint return with an income of $200,000 and over is in the 70 percent tax bracket, and a 3.5 percent tax-exempt yield is the equivalent of 11.67 percent yield before taxes. (See Table 19–2.)

TABLE 21-3

Tax-Exempt Yields Versus Taxable Yields

Taxable Income (in thousands)*	Marginal Tax Rate*	3%	Tax Exempt Interest Yields 3½%	4%
32 to 36 . . . . .42%		5.17%	6.03%	6.90%
36 to 40 45		5.45	6.36	7.27
40 to 44 48		5.77	6.73	7.69
44 to 52 50		6.00	7.00	8.00
52 to 64 53		6.38	7.45	8.51
64 to 76 55		6.67	7.78	8.89
76 to 88 58		7.14	8.33	9.52
88 to 100 60		7.50	8.75	10.00

* These tax rates are for married couples and heads of households filing joint returns.

Income Taxes and Growth Stocks

One reason for the demand for growth stocks is that growth companies frequently pay stock dividends in lieu of cash dividends, or they retain earnings to facilitate growth without resorting to external equity financing by selling more common stock. Stock dividends are far more attractive to the investor who has no need for additional current income, especially investors in the higher tax brackets, because the proceeds from the sale of stock received on stock dividends is treated as capital gain. The capital gains tax rate is lower than the rate on ordinary income, as described earlier.

Technically, the stock dividend only distributes the common stockholder's interest in the company over a larger number of shares. That is, if the common stockholder has 100 shares of common stock and sells 50 shares, his equity in the company will be analogous to the company's having declared a 100 percent stock dividend and his having sold 100 shares. In both cases, his proportionate part of the company's equity will be reduced by 50 percent.

It appears, however, that investors who receive a stock dividend may reap some advantages. A study of stock splits, which have the same net investment effect as stock dividends, showed that a stock dividend and/or split tends to increase in price more than a stock that is not split.[3]

[3] Keith B. Johnson, "An Analysis of the Permanent Price Changes Associated with Common Stock Splits" (D.B.A. dissertation, Washington University, 1963), p. 80.

In attempts to take advantage of lower long-term capital gains income tax rates, investors often lose their perspective. Investors in the lower tax brackets have only to experience a relatively small percent price decline of their stock to eliminate any tax savings. The long-term capital gains rates for 1965 are shown in Table 21–4. In

TABLE 21–4

Effective Long-Term Capital Tax Rates, 1965

Income Tax Bracket		Effective	Income Tax Bracket		Effective
Joint Return	*Single Return*	*Tax Rate*	*Joint Return*	*Single Return*	*Tax Rate*
Up to $ 4,000	Up to $ 2,000	8.0%	Up to $28,000	Up to $14,000	18.0%
Up to 8,000	Up to 4,000	9.5	Up to 32,000	Up to 16,000	19.5
Up to 12,000	Up to 6,000	11.0	Up to 36,000	Up to 18,000	21.0
Up to 16,000	Up to 8,000	12.5	Up to 40,000	Up to 20,000	22.5
Up to 20,000	Up to 10,000	14.0	Up to 44,000	Up to 22,000	24.0
Up to 24,000	Up to 12,000	16.0	Above 44,000	Above 22,000	25.0

other words, an attempt to save income taxes by holding a common stock for more than six months may result in no gain at all, because the price of the stock may decline during the holding period. For example, a couple with a taxable income of up to $4,000 will lose the advantage if the value of their holdings declined only 8 percent.

Need for Liquidity

In the course of one's life, situations are always arising in which cash is needed in amounts over and above the amounts used for daily household expenditures. These needs may be entirely unforeseen, such as catastrophic illness, or may be to satisfy an impulse to purchase a capital asset, such as an automobile. The funds to satisfy these needs and desires may be obtained by selling off a portion of the investment portfolio—usually an expensive means of accomplishing this end. First, the cost of brokerage commissions, etc., on short round-trip transactions in the stock market make acquisition of needed funds by portfolio liquidation expensive. Second, forced liquidations of securities may be ill-timed and can result in substantial capital losses.

For these reasons, an investor is wise to include as part of his portfolio some investments that are liquid or can be converted into cash in a short period of time without appreciable loss. The best investment media for these quick-recourse funds are various institutional dollar contracts, such as savings deposits. In addition, the cash values of life insurance policies also may be regarded as part of the quick-recourse funds. It is not meant to suggest that the investor cancel or cash in his life insurance whenever he feels the need for cash. Most permanent life insurance policies allow the insured to borrow from the issuing company at relatively nominal rates, using the cash value as collateral. When sufficient cash values are available, other quick-recourse funds would be both redundant and expensive.

Proper maintenance of liquidity reduces the need for liquidity in the balance of the portfolio. The investor is then able to buy less marketable issues, which may be better buys in that they may provide opportunities for greater appreciation and higher yield.

Other Selection Considerations

The investor may be well educated and fully informed in investment management matters. After giving full consideration to all factors, he develops an investment program that clearly indicates he should use common stock as his basic investment medium. One remaining personal consideration prevents him from completing his investment program—that is his temperament.

Any rational person dislikes loss. However, some people have an unusually strong reaction to loss, and have such a fear of loss that it is almost an obsession. The slightest slip in the market price of their holdings causes discomfort. This type of person obviously should seek other means of meeting his investment requirements. Even though common stock may be the best media for investment, there is no point in following a course of action that defeats the very purpose of investment management—to allow the investor to reduce the anxiety in investing.

Several alternatives are available to people who cannot tolerate the emotional strain of investing for themselves. Among these choices is use of investment counselors. These portfolio supervision alternatives will be discussed in the next section.

INVESTMENT PORTFOLIO SUPERVISION

Portfolio management involves (1) selecting investments and (2) timing investment purchases. After the initial selection and purchase of securities, continued supervision of the portfolio is needed.

Portfolio Supervision and Timing

It is apparent from the discussion in Chapter 20 that there are several different approaches to timing the purchases and sales of investments. These approaches include efforts to time investments by attempting (1) to forecast changes in business conditions and (2) to analyze fluctuations in stock market prices.

Economic trend trading and technical market analysis approaches are used by many individual investors. Wide ranges of strategies may be used in employing these approaches. On the one extreme, the investor may take an aggressive approach and attempt to exploit market fluctuations. The most extreme example is the tape reader, who actively buys and sells on relatively small changes in market price over short periods in time.

The more moderate economic trend trader combines a study of economic trends, technical market analysis, and careful selection of securities. This type of trader may also be interested in exploiting fluctuations in market prices, but he is discriminating in his purchases because he realizes that today's short-run speculation may become a long-run holding.

The other extreme in timing, using the economic trend trading approach, is the investor who pays attention to price fluctuations but emphasizes selection of media to meet the specifications of his investment program. This investor is interested in buying securities at the lowest possible price. Price fluctuations are not, however, his major concern. He evaluates a common stock. If his valuation indicates a value in excess of the present market price, he will buy the stock, and vice versa. For the most part, this type of investor tends to ignore interim price fluctuations as long as there is no fundamental change in the prospects of the investment.

Security Analysis and Timing

Security analysis is supposed to provide the investor with a valuation of a particular stock, indicating to him whether the stock is undervalued or overvalued in terms of the current market price. Solution of the problem by security analysis assumes that the value determined by analysis is an absolute value that can be used as a norm. Such an approach is an attempt to separate two factors—business conditions and the value of the security—that are, in fact, inseparable. The analyst can use only security analysis to determine the relative value of securities at one particular time. That is, it enables him to determine whether at current market prices the common stock of one company is a better investment than is the common stock of another company.

An interesting attempt to determine absolute values of securities independent of current business conditions is a feature that appears in the *Financial Post*, a Canadian weekly financial newspaper. This exclusive series is an evaluation of 26 selected growth stocks. These charts show, among other things, the price at which a common stock is undervalued and overvalued. Figure 21–1 shows such a chart for Husky Oil Company.

The lines *OV* and *UV* show the prices at which this analyst considers this stock to be overvalued and undervalued. The Husky Oil Company common stock is overvalued at $20 a share and undervalued at $5.00 a share.

FIGURE 21–1

Husky Oil Company

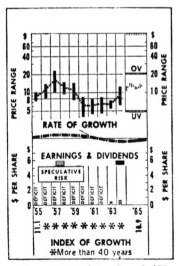

At recent market price of $13, Husky Oil Canada common stock is 160 percent above *UV* level ($5.00), could rise 54 percent to reach *OV* level ($20). Price, 23.2 times latest 12-month earnings of 56 cents per share. No dividend is paid on common. Price range in 1965: $14¼–$10⅛.

Source: *Financial Post*.

Tax Switching

Trading or "switching" may be a perfectly legitimate activity as part of the investor's tax strategy. It is apparent from previous discussion that gains on investment transactions are taxable and losses are deductible. The investor is justified in resorting to trading the stock of one company for the stock of another company without changes in the prospects of these companies.

That an investor may have losses in his portfolio at the end of a taxable year gives rise to a strategy of switching investments to establish a loss for tax purposes. The rule is that to establish a loss for tax purposes the investor must sell a security and not repurchase it for 30 days. The basic objective in tax switching is to sell one security and buy another with similar characteristics. For example, the investor may have owned on October 11, 1965, 100 shares of Standard Oil of New Jersey common stock, which had been purchased at the 1965 high of $90 and was selling on October 11 for $79 a share. On October 11, the investor had a loss of $1,100 in his investment. To establish this loss for tax purposes, the investor must sell these 100 shares of Standard Oil stock and not repurchase the securities for 30 days. If the investor feels that there is a possibility of a substantial rise in the price of Standard Oil stock, he may sell it and purchase an oil company stock of similar quality.

Often, people are reluctant to take losses or gains in securities. Establishing losses is regarded as a personal defeat by many investors. The fallacy of this line of thinking is obvious. The investor has the loss whether he takes it or not. The question is whether he will take it for tax purposes. Conversely, investors also use perverse reasoning in taking profits. Analysis and review of a security may indicate that, in the investor's opinion, the price of a particular common stock is too high. Even in the face of this fact, the investor refuses to sell because he will have to pay a 25 percent capital gains tax. The investor feels that because he cannot buy a similar stock at a 25 percent discount he will hold what he has. The point is that, from a timing standpoint, all common stock may be overpriced; therefore, the investor should sell the stock and increase cash reserves. The basic question is whether in the future the investor will be able to buy the stock at a price low enough to recoup the tax paid after it is sold.

Aids in Portfolio Supervision

As has been repeatedly stated throughout this book, investment management is a continuous process. The investment policy objectives require constant reevaluation because of changes in the level of income, number of dependents, etc. These changes are usually gradual and can be observed during the annual review of the investor's requirements.

Portfolio supervision problems are more immediate and require a continuous day-to-day review of investment commitments if the investor is to achieve the best results. Appraisal of the security holdings should be a continual reexamination of economic conditions, industry and company prospects, and security prices.

Often, the investor may seek to avoid part or all of this rather complex and time-consuming chore by using various devices and various types of assistance. Several choices are available to the investor. He may use one of the formula plans to help eliminate the costly errors of poor timing. He may purchase investment company shares to minimize the selection problem. He may retain professional investment counsel or rely on his broker for advice. With any of these choices or combinations, he cannot completely eliminate the investment management problem. Even in using professional investment counsel the investor must select competent counsel, so he still has a selection problem—at least initially.

An investor may use the broker as an adviser or as a purchasing agent who executes orders, provides information, and suggests investment opportunities. The agent relationship is the more healthy one. In this situation, the investor is not under any obligation to accept the broker's suggestions, and can independently investigate investment opportunities without pressure from the broker to act. At the same time, the broker is not put in the position of providing investment counsel and advice for which he will be held responsible. However, in some cases the investor may rely on the broker for investment advice; then he should be very careful to cultivate and select a man in whom he has confidence. The broker should not be the type who is always trying to sell the investor some speculative situation or "hot deal."

Choosing a Broker. A broker–customer relationship is one of the closest business relationships. To be completely successful, the relationship should be one of mutual confidence, trust, and profit. The broker not only is custodian of an investor's property but also often has access to information that the investor would not want generally known.

First, the firm selected should be financially responsible. One way to have relative assurance of financial responsibility of a brokerage house is to be sure that it is a member of the New York Stock Exchange. There was a time when investors had to consider the financial responsibility of New York Stock Exchange member firms. This does not seem to be a problem now. However, in 1960 one brokerage house was suspended from the New York Stock Exchange because of insolvency—a rare occurrence. In this case, the brokerage house did not have sufficient assets to satisfy all customer's claims. The other New York Stock Exchange members took action to see that the customers would not experience a loss from the insolvency of this member firm.

Second, the investor should select a broker who appreciates his account. All brokers appreciate new business and accounts. However, some well-established customer's men in brokerage houses have such a large clientele, including some large accounts, that they will not give a new account, particularly smaller ones, so much attention or such good service as will a younger man who has not built up large amounts of business. Poor brokerage service can be frustrating and costly because of improperly executed orders, small allotments of new security issues, or unwillingness or inability to furnish information for lack of time.

Because of the closeness of the broker–customer relationship, an investor always should be sure that the man he selects meets the foregoing requirements. After the investor has found the broker who meets these requirements, he has certain obligations to him. First, he should apprise the broker of his investment policy objectives—what he is trying to accomplish. He should share his confidences with the broker and regard these objectives as common ones if he is to cement the most orderly working relationship. Second, the investor should realize that the broker has certain rules and regulations with which he must comply. The investor should cooperate with the broker by not asking him to make exceptions to these rules. Finally, the investor should reward the broker's loyalty and efforts by giving him all of his business so that he will be compensated for the services he performs.

Investment Counsel. An alternative that enables the investor to avoid the portfolio supervision problem is use of professional investment counselors. The investor has the problem of initial selection of a counselor, since they are not uniformly proficient. Selecting proficient counsel is important, because investment counsel is a service offered by professional investment analysts who have only one thing to sell— investment advice. The Investment Advisers Act of 1940, which requires investment counselors to register with the Securities and Exchange Commission and to file certain basic information, may serve to prevent fraud and to discourage incompetents from entering the business. However, because the law sets up no specific standards for training investment counselors, it cannot be assumed that all investment counsel is of uniformly high quality. Brokerage firms, as well as other types of financial institutions, may offer such a service, but this phase of their business will be organized as a separate division. Furthermore, the client is left free to execute his decisions to buy or sell through any broker of his own choosing. The sole financial interest of the investment counselor is in the fee charged for his advice, generally a small percentage of the total market value of the client's portfolio.

When the counselor is mature, adequately trained, and assisted by a competent research staff, investment counsel has many advantages as a possible solution to the investor's problems. First, reliance on counsel is an intelligent recognition that investment management is a highly specialized and continuous operation. Second, the close personal contact between counselor and client enables both to weigh the wisdom of each investment program and to shape the program to suit the investor's individual needs. This personal relationship may also encourage the investor to act promptly on the dictates of rational analysis, unhampered by the influence of buoyant emotion, unfounded fears, or prejudices.

Unfortunately, investment counsel is not an ideal solution to the problems of all investors. The major difficulty is that it is too expensive for the investor of moderate means. From the standpoint of the counselor, no more research may be required to supervise the investment of a few millions of dollars than would be required for an account of a few thousands. For this reason, a minimum fee is usually specified. The large investor finds the burden of counsel fees very modest relative to his investment return, particularly since he can deduct the fees as an expense in reporting his income subject to tax.

Generally, the investor with less than $50,000 of capital will find the burden of investment counsel fees onerous.

Dollar Averaging and Investment Company Shares. The investor may avoid the major problems of portfolio administration by combining the techniques of dollar averaging and the use of investment company shares.

Use of dollar averaging, as discussed earlier, eliminates, for the most part, the problem of timing. Purchase of investment company shares tends to eliminate the problem of selection. A combination plan of investment company shares overcomes the problem that "most of the difficulties in individual investing in equities arise from lack of diversification both *among shares* and *over time.*"[4] However, the problem of selection is not entirely eliminated with this approach, because the investor must still select the proper investment company shares.

The investor may dollar average his purchases of either open-end or closed-end investment company shares. The open-end shares may be dollar averaged by participation in one of the periodic investment plans offered by these companies discussed in Chapter 17. Closed-end investment company shares may be dollar averaged by voluntary purchase of the shares either in the over-the-counter market or on one of the securities exchanges.

Generally, dollar averaging of closed-end shares can be accomplished only by voluntary, systematic purchases in the over-the-counter market or on the securities exchanges, without benefit of any formal plan. One example of this plan is the purchase of Tri-Continental Corporation shares. The common stock of this closed-end investment company is listed on the New York Stock Exchange and may be bought through the New York Stock Exchange's "Monthly Investment Plan," discussed in Chapter 9.

In evaluating the merits of the closed-end investment company versus the open-end investment company combination plans, costs of acquisition are only one factor to be considered. The most important consideration is, of course, management of the company and its performance. Cost factors are so significant in some cases that investment company performance would have to be particularly outstanding to offset them.

---

[4] William C. Greenough, *A New Approach to Retirement Income* (New York: Teachers Insurance and Annuity Association of America, 1955), p. 15.

Summary

The major problems of portfolio management—what to buy and when to buy—may be solved by the investor without professional assistance. In personally supervising his portfolio, the investor accepts complete responsibility for reevaluation of his investments and decisions on whether to buy, sell, or hold.

An alternative approach to the problem of portfolio management is use of outside counsel. The investor may employ this counsel either in the form of professional investment counsel or investment company shares. As a possible choice, the investor may rely on the suggestions of his broker, fortified by the recommendations of advisory services.

REVIEW QUESTIONS AND PROBLEMS

1. What are the two parts of portfolio administration?
2. What are the major investment policy factors that should be met in the selection of investment media?
3. What is the nature of diversification?
4. What is the meaning, if any, of the statement that "Diversification insures that the small investor will not be spectacularly successful"?
5. What are the dangers of overdiversification?
6. Growth stocks should appeal to what type of investor?
7. An investor in the 20 percent income tax bracket is asked if he would rather receive a cash dividend of 4 percent or a stock dividend of an equivalent amount at market. Would his answer have been substantially different if he had been in the 60 percent tax bracket?
8. An investor buys a stock at a price of $10 a share. Soon after the purchase, the stock, for no apparent reason, declines in price to $8. It remains at this price for some time but eventually recovers to $10 a share. If the investor continued to hold the stock, did he sustain a loss as a result of the decline to $8? Explain.
9. Can an investor conceivably consider a common stock as a satisfactory investment if it declines in price below the purchase price and never recovers to the purchase price?
10. Under what conditions would an investor save money by tax switching? Could an investor conceivably worsen his position by switching?
11. An investor comes to you for advice concerning his investment port-

folio. In it you find a stock that is much too speculative for his account and which he should never have bought. He has a sizable loss on his investment in this stock. Would you advise him to sell immediately? What would be the major considerations in this decision?

12. Indicate the investment management problems in the following general rules for common stock investment:

   a) Buy common stock when its intrinsic value is below market price and sell when it is substantially above, without reference to overall business conditions or the general level of stock prices.

   b) Buy a diversified list of high-quality common stocks when business conditions are poor and sell them at the peak of the business upswing.

   c) Buy common stocks when the yields are roughly twice the yields on high-quality long-term bonds. Sell when the yields are about the same as they are on long-term bonds.

APPENDIX 1

Elementary Mathematics of Statistics and Finance

This material is designed to aid the student who has a very limited mathematical and statistical background. For this reason, mathematical proofs are generally omitted. Despite an attempt at utter simplicity, some of the discussion may not be understood by the reader who lacks a minimum working knowledge of elementary algebra. Even such a reader, however, should be able to acquire from this chapter enough ability to handle the usual routine calculations relating to his security investments. The discussion of some selected statistical tools is obviously inadequate but may be of some help to the reader for whom a textbook on statistics would be too forbidding. The student with an adequate background in statistics may omit pages 463–75 entirely.

RATIO, PROPORTION, AND PERCENTAGE

A ratio is a fraction, or an indicated division, such as $\frac{4}{24}$. This fraction may be described as the ratio of 4 to 24 (never as the ratio of 24 to 4). The ratio $\frac{4}{24}$ is obviously equal to $\frac{1}{6}$. This can be written as $\frac{4}{24} = \frac{1}{6}$, and this equation could be read "4 is to 24 as 1 is to 6." This is an illustration of proportion. Let us assume that the number 4—that is, the numerator of $\frac{4}{24}$—measures the current year's profits of a corporation (perhaps in millions of dollars). Let us say that the number 1, the numerator of $\frac{1}{6}$, measures profits 10 years ago. If the denominators, 24 and 6, of the fractions are assumed to measure current sales volume and sales volume 10 years ago, respectively, it is clear that both profits and sales are 4 times as large today as they were 10 years ago. That is why one could say that the rise in profits over the 10-year period is *proportionate* to the gain in sales, as indicated by the equation.

Just as the fraction $\frac{1}{8}$ can be called a ratio, so can the decimal fraction 0.125 be called a ratio because it results from carrying out the indicated division. The decimal fraction is equal to the proper fraction 125/1,000. The fraction is also equal to $12\frac{1}{2}/100$, or $12\frac{1}{2}$ of 100 equal parts of unity. This is more easily stated as $12\frac{1}{2}$ (or 12.5) percent.

We have seen how percentages are computed by division. The yield of a common stock is the result of dividing an estimated annual dividend of $10 by a market price of $80. The result is 0.125 or 12.5 percent. The yield merely states that the dividend is 12.5 percent of market price. Percentages can also be used to measure changes in magnitudes with the passage of time. If an index of stock prices today is 53 and was only 40 a year ago, present stock prices are 132.5 percent "as high as a year ago." Such a measure is called a "relative," because it measures the relationship of some magnitude at a certain time to a magnitude at an earlier "base" period of time. The relative 132.5 is obtained by dividing 53 by 40 to obtain 1.325, moving the decimal point two places to the right.

The relative 132.5 does not measure the percentage *increase* in stock prices. Since the relative measuring stock prices at the "base" price level of 40 is 100, the increase is 32.5 percent ($132.5 - 100.0$). The same result is obtained by computing the absolute increase, amounting to 13 ($53 - 40$), and dividing 13 by 40, moving the decimal point two places to the right. A percentage *decrease* from 53 to 40 is not the same as a percentage *increase* from 40 to 53, because the "base" for computing the decrease is 53 instead of 40. Dividing the decrease of 13 by 53 produces a quotient of 0.245+, or 24.5+ percent.

The student can readily compute the percentage increases and decreases equivalent to equal absolute increases and decreases. Thus, an increase from 100 to 200 (or from 20 to 40) is a 100 percent increase, while a decline from 200 to 100 (or from 40 to 20) is a 50 percent decrease. The following are equivalent increases and decreases, on this basis.

Increase	*Decrease*
100%	.50 %
60%	.37½%
50%	.33⅓%
33⅓%	.25 %
25%	.20 %

The reader must not confuse the principle involved. Equal absolute increases and decreases are different percentage increases and decreases only because the calculation that is assumed involves changing the base from which the percentage is computed. Equal percentage increases and decreases from the *same base* are always equal absolute amounts, provided the percentage increase is not greater than 100 percent, since no greater decrease than 100 percent is possible. Thus, a rise of stock prices from 80 to 100 is a 25 percent increase and an absolute increase of 20 points. Likewise, a decline from 80 to 60 is a 25 percent decrease and an absolute decrease of 20 points.

Taking an average of percentages can produce strange results. Assume that the investor wants to measure the average percentage change in the prices of certain stocks as compared with a year ago. He may either compute the percentage change for each stock and compute an average of the percentages or he can total the market price of the list of stocks at each period of time and compute the percentage change in these totals. The divergent results are shown below.

Stock	Current Price	Price a Year Ago	Percentage Gain
A	6	2	200.0%
B	12	10	20.0
C	106	100	6.0
Total	124	112	10.7
Average of percentage gains of three stocks			75.3+

The method of averaging percentages gives more weight to the percentage gain in the low-priced stock than does the alternative method. The student should be aware of this curious result, but a discussion of properly weighted averages is beyond the scope of this appendix.

AVERAGES

The Mean

What the student may regard as an average—the sum of a set of numbers such as 3, 5, 7, 9, divided by the number of cases, 4—is a special sort of average, called the arithmetic mean. The mean has some interesting properties. The difference between the mean, which is 6 in our illustration and the number 9 in the set of numbers, is 3, and this amount is called the "deviation" of that number from the mean. The sum of the deviations of the numbers smaller than the mean is always equal to the sum of the deviations of the numbers that are larger. Thus, the sum of the deviations of 3 and 5 (namely, $3 + 1 = 4$) is equal to the sum of the deviations of 7 and 9 from the mean.

The deviations in our example are 3, 1, 1, and 3. If one multiplies each deviation by itself—that is, squares each deviation—the numbers 9, 1, 1, and 9, are obtained. The sum of these numbers is 20. If one computes the deviations of the original series of numbers from a number that is *not* the mean (for example, 7), the deviations are different (4, 2, 0, 2). Squaring these numbers produces another series (16, 4, 0, 4), the sum of which is 24, a number larger than 20. This will always be true. The sum of the squares of the deviations from the mean is always less than the sum of the squares of the deviations from any other number that might be taken instead of the mean. This is an interesting property which we shall find useful in understanding correlation, discussed later.

Let us take 3 sets of 10 numbers: (1) the numbers 2, 3, 4, 6, 7, 8, 8, 10, 12, 20; and (2) the numbers 7, 7, 7, 8, 8, 8, 8, 9, 9, 9. The arithmetic mean of both sets is 8. Any average can be defined as a measure of a "central tendency." Obviously the average is a better measure of tendency in the second set of numbers, because no case deviates very far from the mean. This is generally shown by what is known as the "standard deviation." It is usually designated by the Greek letter σ (small sigma). It is computed by taking the sum of the squares of the deviations from the mean, adding these squares, dividing by the number of cases, and extracting the square root of the quotient.[1] The standard deviation of the first set of numbers in our illustration is 4.96; of the second, 0.77. The high standard deviation of the first set of numbers indicates that if the sample is indicative of results from studying a large number of cases, a large proportion of the numbers would fall between 3.04 (the mean of 8 less 4.96) and 12.96 (the mean of 8 plus 4.96). The lower standard deviation of the second set of numbers indicates that the range would fall between 7.23 and 8.77.

Sometimes, the student may wish to study the manner in which

---

[1] Extracting the square root of a number is finding one of two equal factors which, when multiplied, produce that number. Any standard text on arithmetic discusses square root.

one magnitude, such as the tonnage output of steel, varies with another magnitude, such as an index of total industrial production. In plotting yearly or monthly variations on a chart, the degree of relationship between the two magnitudes may be difficult to see, because steel production, for example, may fluctuate in a much wider range than total industrial production. This difficulty can be avoided by expressing the yearly or monthly deviations of each series in terms of the standard deviation of each series, chosen as the unit measure of variation. The calculation involved is simply division of the original data in each series by the standard deviation of that series. Correction of the two series used in our illustration is shown in Table 1.

TABLE 1

Original Deviations		Data Expressed in Standard Deviation Units	
Series 1	*Series 2*	*Series 1*	*Series 2*
−6	7	−1.21	−1.30
−5	7	−1.01	−1.30
−4	7	−0.81	−1.30
−2	8	−0.40	0.00
−1	8	−0.20	0.00
0	8	0.00	0.00
0	8	0.00	0.00
+2	9	+0.40	+1.30
+4	9	+0.81	+1.30
+12	9	+2.42	+1.30

The Mode and the Median

Other measures of central tendency in addition to the arithmetic mean are the mode and the median. We may illustrate with the following series of 17 numbers: 5, 5, 6, 6, 7, 7, 7, 7, 8, 8, 8, 9, 9, 10, 10, 19, 22. The mean of this series is 9. The mode is defined as the magnitude that occurs the greatest number of times. The number 7, which occurs four times, is obviously the mode. When the numbers are arranged in ascending order of magnitude, the median is the middle number. Since there are 17 numbers in all, the ninth number has an equal number of cases (8) on each side of it. The median is obviously 8. In our example, the mean is influenced by the two extreme variations in the series, the numbers 19 and 22. The mode and the median are not so influenced.

Averaging Time Series

When statistics, such as stock prices or levels of industrial production, are available by years, months, weeks, or some other subdivision of time, the statistics are called "time series." The arithmetic mean is sometimes used to smooth out random or seasonal variations; when so used it is called a "moving" or a "trailing" average. In Table

TABLE 2

Date	Original Statistics	3-Month Moving Average	12-Month Moving Average	12-Month Trailing Average
January, 1960	2			
February	3	2		
March	1	3		
April	5	4		
May	6	5		
June	4	4½		
July	3	3	3¾	
August	2	3		
September	4	3		
October	3	4		
November	5	4⅔		
December	6	5		3⅔
January, 1961	4			3⅔

2, a three month moving average is shown. The average of 2 for February, for example, is the sum of the statistics for January, February, and March $(2 + 3 + 1)$ divided by 3, and the average is "centered" at the mid-month, February. The moving average of 3 for March is the sum of the statistics for February, March, and April $(3 + 1 + 5)$ divided by 3.

In the next column to the right, a 12-month moving average centered at July is shown. Since 12 is an even number, no month is exactly the mid-month of the 12-month period. A moving total is computed for the year 1960, the sum of the statistics for each month of the year totaling 44. A second total of 46 is computed by summing the statistics for the period February, 1960, to January, 1961, inclusive. Because July is the seventh month of the first moving total (for the calendar year) and the sixth month of the second moving total, an average of the two totals divided by 12 gives the correct moving average for the month of July. The average of the moving totals is 45. Dividing by 12, the moving average becomes 3¾ for the month of July.

The final column on the right illustrates a 12-month trailing average. The average for December is based on an average of the 12 months from January to December, inclusive. The average for January, 1961, is based on the period February, 1960, to January, 1961, inclusive. A trailing average differs from a moving average in that it is not properly centered but is assumed to relate to the last month for which information is available. A trailing average can be useful for certain purposes, such as dampening the effect of random variations on current statistics; but the student must recognize that it is not properly "centered" and that it may mask significant current trends.

SEASONAL VARIATION

On occasion, the analyst may wish to determine whether monthly variations in certain statistics, such as department store sales or building activity, for example, tend to recur with some degree of regularity, caused by weather, custom, holidays, or other factors. Only by adjusting for such normal variations can one judge whether there has been a *cyclical* change.

We describe a method of computing seasonal variation which is not necessarily the best but is relatively simple. The first step is to compute a properly centered 12-month moving average for each month over a period of years. The original statistic for each month is then divided by the moving average for that month to compute a relative. In the previous illustration, the moving average centered at July, 1960, was 3¾, and the original statistic was 3. Dividing 3 by 3¾ produces a quotient of 0.8. Moving the decimal point two places to the right yields a relative of 80.0.

A similar relative is computed for the month of July in every year for which a moving average has been computed. If moving averages are available for 11 years, for example, there will be 11 relatives for the month of July (as well as for every other month). Let us assume that these relatives for July, arranged in ascending order, are as follows: 65.2, 66.0, 69.9, 71.3, 74.0, 75.0, 80.0, 81.2, 82.9, 83.1, 83.2. If a study of these relatives arranged according to consecutive years, shows no clear downtrend or uptrend, the median may be taken as the probable normal seasonal variation The median of the series is the sixth case, with a value of 75.0. The same computation is made for every month of the year.

If the relative finally chosen as normal for each month were in every case 100.0, this would indicate no need to adjust the original statistics for seasonal influences. This would indicate that in the absence of secular or cyclical changes each monthly statistical magnitude would be one twelfth of the yearly magnitude. A relative of 75.0 for the month of July thus means that for seasonal reasons it is normal that the statistical magnitude for this month be only 75 percent of one twelfth of the annual magnitude.

It is evident that if the relative chosen for each month is correct, the sum of all 12 will be 1,200.0. If they do not total exactly this much, an adjustment must be made. Assume that they total 1,236.0. Dividing by 12 indicates that the average relative is 103.0. That is, each relative is about 3 percent too big. To adjust the July relative of 75.0 for this, one must divide by 1.03 to get the corrected relative of 72.8. When each relative is corrected in this manner, they will total 1,200.0.

CORRELATION

The subject of correlation cannot be fully understood without considerable mathematical background. But correlation is such a useful tool that an attempt to impart at least a partial understanding seems to be justified. The methods we discuss are given without proof, and we do not describe certain refinements that could reduce the labor of calculation.

Suppose the analyst is viewing a statistical time series relating, let us say, to earnings per share of stock in each of the past eight years. Suppose this series proceeds as follows, from the earliest to the latest year: 3, 5, 9, 7, 11, 3, 7, 3. To the extent that the past is any guide to the future, the average of this series of numbers, which is 6, may be the best available guide to an estimate of earnings over the next year. But suppose the analyst discovers another statistical series, perhaps an index of unfilled orders at the beginning of each year, and he begins to study the relationship between this series and earnings per share (assuming no change in capitalization). The figures are listed in Table 3.

Careful study will reveal that earnings are exactly twice unfilled orders, plus 1. Thus, earnings of 3 in the first year are $(2 \times 1) + 1$; while earnings of 5 in the second year are $(2 \times 2) + 1$. Earnings

TABLE 3

Year	Earnings	Index of Unfilled Orders
1	3	1
2	5	2
3	9	4
4	7	3
5	11	5
6	3	1
7	7	3
8	3	1

vary, and unfilled orders vary from year to year; but, if unfilled orders are known at the first of the year, it seems possible to predict earnings for the 12 months ahead if the past relationship still continues to hold good. Thus, if unfilled orders are 5, earnings over the next 12 months could be estimated at 11, a much better guess than the past average of earnings, which is 6.

Exact relationships of this sort are never discovered between economic phenomena. But suppose a reasonably close relationship is suggested, as shown in Table 4. The problem is to define the *average*

TABLE 4

Year	Earnings	Index of Unfilled Orders
1	4	1
2	6	2
3	10	4
4	6	3
5	12	5
6	3	1
7	7	3
8	2	1

relationship between the two statistical series. From our previous discussion, the student might guess that "on the average" actual earnings have come rather close to being twice the index of new orders, plus one. The deviations of actual earnings from theoretical earnings computed in this manner are shown in Table 5. We may say that our theoretical relationship is the average relationship if we can prove

TABLE 5

Year	Index of Unfilled Orders	Theoretical Earnings	Actual Earnings	Deviation of Actual from Theoretical
1	1	3	4	1
2	2	5	4	1
3	4	9	10	1
4	3	7	6	1
5	5	11	12	1
6	1	3	3	0
7	3	7	7	0
8	1	3	2	1

that the sum of the squares of the deviations is less than it would be if we assumed any other relationship. That is a property of the arithmetic mean that we have already discussed.

We shall now illustrate a means of computing the average relationship without having to guess or to resort to trial and error to prove that it is correct. We shall not discuss the proof, since a knowledge of calculus is necessary to understand it. However, in the interest of brevity we shall designate earnings by the latter y, and the index of unfilled orders by the letter x. The statement that earnings are, on the average, equal to twice the index of unfilled orders, plus one, can be stated as: $y = 2x + 1$. It should be noted that this equation is not like a previous one—namely, $\frac{4}{24} = \frac{1}{6}$. These quantities are fixed and are identical, differing only in the form in which the magnitude is expressed. The equation, $y = 2x + 1$, states that y *depends* on x. The index of unfilled orders (x) can take any value, but when any specific value is assigned to it (for example, 3), earnings (y) can take only one value—$(2 \times 3) + 1$, or 7.

We shall now discuss the manner in which the corrected average relationship is calculated. We assume that the form of the equation will be $y = ax + b$, but we do not know that a will be equal to 2, nor that b will be equal to 1. Essentially then, the problem is to discover the correct values for a and for b. As illustrated in Table 6, we first put down in columns each y and each corresponding x, as shown by the actual past record. The next column, headed xy, results from multiplying each y by the corresponding x. The final column-headed x^2 (read "x squared"), results from multiplying each x by itself. We then total all coumns, and note that each column has eight lines, excluding the line for the sum. That is, there are eight "cases" in the series that we are correlating.

TABLE 6

y	x	xy	x^2
4	1	4	1
4	2	8	4
10	4	40	16
6	3	18	9
12	5	60	25
3	1	3	1
7	3	21	9
2	1	2	1
Sums 48	20	156	66

Two equations are then written to find a and b in the equation, $y = ax + b$. The sum of the y's (48) is said to equal the sum of the x's (20) times a, plus the number of cases (8) times b. A second equation is written by stating that the sum of the xy column (156) equals the sum of the x^2 column (66) times a, plus the sum of the x column (20) times b. The solutions will always be of this sort.

These two equations can be solved to find the values of a and b. The two equations and the necessary calculations are as follows.

$$48 = 20a + \ 8b \ (\text{equation } 1)$$
$$156 = 66a + 20b \ (\text{equation } 2)$$

Multiply both sides of equation 1 by 5, and both sides of equation 2 by 2. This is done to make both equations contain the term $40b$. Subtract equation 1 from equation 2 to eliminate the terms with b.

$$312 = 132a + 40b \ (\text{equation 2 multiplied by 2})$$
$$240 = 100a + 40b \ (\text{equation 1 multiplied by 5})$$
$$\overline{\ 72 = \ 32a} \qquad (\text{subtracting equation 1 from 2})$$
$$a = 2.25 \qquad (72 \div 32)$$

To find the value of b, rewrite equation 1, substituting for a its value, 2.25.

$$48 = 45 + 8b \quad (20 \times a = 20 \times 2.25 = 45)$$
$$8b = \ 3 \qquad (48 - 45 = 3)$$
$$b = \tfrac{3}{8} = 0.375 \ (3 \div 8)$$

These values of a and b are then substituted in the original equation, $y = ax + b$. The equation of average relationship is thus $y = 2.25x + 0.375$. This is not the same as the equation we guessed might be correct, $y = 2x + 1$, even though the deviations of actual earnings from theoretical earnings, computed from that equation, conformed to one property of an average—that the sum of deviations above the average value must equal the sum of deviations below the average value. We were not sure whether the sum of the deviations squared was less than any other possible relationship that could be assumed. The sum of the squares of the deviations from the equation

TABLE 7

Actual y	Actual x	Calculated y	Deviation
4	1	2.625	1.375
4	2	4.875	0.875
10	4	9.375	0.625
6	3	7.125	1.125
12	5	11.625	0.375
3	1	2.625	0.375
7	3	7.125	0.125
2	1	2.625	0.625

$y = 2x + 1$ total 6. Let us see whether they total less when we use the correct equation, $y = 2.25x + 0.375$. The deviations are shown in Table 7. We leave for the student to prove that when they are squared and added the sum is 5, or less than in the incorrect equation.

Dividing the sum of the squares of the deviations (5) by the number of cases (8) gives 0.625. Extracting the square root of this number gives 0.7906. This is the standard deviation of the actual data from the value of y when the known value of x is used to estimate y from the equation. The standard deviation of actual y's from the arithmetic mean of the y's (6) is 3.25. Obviously, better estimates of the probable of y seem likely to result when the equation of average relationship to x is used than when sole reliance is placed on an average of past values of y alone.

Mathematical methods are available to compute the average relationship between more than two statistical series. For example, it is possible to compute the average relationship of stock prices to the *combined* influence of earnings and dividends. If we let y represent stock prices; x, earnings; and z, dividends; such a correlation equation will take the form $y = ax + bz + c$, in which a, b, and c are actual numbers. This is called "multiple correlation." The mathematical methods become too complex to treat in a discussion designed to help the investor or business analyst who has a very limited mathematical background.

Paper ruled by vertical and horizontal lines is called coordinate paper. When vertical and horizontal distances are assigned appropriate numbers, it is possible to draw a picture of a mathematical equation such as $y = 2x + 1$. Choosing a value of 2 for x, the equation requires that y must be 5. To plot this point, the value of x is usually assumed to be measured along the horizontal scale (distances to the right of the zero point). The value of y is measured on the vertical scale (distances above zero). The procedure for finding the point at which x is 2 and y is 5 will be the same as if one starts from some point marked zero on a map, moves two units due east, and then proceeds five units due north.

Plotting other points from this equation, such as the point where x is 1 and y is 3, or where x is 3 and y is 7, will reveal that all these points fall in a straight line. Any equation of the form $y = ax + b$ becomes a straight line when plotted on coordinate paper.

By letting x represent a point in time, and by numbering years or months consecutively from earliest to latest as 1, 2, 3, etc., the student can use correlation to compute a line of secular trend. Estimating secular trend, however, requires much common sense and economic analysis, and the mere use of a mathematical tool is no assurance of accuracy.

SIMPLE INTEREST

Problems of calculating simple interest most often arise in connection with the purchase or sale of bonds on dates other than an interest payment date. Interest is a payment for waiting; to the extent that the seller has held a bond for a period of time since he last received interest, he is entitled to the interest that has accrued since this period.

Calculation of accrued interest is slightly different for government bonds than for corporate bonds. Let us illustrate the distinction by assuming that a 3 percent government bond pays interest of $15 twice a year, on January 15 and July 15. Let us assume that the holder sells the bond on August 22. Since it is customary to make delivery of a government bond the day after sale, accrued interest would be computed from July 15 to August 23, the day of delivery. Since July has 31 days, the elapsed time in that month is 16 days ($31 - 15$). To this must be added the 23 days in August to arrive at a total of 39 days on which interest accrued.[2] Interest accruing each day is calculated by dividing $30 by 365, the number of days in a year. The answer is $0.082. Multiplying this by 39 produces $3.20 as the proper amount of interest.

Let us now assume that the holder of a 3 percent *corporate* bond that pays interest January 15 and July 15 sells on August 22. Delivery would normally be 3 days after sale, on August 25. To compute the elapsed time from July 15 to August 25, each month is assumed to contain only 30 days. From July 15 to August 15 is thus assumed to be only 30 days, and adding 10 days more from August 15 to August 25 produces a total of 40 days. This is one day less than actual, but average interest per day is computed by dividing 30 by 360 instead of by 365. The answer is $0.0833. Multiplying by 40 produces $3.33 as the proper amount of accrued interest. The buyer must pay this amount to the seller in addition to the agreed price of the bond, unless he has bought the bond flat. Normally, only defaulted bonds are quoted flat—that is, the price is considered to be full payment for any accrued unpaid interest.

COMPOUND INTEREST

Suppose an investor has a principal of $1,000, which he has lent at 5 percent interest. When he receives his $50 interest at the end of the year, he can theoretically lend it out at 5 percent, thus increasing his principal to $1,050. Next year, he will receive interest of 5 percent, not only on his original principal of $1,000, but also on the $50 of reinvested interest. The amount received at the end of the second year will be 52.50. This will then be added to principal, increasing it to $1,102.50. Because this procedure enables the investor to earn interest on past interest payments he has received and reinvested, the principle of compound interest is said to involve "interest on interest." *As a practical matter it may be very difficult to reinvest small amounts of interest in this manner, yet the whole theory of bond yields rests on the principle of compound interest.*

We have just illustrated the case of compounding interest once a year. Most bonds pay interest twice a year. In that case, the period

---

[2] The student should note that if one counts both July 15 and August 23 as days on which interest accrues the elapsed time is 40 days. Only one of these dates is counted in a proper calculation. Which day should be properly viewed as bearing accrued interest is more a philosophical question than a problem of practical calculation.

of compounding would be six months. The coupon rate of the bond might be an annual rate of 5.0 percent, but for purposes of calculating the effect of the compound interest principle the rate would be taken to be 2.5 percent for each period of 6 months. In the event interest were paid quarterly, the period would be 3 months, and the interest rate per period would be 1.25 percent on a 5.0 percent annual interest rate.

The principle of computing compound interest can best be shown by assuming an initial investment of $1.00. Once the growth of an initial investment of $1.00 has been computed for any given number of periods and at any given rate of interest per period, the growth of an initial investment of any other sum of money can be calculated by simple multiplication.

At a rate of 3 percent per period, an initial investment of $1.00 obviously grows to $1.03 at the end of the first period. The amount of $1.0609 at the end of the second period is obviously the result of adding to $1.03 the interest on $1.03 at 3 percent. Since multiplying $1.03 by one plus the interest rate is the same as multiplying $1.03 by the interest rate and then adding $1.03, the proper amount at the end of the second period is 1.03×1.03. This can be written as $(1.03)^2$, the superior 2 showing the number of times the amount is used as a factor and, hence, corresponding to the number of periods. The general formula for the amount of 1.00 at the end of n periods at an interest rate per period designated by i is $(1 + i)^n$. When the original investment is a principal in excess of $1.00, designated by P, the formula becomes $P(1 + i)^n$.

This amount can be calculated by ordinary multiplication, but the computation is laborious. When the amount of $P(1 + i)^n$, sometimes designated as S, is known and the interest rate i is also known, but n is unknown, it becomes essential to use logarithms to solve for the number of periods. Likewise, when only S and n are known, logarithms must be used to solve for i. The student capable of using logarithms will have no difficulty in using the formula we have given. The student who is not capable will be forced to rely on some table showing the "amount of $1.00" at various rates of compound interest for various periods.

PRESENT VALUE

We have been concerned with the growth at compound interest of an initial investment of $1.00. We now assume that the original investment is not known, and we inquire how much will have to be invested to grow to $1.00 over n periods at the interest rate of i. Obviously, the amount that must be invested initially is less than $1.00. The correct amount is called the "present value" of the right to receive $1.00 after the elapse of n periods and assuming an interest rate of i per period. Obviously, the right to receive $1.00 after the elapse of n periods of time is worth no more than the original investment necessary to produce $1.00 at the end of n periods at an interest rate i. Let V designate the present value of $1.00. When the amount of principal, P, is greater than $1.00, we have proved that the amount to which it will grow is $P(1 + i)^n$. Obviously, if P is chosen as some amount less than $1.00 and equal to V, we may write $V(1 + i)^n = 1$. From this equation, it follows that the present value of $1.00 is $1/(1 + i)^n$, or the reciprocal of the "amount" of $1.00. Tables of present values are available. When only a table of amounts of $1.00 is at hand, present values may, of course, be obtained by computing the reciprocals.

ANNUITIES

When a person receives a fixed amount of money in each period for n periods, he is said to be receiving an annuity. The amounts received each period are called "rents." If it is assumed that the recipient invests each rent received at the close of each period at the interest rate i, there is posed a mathematical problem of determining what the total sum of money will be at the end of the last period. This is known as the "amount of an annuity." It is obviously the amount that will be in an individual's savings bank account if he pursues a policy of depositing the same amount of savings at regular intervals and never withdraws any interest. We offer the formula, without proof, in the interest of brevity. The amount of an ordinary (or immediate) annuity of $1.00, when the rents are received and invested at the *end* of each period is

$$\frac{(1+i)^n - 1.}{i}$$

When the rents are greater than $1.00, the amount is computed by multiplying the amount of an annuity of $1.00 by the dollar amount of the periodic *rent*. Tables are available showing results for various periods and interest rates. When the rents are received and invested at the *beginning* of each period, the annuity is called an "annuity due." The amount of such an annuity at the end of n periods can be obtained by first computing the amount of an ordinary annuity for n periods and multiplying the answer by $(1 + i)$. When interest is compounded more frequently than rents are received and invested, the number of periods (n) must be made equal to the number of rents, and the interest rate (i) must be the *effective* compound rate for the period. If the interest rate for each yearly period, for example, is 5 percent compounded semiannually, the effective compound rate is 5.0625 percent per annum, computed from the formula $[(1 + i') \div 2]^2 - 1$, where i' is the nominal interest rate per year.

The present value of an annuity can be defined as the sum of the present values of all future rentals. For purposes of calculation, a better formula to compute the present value of an annuity is $(1 - V) \div i$. The reader will recall that $V = 1 \div (1 + i)^n$. If the rentals are more than \$1.00, the present value of an annuity of \$1.00 is multiplied by the dollar amount of the periodic rent. The present value of an annuity is important, because the price of a \$1,000 bond, bought to yield $2i$ return[3] to maturity, can be viewed as the present value of the annuity whose rents are the interest payments, plus the present value of \$1,000 at maturity. The price of the bond to yield $2i$ return if the coupon is 5 percent payable twice a year is $25[(1 - V) \div .025] + 1,000V$, where $V = (1 \div 1.025)^n$ and n is the number of six-month periods to maturity.

The concept of the present value of an annuity is also useful in understanding how one computes the fixed annual payment necessary both to pay interest on a debt and to amortize the debt over a given period of years. The present value of an annuity can be defined as the amount of money that must be invested at a given interest rate in order to provide a given number of periodic withdrawals in the future before the fund is exhausted. But these rents can also be viewed as the periodic payments necessary to amortize a debt if the debt is viewed as being the known present value of an annuity. When the present value of an annuity of known rents is computed, the present value of an annuity of \$1.00 is multiplied by the periodic rent. When the present value of an annuity is known, therefore, the rents can be computed by dividing by the present value of an annuity of \$1.00.

---

[3] Yield is $2i$ because yields are stated on an annual basis, whereas i is the rate per period of six months, and hence half the annual rate.

To cite a brief example, suppose that $1,000 is borrowed at 6 percent, to be repaid in equal annual amounts, covering both principal and interest, over a period of 4 years. The installments are presumed to be payable at the end of each year. The present value of an annuity of $1.00 for 4 periods at 6 percent is 3.4651056. Dividing $1,000 by this number indicates the annual installment to be $288.59. We prove in the following table that this is the correct amount to repay the debt with interest.

End of Year	Payment	Interest	Amortization	Balance Owed, $1000.00
1	$288.59	$60.00	$228.59	$771.41
2	288.59	46.28	242.31	529.10
3	288.59	31.75	256.84	272.26
4	288.59	16.34	272.25	.01

BOND TABLES

Computing yields to maturity, or computing prices at which bonds will provide a given yield, can usually be done most easily by consulting published bond tables. In the illustration in Table 8, the bond has an annual coupon rate of $3\frac{1}{2}$ percent, and the interest is paid twice a year. Allowing for compounding of interest, the effective coupon rate is, therefore, actually 3.530625 percent per year. The column to the extreme left lists the yield to maturity of such a bond at corresponding prices shown in columns headed by the length of time to

TABLE 8

Computation of Bond Yields to Maturity
(Annual Coupon Rate, $3\frac{1}{2}$%, Paid Semiannually)

| Yield % | 26 | Years to Maturity | | |
		$26\frac{1}{2}$	27	$27\frac{1}{2}$
2.90	110.90	111.04	111.18	111.32
2.95	109.94	110.06	110.19	110.31
3.00	108.98	109.10	109.21	109.32
3.05	108.04	108.14	108.24	108.34
3.10	107.10	107.19	107.28	107.37
3.15	106.18	106.26	106.33	106.41

maturity. Assume that a $1,000 bond pays interest of $17.50 every 6 months, matures in 26 years, and is quoted in the open market at $1,075.50. Converted to "points" ($10), this price is 107.55. Glancing down the column headed "26," one finds that a price of 107.10 will provide a yield of 3.10 percent, while a price of 108.04 will provide a yield of 3.05 percent. The quoted price is between these two prices; therefore, the yield is between 3.05 and 3.10 percent.

To find the yield more exactly, one must interpolate between these two prices and yields. An increase in price from 107.10 to 108.04 is an absolute increase of 0.94. This increase produces a decrease in yield amounting to 0.05. The difference between the quoted price of 107.55 and 107.10 is 0.45. The yield of a bond selling at 107.55 is therefore less than 3.10 percent by $(0.45 \div 0.94) \times 0.05$, or by roughly 0.024. The estimated yield is therefore 3.076 percent. Interpolation based on proportion does not produce completely accurate results, but results are accurate enough for all but very large bond deals.

Interpolation is frequently necessary for other types of problems. Assume, for example, that one wishes to bid for a $3\frac{1}{2}$ percent bond at a price to yield 3 percent. The bond matures in 26 years and 4 months. This maturity is not shown in the bond table. At a yield of 3 percent, the difference in price between a bond with a maturity of $26\frac{1}{2}$ years and one of 26 years is 0.12 $(109.10 - 108.98)$. If adding 6 months to a maturity of 26 years makes this much difference, adding 4 months should add $(4 \div 6) \times 0.12$, or 0.08. The proper bid for the bond is 109.06 $(108.98 + 0.08)$, plus 2 months' accrued interest amounting to $5.83.[4]

A book of bond tables will show the analyst yields for bonds with coupon rates other than $3\frac{1}{2}$ percent. When the tables cover coupon rates from $\frac{1}{2}$ to 4 percent at intervals of $\frac{1}{8}$ percent, and rates from $4\frac{1}{4}$ to 6 percent at intervals of $\frac{1}{4}$ percent, there will seldom be any necessity to interpolate for a coupon rate that is not given. Books of tables on compound interest, annuities, and bond yields frequently suggest alternative methods of interpolation that could be used when the method we have discussed would involve too great an inaccuracy.

Callable Bonds

When bidding on a yield basis for bonds that are callable at the option of the debtor, the conservative procedure in computing the price is to assume debtor action that is most adverse to the interests

---

[4] We disregard the accrual pending delivery, discussed elsewhere.

of the investor. When a bond is callable after a certain date *at par* and the investor is willing to invest at less than the coupon rate, a premium above par will be paid. In this case, the conservative procedure is to assume that the bond will be called at the call date. For example, suppose that an investor is willing to buy a 4 percent bond with a maturity of 20 years at a yield of 3 percent. The bond is callable at par in 15 years. To yield 3 percent, the price of the bond with a maturity of 20 years is $114.96; but if the bond is called at the end of 15 years, the price to yield 3 percent is 112.01. Obviously, the investor who wants assurance of a 3 percent return should pay no more than 112.01.

On the other hand, if a 4 percent bond with a maturity of 20 years is bought on a 5 percent yield basis, a discount below par will be paid, and the most conservative procedure is to assume that the bond will not be called at the end of 15 years. On a 5 percent yield basis, a 4 percent bond with a maturity of 15 years will sell for 89.53, while a bond with a maturity of 20 years will sell for 87.45. To be certain of at least a 5 percent yield, the investor should pay no more than the lower price.

When a bond is callable before maturity but only at a premium above par, the only general rule is that the investor should compute the price on the assumption that it will not, and pay the lower price. Which price will be lower depends on the size of the premium. Suppose an investor wants to bid on a 5 percent yield basis for a 6 percent bond maturing in 18 years but callable at a 10 percent premium in 13 years. The price, assuming the bond is not called, is found in a bond table to be 111.78.

On a 5 percent yield basis, the price of a 6 percent bond with 13 years to maturity is found in a bond table to be 109.48. To this price, however, must be added the present value of the call premium of $100. Using a table that shows the present value of $1.00, one finds that when n is 26 (periods of 6 months) and the interest rate is 2.5 percent (half the nominal 5 percent annual yield, to allow for compounding), the present value of $1.00 is $0.526. The present value of $100 is, therefore, $52.60, or 5.26 points. Adding this to 109.48 gives a correct price of 114.74. This is higher than the price on the assumption that the bond runs to a maturity of 18 years. The investor will bid the lower price and assume that the bond will not be called.

When the investor already owns a bond and the bond is subject to call at a premium in the future, he may wish to compute the yield to the call date that is implicit in the current market price at which he can sell his bond. Also, when he is thinking of buying a bond that is subject to call in a few months but is attractive if it is not called, he may wish to measure the risk he would take in buying by determining whether the price at which the bond is offered provides any positive yield to call date at all.

Assume that a 6 percent bond, maturing in 5 years but callable at 102 in 6 months, is selling in the market at 104.95. The yield to maturity is 4.87 percent, which may be considerably more than is available from other bonds of comparable quality. A potential investor in the bond may be willing to take the risk that the bond will be called in 6 months because he may have some reason to believe that call is by no means certain. He is unwilling to take this risk, however, if call would actually cause him to lose money. His problem is to compute the yield to call date in order to determine whether he would get any return on his money in the event of call.

The approximate yield can be computed as follows. (1) Divide the market price by the call price to arrive at an adjusted price ($104.95 \div 102 = 102.89$). (2) Divide the annual interest payment, expressed in points, by the call price to arrive at an adjusted yield ($6 \div 102 = 5.88$ percent). (3) Choosing a page in a book of bond yields which relates to a bond with a nominal annual coupon nearest to the adjusted yield (6 percent is nearer than 5¾ percent), use the adjusted price (102.89) to determine a corresponding yield, assuming a maturity at call date but no call premium. (A bond table gives a yield of 0.217 percent for a 6 percent bond with a maturity of 6 months and selling at 102.89). (4) Compute the difference between the nominal coupon rate assumed in step 3 and the adjusted yield ($6.00 - 5.88 = 0.120$). (5) If the coupon rate assumed in step 3 is less than the adjusted yield, add the difference to the yield computed in step 3. If the coupon rate is greater, subtract it from the yield computed in step 3 ($0.217 - 0.120 = 0.097$). The result is only the approximate yield to call date, but results are accurate enough for most purposes. The true yield to call date in our illustration is 0.1 percent.

Scientific Amortization of Premium and Discount

An investor who pays $1056.97 for a 5 percent bond with a maturity of 3 years invests on a 3 percent yield basis. Instead of regarding interest of $25 received in cash every 6 months as constituting his true income, and then recording a loss of $56.97 at maturity, an investor may compute his true income each half year at 1.5 percent and regard the amount of cash received in excess of true income as a partial return of the premium above par that he has paid. In this way, the premium may be completely written off or amortized on his books of account.

Six months after purchase he received $25, but his true income is 1.5 percent of his original investment ($1056.97), or $15.85. The difference between $25 and $15.85 is $9.15, which can be subtracted from his original investment, thus writing it down to $1047.82. At the end of the first year, he receives another payment of $25, but his true income is computed as 1.5 percent of $1047.82, or $15.72. The difference between $25 and $15.72 is $9.28, which again is subtracted from $1047.82 to further reduce his investment cost to $1038.54. The result of continuing this procedure to maturity is shown in Table 9.

TABLE 9

Cost		$1,056.97
First interest date: coupon	$25.00	
True income	15.85	9.15
Carrying value		$1,047.82
Second interest date: coupon	$25.00	
True income	15.72	9.28
Carrying value		$1,038.54
Third interest date: coupon	$25.00	
True income	15.58	9.42
Carrying value		$1,029.12
Fourth interest date: coupon	$25.00	
True income	15.44	9.56
Carrying value		$1,019.56
Fifth interest date: coupon	$25.00	
True income	15.29	9.71
Carrying value		$1,009.85
Sixth interest date: coupon	$25.00	
True income	15.15	9.85
Par received at maturity		$1,000.00

Amortization of a discount, when a bond is bought below par to yield more than the coupon rate, involves no new principle. In this case, the true income will exceed the interest received in cash, and the difference will be added to the carrying value, thus writing up the cost of the bond to par at maturity so that no capital gain is recorded at that time.

VALUE OF RIGHTS

When corporations grant to existing shareholders the privilege of subscribing to a new issue of stock below market price, the investor has the problem of computing the theoretical value of the rights. A right is defined as whatever privilege attaches to ownership of one share of outstanding stock, and usually denotes a privilege of subscribing to a fractional part of a share of new stock. As long as the old stock sells rights-on, a seller of the stock transfers both the stock and the rights that attach thereto. When the stock finally sells ex-rights, only the old stock is transferred, and there is a separate market in the rights until the expiration date.

The theoretical value of a right during the period in which the old stock sells rights-on can be computed from the formula, $M - S \div (N + 1)$, in which M stands for the market price of the old stock; S, for the subscription price of the new stock; and N, for the number of old shares needed to acquire enough rights to buy one share of new stock. For example, if stock is selling with rights-on at a price of 90, and each share of old stock is given the right to buy $\frac{1}{3}$ of a share of new stock at 82, the value of a right is $(90 - 82) \div (3 + 1) = 2$. The formula to compute the theoretical value of a right during the rights-off period is simply $(M - S) \div N$.

The reason for dividing by $N + 1$ in the first formula can be explained by stating that the market price of the stock, M, includes the value of the right itself. Designating the value of the right V, the value of the stock ex-rights is $M - V$. The value of the privilege of buying $1/N$ shares of new stock at S is therefore expressed in the equation $V = (M - V - S) \div N$. By simple algebra:

$$NV + V = M - S$$
$$(N + 1)\,V = M - S$$
$$V = \frac{M - S}{N + 1}$$

CONVERSION PRICE AND CONVERSION PARITY

To say that a bond or a preferred stock is convertible into a certain number of shares of common stock is equivalent to stating that a bond or preferred stock will be accepted at par as payment for stock at a certain price. This price may be called the "conversion price" of the stock. For example, if a preferred stock is convertible into four shares of common, the conversion price of the common stock is 25, or one fourth of 100, the par value of the preferred stock.

The preferred stock may not be selling at par, however. If the preferred stock is selling at 80, conversion parity for the common stock is 20, or one fourth of 80. At any price for the common stock above 20, it will be cheaper to first buy the preferred stock and convert, instead of buying the common stock directly. It is possible to speak of conversion parity for the preferred stock also. When the common stock sells at 20, conversion parity is 80 for the preferred stock.

APPENDIX 2

Income, Savings, and Expenditures of People with Four or More Years of College

Age	Income	Present Value Factor at 4%	Present Value of Income	Excess Income (Income − $5,000)	30% of Col. 4	Savings (Col. 5 + $250)	Expenditures (Col. 1 − Col. 6)	Present Value of Expenditures (Col. 2 × Col. 7)
22	$ 6,030	.9615	$5,798	$1,030	309	$ 559	$ 5,471	$5,260
23	6,306	.9246	5,831	1,306	392	642	5,664	5,237
24	6,582	.8890	5,851	1,582	475	725	5,857	5,207
25	6,858	.8548	5,862	1,858	557	807	6,051	5,172
26	7,134	.8219	5,863	2,134	640	890	6,244	5,132
27	7,409	.7903	5,855	2,409	723	973	6,436	5,086
28	7,685	.7599	5,840	2,685	806	1,056	6,629	5,037
29	7,961	.7307	5,817	2,961	888	1,138	6,823	4,986
30	8,237	.7026	5,787	3,237	971	1,221	7,016	4,929
31	8,513	.6756	5,751	3,513	1,054	1,304	7,209	4,870
32	8,788	.6496	5,709	3,788	1,136	1,386	7,402	4,808
33	9,064	.6246	5,661	4,064	1,219	1,469	7,595	4,744
34	9,340	.6006	5,610	4,340	1,302	1,552	7,788	4,677
35	9,616	.5775	5,553	4,616	1,385	1,635	7,981	4,609
36	9,892	.5553	5,493	4,892	1,468	1,718	8,174	4,539
37	10,167	.5339	5,428	5,167	1,550	1,800	8,367	4,467
38	10,443	.5134	5,361	5,443	1,633	1,833	8,610	4,420

Age	Income	Present Value Factor at 4%	Present Value of Income	Excess Income (Income − $5,000)	30% of Col. 4	Savings (Col. 5 + $250)	Expenditures (Col. 1 − Col. 6)	Present Value of Expenditures (Col. 2 × Col. 7)
39	10,719	.4936	5,291	5,719	1,716	1,966	8,753	4,320
40	10,908	.4746	5,177	5,908	1,772	2,022	8,886	4,217
41	11,097	.4564	5,065	6,097	1,829	2,079	9,018	4,116
42	11,286	.4388	4,952	6,286	1,886	2,136	9,150	4,015
43	11,475	.4220	4,842	6,475	1,943	2,193	9,282	3,917
44	11,664	.4057	4,732	6,664	1,999	2,249	9,415	3,820
45	11,852	.3901	4,623	6,852	2,056	2,306	9,546	3,724
46	12,041	.3751	4,517	7,041	2,112	2,362	9,679	3,631
47	12,230	.3607	4,411	7,230	2,169	2,419	9,811	3,539
48	12,419	.3468	4,307	7,419	2,226	2,476	9,943	3,448
49	12,608	.3335	4,205	7,608	2,282	2,532	10,076	3,360
50	12,640	.3207	4,054	7,640	2,292	2,542	10,098	3,238
51	12,672	.3083	3,907	7,672	2,302	2,552	10,120	3,120
52	12,704	.2965	3,767	7,704	2,311	2,561	10,143	3,007
53	12,736	.2851	3,631	7,736	2,321	2,571	10,165	2,898
54	12,768	.2741	3,500	7,768	2,330	2,580	10,188	2,792
55	12,800	.2636	3,374	7,800	2,340	2,590	10,210	2,691
56	12,832	.2534	3,252	7,832	2,350	2,600	10,232	2,593
57	12,864	.2437	3,135	7,864	2,359	2,609	10,255	2,499
58	12,896	.2343	3,022	7,896	2,369	2,619	10,277	2,408
59	12,928	.2253	2,913	7,928	2,378	2,628	10,300	2,321
60	12,960	.2166	2,807	7,960	2,388	2,638	10,322	2,236
61	12,960	.2083	2,700	7,960	2,388	2,638	10,322	2,150
62	12,960	.2003	2,596	7,960	2,388	2,638	10,322	2,067
63	12,960	.1926	2,496	7,960	2,388	2,638	10,322	1,988
64	12,960	.1852	2,400	7,960	2,388	2,638	10,322	1,912
65	12,960	.1781	2,308	7,960	2,388	2,638	10,322	1,838

Source: U.S. Department of Commerce, Bureau of Census, *Current Population Reports, Consumer Income.*

Index

A

Acacia Mutual Life Insurance Company, 105–6
Advance-decline line, investment timing and, 424–25
Airlines
  analysis of, 289–94
  capitalization of, 291
  financial and operating characteristics, 290–94
  as passenger carriers, 266
  passenger load factor of, 292
  regulatory environment of, 293–94
American Depository Receipts, nature of, 407
Analytical reference standards, 187–89
Annuities
  investment characteristics, 50
  as investments, 49–51
Average cost, as inventory costing method, 240

B

Balance sheet
  capital funds as item on, 231–34
  cash as account on, 224–25
  of commercial banks, 367–71
  consolidated, description of, 235–36
  current assets as classification on, 224–28
  deferred income on, 230
  electric utility composite, 305–6
  of finance companies, 377–81
  fixed assets on, 228
  inventory as account on, 226–28
  liabilities on, 229–34
  long-term debt on, 230–34
  of property and casualty insurance companies, 339–45
  railroad composite, 274–76
  receivables as account on, 225–26
  short-term debt as item on, 229–30
Bank and Quotation Record, 125
Bankers Trust Company, balance sheet of, 369

Banks; see Commercial banks and Mutual savings banks
Bernhard, Arnold, and Company, 122
Best's Insurance Reports, 130
Bond prices, description of, 144
Bond quality and legality for investment, 71–74
Bond yields
  and bond quality, 71
  nature of, 66–71
Bonds
  corporate, general nature of, 56–65; see also Corporate bonds
  definition of coupon rate of, 66
  general nature of, 55–56
  investments of commercial banks, 374
  quality ratings and yields, 71–73
  U.S. Savings, 51–53
  valuation of, 65–71
  value variables, 65–66
  yield differential reflected in quality of, 72–73
  yield to maturity described, 66–71
Book value
  of life insurance common stocks, 328–31
  property and casualty insurance company common stock, 342
Braveman, Philip, 108
Brokers
  commissions allowed on New York Stock Exchange, 163–65
  considerations in choosing, 457–59
  as sources of investment information, 120–21
Business cycle, as factor in industry analysis, 211–14
Business forecasts, monthly economic letters as source of, 138

C

Call options, description of, 170–71
Call provisions of bonds, 60
Call provisions of preferred stock, 96
Canada, gross national product of, 185

Canadian industries and companies
    financial post corporation service as
        source of information, 129
    sources of information, 123
    sources of price quotations of, 126
Capacity factor, calculation of, 307–8
Capital funds
    analysis of, 232–34
    description of, 231–34
Capital gains, income tax treatment of,
    34–35
Capitalization, airlines, 291
Cash, description of, as account classifica-
    tion, 224–25
Cash earnings, concept of, 242–43
Civil Aeronautics Board, function in air-
    line regulation, 293–94
Closed-end investment companies, man-
    agement appraisal measures, 358–59
College Life Insurance Company, 332
Commercial banks
    analysis of operating costs of, 372–74
    balance sheets of, 367–71
    capital-risk asset ratio of, 370
    description of changes in reserves of,
        145–46
    failure of, 45
    gains and losses on securities, 374
    general nature of, 366–67
    income statements of, 373
    loan deposit ratio of, 370–71
    profitability analysis of, 371–74
    regulation of, 366
    savings deposits, financial risk of, 45
    saivngs deposits of, 43–45
    sources of information on, 131
Commissions
    investment company shares, 353–55
    New York Stock Exchange, 354–55
Common stock
    book value of, 90–91
    buying on margin, 165–67
    characteristics of, 77–81
    commissions on sale of, 163–64
    description of options on, 169–71
    finance company, selection of, 384
    growth, 89–90
    intrinsic value of, 176–77
    investment company acquisition costs
        of, 353–55
    in the investment program, 108–11
    life insurance, estimating book value of,
        328–31
    market analysis as valuation method of,
        175–76
    par value of, 77–78
    preemptive rights of, 78–81

Common stock—*Cont.*
    price index, Standard and Poor's (500
        stocks) 1928–64, 109
    prices
        description of quotations of, 143
        forecasting major economic trends
            and, 412–16
    primary marketing of, 150–55
    property and casualty insurance com-
        panies, 345
    qualitative analysis of, 177–78
    quantitative analysis of, 178
    record of electric utility, 319
    selection of electric utility, 317–18
    selection measures of, 255–57
    short sales of, 167–69
    sources of information on prices of, 125–
        26
    valuation of, 83–93
    voting rights of, 77
    warrants as options to purchase, 81–82
Common stock prices, reading the financial
    page, 142–44
Common stock yields, 84–85
Company annual reports, as source of in-
    formation, 128–29
Confidence index, investment timing and,
    422–24
Constant dollar value of stocks plan, 427–
    30
Constant stock-bond ratio plan, 430–32
Consumer buying habits, as factor in in-
    dustry analysis, 205–6
Consumer credit, nature of, 375–76
Continental Insurance Company, 337–39,
    343
Conversion privilege of corporate bonds,
    62–64
Convertible bonds, value of, 63
Corporate bonds
    analysis of maturities of, 287–88
    call provisions of, 60
    conversion provision in, 62–64
    equipment trust obligations, 285
    guaranteed, 283–84
    maturity of, 60–61
    measures of quality of, 252–54
    methods of recovering principal, 59–61
    mortgage, 284–85
    security and asset protection of, 57–59
    sinking funds of, 60–61
    types of security, 57–59
        secured, 57–58
        subordinated, 58–59
        unsecured, 58
Cumulative provision of preferred stock,
    93–94

Current expenditure requirements, computation of, 13

D

Debenture bonds, nature of, 58
Debt
long-term, as balance sheet item, 230–34
service analysis of, 243–44
short-term, as balance sheet item, 229–30
Depreciation
description of methods of, 240–43
electric utility, 313–14
Detroit Edison Co., operating revenues of, 312
Dilution
description of, 234–35
the nature of, 310–11
Disability
economic effects of, 18–19
frequency of, 19
as investment requirement, 17–19
and life value, 12
and medical expense insurance, 19–20
need of insurance against effects of, 18–21
as personal financial hazard, 10
Disability income insurance
calculation of amount needed, 18
nature of, 20–21
Diversification, description of, 444–45
Dividends
measures of payout, 254–55
present value of, 83–87
Dollar averaging plan, 435–37
investment company shares and, 460
Dow Theory, 418–19
Dow-Jones Industrial Average, description of, 143
Dreyfus Corporation, systematic purchase plan of, 353
Dun and Bradstreet, Municipal Service Reports, 392

E

Earnings
basis for valuation of common stock, 87–89
dilution of, 310
Economic data, general, sources of, 136–40
Economic trends and investment timing, 411–16
Economic value of man
factors determining, 11
influence of income pattern on, 12

Electric utilities
analysis of income statement of, 311–16
calculation of load of, 306–7
capacity measures of, 307–8
customer classification of, 311–12
dilution of earnings of, 309–10
expense ratios of, 315–16
financial expenses of, 317
financial management of, 308–10
fixed charges earned ratio, 316–17
industry growth of, 300–303
measures of plant utilization, 305–8
objectives of financial statement analysis, 303
operating expense analysis of, 312–16
postwar record of common stocks, 319
regional growth patterns of, 301–2
selection of common stock of, 317–18
special characteristics of, 300
stability of production of, 302–3
Equipment trust certificates, 285
Equity interest, definition of, 76–77
Equity investments, 4–5

F

Family income, allocation of, 10–11
Federal Aviation Agency, function in airline regulation, 293
Federal Deposit Insurance Corporation and commercial banks, 45
Federal individual income taxes, general nature of, 33–35
Federal Power Commission, electric power statistics, 130
Federal Reserve banks, description of financial condition of, 145
Federal Reserve Board of Governors, margin requirements, 166
Federal Savings and Loan Insurance Corporation, purpose of, 43
Finance companies
analysis of operations of, 381–84
balance sheets of, 377–81
capital structure of, 380–81
costs of operation of, 382–83
factors in analysis of, 377
general nature of, 375–76
income sources of, 381
investment characteristics of, 376–77
regulation of, 366
unearned income of, 378–80
Financial Post, The, 126
Financial Post Corporation Service, The, 129
Financial risk
definition of, 28
as factor in common stock valuation, 83

Financial risk—*Cont.*
influence on bond values, 66
nature of, 27–28
portfolio quality and, 444–47
and savings and loan associations, 41–43
stability of income and assumption of, 112
Financial statement analysis
accounting practices and comparability of data, 219
and the balance sheet, 223–36
capital funds analysis, 232–34
choice of tools in, 221–22
consolidated balance sheets as factor in, 235–36
debt service analysis, 243–44
electric utilities, 303–17
electric utility income statements, 311–16
equity value factors in, 234–35
factors in finance company, 377
importance of interpretation in, 222–23
income statement in, 236–44
life insurance companies, 323–31
major factors in, 247
preparation of statements for, 220–21
property and casualty company earnings adjustments, 337–39
railroad income statement, 278–83
railroads, 273–89
reconstructed electric utility operating statements, 313
use of cash earnings concept in, 242–43
Financial statements
comparability of, 189–90
interpretation of analysis of, 190–91
introduction to analysis of, 218–23
Fire and casualty insurance companies, sources of information on, 130
First in, first out, description of, 238–39
First National Bank of Chicago, finance company composite data of, 380
Fixed charge coverage
analysis of, 285–87
measures of, 253–54
standards for railroads, 288–89
Fixed charges earned ratio, 316–17
Fixed dollar contracts, 4–5
choices of, 39
in the investment program, 107–8
Foreign securities
American depository receipts and, 407
general nature of, 403–7
political stability and, 405
transfer problems of, 407
Formula plans

Formula plans—*Cont.*
constant dollar value of stocks plan, 427–30
constant stock-bond ratio plan, 430–32
dollar averaging plan, 435–37
equalizing type, description of, 427
general nature of, 426–27
variable stock-bond ratio plan, 432–35

G

General Contract Finance Corporation, 376
Government actions, as factor in industry analysis, 208–9
Granville, Joseph, 417
Greenough, William C., 111
Growth
company, measures of, 247–48
of the industry and foreign competition, 207–8
of the industry and its investment implications, 199–202
of the industry and population characteristics, 206–7
Growth stock valuation, 89–90
Growth stocks
income taxes and, 451–52
portfolio administration and, 448–50

H

Health and accident insurance, as protection against disability, 18
Hope Natural Gas decision, significance of, 299–300

I

Income, deferred, description of, 230
Income bonds, definition of, 62
Income statement
of commercial banks, 373
cost of goods sold on, 238–40
cost of operations as classification of, 243–73
depreciation charges on, 240–42
property and casualty insurance companies, 338
sales as account on, 236–37
Income taxes
and investment policy, 33–35, 113–14
portfolio administration and, 450–51
special treatment of capital gains, 34–35
tax switching of securities and, 456
Index of Industrial Production, description of, 137–38
Industry analysis; *see also* Transportation industry
changes in industry prospects, 202–8

Industry analysis—*Cont.*
    classification of industries, 195–97
    commodity prices as factor in, 209–11
    cyclical characteristics as factor in, 211–14
    electric utilities, 300–303
    governmental actions as factor in, 208–9
    industry growth as factor in, 199–202
    population characteristics and, 206–7
    procedure in, 184–86
    sources of information, 131
    special factors in, 208–14
    stages of industry development in, 198–99
Industry growth, economics of, 197–208
Industry statistics, 133–36
Institutional fixed dollar contracts
    commercial bank savings deposits, 43–45
    importance of, 5–6
    investment characteristics of, 40–41
    and purchasing power risk, 40
    and risk, 39
    savings and loan share accounts, 41
    types of, 40
    variations in quality of, 41
Insurance
    disability income, 20–21
    medical expense, 19–20
Interest rate risk
    influence on bond values, 65–66
    nature of, 30–31
    U.S. government securities and, 402–5
Interest rates, sources of information, 144–46
Interstate Commerce Commission, role in regulation of rail rates, 269–71
Interstate Finance Corporation
    balance sheet of, 379
    income statement of, 382
Intrinsic value, approach to security analysis, 176–77
Inventory, costing of, 238–40
    description of as balance sheet item, 226–28
Investment analysis, definition of, 174–75
Investment banker, function of, 151–53
Investment companies
    capital structure of, 349–50
    growth of, 347
    investment policies and objectives of, 350–52
    investor's experience indexes of, 359–63
    nature of, 347–55
    organization of, 348–49
    purchase costs of shares, 353–55
    selection considerations, 355–64

Investment companies—*Cont.*
    source of information on, 131
    systematic purchase plans of, 352–53
Investment counsel, mail order, 121–22
Investment counselor, use of, 459–60
Investment information
    company annual report as source of, 128–29
    free advice, 119–21
    industry sources, 131–36
    mail order investment counsel, 121–22
    standard financial services, 122–25
Investment planning
    and disability, 17–21
    and income taxes, 33–35
    and investor temperament, 37
    and life insurance, 16–17
    and personal savings, 14–15
    and personal scale of living, 14
    and premature death, 15–16
    and retirement, 21–22
    and social security, 16–17
    and unemployment, 22–23
    use of life economic value in, 12
Investment policy
    and federal income taxes, 113–14
    of investment companies, 350–52
    and liquidity considerations, 35–36
    and personal considerations, 37–38
    portfolio administration and, 443–53
    stability and level of income, 112–13
Investment portfolio, of property and casualty insurance companies, 340
Investment programming
    the balanced program, 110
    and common stock, 108–10
    definition of, 100
    and income taxes, 113–14
    and life insurance, 101–6
    and quality of investments, 114–16
    and retirement, 106–12
    use of fixed dollar contracts, 107–8
Investment requirements, 15–23
    disability as an, 17–21
    premature death as, 15–16
    retirement, 21–22
    and unemployment, 22–23
Investment timing
    approaches to, 410–11
    confidence index and, 422–24
    Dow Theory and, 418–19
    forecasting major economic trends and, 411–16
    formula plans, 426–38
    general nature of problem of, 409–10
    odd-lot theory and, 418–22
    portfolio administration and, 441–42

Investment timing—*Cont.*
 technical market analysis and, 416–25
Investments
 nature of, 7
 the subject of, 2
 why study, 2–4

J

Journal of Commerce, 125

L

Last in, first out, description of, 239–40
Leverage
 of closed-end investment companies, 349–50
 of commercial banks, 368–70
 description of effects of, 231–32
 electric utility, 308–10
 finance company, 380–81
 of property and casualty insurance companies, 341
Liberty Loan Corporation
 balance sheet, 379
 income statement of, 382
Life and Casualty Insurance Company of Tennessee, 327
Life insurance
 basic types of, 102–4
 and cash surrender values, 47
 choosing a company, 104–6
 choosing a policy, 104
 endowment, 103–4
 as an investment, 45–51
 and investment planning, 16–17
 and investment programming, 101–6
 and level premium plan, 47–49
 limited payment, 103
 nature of, 45–49
 ordinary, 103
 purpose of, 101–2
 term, 102–3
Life insurance companies
 book value of common stocks, 328–31
 costs of operations of, 324–26
 earnings adjustments for, 327–28
 importance of growth of, 331–32
 lapse ratios and their importance, 330
 nature of operations, 322–26
 net gain from operations of, 326–28
 policy reserves of, 323–24
 sources of information on, 130–31
Life insurance premiums, calculation of, 45–47, 323–24
Liquidity, nature of, 35–36
Load factor, calculation of electric utility, 306–7

M

Maclean-Hunter Publishing Company, 123
Maintenance expenses, of railroads, 280–82
Management
 interview as means of evaluating, 192–93
 sources of information on, 127–28
Margin, buying common stock on, 165–67
Market analysis
 as approach to security analysis, 175–76
 investment timing and, 416–25
Market risk
 importance of price fluctuations, 178–79
 and inflation, 32–33
 nature of, 31–33
Market value of common stocks, nature of, 91–93
Marketability
 definition of, 36
 municipal bond, 390
Maturity
 definition of bond, 60–61
 definition of serial bond, 68
Medical expense insurance, nature of, 19–20
Mellon National Bank, balance sheet of, 369
Mergers, movement among railroads, 272–73
Moody's bond ratings
 and bond yields, 71–74
 description of, 125
Moody's Investors Service, 130
 description of, 123
Municipal bonds
 analysis of, 390
 economic background analysis and, 393–94
 efficient fiscal management and value of, 393
 general characteristics of, 386–88
 holders of, 389
 investment characteristics of, 388–94
 legality of, 390–91
 measures of ability to pay, 391–93
 revenue bonds, 394–98; *see also* Revenue bonds
Mutual funds; *see* Open-end investment companies *and* Investment companies
Mutual savings banks, savings deposits of, 43–45

N

National Bureau of Economic Research, statistical business indications of, 412–16

National income, indexes of for selected countries, 185
National income data, sources of information on, 138–39
New York Stock Exchange; *see also* Securities markets
  commissions charged on, 163–65
  listing statements of, 127
  margin requirements of, 167
  monthly investment plan, 165
Northwestern Mutual Life Insurance Company, 105–6

O

Odd-lot
  description of, 156
  index, calculation of, 420–21
  theory, 419–22
Open-end investment companies
  management appraisal measures, 356–58
  systematic purchase plans, 352–53
Operating ratio, electric utility adjusted, 312–13
Organized securities exchanges, 155–57
Over-the-counter market, description of, 157–58

P

Par value of common stock, 77–78
Participation provision of preferred stock, 94–95
Passenger transportation market, 265–68
Personal financial hazards, 10
  and disability income insurance, 18
  types of protection, 11
Plant equipment, as account on balance sheet, 228
Political stability and investment, 6
Portfolio administration
  capital gains and, 448–49
  diversification and, 444–45
  income taxes and, 450–51
  investment timing and, 441–42, 454
  liquidity and, 452–53
  media quality and, 442–47
  media selection and, 441–47
  tax switching and, 456
Portfolio liquidity, 35–36
  and marketability, 36
Portfolio supervision and investor ability, 37
Post options, description of, 169–70
Preemptive rights, nature of, 78–79; *see also* Rights
Preferred stock
  call provisions, 96

Preferred stock—*Cont.*
  characteristics and value of, 93–98
  claim on assets, 95–96
  claim on income, 93–94
  participation provision, 94–95
  sinking fund provisions of, 96
  special features of, 76–77
  voting rights of, 95
  yields on, 96–97
Premature death
  as investment requirement, 15–16
  life insurance as protection against economic hazards of, 101–2
  and life value, 12
  as personal financial hazard, 10
Price index, consumer, 29
Price-earnings ratio
  for Standard and Poor's 500 stocks 1954–64, 88
  use of, 256–57
Private placements, of securities, 154–55
Property and casualty insurance companies
  balance sheet of, 339–45
  common stock, adjusted book value of, 342–45
  earnings adjustments of, 337–39
  importance of investment income of, 337
  profits of, 334
  underwriting expense of, 335–37
Prospectus
  "red herring", description of, 128
  as source of company information, 127–28
Public utility; *see also* Electric utilities
  regulation of, 297–300
  securities, competitive bidding required for, 151
  source of information on, 129–30
  special economic characteristics of, 296–97
Purchasing power of dollar, 29–30
Purchasing power risk
  cumulative effects of, 107–8
  exposure of annuities and life insurance to, 50–51
  and institutional fixed dollar contracts, 40
  nature of, 28–30
  and the retired investor, 115–16
Putnam Fund of Boston, performance index of, 357, 361–63

Q

Qualitative analysis, 191–93
Quality of investments and the investment program, 114–16

Quality ratings, municipal bond, 389

R

Railroad securities, competitive bidding required for, 151
Railroads
    analysis of bonds of, 283–89
    analysis of fixed charge coverage of, 286–87
    analysis of traffic of, 276–78
    competitors of, 269
    equipment trust obligations of, 285
    freight transportation market, 263–65
    guaranteed bonds of, 283–84
    importance of location, 277–78
    maintenance expenses of, 280–82
    measures of plant and equipment utilization, 276
    merger movement of, 272–73
    mortgage bonds of, 284–85
    operating expenses, analysis of, 278–82
    passenger traffic and, 267–68
    passenger transportation market, 265–68
    regulation of rates and service, 269–71
    selection of bonds of, 288–89
    sources of information on, 129–30
    transportation expenses of, 279–80
    work rules and cost of operation of, 271–72
Rates
    regulation of public utility, 279–300
    regulation of railroad, 269–71
Ratio analysis
    adjusted operating ratio of electric utilities, 312–13
    asset turnover, 249
    choice of tools in, 221–22
    common stock selection measures, 255–57
    current ratio, 252
    dividend payout ratio, 254–55
    earning power ratios, 250
    earnings quality, measures of, 250–51
    electric utility expense ratios, 314
    fixed charges earned, electric utilities, 316–17
    fixed charges earned ratio, 285–87
    general description of, 187
    measure of asset management effectiveness, 370–71
    measures of
        commercial bank leverage, 370
        credit capacity, 252–54
        electric utility plant utilization, 305–8
        growth, 247–48

Ratio analysis—*Cont.*
    measures of—*Cont.*
        plant and equipment utilization, 276
        profitability, 248–50
        property and casualty underwriting expense, 335–37
        quality of receivables, 226
        railroad traffic density, 276–77
        working capital adequacy, 251–52
    municipal bond measures of ability to pay, 391–93
    operating ratio as tool, 237
    operational effectiveness ratios, 249–50
    price-earnings ratio, description of, 246
    profit margin analysis, 249
    railroad maintenance ratios, 280–82
    revenue bonds, 395–96
Receivables
    description of, as account classification, 225–26
    tests of quality, 226
Regulation, of public utilities, 297–300
Research and development, as factor in security analysis, 203–5
Retirement
    and the investment program, 106–12
    investment program after, 111–12
    as an investment requirement, 21–22
    as personal financial hazard, 10
Revenue bonds
    analysis of, 395
    defaults on, 397
    general nature of, 394–98
    terms of issue, 397–98
Rights
    nature of, 78–79
    value of, 79–81
Risk
    description of businessman's risk, 112
    financial, 27–28
    general nature of, 7
    and institutional fixed dollar contracts, 319
    interest rate, 30–31
    market, 31–33
    the nature of, 26–27
    purchasing power, 28–30

S

Sales, description of, 236–37
Savings,
    allocation of, 4
    assumed rate of, 13–14
Savings deposits, commercial banks, 45
Savings and loan associations,
    financial risk and, 41–43

Savings and loan associations—*Cont.*
nature of, 41–43
yields on investments in, 42
Securities
primary marketing of, 150–55
private placement of, 154–55
Securities Act of 1933, major provisions of, 152–53
Securities and Exchange Commission
regulations of short sales, 167
role in public sale of securities, 151–54
Securities markets
common stock options, 169–71
description of transactions on stock exchanges, 160–69
market for inactive issues, 158–59
the over-the-counter market, 157–58
secondary offerings in, 159
selling short in, 167–69
stock exchanges, description of, 155–57
Security analysis; *see also* Industry analysis
airlines, 289–94
approaches to, 175–80
as a career, 2-4
comparability of financial statements, 189–90
importance of interpretation in, 190–91, 222–23
industry growth as factor in, 197–208
investment timing and, 454–56
market price fluctuations and, 178–79
procedure in, 180–94
qualitative factors in, 191–93
use of analytical reference standards in, 187–89
use of balance sheet in, 223–36
use of management interview in, 192–93
use of ratios in, 187
Security prices, sources of, 125–26
Sinking fund and bonds, 60–61
Sinking fund provisions of preferred stock, 96
Social security and investment planning, 16–17
Specialist, function of, 156–57
Standard financial statements, description of, 220–21
Standard Listed Stock Reports, description of, 182–84
Standard and Poor's
bond ratings, description of, 125
bond ratings and bond yields, 71–73
common and preferred stock ratings description of, 125
Industry Surveys, 131–32
investment service, description of, 123

Standard and Poor's—*Cont.*
investment services, use in security analysis, 181–84
Stein, Roe and Farnham, Balanced Fund, performance index, 357, 361–63
Stock exchanges, 155–57
description of transactions on, 160–69
Stock broker, as a career, 2–4
Stop loss orders, description of, 161–62

T

Term life insurance, 102–3
Textron, Inc., percentage distribution of product lines, 196
Timing of investments and uncertainty, economic, 7–8
Ton-mile, definition of, 263
Transportation industry
characteristics of, 262–73
freight transportation market, 263–65
Tri-Continental Corporation
description of capital structure of, 349–50
performance index of, 359

U

Uncertainty, economic and individual investment, 7–8
Unemployment
as an investment requirement, 22–23
as personal financial hazard, 10
United Home Life Insurance Company, 332
United States Government, description of daily Treasury statement of, 147
U.S. Government securities
certificates of indebtedness, 399–400
characteristics of, 399–402
classification of, 386
government corporation and agency bonds, 401–2
nonmarketable securities, 401
risks of, 402–3
sources of information on, 131
treasury bills, 399
treasury bonds, 400–1
treasury notes, 400
U.S. savings bonds as investments, 51–53

V

Valuation of common stock
importance of market price fluctuations in, 178–79
use of market analysis in, 175–76
Valuation of growth stock, 89–90
Value
of bonds, determination of, 65–71

Value—*Cont.*
of common stock, concepts of, 83–93
multiple of earnings approach, 87–89
use of dividends in determining, 83–87
market, of common stock, 91–93
of rights, 79–81
of warrants, 82
Value Line Investment Survey, 122
Value Line Survey, system, portfolio administration and, 445–46
Variable stock-bond ratio plan, 432–35
Vassar College, use of formula plan, 433–35
Voting rights
of common stock, 77

Voting rights—*Cont.*
of preferred stock, 95

W

Wall Street Journal, 125
Warrants
description of, 81–82
value of, 82
Western Casualty and Surety Company, 340
Wiesenberger, Arthur and Company, investment company performance indexes of, 356–58

Y

Yields, municipal bond, 391

This book has been set in 11 point Caledonia, leaded 2 points; and 10 point Caledonia, leaded 1 point. Chapter numbers and titles are in Melior. The size of the type page is 27 by 45½ picas.